A·N·N·U·A·L E·D·I·T·I·O·N·S

Marketing

Twenty-Sixth Edition

04/05

EDITOR

John E. Richardson

Pepperdine University

Dr. John E. Richardson is professor of marketing in The George L. Graziadio School of Business and Management at Pepperdine University. He is president of his own consulting firm and has consulted with organizations such as Bell and Howell, Dayton-Hudson, Epson, and the U.S. Navy as well as with various service, nonprofit, and franchise organizations. Dr. Richardson is a member of the American Marketing Association, the American Management Association, the Society for Business Ethics, and Beta Gamma Sigma honorary business fraternity.

McGraw-Hill/Dushkin

530 Old Whitfield Street, Guilford, Connecticut 06437

Visit us on the Internet
http://www.dushkin.com

1, 4, 5, 6, 10, 13, 16

Credits

1. **Marketing in the 2000s and Beyond**
   Unit photo—© 2004 by Sweet By & By/Cindy Brown.
2. **Research, Markets, and Consumer Behavior**
   Unit photo—© 2004 by Sweet By & By/Cindy Brown.
3. **Developing and Implementing Marketing Strategies**
   Unit photo—© 2004 by PhotoDisc, Inc.
4. **Global Marketing**
   Unit photo—TRW Inc. photo.

Copyright

Cataloging in Publication Data
Main entry under title: Annual Editions: Marketing. 2004/2005.
1. Marketing—Periodicals. I. Richardson, John E., *comp*. II. Title: Marketing.
ISBN 0–07–286130–4   658'.05   ISSN 0730–2606

Twenty-Sixth Edition

Cover image © 2004 PhotoDisc, Inc.
Printed in the United States of America   234567890BAHBAH54   Printed on Recycled Paper

Editors/Advisory Board

Members of the Advisory Board are instrumental in the final selection of articles for each edition of ANNUAL EDITIONS. Their review of articles for content, level, currentness, and appropriateness provides critical direction to the editor and staff. We think that you will find their careful consideration well reflected in this volume.

To the Reader

In publishing ANNUAL EDITIONS we recognize the enormous role played by the magazines, newspapers, and journals of the public press in providing current, first-rate educational information in a broad spectrum of interest areas. Many of these articles are appropriate for students, researchers, and professionals seeking accurate, current material to help bridge the gap between principles and theories and the real world. These articles, however, become more useful for study when those of lasting value are carefully collected, organized, indexed, and reproduced in a low-cost format, which provides easy and permanent access when the material is needed. That is the role played by ANNUAL EDITIONS.

The new millennium should prove to be an exciting and challenging time for the American business community. Recent dramatic social, economic, and technological changes have become an important part of the present marketplace. These changes—accompanied by increasing domestic and foreign competition—are leading a wide array of companies and industries toward the realization that better marketing must become a top priority now to ensure their future success.

How does the marketing manager respond to this growing challenge? How does the marketing student apply marketing theory to the real world practice? Many reach for the *Wall Street Journal, Business Week, Fortune,* and other well-known sources of business information. There, specific industry and company strategies are discussed and analyzed, marketing principles are often reaffirmed by real occurrences, and textbook theories are supported or challenged by current events.

The articles reprinted in this edition of *Annual Editions: Marketing 04/05* have been carefully chosen from numerous public press sources to provide current information on marketing in the world today. Within these pages you will find articles that address marketing theory and application in a wide range of industries. In addition, the selections reveal how several firms interpret and utilize marketing principles in their daily operations and corporate planning.

The volume contains a number of features designed to make it useful for marketing students, researchers, and professionals. These include the *Industry/Company Guide*, which is particularly helpful when seeking information about specific corporations; a *topic guide* to locate articles on specific marketing subjects; *World Wide Web* pages; the *table of contents* abstracts, which summarize each article and highlight key concepts; a *glossary* of key marketing terms; and a comprehensive *index*.

The articles are organized into four units. Selections that focus on similar issues are concentrated into subsections within the broader units. Each unit is preceded by a list of unit selections, as well as a list of key points to consider that focus on major themes running throughout the selections, Web links that provide extra support for the unit's data, and an overview that provides background for informed reading of the articles and emphasizes critical issues.

This is the twenty-sixth edition of *Annual Editions: Marketing.* Since its first edition in the mid-1970s, the efforts of many individuals have contributed toward its success. We think this is by far the most useful collection of material available for the marketing student. We are anxious to know what you think. What are your opinions? What are your recommendations? Please take a moment to complete and return the *article rating form* on the last page of this volume. Any book can be improved and this one will continue to be, annually.

John E. Richardson

John E. Richardson

Editor

Contents

UNIT 1
Marketing in the 2000s and Beyond

Thirteen selections examine the current and future status of marketing, the marketing concept, service marketing, and marketing ethics.

Part A.   Changing Perspectives

Part B.   The Marketing Concept

The concepts in bold italics are developed in the article. For further expansion, please refer to the Topic Guide and the Index.

UNIT 2
Research, Markets, and Consumer Behavior

Eleven selections provide an analysis of consumer demographics and lifestyles, the growth of maturation of markets, and the need for market research and planning.

The concepts in bold italics are developed in the article. For further expansion, please refer to the Topic Guide and the Index.

UNIT 3
Developing and Implementing Marketing Strategies

Thirteen selections analyze factors that affect the development and implementation of marketing strategies.

The concepts in bold italics are developed in the article. For further expansion, please refer to the Topic Guide and the Index.

The concepts in bold italics are developed in the article. For further expansion, please refer to the Topic Guide and the Index.

UNIT 4
Global Marketing

Six selections discuss the increasing globalization of markets, trends in world trade, and increasing foreign competition.

The concepts in bold italics are developed in the article. For further expansion, please refer to the Topic Guide and the Index.

Topic Guide

This topic guide suggests how the selections in this book relate to the subjects covered in your course. You may want to use the topics listed on these pages to search the Web more easily.

On the following pages a number of Web sites have been gathered specifically for this book. They are arranged to reflect the units of this *Annual Edition.* You can link to these sites by going to the DUSHKIN ONLINE support site at *http://www.dushkin.com/online/.*

ALL THE ARTICLES THAT RELATE TO EACH TOPIC ARE LISTED BELOW THE BOLD-FACED TERM.

Advertising

10. Services Communications: From Mindless Tangibilization to Meaningful Messages
16. Surviving Innovation
19. Emailing Aging Boomers vs. "Seniors"
21. Asian-American Consumers as a Unique Market Segment: Fact or Fallacy?
26. In Praise of the Purple Cow
28. The Hole Story: How Krispy Kreme Became the Hottest Brand in America
31. Most Valuable Players
32. The Old Pillars of New Retailing
34. 10 Top Stores Put to the Test
35. Tips for Distinguishing Your Ads From Bad Ads
36. Living Up and Down the Dial
37. Counting Eyes on Billboards
42. Cracking China's Market
43. The Lure of Global Branding

Branding

1. The Next 25 Years
8. Start With the Customer
9. What Drives Customer Equity
10. Services Communications: From Mindless Tangibilization to Meaningful Messages
15. Product by Design
16. Surviving Innovation
18. Defining Luxury: Oh, the Good Life
20. Race, Ethnicity and the Way We Shop
21. Asian-American Consumers as a Unique Market Segment: Fact or Fallacy?
26. In Praise of the Purple Cow
28. The Hole Story: How Krispy Kreme Became the Hottest Brand in America
34. 10 Top Stores Put to the Test
38. Segmenting Global Markets: Look Before You Leap
39. International Marketing Research: A Management Briefing
42. Cracking China's Market
43. The Lure of Global Branding

Competition

25. The Very Model of a Modern Marketing Plan
28. The Hole Story: How Krispy Kreme Became the Hottest Brand in America
30. Which Price is Right?
31. Most Valuable Players
32. The Old Pillars of New Retailing
38. Segmenting Global Markets: Look Before You Leap

Consumer behavior

4. The Customer Profitability Conundrum: When to Love 'Em or Leave 'Em
7. Why Customer Satisfaction Starts With HR
9. What Drives Customer Equity
11. Why Service Stinks
15. Product by Design
17. A Beginner's Guide to Demographics
18. Defining Luxury: Oh, the Good Life
20. Race, Ethnicity and the Way We Shop
21. Asian-American Consumers as a Unique Market Segment: Fact or Fallacy?

22. Defining Moments: Segmenting by Cohorts
23. What Are Your Customers Saying?
24. Tough Love
30. Which Price is Right?
32. The Old Pillars of New Retailing
34. 10 Top Stores Put to the Test
37. Counting Eyes on Billboards
38. Segmenting Global Markets: Look Before You Leap
40. Small Packets, Big Business

Consumer demographics

1. The Next 25 Years
4. The Customer Profitability Conundrum: When to Love 'Em or Leave 'Em
7. Why Customer Satisfaction Starts With HR
9. What Drives Customer Equity
10. Services Communications: From Mindless Tangibilization to Meaningful Messages
11. Why Service Stinks
15. Product by Design
17. A Beginner's Guide to Demographics
18. Defining Luxury: Oh, the Good Life
19. Emailing Aging Boomers vs. "Seniors"
20. Race, Ethnicity and the Way We Shop
21. Asian-American Consumers as a Unique Market Segment: Fact or Fallacy?
22. Defining Moments: Segmenting by Cohorts
24. Tough Love
30. Which Price is Right?
34. 10 Top Stores Put to the Test
37. Counting Eyes on Billboards
40. Small Packets, Big Business
41. Time for Marketers to Grow Up?

Direct marketing

23. What Are Your Customers Saying?
26. In Praise of the Purple Cow
27. Have It Your Way
31. Most Valuable Players
33. When Worlds Collide

Distribution planning

2. High Performance Marketing
3. Marketing High Technology: Preparation, Targeting, Positioning, Execution
4. The Customer Profitability Conundrum: When to Love 'Em or Leave 'Em
32. The Old Pillars of New Retailing
33. When Worlds Collide
34. 10 Top Stores Put to the Test
39. International Marketing Research: A Management Briefing

Economic environment

1. The Next 25 Years
5. Entrepreneurs' Biggest Problems—And How They Solve Them
19. Emailing Aging Boomers vs. "Seniors"
24. Tough Love
30. Which Price is Right?
36. Living Up and Down the Dial
38. Segmenting Global Markets: Look Before You Leap

World Wide Web Sites

The following World Wide Web sites have been carefully researched and selected to support the articles found in this reader. The easiest way to access these selected sites is to go to our DUSHKIN ONLINE support site at *http://www.dushkin.com/online/*.

AE: Marketing 04/05

The following sites were available at the time of publication. Visit our Web site—we update DUSHKIN ONLINE regularly to reflect any changes.

General Sources

CyberAtlas Demographics
http://cyberatlas.internet.com/big_picture/demographics/article/0,,5901_150381,00.html

The Baruch College–Harris poll commissioned by *Business Week* is used at this site to show interested businesses who is on the Net in the United States. Statistics for other countries can be found by clicking on Geographics.

General Social Survey
http://www.icpsr.umich.edu/GSS99/

The GSS (see DPLS Archive: *http://DPLS.DACC.WISC.EDU/SAF/*) is an almost annual personal interview survey of U.S. households that began in 1972. More than 35,000 respondents have answered 2,500 questions. It covers a broad range of variables, many of which relate to microeconomic issues.

Krislyn's Favorite Advertising & Marketing Sites
http://www.krislyn.com/sites/adv.htm

This is a complete list of sites that include information on marketing research, marketing on the Internet, demographic sources, and organizations and associations. The site also features current books on the subject of marketing.

Retail Learning Initiative
http://www.retailsmarts.ryerson.ca

This series of small business and retail marketing links from Canada connects to many more business links in the United States and to workshops and dialogue forums.

STAT-USA/Internet Site Economic, Trade, Business Information
http://www.stat-usa.gov

This site, from the U.S. Department of Commerce, contains Daily Economic News, Frequently Requested Statistical Releases, Information on Export and International Trade, Domestic Economic News and Statistical Series, and Databases.

U.S. Census Bureau Home Page
http://www.census.gov

This is a major source of social, demographic, and economic information, such as income/employment data and the latest indicators, income distribution, and poverty data.

UNIT 1: Marketing in the 2000s and Beyond

American Marketing Association Code of Ethics
http://www.marketingpower.com/

At this American Marketing Association site, use the search mechanism to access the organization's Code of Ethics for marketers.

Futures Research Quarterly
http://www.wfs.org/frq.htm

Published by the World Future Society, this publication describes futures research that encompasses both an evolving philosophy and a range of techniques, with the aim of assisting decision-makers in all fields to understand better the potential consequences of decisions by developing images of alternative futures. From this page explore the current and back issues and What's Coming Up!

Center for Innovation in Product Development (CIPD)
http://web.mit.edu/cipd/research/prdctdevelop.htm

CIPD is one of the National Science Foundation's engineering research centers. It shares the goal of future product development with academia, industry, and government.

Marketing in the Service Sector
http://www.ext.colostate.edu/pubs/ttb/tb010424.html

At this site, Frank Leibrock discusses and recommends two books by Harry Beckwith that target marketing in the service sector. Read his reasons for thinking they make sense to owners of small businesses, then read the books themselves.

Professor Takes Business Ethics to Global Level
http://www.miami.com/mld/miamiherald/4426429.htm

This is a discussion by Professor Robert W. McGee of the challenges that the new century brings to business and its relation to ethical issues at a global level. The article by Mike Seemuth provides interesting reading about the important part that government plays in business decisions. Tariffs and protectionism are highlighted.

Remarks by Chairman Alan Greenspan
http://www.federalreserve.gov/boarddocs/speeches/2000/20000322.htm

These remarks were made by chairman Alan Greenspan on March 22, 2000, concerning the challenges that face American businesses, workers, and consumers as the U.S. economy embarked on the new century.

UNIT 2: Research, Markets, and Consumer Behavior

Canadian Innovation Centre
http://www.innovationcentre.ca/company/Default.htm

The Canadian Innovation Centre has developed a unique mix of innovation services that can help a company from idea to market launch. Their services are based on the review of 12,000 new product ideas through their technology and market assessment programs over the past 20 years.

CBA.org: Research and Develop
http://www.cba.org/CBA/National/Marketing/research.asp

This interesting article, written by Elizabeth Cordeau, president of a Calgary-based management consulting firm to law firms and legal associations (featured on the Web by CBA, the information service of the Canadian Bar Association), claims that good marketing begins with excellent market research.

Industry Analysis and Trends
http://www.bizminer.com/market_research.asp

The importance of using market research databases and pinpointing local and national trends, including details of industry and small business startups, is emphasized by this site of the Brandow Company that offers samples of market research profiles.

Marketing Intelligence
http://www.bcentral.com/articles/krotz/123.asp

This article discusses five market intelligence blunders made by the giant retailer K-Mart. "There were warning signs that Kmart management mishandled, downplayed or just plain ignored," Joanna L. Krotz says.

Maritz Marketing Research
http://www.maritzresearch.com

Maritz Marketing Research Inc. (MMRI) specializes in custom-designed research studies that link the consumer to the marketer through information. Go to Maritz Loyalty Marketing in the Maritz Companies menu to find resources to identify, retain, and grow your most valuable customers. Also visit Maritz Research for polls, stats, and archived research reports.

USADATA
http://www.usadata.com

This leading provider of marketing, company, advertising, and consumer behavior data offers national and local data covering the top 60 U.S. markets.

WWW Virtual Library: Demography & Population Studies
http://demography.anu.edu.au/VirtualLibrary/

More than 150 links can be found at this major resource to keep track of information of value to researchers in the fields of demography and population studies.

UNIT 3: Developing and Implementing Marketing Strategies

American Marketing Association Homepage
http://www.marketingpower.com

This site of the American Marketing Association is geared to managers, educators, researchers, students, and global electronic members. It contains a search mechanism, definitions of marketing and market research, and links.

Consumer Buying Behavior
http://www.courses.psu.edu/mktg/mktg220_rso3/sls_cons.htm

The Center for Academic Computing at Penn State posts this course data that includes a review of consumer buying behaviors; group, environment, and internal influences; problem-solving; and post-purchasing behavior.

Product Branding, Packaging, and Pricing
http://www.fooddude.com/branding.html

Put forward by fooddude.com, the information at this site is presented in a lively manner. It discusses positioning, branding, pricing, and packaging in the specialty food market, but it applies to many other retail products as well.

UNIT 4: Global Marketing

CIBERWeb
http://ciber.centers.purdue.edu

The Centers for International Business Education and Research were created by the U.S. Omnibus Trade and Competitiveness Act of 1988. Together, the 26 resulting CIBER sites in the United States are a powerful network focused on helping U.S. business succeed in global markets. Many marketing links can be found at this site.

Emerging Markets Resources
http://www.usatrade.gov/website/ccg.nsf

Information on the business and economic situation of foreign countries and the political climate as it affects U.S. business is presented by the U.S. Department of Commerce's International Trade Administration.

International Business Resources on the WWW
http://globaledge.msu.edu/ibrd/ibrd.asp

This Web site includes a large index of international business resources. Through *http://ciber.bus.msu.edu/ginlist/* you can also access the Global Interact Network Mailing LIST (GINLIST), which brings together, electronically, business educators and practitioners with international business interests.

International Trade Administration
http://www.ita.doc.gov

The U.S. Department of Commerce is dedicated to helping U.S. businesses compete in the global marketplace, and at this site it offers assistance through many Web links under such headings as Trade Statistics, Cross-Cutting Programs, Regions and Countries, and Import Administration.

World Chambers Network
http://www.worldchambers.net

International trade at work is viewable at this site. For example, click on Global Business eXchange (GBX) for a list of active business opportunities worldwide or to submit your new business opportunity for validation.

World Trade Center Association On Line
http://iserve.wtca.org

Data on world trade is available at this site that features information, services, a virtual trade fair, an exporter's encyclopedia, trade opportunities, and a resource center.

We highly recommend that you review our Web site for expanded information and our other product lines. We are continually updating and adding links to our Web site in order to offer you the most usable and useful information that will support and expand the value of your Annual Editions. You can reach us at: *http://www.dushkin.com/annualeditions/*.

UNIT 1

Marketing in the 2000s and Beyond

Unit Selections

Key Points to Consider

- Dramatic changes are occurring in the marketing of products and services. What social and economic trends do you believe are most significant today, and how do you think these will affect marketing in the future?

- Theodore Levitt suggests that as times change the marketing concept must be reinterpreted. Given the varied perspectives of the other articles in this unit, what do you think this reinterpretation will entail?

- In the present competitive business arena, is it possible for marketers to behave ethically in the environment and both survive and prosper? What suggestions can you give that could be incorporated into the marketing strategy for firms that want to be both ethical and successful?

 **Links: www.dushkin.com/online/**
These sites are annotated in the World Wide Web pages.

American Marketing Association Code of Ethics
http://www.marketingpower.com/

Futures Research Quarterly
http://www.wfs.org/frq.htm

Center for Innovation in Product Development (CIPD)
http://web.mit.edu/cipd/research/prdctdevelop.htm

Marketing in the Service Sector
http://www.ext.colostate.edu/pubs/ttb/tb010424.html

Professor Takes Business Ethics to Global Level
http://www.miami.com/mld/miamiherald/4426429.htm

Remarks by Chairman Alan Greenspan
http://www.federalreserve.gov/boarddocs/speeches/2000/20000322.htm

"If we want to know what a business is we must start with its purpose.... There is only one valid definition of business purpose: to create a customer. What business thinks it produces is not of first importance—especially not to the future of the business or to its success. What the customer thinks he is buying, what he considers 'value' is decisive—it determines what a business is, what it produces, and whether it will prosper."

—Peter Drucker,
The Practice of Management

When Peter Drucker penned these words in 1954, American industry was just awakening to the realization that marketing would play an important role in the future success of businesses. The ensuing years have seen an increasing number of firms in highly competitive areas—particularly in the consumer goods industry—adopt a more sophisticated customer orientation and an integrated marketing focus.

The dramatic economic and social changes of the last decade have stirred companies in an even broader range of industries—from banking and air travel to communications—to the realization that marketing will provide them with their cutting edge. Demographic and lifestyle changes have splintered mass, homogeneous markets into many markets, each with different needs and interests. Deregulation has made once-protected industries vulnerable to the vagaries of competition. Vast and rapid technological changes are making an increasing number of products and services obsolete. Intense international competition, rapid expansion of the Internet-based economy, and the growth of truly global markets have many firms looking well beyond their national boundaries.

Indeed, it appears that during the new millennium marketing will take on a unique significance—and not just within the industrial sector. Social institutions of all kinds, which had thought themselves exempt from the pressures of the marketplace, are also beginning to recognize the need for marketing in the management of their affairs. Colleges and universities, charities, museums, symphony orchestras, and even hospitals are beginning to give attention to the marketing concept—to provide what the consumer wants to buy.

The selections in this unit are grouped into four areas. Their purposes are to provide current perspectives on marketing, discuss differing views of the marketing concept, analyze the use of marketing by social institutions and nonprofit organizations, and examine the ethical and social responsibilities of marketing.

The five articles in the first subsection provide significant clues about salient approaches and issues that marketers need to address in the future in order to create, promote, and sell their products and services in ways that meet the expectation of consumers.

The four selections that address the marketing concept include Theodore Levitt's now-classic "Marketing Myopia," which first appeared in the *Harvard Business Review* in 1960. This version includes the author's retrospective commentary, written in 1975, in which he discusses how shortsightedness can make management unable to recognize that there is no such thing as a growth industry.

The second article shows convincing evidence that HR drives customer satisfaction. The next article reflects the importance of letting the customer come first at top-performing service companies. The last article in this subsection, "What Drives Customer Equity," discloses the significance of customer equity as a significant determinant of the long-term value of a company.

In the Services and Social Marketing subsection, the first article describes the unique challenge that service businesses face: how to effectively communicate the necessary benefits of their service offerings. The final article in this subsection reveals how sometimes service is focused on elite consumers—while putting other consumers in a secondary position.

In the final subsection, a careful look is taken at the strategic process and practice of incorporating ethics and social responsibility into the marketplace. "Trust in the Marketplace" discusses the importance of gaining and maintaining customers' trust. "A Matter of Trust" reveals the importance of training sales reps to sell their companies' ethics and integrity along with their products and services.

THE NEXT 25 YEARS

Population projections calculated exclusively for *American Demographics* for the next quarter century forecast a larger, older and more diverse nation, one with many opportunities—and challenges—for businesses.

BY ALISON STEIN WELLNER

In 2025, the oldest Baby Boomers will celebrate their 79th birthday. The youngest members of Gen Y will mark their 31st birthday, and the oldest Gen Xers will be two years away from being eligible for Social Security benefits—assuming they still exist.

It's always difficult to predict the future, and crystal balls are particularly cloudy when it comes to speculation about what this country will be like politically, socially and culturally a quarter century from now. In statistician-speak, too many variables are interacting in unpredictable ways for a steady hand to paint a detailed picture of tomorrow. But there is an exception: demographics. The demographic book on 2025 is already written, as most of the people who will be alive in 22 years in this country are alive today.

So what are the fundamental demographic trends that will shape the consumer market over the next 25 years? To help answer that question, *American Demographics* teamed up with MapInfo, a Troy, N.Y.-based market research firm, to create population projections to 2025. We found that the trends likely to influence business agendas of tomorrow are already gaining momentum today—and the smartest companies have started developing strategies to suit the three largest and most likely demographic trends that will shape the marketplace of tomorrow. Even in a down economy, these companies are aware that they'll need to meet the needs of a population that's growing at a feverish pace. They're tweaking marketing plans to suit a nation that will increasingly be dominated by people over age 65. They're working to understand emerging ethnic groups now, instead of waiting another 10 years, realizing that the majority white population is on its way to becoming a minority.

But even demographic projections are fallible: Consumers have the ability to throw them off course. By definition, projections make assumptions based on past behavior, and future behavior may or may not follow the same patterns. To create projections such as these, demographers analyze birth rates, death rates and immigration, and project forward three different numbers—one that indicates the highest possible number, one that indicates the lowest and one that's in between, a number known as "the middle series." The projections that follow mostly rely on the middle series—which means they assume people will continue to have children at about the same rate, deaths will continue at about the same rate and immigration will fall between the current rate and its highest number. To the extent that demographics are destiny, here's what's in the cards.

America the Crowded

On the business agenda:

- More opportunity, more niche markets
- Environmental concerns moving front and center

If your idea of America conjures up visions of unlimited wide, open spaces, or of houses on acres and acres of land, you may be in for quite a shock during the next two decades. By 2025, the U.S. population is expected to exceed 350 million people—an increase of about 70 million and a boost of 25 percent, according to projections by MapInfo.

This puts the nation on a growth trajectory that's similar to the one experienced just after World War II, when the GIs came home and helped create the Baby Boom in the 1950s and 1960s. Population growth slowed during the 1970s and 1980s but experienced a surge during the

growth industry: people

The country's population growth over the next 25 years is expected to far exceed its growth over the past 20 years.

Sources: U.S. Census Bureau; MapInfo

1990s. Expect record-shattering growth to continue, as Americans live longer, birth rates hold steady and immigration continues apace. This wide expanse of growing humanity means that nearly every market segment will expand in numbers over the next 25 years, because more people means more pocketbooks.

However, this *massive* market does not herald a return to the *mass* market. "This [population] growth will combine with increasing diversity to create an ever-growing list of market segments," says Josh Calder, chief editor of the Global Lifestyles project, a research venture of Social Technologies, an Arlington, Va.-based consultancy. "I saw a professionally made bumper sticker the other day that said, 'Proud to be Sikh and American.' Such niches driven by ethnicity, attitudes and interest will proliferate," he adds.

As the population increases, niche markets may become unwieldy for businesses to target with a single marketing strategy. For example, many companies have one marketing strategy to reach Hispanic consumers. But by 2025, the Hispanic market will double, to 70 million consumers. As a result, the niche market of today will become a mass market in its own right, segmented not only by nationality (i.e., Mexican, Guatemalan) but also by spending behavior and other psychographic characteristics. Vickie Abrahamson, cofounder and executive vice president of Minneapolis-based Iconoculture, a trends consulting firm, dubs this movement "beehiving." Says Abrahamson, "Beehiving is the growth of tight-knit, alternative communities sharing common values and passions. Marketers must tap in to beehive rituals, customs and language to build trust and patronage."

Of course, population growth can present some challenges. "Don't you ever wonder how we'll have all the resources to take care of everyone on this planet? It's stunning to think about," says Richard Laermer, marketing expert and author of *TrendSpotting* (Perigee, 2002). A larger U.S. population will require more water and more land to provide food; it also means that more pollution will be created, according to a 2001 report by Lori Hunter, an analyst at the Santa Monica, Calif.-based think tank RAND. Indeed, population growth means that natural resources will be stretched in the coming years, says Dan McGinn, president of the McGinn Group, a marketing communications firm in Arlington, Va. "More people means more demand for resources, which means shortages of resources. Land, water, power—there will be less to go around," he adds. Expect to see escalating conflicts at the local level over land use, in which the benefits of population growth will be pitted against the cost to the environment. Also expect products and services to be scrutinized more closely for their environmental impact.

the graying future

Those over the age of 60 will likely dominate by 2025.

	2000	2025	DIFFERENCE	PERCENT DIFFERENCE
Total	281,421,906	351,070,000	69,648,094	24.7%
Under 5 years	19,175,798	23,183,000	4,007,202	20.9%
5–9	20,549,505	22,845,000	2,295,495	11.2%
10–14	20,528,072	23,166,000	2,637,928	12.9%
15–19	20,219,890	23,449,000	3,229,110	16.0%
20–24	18,964,001	22,481,000	3,516,999	18.5%
25–29	19,381,336	21,257,000	1,875,664	9.7%
30–34	20,510,388	21,615,000	1,104,612	5.4%
35–39	22,706,664	22,728,000	21,336	0.1%
40–44	22,441,863	22,374,000	-67,863	-0.3%
45–49	20,092,404	21,031,000	938,596	4.7%
50–54	17,585,548	19,318,000	1,732,452	9.9%
55–59	13,469,237	18,452,000	4,982,763	37.0%
60–64	10,805,447	18,853,000	8,047,553	74.5%
65–69	9,533,545	19,844,000	10,310,455	108.1%
70–74	8,857,441	17,878,000	9,020,559	101.8%
75–79	7,415,813	14,029,000	6,613,187	89.2%
80–84	4,945,367	9,638,000	4,692,633	94.9%
85+	4,239,587	8,930,000	4,690,413	110.6%

Source: MapInfo and American Demographics

The Mighty Mature Market

On the business agenda:

- The senior market gaining new allure
- Creating ageless multigenerational brands

the mixed society

By 2025, white non-Hispanics will hold a mere 60 percent majority.

	WHITE, NON-HISPANIC	BLACK, NON-HISPANIC	ASIAN/PACIFIC ISLANDER, NON-HISPANIC	NATIVE AMERICAN, NON-HISPANIC	HISPANIC
Population, all ages	210,984	45,567	23,564	2,787	68,168
Percent of total population	60.1%	13.0%	6.7%	0.8%	19.4%
Population, under 5 years	11,872	3,103	1,642	196	6,370
5–9	12,034	3,065	1,583	199	5,964
10–14	12,319	3,180	1,677	221	5,769
15–19	12,495	3,359	1,652	224	5,719
20–24	11,985	3,170	1,641	213	5,472
25–29	11,418	2,907	1,703	201	5,028
30–34	11,993	2,865	1,780	187	4,790
35–39	12,938	3,198	1,771	190	4,631
40–44	13,311	3,176	1,634	202	4,051
45–49	12,834	2,836	1,524	180	3,657
50–54	11,888	2,596	1,356	148	3,330
55–59	11,664	2,419	1,263	130	2,976
60–64	12,502	2,343	1,141	114	2,753
65–69	13,838	2,413	978	107	2,508
70–74	13,071	1,978	800	93	1,936
75–79	10,531	1,429	606	72	1,391
80–84	7,471	816	400	49	902
85–89	3,950	385	217	29	496
90–94	1,859	199	118	17	264
95–99	745	90	54	10	116
100+	267	41	22	6	45
Median age	43.2 years	36.9 years	35.3 years	33.8 years	29.8 years

NOTE: Population numbers in thousands

Source: MapInfo

The biggest growth market, by far, will be the 65 and older set. In 2000, this group included 35 million people, about 12 percent of the population. By 2025, as Baby Boomers age and life expectancy continues to increase, the number of seniors will double, to more than 70 million people. To put this in perspective, the U.S. will have twice as many seniors in 2025 as it has African Americans today.

The graying of America means that companies will have to do more than pay lip service to the idea of marketing to older people. "The era of youth domination in business and marketing will be over," contends Maddy Dychtwald, the author of *Cycles: How We Will Live, Work, and Buy* (Free Press, 2003). "We've always been very youth focused because the percentage of young people has always overwhelmed the percentage of older adults. Since this domination will be balancing out, we will see more industries and companies begin to seek customers outside of the 18-to-34 demographic," she says. Dychtwald cites a recent Pepsi commercial as an indication of things to come. The ad features a teenage boy in the middle of a mosh pit at a rock concert. He turns around to discover his father rocking out nearby. "The Pepsi Generation is not just about youth anymore," she says. "In fact, it's becoming multigenerational, which is good news for business. It increases their potential target market dramatically."

Still, businesses are not going to suddenly lose all interest in the 18-to-34 demographic. "America loves

magnet markets

Metros with a high diversity quotient, or that have a large senior population are expected to grow the fastest over the next 25 years; areas with a low diversity quotient are more likely to shrink.

METROPOLITAN AREA	2000	2005	2010	2015	2020	2025	CHANGE	PERCENT CHANGE
Laredo, TX	194,636	227,570	261,073	295,656	331,176	367,815	173,179	89.0%
Punta Gorda, FL	142,297	166,531	190,665	215,186	240,104	265,542	123,245	86.6%
Las Vegas, NV-AZ	1,581,525	1,836,721	2,093,204	2,355,460	2,622,811	2,897,008	1,315,483	83.2%
Austin-San Marcos, TX	1,259,929	1,452,492	1,645,797	1,843,311	2,044,712	2,251,148	991,219	78.7%
Provo-Orem, UT	370,532	423,693	476,961	531,378	586,832	643,683	273,151	73.7%
Phoenix-Mesa, AZ	3,276,401	3,689,337	4,105,093	4,531,884	4,968,122	5,416,621	2,140,220	65.3%
Naples, FL	253,806	285,648	317,698	350,581	384,177	418,739	164,933	65.0%
Medford-Ashland, OR	181,824	203,962	226,198	248,931	272,152	295,966	114,142	62.8%
West Palm Beach-Boca Raton, FL	1,137,775	1,275,564	1,412,373	1,551,564	1,692,865	1,837,450	699,675	61.5%
Wilmington, NC	234,816	262,761	290,765	319,409	348,657	378,676	143,860	61.3%
Orlando, FL	1,654,675	1,847,142	2,042,204	2,243,626	2,450,435	2,663,763	1,009,099	61.0%
Huntington-Ashland WV-KY-OH	315,379	315,296	315,753	317,042	319,011	321,537	6,158	2.0%
Toledo, OH	618,056	617,729	618,309	620,615	623,998	628,522	10,466	1.7%
Pittsburgh, PA	2,356,378	2,354,353	2,355,811	2,363,989	2,376,583	2,393,744	37,366	1.6%
Buffalo-Niagara Falls, NY	1,168,948	1,167,651	1,168,075	1,171,903	1,177,887	1,186,172	17,224	1.5%
Jamestown, NY	139,663	139,488	139,511	139,933	140,634	141,593	1,930	1.4%
Lawton, OK	114,886	114,695	114,692	115,022	115,523	116,298	1,412	1.2%
Muncie, IN	118,722	118,689	118,752	119,037	119,485	120,099	1,377	1.2%
Parkersburg-Marietta, WV-OH	151,138	150,877	150,821	151,185	151,848	152,807	1,669	1.1%
Youngstown-Warren, OH	594,416	593,378	593,165	594,563	597,065	600,601	6,185	1.0%
Sharon, PA	120,219	119,972	119,890	120,154	120,620	121,271	1,052	0.9%
Binghamton, NY	251,897	250,751	249,948	249,860	250,236	251,055	-842	-0.3%

Source: Woods & Poole Economics; MapInfo 2003

youth—and all things associated with it," points out Ann A. Fishman, president of Generational Target Marketing Corp., in New Orleans. Adds Rob Duboff, senior vice president of Bowne Decision Quest, based in Waltham, Mass., "Even if there is no increase in the 18-and-under age segment, many marketers will continue to target it as these people start to establish their adult buying habits."

Instead, companies will have to learn to establish brands that attract older consumers without alienating younger ones, says Dychtwald. "It's becoming clear that people aren't over the hill at 50 anymore. Smart marketers will capitalize on this knowledge and create the image of an ageless society where people define themselves more by the activities they're involved in than by their age." Although grandparents can be age 45, 65 or 85, what they have in common is that they all want to buy gifts for their grandchildren, she reports. "You could have college

students ages 20, 30 and 60. It's all part of a more cyclic life, where people cycle in and out of different life-stage events based on their interests rather than their age," explains Dychtwald.

The Consumer Kaleidoscope

On the business agenda:

- Devising marketing campaigns that appeal to many demographic segments
- Figuring out how to address the shrinking white majority

By 2025, the term "minority," as it's currently used, will be virtually obsolete. Non-Hispanic whites will still be the majority race in America—but just barely. According to MapInfo's projections, the share of non-Hispanic whites will fall to 60 percent by 2025, from 70 percent today. And the Hispanic population will almost double, to more than 68 million, from 35 million today, growing to 19 percent of the population from 12 percent. The number of Asians in the U.S. will also double, reaching 24 million, or 7 percent of the population, from its current 4 percent.

Companies that have not yet developed a multicultural marketing strategy will have to "wake up and smell the Thai tacos," quips Abrahamson. "If a company today is concentrating solely on a white audience, then it is living in another galaxy, far, far away," she says. Indeed, as the multicultural market becomes a multibillion-dollar market, companies that are already focusing on nonwhite consumers will find themselves at a distinct advantage, says Mark Seferian, director of business development at EchoboomX, a marketing firm based in Denver. "The companies that are currently working to understand emerging ethnic groups will have a huge advantage over the companies that wait another 10 years," he says. (This will be particularly true in fast-growing metro areas, which will tend to be more diverse. See chart, "The Mixed Society.")

Many businesses will not be able to adapt to the realities of the new marketplace, argues McGinn. "Diversity will be much more than a buzzword—diversity will be the key to economic survival," he says. Ethnic newspapers, magazines, television and radio will see phenomenal growth over the coming decades, McGinn believes, and the mainstream media will have to join forces with these ethnic specialists to stay in business. "Companies will not be able to keep swimming in the mainstream, because there is no mainstream. Instead, it's a series of parallel creeks, some constantly filling, some drying up a little," he says.

One of those "drying" creeks will be the declining majority—the white consumer market, which will experience slow growth over the next 25 years. Companies that market to white America will have to rethink their strategies, according to Rob Frankel, a branding expert based in Los Angeles. "The more cynical side of me suspects a subtle 'white market' will define itself, probably premium-positioned, probably leveraging white angst at lost population dominance," he says. If the current gap in wealth and income between white and nonwhite consumers holds for the next 25 years, businesses will find ample reason to target the nation's 210 million non-Hispanic white consumers.

Will tomorrow's multicultural marketing strategies continue to be segmented by race, with one strategy for "mainstream," one for African American consumers, another for Asians, another for Hispanics? Or will an increasingly multicultural population prefer inclusive, "fusion" strategies that attempt to encompass many different nationalities or racial identities in one campaign, such as those pioneered by clothing retailers Benetton and The Gap? The answer will depend on how Americans come to view their racial identity over the next two and a half decades. For instance, the increasing number of multiracial consumers may not necessarily lead to a consumer culture that blends racial identities, because there's growing evidence that multiracial consumers will think of themselves as a distinct racial group. Former Census Bureau director Kenneth Prewitt points to a growing number of organizations on college campuses aimed at helping multiracial students assert their group identity.

It will become a major challenge for businesses to grasp such subtle matters of cultural identity. To do this, companies will have to rely more heavily on in-depth market research techniques, such as ethnographic research, or new qualitative methods that rely on cognitive science, which promise to give markets an understanding of their consumer's culture, says Seferian. Ethnography enables marketers to understand a culture other than their own through direct observation, absorbing subtle differences in communication styles, behavior patterns and lifestyle. (For more on ethnography, see "Watch Me Now," *American Demographics,* July/August 2002, and "The New Science of Focus Groups," in the March 2003 issue.)

In a nation no longer dominated by one group, most businesses will be marketing to a consumer base that will include a patchwork of racial and ethnic identities. Understanding the differences in consumers' cultural identities will make the difference between failure and success.

High Performance Marketing

Marketing must become a leader for change across the corporation

By Jagdish N. Sheth and Rajendra S. Sisodia

EXECUTIVE briefing

Marketing productivity as we define it includes both efficiency and effectiveness to generate loyal and satisfied customers at low cost. However, many companies either create loyal customers at an unacceptably high cost or alienate customers—and employees—in their search for marketing efficiencies. We believe marketing needs to change in order to reestablish itself as a fundamental driver of business success and that the solution lies in "high performance marketing."

Two major changes have emerged in marketing practice over the past five years. The first is the use of the Internet in marketing. An era of intense experimentation with this technology has taught us several lessons. For example, applicability for business-to-consumer e-commerce turned out to be much narrower than most marketers expected. E-mail marketing appeared to be an efficient marketing channel at first, but its abuse and overuse may soon dilute its effectiveness just as direct mail became synonymous with junk mail and telemarketing degenerated from a cost-effective two-way interactive channel into sometimes intrusive customer harassment.

The Internet has empowered customers—usually to the disadvantage of marketers. Now customers can readily search for the best "deal" on every transaction and can communicate with each other to spread word—both positive and negative—about their product purchase experiences. Marketers have been at least moderately successful in the use of "mass personalization" technologies such as collaborative filtering to tailor recommendations to customers and generate some incremental sales.

The second major development has been the popularization of customer relationship management (CRM) software and the rise of 1-to-1 marketing. The CRM industry has exploded in the last few years, growing at 40% per year as more than 2,000 vendors have emerged, promising to achieve the seamless integration of sales, marketing, and customer service around the needs of individual customers. The CRM software market is expected [to] reach $10 billion in 2001 (according to AMR Research), while the worldwide CRM services business reached $34 billion in revenues in 1999, growing at an annual 20% rate with a projected reach of $125 billion by 2004, according to IDC.

These developments, though momentous, have not brought marketing appreciably closer to our stated ideal of "effective efficiency." In many ways, the marketing function remains as troubled as ever. Major new problems have arisen, such as the ability of customers to readily organize themselves into powerful groups speaking with a unified voice, while others have subsided somewhat. For example, as media continue to get fragmented and more addressable, marketing noise levels have decreased somewhat.

The Trouble With Marketing

Marketing is still not truly customer-centric. For all the lip service that has been paid, marketers are still attempting to control and drive customers to behave in ways they want, rather than organizing their own activities around customer needs. The Internet has not altered this in any significant way.

Most CRM implementations have been expensive failures. CRM, fundamentally, is really just fine-tuned target marketing, albeit with better coordination between sales, marketing, and customer service than we have had in the past. Many companies rushed to embrace CRM as a cure-all that would make them more customer-focused and successful, ignoring the reality that no software can overcome the lack of a customer-centric culture and mindset. Even for companies already possessing a strong customer-centric orientation, there is no guarantee that grafting a CRM system on top will lead to major improvements; it can even lead to deteriorated performance if it takes away from employees' flexibility and responsiveness in dealing with customers.

Most CRM systems do little to improve the customer experience; they just enable marketers to better deploy their resources. Overall, companies have probably lost more money than they have gained through these implementations. In fact, it is estimated that 60% to 80% of CRM projects do not achieve their goals, and 30% to 50% fail outright. CRM implementations in most companies have been initiated by CEOs and led by CIOs; the marketing function has rarely taken the lead or even been actively involved in the decision making. CEOs have embraced CRM technology as a way to finally get some precision and accountability in their marketing efforts. However, the treatment has rarely matched the disease, with the unsurprising result that the marketing function remains as malaise-ridden as ever.

Marketing spending continues to yield poor returns, especially on advertising and branding. For example, many dot-coms spent the bulk of their venture funding on outrageously expensive advertising campaigns, under the delusion that having a recognizable brand would solve all of their other business problems.

The promise of radically efficient business models that leverage the uniqueness of the Internet has given way to widespread disillusionment and a seeming return to "business as usual." However, the root cause of the dot-com debacle was not poor technology or lack of capital, but companies' failure to understand customer behavior. They were left dumbfounded when the anticipated huge changes in behavior required for success didn't happen. Companies especially failed to understand the psychology of consumer resistance to innovation and failed to develop strategies to overcome such resistance.

We believe marketers have not yet fully examined how their function needs to change in order to reestablish itself as a primary driver of business success. High performance marketing (HPM) may be the solution to their problems.

High Performance Organizations

Jordan defines high performance organizations as "groups of employees who produce desired goods or services at higher quality with the same or fewer resources. Their productivity and quality improve continuously, from day to day, week to week, and year to year, leading to the achievement of their mission." (See Additional Reading)

High performance organizations share many characteristics. In addition to identifying and eliminating non-value-added activities, leveraging technology in the service of their mission, and having a strong, organization-wide customer orientation, they also have inspirational and transformational leadership that focuses their

resources and energies on achieving a clearly defined mission.

Organizations that perform well empower employees to act autonomously to achieve the corporate mission and provide incentives to individual employees to align their behaviors with the achievement of better outcomes for customers. They also have organizational cultures that embody a high degree of trust—what Carnevale calls "an expression of faith and confidence that a person or an institution will be fair, reliable, ethical, competent, and non-threatening."

High performance organizations tend to use systems thinking, so all employees have a dynamic understanding of how the "living" organization functions and the interdependencies between components and subsystems. They are flexible and adaptable to changing circumstances, emphasizing continuous improvement, reinvention, and innovation.

High Performance Marketing

The operations and manufacturing functions at many leading companies today can be described as "high performance" because they have demonstrated continuous quality improvements and cost reductions. More than anything else, marketers will have to start thinking in new and creative ways about everything in their domain—markets, customers, budgets, organizational structures, information, and incentives. We propose the marketing function needs to adopt the following tenets in order to move toward true high performance.

Customer centricity. Customer-centric marketing will lead to non-intuitive consequences. First, whereas traditional marketing has been concerned with demand management, customercentric marketing will lead the marketing function toward "supply management"—the ability to rapidly respond to customer requirements rather than focusing on controlling them. Second, traditional marketing practices emphasize the acquisition of customers, while customer-centric marketing emphasizes the retention of the "right" customers along with the "outsourcing" of the rest. Third, whereas traditional firms and customers are institutionally separate with little interaction, customer-centric marketing will lead to customers and firms co-creating products, pricing, and distribution. Fourth, customer-centric marketing will be characterized by more "fixed costs" and fewer variable costs; companies will make infrastructure investments that greatly reduce transaction costs. Finally, the vocabulary, metrics, and organizations will evolve toward a customer focus rather than product focus or segment focus. For example, Procter & Gamble renamed its channel sales organization "customer business development" in early 1999.

Investment orientation. In most companies, sales and marketing expenditures are several times greater than capital expenditures. Yet capital expenditures are subject to a far greater amount of analysis and evaluation than marketing expenditures. Most marketing activities involve a substantial lag between action and effect. When marketing is treated as an expense, the causality often becomes reversed, as marketing budgets tend to be determined by sales forecasts. Treating marketing as an investment forces companies to come to grips with the temporal relationship between current marketing actions and future marketplace reactions.

Well-spent marketing resources applied to a brand in its early years can build a stock of value that can be sustained or even enhanced with very small amounts of spending. Marketing investments can pay off if they are well-timed and targeted. Investments made at the right stage of the product life cycle and directed at the most profitable customers deliver superior returns.

Systems thinking. Systems modeling is an integrative approach that combines systems thinking and the principles of cybernetics. It incorporates causal-loop diagramming to show sequences of cause-and-effect relationships as well as stock-and-flow diagrams to represent systemic effects of feedback on the accumulations and rates of flow in the system. These two system representations are coupled in order to simulate the behavior of the system. Modeling and simulating the system helps managers recognize and understand the dynamic patterns of system behavior. Systems dynamics offers a great deal of potential to marketers, but is hardly used. For example, it is a useful approach to model the customer acquisition and retention process.

Incentive alignment. The incentives provided to marketing employees are haphazard and often at odds. Most advertising agencies are still paid a commission proportional to the volume of advertising run, creating a disincentive for higher impact advertising that needs fewer exposures. Many salespeople are still compensated on short-term customer acquisition measures, with little regard for customer profitability or longevity.

The guiding principle in creating incentive systems is to use market mechanisms wherever possible. In their book, *Free to Choose* (1990, Harcourt Brace), Milton and Rose Friedman present a framework for evaluating the relative productivity of spending in different circumstances. The "Friedman Matrix" categorizes business spending along two dimensions: whose money is spent and for whose benefit the money is spent. The way to align employee and company interests is to organize every spending decision in such a manner that employees act as though they are spending their own money for their own benefit. This will ensure that they are both effective and efficient in their resource allocation.

The framework suggests that resources are spent most optimally when they are "owned" by an individual and spent by that individual for his or her own purposes. In buying a family car, for example, individuals are likely to spend what they know they can afford and get a car

that satisfies their needs. On the other hand, individuals able to spend someone else's money on themselves (e.g., buying an expense account meal) are likely to get what they want (effective), but will probably spend more than if they were paying their own money (inefficient). A third situation exists when an individual spends his or her own money (staying within a budget) to purchase a gift for someone else; while efficient, this is unlikely to optimally satisfy the recipient (ineffective). Finally, when individuals (e.g., bureaucrats) are charged with spending other people's money (e.g., taxpayers) on things that do not affect them directly (e.g., welfare), spending is neither effective nor efficient.

Incentive alignment is a guiding principle for moving toward high performance marketing. Examples include creating sales force compensation schemes to reward customer retention and profitability (as the insurance industry has done in recent years) and incentivizing new product development teams to create high quality new products in a short time without consuming inordinate resources.

Avoid incremental thinking. When it comes to changes in how the marketing function is defined, organized, and compensated, incremental thinking will not suffice. Given product parity and near-perfect information availability and matching, the quality of a firm's marketing strategy and execution will be prime drivers of market capitalization.

For too long, the marketing function has been content to focus on relatively trivial tactics and has been lackadaisical about taking a prominent role in shaping the overall fortunes of the corporation. In other words, marketing has not aspired to a higher level and has demonstrated no zeal or passion to elevate its respect and relevance within the corporation. Other functional areas have rallied around ambitious and organization-transforming initiatives, such as TQM and Six Sigma (driven by operations), Economic Value Added (driven by CFOs), and the Balanced Scorecard (driven by accounting).

Marketing needs to break out of its "doer rather than leader" role and its preoccupation with the mundane. We believe marketing needs to become a leader for change and transformation across the corporation. Marketing must take hold of the leadership levers for the corporation. The best way for it to do so is to leverage its fundamental identity as the voice of the customer within the corporation. Marketing needs to go outside the box and break many of the self-imposed rules that have relegated it to a constricted role.

Understand market growth. One of the biggest gaps remaining in marketing know-how is an understanding of what determines market growth. Marketers must attempt to grow the total market, not just try to protect and grow their market share. Several factors can contribute to market growth, such as an emphasis on emerging markets and the creative "dematuring" or revitalization of mature markets through the fusion of non-traditional technologies (as Yamaha did by incorporating digital electronics into pianos) or injecting elements of fashion and personalization (as some European manufacturers have done with small appliances). Commodity markets in developing markets such as India and China are ripe for dematuring, through the introduction of packaging, processing, and other value-adding functions.

View customers differently. Just as we have gone through significant changes in how we think about employees and shareholders, we will need to engage in some fresh thinking about customers. Customers should be viewed and managed as assets of the organization to be invested in, depreciated, and replaced. In addition to the outsourcing of customers (e.g., using business partners to serve certain customer groups), companies also need to think about trading, sharing, firing, and outright selling customers.

Harness marketing information. In *2020 Vision* (1992, Simon & Schuster), Stan Davis and Bill Davidson described the "information exhaust" that companies generate through their ongoing transactions and relationships with customers. In the past, most of this exhaust was discharged into the atmosphere and disappeared. Smart companies, however, have developed ways to "turbocharge" the core business by harnessing this information flow. Through feedback mechanisms, this allows the marketing "engine" to operate at a higher level of efficiency. Information exhaust also can generate highly profitable sidelines that in some cases may become more profitable than the core business. For example, by focusing on the lifetime value of customers, General Motors' U.S. operation sees the potential for substantial synergies across its automotive, consumer credit, mortgage, and even its communications businesses.

Firms can use this thinking to guide strategic decisions on entering new businesses. For example, entry into the credit card business is often dictated not by the economics of that business per se, but by the usable information used to improve the core business. Similar examples can be found in the magazine and software industries, as the recent merger of AOL and Time Warner demonstrates. Given their potential value, it is imperative that firms develop sound mechanisms for sharing information and managing marketing knowledge. Marketing employees need to receive incentives to share information that could be of broader value to the corporation.

Prepare for a new role. Senior management needs to reconsider how to control and integrate the marketing function for best results—to determine the proper role of the marketing function in a corporation where virtually all functions have become market-oriented. To start with, the sales-marketing-customer service separation must end, and marketers must take on the responsibility for attracting as well as retaining and growing profitable customers. Additionally, marketing has to be accorded greater say over key decision areas such as procurement, pricing,

product development, and logistics, all of which have been gradually taken away from marketing departments.

In the future marketing will get wider but shallower; it will encompass a wider range of activities but will perform fewer of them in house. Many activities will be outsourced to best-in-class external suppliers, while others will be performed in various parts of the corporation. The marketing manager's job will evolve from a "doer" to a coordinator of internal and external resources pertinent to customer retention and profitable growth.

The marketing function will also, in a more deliberate way, formally incorporate upstream linkages that were once the domain of the purchasing department. Key suppliers will become an integral part of the marketing team and will be involved in strategic planning and new product development. For example, this is already happening in the automotive industry.

Employ dynamic budgeting. The budgeting process is probably one of the biggest contributors to marketing's problems. Budgeting is static, forecast-driven (based on notoriously inaccurate forecasts subject to intense and deliberate distortions and game playing), counterintuitive (e.g., mixing cause and effect in advertising), and subject to the "use it or lose it" rule. Budgets escalate year after year in prosperous times, with little consideration for changes in actual needs over time.

Static budgeting needs to be replaced with dynamic budgeting, where resources are requested and allocated based on an "as needed and justified" basis. Rather than budget by scale or in some proportion to the top line, budgeting should be driven by the size of the opportunity, the anticipated ROI, and increase in shareholder value. This requires decoupling the marketing budgeting for a brand from the current brand's revenue level and instead coupling it to the opportunity for revenue and profit growth that the brand presents. In situations where more traditional budgeting procedures persist, managers need to receive direct incentives not to fully use their budgets, just as U.S. farmers are often given incentives not to plant crops.

Consider how marketing budgets and customer-related responsibilities are typically allocated in companies. The marketing budget usually covers advertising, sales promotions, market research, and some portion of distribution costs. It may include the cost of the sales force, though in many companies it does not. It almost never includes the cost of customer service, and usually does not include product development.

It is not unusual to find situations where sales, customer service, and new product development are funded out of budgets that are not under marketing's control. Clearly, we need to create transparent incentive schemes to focus all marketing personnel on the essentials: the profitability of what they do and the maintenance of high levels of customer satisfaction and retention.

Change marketing metrics. Marketing employees for too long have been measured on market share, with little or no consideration to the profitability of that market share. Of late, there has been some movement toward thinking more about the bottom-line impact or measuring marketing based on its profit impact.

Ultimately, the measure that matters most for a business is shareholder value or market capitalization. It is a summary descriptor of all the value the business has created and is expected to create in the future. The question for the marketing function is: How can it affect the company's market capitalization? The measure of marketing's success must move from "share of market" to "share of market capitalization" within the industry. Operationalizing this will be one of the key challenges for marketing in the years to come.

Filling the Void

Reflecting the greater emphasis on shareholder value in recent years, the CFO today drives most companies. However, a preoccupation with finances can be dangerous because it can lead companies to lose sight of the true driver of business success—the long-term satisfaction and retention of profitable customers.

In our view, marketing has a great opportunity to create excitement around becoming customer-centric and in the process can satisfy both the CEO and the CFO. If, on the other hand, it continues to take a back seat within the corporation, it will be abdicating its fiscal responsibilities. High performance marketing is really "inspirational marketing" that can rally the corporation to set and achieve much higher goals than ever before. While it has a number of tenets as discussed earlier, its defining characteristic is that it is customer-centric. In order to operationalize customer-centric marketing fully, it is

essential that companies create a new senior executive role that takes an outside-in perspective rather than the inside-out perspective adopted by others. This role is that of a "chief customer officer" (CCO).

The CCO position, while currently seen mostly in small high-tech companies, is expected to become commonplace. The Meta Group projects that 25% of Global 2000 businesses will have a CCO by 2003, while Gartner expects 15% of U.S. companies to have such a position by 2003. Cisco Systems has been a pioneer in this regard; it established the position of senior vice president of customer advocacy in 1991, with Cisco's customer service, product design, and IT groups reporting to it.

There is a void at the top of most major corporations, and marketing must move quickly to fill it. If it does not, marketing will continue to become more marginalized, and all stakeholders—customers, employees, and shareholders—will suffer as a result.

Additional Reading

Carnevale, David G. (1995), *Trustworthy Government: Leadership and Management Strategies for Building Trust and High Performance.* New York: Jossey-Bass.

Jordan, Sephena A. (1999), "Innovative Cultures + Empowered Employees = High Performance Organizations," *Public Productivity & Management Review,* (23:1),109–113.

Sheth, Jagdish N., Rajendra S. Sisodia, and Arun Sharma (2000), "The Antecedents and Consequences of Customer-Centric Marketing," *Journal of the Academy of Marketing Science,* (28:1), 55–66.

About the Authors

Jagdish N. Sheth is the Charles H. Kellstadt professor of marketing at the Goizueta Business School at Emory University in Atlanta.

Rajendra S. Sisodia is trustee professor of marketing at Bentley College in Waltham, Mass. He may be reached at rsisodia@bentley.edu.

From *Marketing Management,* September/October 2001, pp. 18-23. © 2001 by the American Marketing Association. Reprinted by permission.

Marketing High Technology: Preparation, Targeting, Positioning, Execution

A range of strategies are available to the high-tech marketing manager taking a shot at launching the latest technology.

Chris Easingwood and Anthony Koustelos

Commercialization of new high-tech products is often the costliest stage of the entire product development process. Yet even when the process is well managed, the risk of failure remains high. New high-tech products usually have just one shot at the market. Get it wrong and the consequences are invariably fatal. And although the launch strategy is critical, this stage is largely neglected in the business press and academic literature on high-tech marketing, innovation, and new product development.

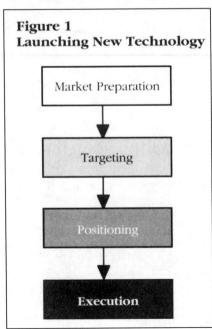

Figure 1
Launching New Technology

- Market Preparation
- Targeting
- Positioning
- **Execution**

Persuading a market to adopt a new technology is generally comprised of four stages, shown in Figure 1. The first step, market preparation, involves readying customers and other companies for the change. Typically this stage takes place while the product is still in development, though not necessarily so. The second stage in planning the marketing of the product is targeting, followed by positioning based on the expected competitive situation. The final stage involves execution and consists of the strategies that are often the most visible part of the mix, used to achieve specific results. Each of the four stages will be described in turn.

MARKET PREPARATION

Market preparation is intended to get the market ready for the new technology by building awareness and, most important, forming relationships. Figure 2 shows some examples.

Cooperation/Licensing/Alliances

In many cases, the way a marketer chooses to set up the market is crucial. Some form of cooperation is increasingly seen not as an option but as a necessity. Few companies can go it alone, at least not when the launch of major technology is concerned.

Alliances and licensing arrangements encourage the adoption of technological standards for at least two good reasons.

One is because of the expected boost to sales. Customers are reluctant to adopt when faced with competing and incompatible technologies (recall the days of the VHS and Betamax videocassette formats). They realize that markets rarely allow two competing technologies to thrive, and eventually coalesce around the preferred one, condemning the other(s) to decline.

The other reason is that companies sometimes seek to establish their own technology as the standard, to preempt those of rivals and avoid having a competing standard imposed. This was very much the reason for Psion, Motorola, Ericsson, and Nokia forming a consortium called Symbian. The four agreed to adopt Psion's computer operating system, called EPOC, in the hope that this would become the industry standard for the next generation of wireless communication devices, such as mobile phones and palm-top computers. The mobile phone is expected to become "smart," sending and receiving data, downloading from the Internet, and storing large amounts of information. The alliance is also an attempt to prevent Microsoft's Windows CE operating system in consumer electronics from becoming the standard. Ericsson, Motorola, and Nokia each had to abandon its own operating system in adopting Psion's—a sacrifice that may prove worthwhile, given *Fortune's* claim that David Potter, Psion's CEO, is the man Microsoft's Bill Gates fears the most (Wallace 1998).

Figure 2
Market Preparation: Some Examples

Form alliances	Psion, Motorola, Ericsson, and Nokia adopting Psion's computer operating system to thwart Microsoft's Windows CE operating system
Supply to OEMs	IBM licensing its hard disk drives
Provide pre-launch information	Apple providing information on the Macintosh NC

Sometimes the alliances formed can be informal or "loose," arising through mutual advantage. This is because, more and more, technological products rarely stand alone. They depend on the existence of other products and technologies. A good example is the World Wide Web, with its groupings of businesses that include browsers, on-line news, e-mail, network retailing, and financial services. Arthur (1996) calls these networks of products and services that support and enhance each other "mini-ecologies." They are increasingly the basic frameworks of knowledge-based industries, and companies have to secure themselves a place in these loose alliances built around a mini-ecology.

Supply to OEMs

Market preparation can also be tackled by sharing the new technology with original equipment manufacturers (OEMs). This increases the awareness of the product and the technology, and boosts sales via expansion to new markets. IBM developed two powerful hard disk drives, Travel-Star 8GS and 3GN, for its own ThinkPad notebooks, but decided to license them to Acer, Gateway 2000, Dell, and other OEMs as well, which plan to use the drives in their portable PCs. This market preparation tactic enables the producer to retain full ownership of its technology while at the same time expanding market potential beyond its own marketing capacity, albeit at a lower margin.

Provide Pre-Launch Information

The type of information released before launch, and the manner in which it is delivered, can be a key tactical decision in the product launch. The publicly visible demonstration of this strategy is the article in the press, detailing the time the product will reach the market, the basis of the technology, and other information. Intel has been releasing details of its new MMX technology-based Pentium-II chip. Articles have also appeared on the Macintosh NC, Apple's forthcoming network computer, based on the company's powerful new chip, PowerPC 750. Those who typically need to be informed before the launch are the distribution network, service suppliers (such as software houses), and the media, who in turn inform potential customers.

The information to be released has to be planned carefully so as to arouse sufficient interest in the new product without losing a competitive edge in a market where imitation can materialize with lightning speed. A careful balance must be drawn that allows for the need to have influential components of the market's infrastructure informed without giving a technological lead away to competitors.

Educate the Market

A special form of providing pre-release information is an education program. This is very ambitious and more long-term than merely releasing information, and thus it is less common. It is exactly what Intel did in the early days of the microchip. Rather than marketing the product directly—there were just too many markets with too many applications for that—it set about educating the various markets on the potential of the technology, leaving them with much greater in-depth knowledge to work out how the product might be used in their particular markets.

However, education has to be managed and timed carefully. Otherwise, the company sells the vision before it has the product to deliver that vision. Not surprisingly, smaller companies shy away from trying to educate markets, leaving it to larger corporations with their greater resources and longer planning horizons.

Create Special Distribution Arrangements

Finally, technology may be launched into new markets as well as currently served markets, which would entail establishing new channels of distribution. Distribution rights may be given to competitors in these new markets. New distribution can also be gained through joint ventures, possibly involving collaborative development of the technology.

TARGETING

Adoption of a new technology is likely to be faster if the marketing strategy is compatible with the segment targeted. Easingwood and Lunn (1992) examined the diffusion of telecommunications products and found that clearly targeted products diffused more rapidly than non-targeted ones (see Figure 3 for examples).

Target Innovative Adopters

Targeting innovative adopters can take two main forms: (a) targeting both companies and innovative individuals within those companies, or (b) targeting sectors.

Innovative Companies and Individuals. Based on the familiar model, the technology adoption life cycle, this strategy identifies innovative adopters because they are prepared to buy without seeing the product up and running elsewhere. They do not insist that the technology have a "track record." Moore (1991) divides these early buyers—only a small percentage of the total potential market, but hugely influential—into technological enthusiasts, or "techies," and visionaries. Techies are intrigued by technology and will explore a

---

Figure 3
Targeting: Some Examples

Target innovative adopters	NTT taking its global photo transmission system to sectors, such as the insurance industry, that are likely to be early adopters
Target pragmatists	Amgen using a large sales force to promote its hepatitis C drug to *all* hospital specialists
Target conservatives	Microsoft aiming its integrated software product Works at the PC conservative market
Target current customers	IBM Software Group working with many of the Global 5000
Target competitors' customers	Xerox targeting its digital copiers at Hewlett-Packard customers

---

product's potential for themselves. Their endorsement is vital because it means the product does, in fact, work. Visionaries are the managers with clout, often very senior, who can see a product's potential for overturning existing ways of operating, delivering significant value and competitive advantage to those organizations prepared to grasp the new technology.

Technological enthusiasts and visionaries, although placed together in this innovative group, are very different in some regards. Techies are excited by the technology itself, whereas the visionaries try to find its greater worth—some single, compelling application that uses the full range of the new technology. A visionary is motivated by a potentially significant leap forward, not by the newness of the technology.

Visionaries are a rare breed. They not only have the ability to see the potential when no one else can, they also have the management drive and charisma to persuade the rest of an organization to back the vision. They anticipate a radical discontinuity between the old ways and the new, realizing that this rarely happens smoothly, and so they will tolerate the glitches and setbacks that inevitably occur before this is achieved.

The only way to work with visionaries, says Moore, is to use a small, high-level sales force. Constantly looking to leverage technology, visionaries typically maintain good relationships with techies, so this segment should not be neglected. And techies can be reached fairly easily through the technical and business press. It is their job to stay alert to all developments, wher-

ever their sources, not just to focus on their own industry.

Early Adopting Sectors. Innovators can sometimes be hard to identify, but they are worth searching out. They start the ball rolling. However, an alternative to identifying individuals with these special attractive characteristics is to target whole sectors that are likely to be early buyers.

USDC developed an active-matrix flat panel display screen—in effect, the first "paper-quality" screen, with each pixel linked to its own transistor—and targeted the product at some of the world's leading air forces, a sector with a pressing need for the latest technology.

In the telecommunications sector, NTT has developed Digital Photo System, a means of transmitting a photo by a digital camera over the airways via cellular phones to a laptop computer and from there to a printer. The whole process takes about 10 seconds and can be done globally. The service was aimed initially at the newspaper and insurance sectors, both of which would particularly benefit from an acceleration in the speed of the internal processing of photographs.

Target the Pragmatists

Sometimes called the "early majority," pragmatists (as Moore calls them) are the large group of adopters following behind the techies and visionaries, though Moore argues that the gap between the two groups is so large it deserves to be called a chasm. Pragmatists typically comprise large organizations with a clear need to adopt new technologies to retain or improve competi-

tiveness, but with a reluctance to do so. The dislocation would be so extensive and the size of the investment required to switch the whole firm over to the new technology so large that they are risk-averse. People in this group are reasonably comfortable about taking on new technology, but only when some well-established references exist. Their preference is for evolution, not revolution. They are looking for something that can be slotted into existing ways of doing things. "If the goal of visionaries is to take a quantum leap forward," explains Moore, "the goal of pragmatists is to make a percentage improvement—incremental, measurable, predictable progress."

Marketing to pragmatists is a matter of:

- attending the industry conferences and trade shows;
- getting frequent mentions in the industry magazines;
- being installed in other companies in the same industry;
- developing industry-specific applications;
- having alliances with other key suppliers to the industry.

As Moore observes, pragmatists like to hear companies talk about their new products as "industry standards." What they hate to hear is products described as "state-of-the-art." This makes them extremely edgy. Pharmaceutical companies are well known for targeting their new drugs at hospital specialists working in the leading teaching hospitals. However, they do not neglect the pragmatists either. Amgen has assembled a sales team of about 50 people to promote its new hepatitis C drug to all the hematologists and gastroenterologists working in hospitals who may have to treat patients with the ailment.

Target Conservatives

The "conservatives," or "late adopters," really are not that keen on new technology. By and large, they would really rather not adopt any if they could get away with it, but competitive pressures may force them to do so. They are not that confident in their ability to adapt to new technology, so they like to see evidence of support. By the time the technology gets to them, there will probably be an established standard. Conservatives like to buy pre-assembled packages, with everything bundled. "They want high-tech products to be like refrigerators," says Moore. "You open the door, the light comes on automatically, your food stays cold, and you don't have to think about it."

However, it can he a big mistake to neglect this section of the market. For one thing, it is large—probably around a third of the whole market. It is often not developed as systematically as it should be, possibly because high-tech companies do not generally find it easy to empathize with this group. The product development costs are apt to be fully amortized at this stage, so extending the product's life should be highly profitable.

Because of conservatives' reluctance to come to grips with a new technology and its implications, a product has to be made increasingly easy to adopt if a high-tech company is to succeed with this group. The DOS PC operating system stalled when it reached the late adopter segment—the home market, the home office, the small business. This segment does not have the support offered in large companies and was disinclined to teach itself DOS. It took the greater simplicity of Windows 3.0 to bring it into the market. Microsoft has aimed its product Works, an integrated, all-in-one word processor, spreadsheet, and database (none of which are state-of-the-art), at the PC conservative market.

Target Current Customers

Existing customers can be an obvious target group for well-established companies. So it makes sense for IBM Software Group, the world's second largest software firm—which has very strong customer relationships with the Global 5000, the world's largest companies—to think first of its current customers. Although current customers ought to be the most secure market, this is not necessarily the case. They can he hard to satisfy and quite costly to retain. Such is Intel's experience. It is having to cut the prices of some of its computer chips in an attempt to retain big corporate customers such as Compaq and Packard Bell. The latter are threatening to switch to Cyrix, the rival microprocessor producer, as they do everything possible to reduce the costs of their lowest-priced PCs.

Targeting existing customers is a strategy particularly appropriate to rapidly changing, advanced technologies. It can be particularly relevant for complex technologies when the decision to adopt often relies on a high degree of technical expertise and mutual trust between buyer and supplier.

Target Competitors' Customers

Finally, competitors' customers can present a prime opportunity, especially when the company's own product is competitive and the competitor has a large market share. Xerox would claim that this is the case for the new digital copiers designed by its Office Document Product Group. The copiers, which have faxing, scanning, and printing capabilities when connected to the personal computers of Hewlett-Packard's customers, are targeted toward HP and its dominance in the printer market.

Such a practice is commonplace in the pharmaceutical industry. Amgen has pitched its new hepatitis C treatment drug, Infeger, at those customers for whom the existing treatments, such as Schering-Plough's Intron A or Roche Holdings' Roferon A, have not been successful.

Of course, this strategy is very aggressive. For brand new technologies, it may be counterproductive. Aggressive competitive tactics may be seen as undermining the credibility of the entire technology, rather than just the competitor's product, as may have been intended.

POSITIONING

Some new technologies are so specialized that targeting and positioning strategies are too unambiguous and virtually redundant. Other new technologies are so wide-ranging in their potential applications that the market needs some strong clues as to targeting and positioning before it will respond. Many products fall between these two extremes.

Positioning can be based on tangible (technological) or intangible characteristics (such as image), with technologically intensive industrial markets favoring the former. Where the market is not so technologically informed, or the benefits of the new technology are not so easily differentiated from competitors, positioning characteristics are likely to be more intangible. Positioning possibilities can be numerous, but some of those used most often are described here (see Figure 4 for examples).

Emphasize Exclusivity

A way to differentiate the product offer is by emphasizing how exclusive it is. In other words, can the product be placed in the upper segment of the market, where the margins are usually higher? For example, by focusing on quality, engineering, and adjustability, Recaro is offering a top-of-the-range child's safety seat—the Recaro-Start—that appeals to wealthier parents who place high priority on their children's safety. The company is playing heavily on its reputation for producing high-tech safety seats for Porsche and Aston-Martin.

Emphasize a Low Price

It used to be that low prices were considered an inappropriate lever for high-tech products and services. The market's reluctance to purchase was due to the misgivings it held about the new product's performance, which was largely unproven. The best strategy, marketers believed, was to address this reluctance directly by lowering the perceived risk that the product would not come up to expectations, or by reducing the perceived likelihood that it might be made redundant by a superior technology. In any case, high margins were needed to recoup the high costs of development.

Well, not necessarily anymore. Low price is used more and more in high-tech markets. For instance, phone companies will have to pay just $5 per device to use EPOC from Symbian, versus a reported $25 for Microsoft's Windows CE.

Emphasize Technological Superiority

Focusing on the technological superiority of a new high-tech product is common. When technology is changing rapidly and perhaps radically, it would seem that positioning a product on the basis of the latest technology built into it should reflect the product's true *raison d'etre*.

Figure 4
Positioning: Some Examples

Emphasize exclusivity	Recaro (supplier to Porsche and Aston Martin) with its top-of-the-range child's safety seat
Emphasize a low price	Just $5 per mobile phone for the operating system from Symbian ($25 quoted for the alternative)
Emphasize technological superiority	Xerox focusing on the superiority of digital copiers over the old technology
Emphasize a "safe bet"	Lucent Technologies designing its digital phones to be compatible with international standards

Xerox's new digital copiers are priced about 10 percent higher than old-style copiers because of the greater quality and reliability they offer compared to the old "light lens" technology copiers. This practice is also observed in the computer component manufacturing industry, where such new products as "bonded modems," storing units, and processor chips justify their premium pricing through their advanced technological features.

However, emphasizing such superiority does have its drawbacks. First, by stressing technological features, the marketer is assuming a certain level of knowledge that may not be present in at least part of the target market. Second, the preoccupation with technological specifications may obscure the genuine benefits customers could realize from the technology. Given the buying center nature of many high-tech adoption decisions involving technical specialists and nonspecialists, not all of whom are capable of translating technical specifications into everyday benefits, it may be more successful to come up with a more benefit-specific positioning tactic.

Emphasize a 'Safe Bet'

Stressing customer protection in the product is important because it enhances the product's credibility element and reduces the associated risk of moving to a new technology. Lucent Technologies focused on the fact that the specifications of both of its two newly introduced digital phones fall under established standards. One of the phones operates on the Code Division Multiple Access (CDMA) technology standard of the United States. The other, which is a "dual mode/dual band" handset, operates on the Time Division Multiple Access (TDMA) standard introduced by AT&T to serve the entire European market, where the existence of different networks can otherwise hinder compatibility.

EXECUTION

As the final stage and therefore the one that completes the product's projection into the marketplace, execution is designed to trigger a positive purchase decision. The strategies used depend on the objectives of the launch itself, which in turn depend on the state of technology and the awareness the market has of it. For a very new technology, of which the market is unaware, execution tends to focus on conveying the generic benefits. At the other extreme, where the technology is well known to the market, the launch objectives focus more on establishing a brand name and competitive advantage. Figure 5 provides examples.

Use Opinion Leaders

It makes good sense to obtain the support of opinion leaders. As Moore states, "No company can afford to pay for every marketing contact made. Every programme must rely on some on-going chain-reaction effects, what is usually called 'word of mouth.'" Word-of-mouth is invaluable, of course, but the support of opinion leaders, who are industrial rather than public celebrities, can also be taken on board more formally, such as in advertising or through appearances at company seminars.

Compaq and NEC Technologies have managed to secure the endorsement of a number of well-known technical journalists for their FPDS screen. Pharmaceutical companies try to communicate the views of prominent doctors on their new drugs to influence the views of general practitioners and other doctors.

Reduce the Risk of Adoption

It is sometimes possible to reduce adoption risks. Can the product be offered on an introductory trial? Can it be leased? Luz Engineering, a producer of industrial solar heaters costing between $2–4 million, came up with a novel variation on this approach. Now Luz is prepared to sell its systems. However, it is also prepared to install and operate the solar heaters itself, in which case the client merely contracts to buy steam at 350°F for 20 years at a discount from the prevailing local power company rate. This is a "no-lose deal" from the client's perspective. The client pays for none of the installation and operating costs, but enjoys most of the expected benefits of the technology, without the associated risks.

Cultivate a Winner Image

Individuals and organizations can easily be confused by too much choice. Their first reaction, when faced with a confusing purchasing decision, is to postpone it. But when this is no longer possible, they vote for the safe choice: the market leader. There is safety in numbers. And this position can be reinforcing in technology markets. Other companies will recognize the leadership position and design supporting products and services around the market leader, which will thus become even more the preferred choice. The number one product becomes easier to use, cheaper to use, and better supported. There is a "winner take most" tendency, as Arthur states—the phenomenon of increasing returns. The bigger you get, the more apt you are to get bigger still. Conversely, the smaller you get, the more apt you are to shrink even more. Success breeds success, failure breeds failure. You have to become

Figure 5
Execution: Some Examples

Use opinion leaders	Compaq and NEC Technologies securing endorsements from technical journalists
Reduce the risk of adoption	Luz Engineering installing and running its industrial solar heaters that supply clients with energy at guaranteed prices
Cultivate a winner image	IBM advertising its position as recipient of the most U.S. patents for the fifth year running
Concentrate on a particular application	Lotus Notes focusing on worldwide accounting and consulting firms

a "gorilla," because if you do not, you'll be a "chimpanzee" or, more likely, a "monkey."

Thus, companies should try to cultivate a winner image for themselves and their products. However, this often involves allocating considerable resources to a big media splash aimed at communicating the (preordained) success of the new product. So this strategy is most popular with large companies. When Microsoft launched Windows 95, it did not pull its punches or spare its expenses. In the U.S., the Empire State Building was bathed in Windows colors. In the U.K., the *Times*, sponsored by Microsoft, doubled its print run and was given away free. In Australia, the Sydney Opera House was commandeered. The worldwide event, accompanied by the Rolling Stones' hit "Start Me Up," was said to have cost $200 million, but was hugely successful: one million copies sold in the U.S. in the first four days, compared to the 60 days it took the upgrade to MS-DOS to reach that level.

Of course, the approach to this position can be more subtle. In the last year, IBM received more U.S. patents than any other company, taking the top spot for the fifth consecutive year in a list that used to be dominated primarily by Japanese firms. This achievement has been stressed by IBM through articles in the technology sections of top-rated journals. It has also been the theme of an advertising campaign that aims to build a leader image for the company.

Sometimes the leadership position cannot be established across the entire market, in which case it should be established in a market segment. It is important to be the biggest fish in the pond, even if it means searching out a very small pond.

A market leader position is particularly important for pragmatists. These are the people who are contemplating committing their organizations to the new product—a much less risky gamble if the new product is the market leader.

A company that can establish a lead in a segment is in a very strong position. All the major customers have committed themselves to the product and so want it to remain the standard. The company can only lose such a position by shooting itself in the foot. Moore believes that segments conspire, unconsciously, "to install some company or product as the market leader and then do everything in their power to keep [it] there." This, of course, puts up huge barriers to entry for other competitors. If the leader plays its cards right, it can end up "owning" the segment.

Concentrate on a Particular Application

Concentrating on a particular application is all about crossing the chasm, the huge gulf that separates the techies and visionaries, few in number, from the much larger mainstream market dominated by pragmatists. The way across the chasm is to target the company's resources to one or two very specific niche markets where it can dominate rapidly and force out competitors. It can then use the dominance of the first niche to attack the surrounding niches.

Moore uses the analogy of the Allies' D-Day invasion strategy in World War II: assembling a huge invasion force and focusing it on one narrowly defined target, the beaches of Normandy, routing the enemy, then moving out to dominate surrounding areas of Normandy. In other words, establish a beachhead, then broaden the basis of operations.

Serving the needs of a particular segment is all about focusing the company's resources on customizing the product to the needs of that segment. The segment wants a customized solution. It wants the "whole product" with all relevant services, not 80 percent of the whole product with the responsibility of supplying the missing 20 percent itself. Sales in several segments would soon stretch the company's development resources to the breaking point as it tried to customize the product to each segment's needs. Lotus Notes managed to escape the chasm when it focused on the global account management sector; particularly on worldwide accounting and consulting firms.

In addition, niche sales are driven by references and word-of-mouth within that niche. Failure to build up a core level of business in a particular segment means that momentum in any one single segment is never established. Pragmatists and conservatives talk to people in their own industry and look for solutions that have been proven to work there.

Tactical Alliances. Companies sometimes have the opportunity to form tactical alliances with smaller firms to help put a "complete product" in place. Market niches will coalesce behind a product much more readily—elevating it effectively to the position of a standard—if that product is supported by a number of products that fill in the gaps the market values but that the main product could not possibly supply. Producers of software packages often welcome the entry of smaller firms with their add-on programs to help provide the fully rounded complete product. It is a matter of gathering the appropriate partners and allies to jointly deliver a more complete product.

This is, however, very different from the cooperation/licensing/alliance approach discussed earlier, which is more formal and strategic. Tactical alliances tend to occur spontaneously at a later stage in a technology's development as smaller companies, realizing that a product has the potential to become a standard, desire to become associated with that standard.

Introducing a new technology offers a marketplace the first opportunity to experience the brand new product. So the manner in which the introduction is handled is critical. Everything has to come together in what is usually a narrow window of opportunity. Get it wrong, and there may be little time to put things right. By this stage, the investment in the new technology may be considerable, yet the chances of rejection or indifference are quite high.

The strategies proposed here are all designed to reduce the risks of failure. Of course, a complete and consistent strategy will assemble one or more components from each of the preparation, targeting, positioning, and execution stages.

Technology-intensive products and companies are at the leading edge of many Western countries' economies. By examining the range of illustrations included here, it is hoped that managers can help the new technology take its intended role in these economies.

References

W. Brian Arthur, "Increasing Returns and the New World of Business," *Harvard Business Review*, July–August 1996, pp. 100–109.

Christopher Easingwood and Simon O. Lunn, "Diffusion Paths in a High-Tech Environment: Clusters and Commonalities," *R&D Management, 22*, 1 (1992): 69–80.

Geoffrey A. Moore, *Crossing the Chasm: Marketing and Selling High-Technology Products to Mainstream Customers* (New York: HarperBusiness, 1991).

Geoffrey A. Moore, *Inside the Tornado: Marketing Strategies from Silicon Valley's Cutting Edge* (New York: HarperBusiness, 1995).

Charles P. Wallace, "The Man Bill Gates Fears Most," *Fortune*, November 23, 1998, pp. 257–260.

Chris Easingwood is the Caudwell Professor of Marketing and Head of Marketing and Strategy at Manchester Business School, Manchester, England, where **Anthony Koustelos** was an MBA student before becoming a market analyst with the Competitive Intelligence Unit, Business Development Group, DHL Worldwide Network NV/SA Brussels, Belgium.

The Customer Profitability Conundrum: When to Love 'Em or Leave 'Em

The customer may always be right, according to the old adage. But here is a not-so-old adage that is just as true: The customer may not always be profitable. That is why many companies these days are taking a hard look at their customers to determine which of them are worth serving and which should take their business elsewhere. The notion of eliminating customers may seem counterintuitive but in many industries—consumer products manufacturing, health insurance, banking and telecommunications among them—analyzing customer behavior and responding with strategies to make them as profitable as possible is essential to long term success.

> "Companies are beginning to look more closely at their customers to determine which of them are worth serving and which should take their business elsewhere."

The customer may always be right, according to the old adage. But here is a not-so-old adage that is just as true: The customer may not always be profitable. That is why increasing numbers of companies are beginning to look more closely at their customers to determine which of them are worth serving and which should take their business elsewhere. Put simply, it is sometimes necessary to identify and get rid of your worst customers—preferably by encouraging such customers gently but firmly to migrate to your competitors.

The idea of eliminating customers seems counterintuitive, almost sacrilegious: What company wants to lose customers? But faculty members at the University of Pennsylvania's Wharton School and consultants at Booz Allen Hamilton say in many industries—consumer products manufacturing, health insurance, banking and telecommunications among them—analyzing customer behavior and responding with strategies to make them as profitable as possible is essential to improving overall corporate profitability and making the most efficient use of scarce resources.

These experts caution, however, that terminating a relationship should be a last resort, after all efforts to transform a bad customer into a profitable one have been tried and failed.

"Some of my clients now tell me they're sorry they listened to consultants five years ago when we told them to get rid of unprofitable customers," says Chris Dallas-Feeney, senior vice president in Booz Allen's New York office. "In banks, where I spend a good bit of my time, executives in the 1990s were told to get out of the mass market and focus on more affluent, profitable customers. Today, they're saying, 'To heck with that, we want to serve every customer we can.' As consultants we have to amass significant evidence to prove a particular customer segment is a dog and therefore you shouldn't bother."

One Wharton marketing researcher, Peter Fader, goes even further, challenging the very idea that a company can know when to reward good customers and fire unprofitable ones, especially in the business-to-consumer sector. "Despite our desire to explain everything that a customer does, much customer behavior is very random," he says. "You might have a hot period where a customer is buying a lot of your product, then a cold period. People's tastes and habits evolve over time. It's hard to look at the past and say with a great sense of confidence, 'This will be a good customer and this will be a bad one.'"

Although most marketing strategists argue that managing relationships based on customer profitability is both possible and beneficial, it is surprising how few marketing departments collect even basic data. "It's amazing to me how many large corporations track their sales but don't do a very good job of tracking sales to whom," says Wharton marketing professor David J. Reibstein. "Shipping departments handle some of that information, but knowing who bought what hasn't always been tracked closely by the marketing people."

But that is changing as companies across industries have reorganized and restructured their businesses to be less product-oriented and more customer-focused. Notes Wharton marketing professor Barbara Kahn: "When companies were product-focused, they would prune unprofitable products. Now, they also look increasingly at the profitability of customers."

What's a Bad Customer?

Gary Ahlquist, a senior vice president of Booz Allen Hamilton, based in Chicago, says: "In most industries bad customers are those who do three things: they order rarely, they pay slowly or not at all, and they make unreasonable demands. They want a product or service but they don't want to pay for it. So they end up being tough to deal with or unprofitable."

Mitch Rosenbleeth, a vice president in Booz Allen's Dallas office and co-author of a recent report titled "Capturing Value Through Customer Strategy," says the process of identifying unprofitable customers is challenging for companies to embrace because the value is not obvious and it is painstaking.

"We just finished a project for a client where, when we looked at customer profitability, 30% of the customers created 200% of the client's profits," Rosenbleeth says. "About 50% of the customers weren't very profitable and the remaining 20% destroyed profits. So should the client have cut those 20% loose? That wasn't the answer."

Instead, the solution was to segment customers into what Rosenbleeth calls tailored business streams. "You structurally change the way you serve different customers to make each segment as profitable as possible," he explains. For ex-

ample, a company might continue to serve the best 30% of its customers as it always has, but create different business models for the others. For the unprofitable bottom 20% of customers, it could create a model that either makes those customers profitable or encourages them to go elsewhere. For the 50% in the middle, the company could create a model that drives their profitability higher. Too few companies "take the trouble to obtain a true customer profitability picture," Rosenbleeth says, "and even those that do rarely have a view of the customer's present profitability, let alone the total lifetime value of a customer."

If customers are fired, should a company ever try to get them back? "It's more expensive to acquire a new customer than to retain an existing one," Kahn says. "It's even more expensive to bring back a customer that you've gotten rid of. It's costly and it's a mistake you don't want to make. That's why I believe firing customers should be a last resort."

Love 'Em or Leave 'Em

Much is at stake in being able to manage customers effectively. By failing to winnow the good customers from the bad ones and deal with them accordingly, companies that are dominant in an industry expose themselves to withering competitive attacks by new entrants, according to Eric Clemons, professor of operations and information management at Wharton. This can be illustrated by developments in recent years in the financial services industry, specifically credit-card companies, perhaps the most-studied sector when it comes to customer segmentation.

Clemons is co-author, with Matt Thatcher of the University of Arizona, of a case study analyzing how a small, relatively unknown institution called Capital One became one of the world's largest—and most profitable—credit-card issuers in a few short years during the late 1980s and 1990s. The company, a pioneer in customer segmentation, achieved its robust growth by exploiting an innovative approach to targeted marketing, based on customer profitability analysis.

Capital One attributes its success to efforts in applying information technol-

ogy tools to customer acquisition and retention. Specifically, the company has relied on what it calls its Information-Based Strategy (IBS), a proprietary set of analytical tools, to tailor its products to the appropriate customers and ensure that each customer is serviced efficiently.

In the case study, Clemons and Thatcher coined colorful terms for two groups of customers—*love 'ems* (the customers who are profitable) and *kill yous* (the unprofitable customers). Most retail banks in 1988 charged uniform prices to all consumers for banking services despite major differences in costs in serving the love 'ems and the kill yous. That situation provided an opportunity for a new entrant, like Capital One, to go after the love 'ems of entrenched banks that were failing to segment customers. The new entrant's strategy: offer fees that were lower than the love 'ems were charged by their current bank, but high enough to generate profits for the new entrant.

A breakthrough for Capital One took place when the company used what it called "test and learn" models to determine which combination of product, price and credit limit could be profitably offered to customers who could be segmented by a wide range of publicly available credit and demographic information. Through the test-and-learn tools, Capital One found that it could offer a balance-transfer product, which offers a lower initial annual percentage rate (APR) to card applicants who transfer balances from a competitor's card.

"It turns out that this transfer of balances by customers from higher APR credit cards to a lower one provides the card issuer with an important signal," Clemons and Thatcher write. "Customers who do not carry balances find no value in a lower APR and will not take the time and effort to switch cards. More importantly, the customers that the balance transfer product will attract are those customers who have a balance they cannot presently pay off but which they will eventually pay off slowly. Therefore, they care about the lower APR."

Customer-segmentation techniques such as these have paid off handsomely for Capital One and eroded the market share of once-dominant players in the credit-card business. Since 1992 the dollar value of loans managed by Capital One has risen from $1.7 billion to $56.9 billion, and Capital One is now one of the top 10 credit-card companies in the U.S., according to The Nilson Report's 2002 ranking of the top U.S. issuers of general purpose credit cards.

The lessons of Capital One's success can be extended to many other industries, says Clemons. He adds: "If companies in an incumbent industry can't fire the kill yous, and a new entrant can go after the love 'ems, incumbent industries can fall apart."

A Multi-industry Perspective

Here are examples of how other industries are managing customer profitability:

Wireless telephony. Dominic Endicott, a vice president in Booz Allen's Boston office, says wireless companies have wonderful opportunities to segment customers by profitability. He cites several reasons. First, each wireless player has between 10 million and 30 million customers, which means they have many chances to increase the value of each customer. Companies can target certain segments and offer a new value proposition, while improving the value of calling packages for existing customers.

According to Endicott, any business with lots of customers with a subscription history is ripe for this sort of segmentation, including cable TV operators and Internet service providers. Wireless companies even have the ability to reach customers any time by sending messages to their phones. If a customer has experienced a lot of dropped calls, a company not only knows this but can compensate her for the trouble, say, with an additional hour of peak-time calls. By contrast, Endicott says, "With a product in a supermarket, you're lucky if you get scanner data telling you that a person buys soap once a month."

Despite these ready advantages, wireless companies have yet to take full advantage of customer profitability management. Since their inception, wireless firms have pulled out all the stops to acquire customers but have placed little

emphasis on managing the value of the customer base.

Endicott says that, in his experience, most wireless operators are "woefully" ill prepared to do this well. "We found it requires comprehensive changes, beginning with the kind of information you gather, the kind of analytics you do and how you organize policies and process across the organization. It is difficult to change the acquisition culture of most wireless companies, which drives them to acquire more and more customers without regard to the qualities of their customer base. This is the first year they've seen a slowdown in growth. It takes a lot of time to change that. But I'm not sure other industries are doing it much better."

Consumer products. Major consumer-products manufacturers have any number of ways to use business streams that are tailored to the needs of customers, explains Les Moeller, vice president in Booz Allen's Cleveland office. For instance, a consumer-products company can use different models to serve three customer segments: a mega-retailer such as Wal-Mart; a national supermarket chain that is a major player but smaller than Wal-Mart; and a small regional or local retailer.

It turns out that larger customers, like Wal-Mart and some regional grocery chains, are better able to order in more efficient quantities, because of their size and distribution capabilities. The real trick is to get those orders from larger customers and to get the inefficient smaller accounts to order and take delivery through a more efficient delivery system, or pay for their increased service requirements.

Moeller, says achieving higher efficiency requires both the retailer and the manufacturer to make complex choices. Should, for instance, the buyer order a full truckload of a product? Or, if the buyer orders a pallet, does it order a full pallet of one stock keeping unit (SKU, or barcode), or does it order layers of one SKU? Or does it order layers that consist of mixed SKUs?

Moeller describes the process this way: "When a product comes off the production line, it's one SKU and it all ends

up on one pallet. If you order a full pallet of one product, all the same size—laundry detergent with bleach or lemon-scented dish detergent—the forklift operator picks that pallet up and puts it on the delivery truck. It's simple. But if that buyer doesn't move enough products in his stores to warrant buying a full pallet of a single item, he may have to mix, on one pallet, regular dish detergent with the lemon-scented kind. That means the warehouse worker has to break pallets apart and reconfigure pallets to fill an order. That can become very expensive." Once the product is delivered to the buyer, other costs come into play: Who, for example, unloads the truck and how much time is allotted to unload it?

There are ways, however, for consumer-products companies to ensure that the buyers are getting the right kind of service and are still a profitable segment to serve. If the retailer is large enough, the consumer-products company can provide incentives to entice them to buy full pallets. If the retailer is not large enough to buy full pallets, they should be pushed to buy from a distributor instead of directly from the factory. This way, the supplier can keep its costs down, while at the same time getting its products on shelves.

Or, a buyer could strike a deal with the supplier regarding delivery. If the truck arrives on time, the buyer agrees to unload the truck within 30 minutes. That way, the driver can quickly get back on the road and make more deliveries. In return, the supplier gives the buyer, say, $50 for every truck that is unloaded in the allotted half-hour. Another option would be for the consumer-products company to offer a deal whereby the buyer orders in full pallets, or even full truckloads, unloads the truck in 30 minutes, and always pays its bill on time. In return, the supplier gives the buyer a rebate of $300 per delivery. "These are the kinds of incentive programs that consumer products companies can put into place to make their customers more profitable and their supply chain more efficient," Moeller says.

Health insurance. Health insurers face a somewhat different set of circumstances in trying to develop tailored business streams to deal with good and bad customers. Typically, people obtain health insurance in one of three ways: through their employers, which is most common; as individuals dealing directly with an insurer, which is the least common way; or through a government program like Medicare or Medicaid. To a health insurer, a good customer is someone for whom their employer pays a premium and never files a claim. Bad customers are people who are genetically-predisposed to a particular illness, or who are sick or injured as a result of an event beyond their control, such as an accident.

"It's a scarier notion to turn clients away than it is to hope against hope that you can make profitable the 500 clients you should get rid of," says Booz Allen's Chris Dallas-Feeney.

"In the past, insurers have dealt with unprofitable customers through retroactive analysis," explains Booz Allen's Ahlquist. "They analyze claims information and see where they've had bad risks with employers in the past. They aggregate that data to the employer level, and then determine how much to charge the employer in the future. Or, they may decide not to offer coverage to that employer if the employer was involved in a hazardous business like coal mining."

Even today, the retrospective model prevails. But some insurers are trying to use prospective models. For example, if a company is bidding for the health-insurance business of a law firm, it might analyze data from another law firm and engage in predictive modeling on what it believes its exposure will be, and price coverage based on this analysis.

Once it has the new law firm as an account, the insurance company will try to get more information on individuals so that it can begin to put them into cost-control programs, such as conducting ongoing health assessments or special programs for diabetics. So an insurer,

knowing that of the 100 people in the law firm some will contract Type 2 diabetes, can price its premiums accordingly. It can also require that such patients be monitored by their doctors on a regular basis and encouraged to take steps (perhaps a combination of medication, a healthy diet, exercise and weight loss) to mitigate or eliminate the long-term effects of the disease. "Type 2 diabetes can be managed so that the person does not incur huge costs later in life due to loss of vision or some other problem," Ahlquist says.

"Monitoring programs such as these are a way to provide incentives for the individuals who are prone to be ill to try to become healthier, and, therefore, more profitable for the insurer. Of course, if there are many unprofitable customers in the account, the insurer can either drop coverage or re-price it." However, most people covered by employer insurance plans cannot be "fired" by insurance companies because dropping coverage is usually prohibited under terms of the contract with the employer.

Hope Springs Eternal

Convincing businesses that it is sometimes necessary to get rid of customers is not easy. Booz Allen's Dallas-Feeney, who is co-author with Rosenbleeth of "Capturing Value Through Customer Strategy," describes how companies strenuously resist any suggestion that some customers have to go.

"Customers who tend to be unprofitable may not be as bad as they may look, and the ones that appear profitable may not be as good as they appear."

"It's a scary notion for companies to think they have to make more money on fewer clients because it means you really have to win their commitment and loyalty to you. It's a scarier notion to turn clients away than it is to hope

against hope that you can make profitable the 500 clients you should get rid of. I call this the 'hope springs eternal' way of thinking. The reason salespeople are successful is because they are generally optimistic and don't want to get rid of customers. And that's a good thing. But a company can't afford to let optimism stand in the way of making a tough decision about customers when it's necessary."

"Companies have difficulty analyzing the profitability of customer bases at the level of the individual person... However, it is a long-accepted practice to make predictions about groups of people."

Wharton's Fader is skeptical about much of the thinking behind the notion of managing individual customers' profitability. I think it's insane to do," Fader says of the idea of customer management at the individual level. "For one thing, it is hard to diagnose past behavior to understand why people did what they did. Historical behavioral data is rich and interesting, but it has its limits as a guide to the future." He is especially adamant in doubting the wisdom of firing unprofitable accounts in the business-to-consumer sector, although he does say that managing business-to-business customers is often feasible and worthwhile.

He also says that customers who tend to be unprofitable may not be as bad as they may look, and the ones that appear profitable may not be as good as they appear.

"Any time you rank customers, you'll find that the extremes tend to regress toward the mean and become more average over time. If you have an incentive or rewards program for good customers, you'll find that, eventually, they may not be as good as they used to be. This is especially true when you're talking about very sporadic behavior, as we are here. If a person applies for a bank loan only once in a while, how can the bank know if the customer is abandoning the bank or just has no need for the bank's services at the moment?"

"Every unprofitable customer should get a chance to become a better customer. But some customers will remain unprofitable no matter what steps a company takes to change its cost structure."

Fader acknowledges that companies have difficulty analyzing their customer bases at the level of the individual person because each customer behaves randomly. However, it is a long-accepted practice to make predictions about groups of people. Actuaries do it all the time. They can forecast accurately what percentage of a group of people will perish in auto accidents, but cannot name the individuals who will die.

"No matter how much data you have on a customer, it's hard to capture everything that's going on," Fader says. "But when you aggregate a bunch of people together it is possible to make very accurate statements about the cohort as a whole. You can, for example, study a group and say with confidence that 25%

of these customers will buy products twice from us this year. That's the way a customer base should be analyzed. I worry about clients or vendors who sell or use CRM services that claim to be able to pinpoint customers and their behavior. It's voodoo."

Fader argues that data mining "is wonderful for the original reasons it was developed, like credit card scoring to determine who should get cards. Data mining can help you figure out what makes group A different from B. There are lots of applications for that framework. But it doesn't work well where behavior is evolving. Data mining is pretty darn limited when you move outside of a static snapshot."

It is more difficult in B2B relationships than in B2C to lump customers together, and analyze them on that basis, Fader says. However, the benefits of one-to-one marketing can be greater in B2B relationships where the monetary value of each customer is much larger than in B2C.

Don't Shoot from the Hip

Fader's opinions represent the minority view. Dallas-Feeney, the Booz Allen consultant in New York, says managing customers can be done and done well, as long as it is not misunderstood. It involves, he says, more than just firing customers.

"None of our clients would say, 'OK, your analysis tells me I should exit this many customers, so let's get rid of them

immediately.' Every one of those customers—with the obvious exceptions of bad credit—will be presented with a set of incentives so that a company can say, 'Hey, if we can make this relationship better, we'll keep you. But we can't be successful unless you do the following.'"

The overarching philosophy is that every unprofitable customer should get a chance to become a better customer, with the sales force being given the responsibility of turning those customers around. But some customers will remain unprofitable no matter what steps a company takes to change its cost structure.

Says Dallas-Feeney: "Everything we've been talking about amounts to a reality check that companies should do with every customer on a regular basis. They should look at their relationships and see whether those relationships are working for both parties."

strategy+business (www.strategy-business.com) and Knowledge@Wharton (http://knowledge.wharton.upenn.edu) publish white papers on contemporary global business issues, featuring the latest research and ideas from partners at Booz Allen Hamilton and faculty from the University of Pennsylvania's Wharton School. strategy+business is a quarterly business thought-leadership magazine published by Booz Allen Hamilton. Knowledge@Wharton is an online resource for executives published biweekly by the Wharton School.

Entrepreneurs' Biggest Problems—And How They Solve Them

Among the ingredients for success: flexibility, realism and passion

By Paulette Thomas

EVEN THE MOST realistic entrepreneur underestimates the difficulties in building a business.

Sure, everyone foresees challenges in raising capital, managing employees, assessing the competition—all the demands that sound like business-school courses. But ask anyone in the real world: Those are just the barest start.

You never know what else the gods will throw your way. A war? A recession? Technology evolving and obsolescing before your eyes? Excessive growth? There's no end to the obstacles your business may encounter.

So what sets apart the entrepreneurs who surmount these obstacles from those who don't? What qualities do they need to possess to find solutions in an era of speedy, unpredictable change?

The answers are more obvious than you might think. For the entrepreneurs whose problems and solutions we present in this report, a clear set of characteristics made all the difference between success and failure. Having these qualities is no guarantee of success. But if you don't have them, you'd better figure out how to get them.

A CLEAR STRATEGY. A well-defined plan can keep a ship on course when the winds would otherwise blow it off the map. **Metaphase Design Group** Inc., of St. Louis, for example, has defined its mission as pursuing only in-depth, high-end, intensively researched design work for its clients. Its product isn't cheap, but it has stuck to its gold-standard plan amid a recession and cost-cutting everywhere. Adhering to that strategy gives its

Stay Focused

leaders the backbone to turn away lesser business that dilutes its mission. And they are thriving through the weak economy.

FLEXIBILITY. Successful entrepreneurs have a plan, full of detail and rich in data. But they are willing to abandon it when the customers don't follow. They cut losses and retool fast.

Neil Peterson started Flexcar in Seattle, an innovative time-sharing plan that he hoped would attract business from car buyers who didn't want to buy and were frustrated with the rigid, traditional rental agencies. Though it was popular in Europe, he wasn't making headway in the U.S., where drivers take for granted the convenience of a car and its place as a status symbol. Meeting that resistance, he refined his marketing campaign to steer it toward universities and businesses, where the sales pitch made sense. *Changed target mkt,*

A REALISTIC VIEW. Some entrepreneurs, enamored of their vision, swallow it whole and lose the dispassionate judgment they must exercise. "They have to be able to strip away the hype and be brutally honest with themselves and their backers," says James Schrager, professor of entrepreneurship and strategy at the University of Chicago's graduate school of business.

This is particularly important following the mass hypnosis of the dot-com era. "Investors want to see seasoned analysis, logical reasoning," he says.

Such clear-eyed thinking helped the founders of **Hat World** Inc. in Indianapolis recognize that they were in over their heads when an acquisition trebled the company's size overnight. Rather than celebrate and have a big time presiding over a huge operation, its founders pulled back to hire an experienced chief executive fast.

ETHICAL BEHAVIOR. Need we say it following Enron, Tyco and the host of other governance scandals that have befallen Corporate America? Investors and government regulators are operating on Level Orange vigilance. Bad behavior has a way of catching up with a business.

"You should fix the problem honestly," says the University of Chicago's Dr. Schrager, "or if you can't fix it honestly, you shouldn't be in that business. It's that simple."

A ROBUST NETWORK. Successful entrepreneurs turn to their Rolodex in times of need. They make it a point to do favors when they can, because they know that their turn to ask for help will come.

Jill Blashack built **Tastefully Simple**, an Alexandria, Minn., gourmet-food distributor, which sells through home parties. She went from $100,000 in sales in 1995 to $78 million last year—all on a network that grew exponentially. A friend was her first investor. A friend led her to the president of a similar company that shared strategies and results with her. And the at-home-party model worked as friends and acquaintances all added their own networks.

A GLOBAL PERSPECTIVE. Global markets may provide solutions to problems that were unthinkable a decade or two ago. Shifting labor across borders or invading new markets can alter the course of a business.

Mark Goldstein, a Pittsburgh immigration attorney, was doing great business in the 1990s as he helped companies deal with immigration issues as they hired software engineers from India. When the tech boom ebbed, he turned that inside out, and began searching for overseas companies looking to break into U.S. markets.

my on-line course

AN ABILITY TO DEAL WITH TECHNOLOGY. Every entrepreneur has to make peace with the fact that technology changes nearly all aspects of his or her business, even if the company isn't in tech. It might lower costs—for you or a competitor. It could make your product obsolete or make it the must-have.

Evolve or get left behind, says James Bird, a corporate-film producer in Cincinnati. Mr. Bird recently made the switch to high-definition video-production work to set his business apart from his competitors.

PASSION. Not much can surpass the single-minded drive of an entrepreneur committed to solving a problem.

Grant Goodman, in Phoenix, runs a heavy-trucking company and uses environmentally friendly biodiesel fuel to reduce pollution in his city. The higher costs deterred him, but only temporarily; he's planning to manufacture his own biodiesel fuel, at least at break-even costs.

His passion for the best way to do business is helping to solve environmental problems for others. And selling his services as a "green" company can't hurt either.

MS. THOMAS, A WRITER IN PITTSBURGH, IS THE CASE STUDIES COLUMNIST FOR THE WALL STREET JOURNAL.

Unforseen events —

Marketing myopia

(With Retrospective Commentary)

Shortsighted managements often fail to recognize that in fact there is no such thing as a growth industry

Theodore Levitt

How can a company ensure its continued growth? In 1960 "Marketing Myopia" answered that question in a new and challenging way by urging organizations to define their industries broadly to take advantage of growth opportunities. Using the archetype of the railroads, Mr. Levitt showed how they declined inevitably as technology advanced because they defined themselves too narrowly. To continue growing, companies must ascertain and act on their customers' needs and desires, not bank on the presumptive longevity of their products. The success of the article testifies to the validity of its message. It has been widely quoted and anthologized, and HBR has sold more than 265,000 reprints of it. The author of 14 subsequent articles in HBR, Mr. Levitt is one of the magazine's most prolific contributors. In a retrospective commentary, he considers the use and misuse that have been made of "Marketing Myopia," describing its many interpretations and hypothesizing about its success.

Every major industry was once a growth industry. But some that are now riding a wave of growth enthusiasm are very much in the shadow of decline. Others which are thought of as seasoned growth industries have actually stopped growing. In every case the reason growth is threatened, slowed, or stopped is *not* be-

cause the market is saturated. It is because there has been a failure of management.

Fateful purposes: The failure is at the top. The executives responsible for it, in the last analysis, are those who deal with broad aims and policies. Thus:

• The railroads did not stop growing because the need for passenger and freight transportation declined. That grew. The railroads are in trouble today not because the need was filled by others (cars, trucks, airplanes, even telephones), but because it was *not* filled by the railroads themselves. They let others take customers away from them because they assumed themselves to be in the railroad business rather than in the transportation business. The reason they defined their industry wrong was because they were railroad-oriented instead of transportation-oriented; they were product-oriented instead of customer-oriented.

• Hollywood barely escaped being totally ravished by television. Actually, all the established film companies went through drastic reorganizations. Some simply disappeared. All of them got into trouble not because of TV's inroads but because of their own myopia. As with the railroads, Hollywood defined its business incorrectly. It thought it was in the movie business when it was actually in the entertainment business. "Movies" implied a specific, limited product. This produced a

fatuous contentment which from the beginning led producers to view TV as a threat. Hollywood scorned and rejected TV when it should have welcomed it as an opportunity—an opportunity to expand the entertainment business.

Today TV is a bigger business than the old narrowly defined movie business ever was. Had Hollywood been customer-oriented (providing entertainment), rather then product-oriented (making movies), would it have gone through the fiscal purgatory that it did? I doubt it. What ultimately saved Hollywood and accounted for its recent resurgence was the wave of new young writers, producers, and directors whose previous successes in television had decimated the old movie companies and toppled the big movie moguls.

There are other less obvious examples of industries that have been and are now endangering their futures by improperly defining their purposes. I shall discuss some in detail later and analyze the kind of policies that lead to trouble. Right now it may help to show what a thoroughly customer-oriented management can do to keep a growth industry growing, even after the obvious opportunities have been exhausted; and here there are two examples that have been around for a long time. They are nylon and glass—specifically,

E. I. duPont de Nemours & Company and Corning Glass Works.

Both companies have great technical competence. Their product orientation is unquestioned. But this alone does not explain their success. After all, who was more pridefully product-oriented and product-conscious than the erstwhile New England textile companies that have been so thoroughly massacred? The DuPonts and the Cornings have succeeded not primarily because of their product or research orientation but because they have been thoroughly customer-oriented also. It is constant watchfulness for opportunities to apply their technical knowhow to the creation of customer-satisfying uses which accounts for their prodigious output of successful new products. Without a very sophisticated eye on the customer, most of their new products might have been wrong, their sales methods useless.

Aluminum has also continued to be a growth industry, thanks to the efforts of two wartime-created companies which deliberately set about creating new customer-satisfying uses. Without Kaiser Aluminum & Chemical Corporation and Reynolds Metals Company, the total demand for aluminum today would be vastly less.

Error of analysis: Some may argue that it is foolish to set the railroads off against aluminum or the movies off against glass. Are not aluminum and glass naturally so versatile that the industries are bound to have more growth opportunities than the railroads and movies? This view commits precisely the error I have been talking about. It defines an industry, or a product, or a cluster of know-how so narrowly as to guarantee its premature senescence. When we mention "railroads," we should make sure we mean "transportation." As transporters, the railroads still have a good chance for very considerable growth. They are not limited to the railroad business as such (though in my opinion rail transportation is potentially a much stronger transportation medium than is generally believed).

What the railroads lack is not opportunity, but some of the same managerial imaginativeness and audacity that made them great. Even an amateur like Jacques Barzun can see what is lacking when he says:

"I grieve to see the most advanced physical and social organization of the last century go down in shabby disgrace for lack of the same comprehensive imagination that built it up. [What is lacking is] the will of the companies to survive and to satisfy the public by inventiveness and skill."[1]

Shadow of obsolescence

It is impossible to mention a single major industry that did not at one time qualify for the magic appellation of "growth industry." In each case its assumed strength lay in the apparently unchallenged superiority of its product. There appeared to be no effective substitute for it. It was itself a runaway substitute for the product it so triumphantly replaced. Yet one after another of these celebrated industries has come under a shadow. Let us look briefly at a few more of them, this time taking examples that have so far received a little less attention:

• *Dry cleaning*—This was once a growth industry with lavish prospects. In an age of wool garments, imagine being finally able to get them safely and easily clean. The boom was on.

Yet here we are 30 years after the boom started and the industry is in trouble. Where has the competition come from? From a better way of cleaning? No. It has come from synthetic fibers and chemical additives that have cut the need for dry cleaning. But this is only the beginning. Lurking in the wings and ready to make chemical dry cleaning totally obsolescent is that powerful magician, ultrasonics.

• *Electric utilities*—This is another one of those supposedly "no-substitute" products that has been enthroned on a pedestal of invincible growth. When the incandescent lamp came along, kerosene lights were finished. Later the water wheel and the steam engine were cut to ribbons by the flexibility, reliability, simplicity, and just plain easy availability of electric motors. The prosperity of electric utilities continues to wax extravagant as the home is converted into a museum of electric gadgetry. How can anybody miss by investing in utilities, with no competition, nothing but growth ahead?

But a second look is not quite so comforting. A score of nonutility companies are well advanced toward developing a powerful chemical fuel cell which could sit in some hidden closet of every home silently ticking off electric power. The electric lines that vulgarize so many neighborhoods will be eliminated. So will the endless demolition of streets and service interruptions during storms. Also on the horizon is solar energy, again pioneered by nonutility companies.

Who says that the utilities have no competition? They may be natural monopolies now, but tomorrow they may be natural deaths. To avoid this prospect, they too will have to develop fuel cells, solar energy, and other power sources. To survive, they themselves will have to plot the obsolescence of what now produces their livelihood.

• *Grocery stores*—Many people find it hard to realize that there ever was a thriving establishment known as the "corner grocery store." The supermarket has taken over with a powerful effectiveness. Yet the big food chains of the 1930s narrowly escaped being completely wiped out by the aggressive expansion of independent supermarkets. The first genuine supermarket was opened in 1930, in Jamaica, Long Island. By 1933 supermarkets were thriving in California, Ohio, Pennsylvania, and elsewhere. Yet the established chains pompously ignored them. When they chose to notice them, it was with such derisive descriptions as "cheapy," "horse-and-buggy," "cracker-barrel storekeeping," and "unethical opportunists."

The executive of one big chain announced at the time that he found it "hard to believe that people will drive for miles to shop for foods and sacrifice the personal service chains have perfected and to which Mrs. Consumer is accustomed."[2] As late as 1936, the National Wholesale Grocers convention and the New Jersey Retail Grocers Association said there was nothing to fear. They said that the supers' narrow appeal to the price buyer limited the size of their market. They had to draw from miles around. When imitators came, there would be wholesale liquidations as volume fell. The current high sales of the supers was said to be partly due to their novelty. Basically people wanted convenient neighborhood grocers. If the neighborhood stores "cooperate with their suppliers, pay attention to their costs, and improve their service," they would be able to weather the competition until it blew over.[3]

It never blew over. The chains discovered that survival required going into the supermarket business. This meant the wholesale destruction of their huge investments in corner store sites and in established distribution and merchandising methods. The companies with "the courage of their convictions" resolutely stuck to the corner store philosophy. They kept their pride but lost their shirts.

Self-deceiving cycle: But memories are short. For example, it is hard for people who today confidently hail the twin messiahs of electronics and chemicals to see how things could possibly go wrong with these galloping industries. They probably also cannot see how a reasonably sensible businessman could have been as myopic as the famous Boston millionaire who 50 years ago unintentionally sentenced his heirs to poverty by stipulating that his entire estate be forever invested exclusively in electric streetcar securities. His posthumous declaration, "There will always be a big demand for efficient urban transportation," is no consolation to his heirs who sustain life by pumping gasoline at automobile filling stations.

Yet, in a casual survey I recently took among a group of intelligent business executives, nearly half agreed that it would be hard to hurt their heirs by tying their estates forever to the electronics industry. When I then confronted them with the Boston streetcar example, they chorused unanimously, "That's different!" But is it? Is not the basic situation identical?

In truth, *there is no such thing* as a growth industry, I believe. There are only companies organized and operated to create and capitalize on growth opportunities. Industries that assume themselves to be riding some automatic growth escalator invariably descend into stagnation. The history of every dead and dying "growth" industry shows a self-deceiving cycle of bountiful expansion and undetected decay. There are four conditions which usually guarantee this cycle:

1. The belief that growth is assured by an expanding and more affluent population.
2. The belief that there is no competitive substitute for the industry's major product.
3. Too much faith in mass production and in the advantages of rapidly declining unit costs as output rises.
4. Preoccupation with a product that lends itself to carefully controlled scientific experimentation, improvement, and manufacturing cost reduction.

I should like now to begin examining each of these conditions in some detail. To build my case as boldly as possible, I shall illustrate the points with reference to three industries—petroleum, automobiles, and electronics—particularly petroleum, because it spans more years and more vicissitudes. Not only do these three have excellent reputations with the general public and also enjoy the confidence of sophisticated investors, but their managements have become known for progressive thinking in areas like financial control, product research, and management training. If obsolescence can cripple even these industries, it can happen anywhere.

Population myth

The belief that profits are assured by an expanding and more affluent population is dear to the heart of every industry. It takes the edge off the apprehensions everybody understandably feels about the future. If consumers are multiplying and also buying more of your product or service, you can face the future with considerably more comfort than if the market is shrinking. An expanding market keeps the manufacturer from having to think very hard or imaginatively. If thinking is an intellectual response to a problem, then the absence of a problem leads to the absence of thinking. If your product has an automatically expanding market, then you will not give much thought to how to expand it.

One of the most interesting examples of this is provided by the petroleum industry. Probably our oldest growth industry, it has an enviable record. While there are some current apprehensions about its growth rate, the industry itself tends to be optimistic.

But I believe it can be demonstrated that it is undergoing a fundamental yet typical change. It is not only ceasing to be a growth industry, but may actually be a declining one, relative to other business. Although there is widespread unawareness of it, I believe that within 25 years the oil industry may find itself in much the same position of retrospective glory that the railroads are now in. Despite its pioneering work in developing and applying the present-value method of investment evaluation, in employee relations, and in working with backward countries, the petroleum business is a distressing example of how complacency and wrongheadedness can stubbornly convert opportunity into near disaster.

One of the characteristics of this and other industries that have believed very strongly in the beneficial consequences of an expanding population, while at the same time being industries with a generic product for which there has appeared to be no competitive substitute, is that the individual companies have sought to outdo their competitors by improving on what they are already doing. This makes sense, of course, if one assumes that sales are tied to the country's population strings, because the customer can compare products only on a feature-by-feature basis. I believe it is significant, for example, that not since John D. Rockefeller sent free kerosene lamps to China has the oil industry done anything really outstanding to create a demand for its product. Not even in product improvement has it showered itself with eminence. The greatest single improvement—namely, the development of tetraethyl lead—came from outside the industry, specifically from General Motors and DuPont. The big contributions made by the industry itself are confined to the technology of oil exploration, production, and refining.

Asking for trouble: In other words, the industry's efforts have focused on improving the *efficiency* of getting and making its product, not really on improving the generic product or its marketing. Moreover, its chief product has continuously been defined in the narrowest possible terms, namely, gasoline, not energy, fuel, or transportation. This attitude has helped assure that:

• Major improvements in gasoline quality tend not to originate in the oil industry. Also, the development of superior alternative fuels comes from outside the oil industry, as will be shown later.

• Major innovations in automobile fuel marketing are originated by small new oil companies that are not primarily preoccupied with production or refining. These are the companies that have been responsible for the rapidly expanding multipump gasoline stations, with their successful emphasis on large and clean layouts, rapid and efficient driveway service, and quality gasoline at low prices.

Thus, the oil industry is asking for trouble from outsiders. Sooner or later, in this land of hungry inventors and entrepreneurs, a threat is sure to come. The possibilities of this will become more apparent when we turn to the next dangerous belief of many managements. For the sake of continuity, because this second belief is tied closely to the first, I shall continue with the same example.

Idea of indispensability: The petroleum industry is pretty much persuaded that there is no competitive substitute for its major product, gasoline—or if there is, that it will continue to be a derivative of crude oil, such as diesel fuel or kerosene jet fuel.

There is a lot of automatic wishful thinking in this assumption. The trouble is that most refining companies own huge amounts of crude oil reserves. These have value only if there is a market for products into which oil can be converted—hence the tenacious belief in the continuing competitive superiority of automobile fuels made from crude oil. ✭

This idea persists despite all historic evidence against it. The evidence not only shows that oil has never been a superior product for any purpose for very long, but it also shows that the oil industry has never really been a growth industry. It has been a succession of different businesses that have gone through the usual historic cycles of growth, maturity, and decay. Its overall survival is owed to a series of miraculous escapes from total obsolescence, of last-minute and unexpected reprieves from total disaster reminiscent of the Perils of Pauline.

Perils of petroleum: I shall sketch in only the main episodes.

First, crude oil was largely a patent medicine. But even before that fad ran out, demand was greatly expanded by the use of oil in kerosene lamps. The prospect of lighting the world's lamps gave rise to an extravagant promise of growth. The prospects were similar to those the industry now holds for gasoline in other parts of the world. It can hardly wait for the underdeveloped nations to get a car in every garage. oil - light ⟶ light bulb

In the days of the kerosene lamp, the oil companies competed with each other and against gaslight by trying to improve the illuminating characteristics of kerosene. Then suddenly the impossible happened. Edison invented a light which was totally nondependent on crude oil. Had it not been for the growing use of kerosene in space heaters, the incandescent lamp would have completely finished oil as a growth industry at that time. Oil would have been good for little else than axle grease.

Then disaster and reprieve struck again. Two great innovations occurred, neither originating in the oil industry. The successful development of coal-burning domestic central-heating systems made the space heater obsolescent. While the industry reeled, along came its most magnificent boost yet—the internal combustion engine, also invented by outsiders. Then when the prodigious expansion for gasoline finally began to level off in the 1920s, along came the miraculous escape of a central oil heater. Once again, the escape was

provided by an outsider's invention and development. And when that market weakened, wartime demand for aviation fuel came to the rescue. After the war the expansion of civilian aviation, the dieselization of railroads, and the explosive demand for cars and trucks kept the industry's growth in high gear.

Meanwhile, centralized oil heating—whose boom potential had only recently been proclaimed—ran into severe competition from natural gas. While the oil companies themselves owned the gas that now competed with their oil, the industry did not originate the natural gas revolution, nor has it to this day greatly profited from its gas ownership. The gas revolution was made by newly formed transmission companies that marketed the product with an aggressive ardor. They started a magnificent new industry, first against the advice and then against the resistance of the oil companies.

By all the logic of the situation, the oil companies themselves should have made the gas revolution. They not only owned the gas; they also were the only people experienced in handling, scrubbing, and using it, the only people experienced in pipeline technology and transmission, and they understood heating problems. But, partly because they knew that natural gas would compete with their own sale of heating oil, the oil companies pooh-poohed the potentials of gas.

The revolution was finally started by oil pipeline executives who, unable to persuade their own companies to go into gas, quit and organized the spectacularly successful gas transmission companies. Even after their success became painfully evident to the oil companies, the latter did not go into gas transmission. The multibillion dollar business which should have been theirs went to others. As in the past, the industry was blinded by its narrow preoccupation with a specific product and the value of its reserves. It paid little or no attention to its customers' basic needs and preferences.

The postwar years have not witnessed any change. Immediately after World War II the oil industry was greatly encouraged about its future by the rapid expansion of demand for its traditional line of products. In 1950 most companies projected annual rates of domestic expansion of around 6% through at least 1975. Though the ratio of crude oil reserves to demand in the Free World was about 20 to 1, with 10 to 1 being usually considered a reasonable work-

ing ratio in the United States, booming demand sent oil men searching for more without sufficient regard to what the future really promised. In 1952 they "hit" in the Middle East; the ratio skyrocketed to 42 to 1. If gross additions to reserves continue at the average rate of the past five years (37 billion barrels annually), then by 1970 the reserve ratio will be up to 45 to 1. This abundance of oil has weakened crude and product prices all over the world.

Uncertain future: Management cannot find much consolation today in the rapidly expanding petrochemical industry, another oil-using idea that did not originate in the leading firms. The total United States production of petrochemicals is equivalent to about 2% (by volume) of the demand for all petroleum products. Although the petrochemical industry is now expected to grow by about 10% per year, this will not offset other drains on the growth of crude oil consumption. Furthermore, while petrochemical products are many and growing, it is well to remember that there are nonpetroleum sources of the basic raw material, such as coal. Besides, a lot of plastics can be produced with relatively little oil. A 5,000-barrel-per-day oil refinery is now considered the absolute minimum size for efficiency. But a 5,000-barrel-per-day chemical plant is a giant operation.

Oil has never been a continuously strong growth industry. It has grown by fits and starts, always miraculously saved by innovations and developments not of its own making. The reason it has not grown in a smooth progression is that each time it thought it had a superior product safe from the possibility of competitive substitutes, the product turned out to be inferior and notoriously subject to obsolescence. Until now, gasoline (for motor fuel, anyhow) has escaped this fate. But, as we shall see later, it too may be on its last legs.

The point of all this is that there is no ✭ guarantee against product obsolescence. If a company's own research does not make it obsolete, another's will. Unless an industry is especially lucky, as oil has been until now, it can easily go down in a sea of red figures—just as the railroads have, as the buggy whip manufacturers have, as the corner grocery chains have, as most of the big movie companies have, and indeed as many other industries have.

The best way for a firm to be lucky is to make its own luck. That requires knowing what makes a business successful. One of the greatest enemies of this knowledge is mass production.

Production pressures

Mass-production industries are impelled by a great drive to produce all they can. The prospect of steeply declining unit costs as output rises is more than most companies can usually resist. The profit possibilities look spectacular. All effort focuses on production. The result is that marketing gets neglected.

John Kenneth Galbraith contends that just the opposite occurs.[4] Output is so prodigious that all effort concentrates on trying to get rid of it. He says this accounts for singing commercials, desecration of the countryside with advertising signs, and other wasteful and vulgar practices. Galbraith has a finger on something real, but he misses the strategic point. Mass production does indeed generate great pressure to "move" the product. But what usually gets emphasized is selling, not marketing. Marketing, being a more sophisticated and complex process, gets ignored.

The difference between marketing and selling is more than semantic. Selling focuses on the needs of the seller, marketing on the needs of the buyer. Selling is preoccupied with the seller's need to convert his product into cash, marketing with the idea of satisfying the needs of the customer by means of the product and the whole cluster of things associated with creating, delivering, and finally consuming it.

In some industries the enticements of full mass production have been so powerful that for many years top management in effect has told the sales departments, "You get rid of it; we'll worry about profits." By contrast, a truly marketing-minded firm tries to create value-satisfying goods and services that consumers will want to buy. What it offers for sale includes not only the generic product or service, but also how it is made available to the customer, in what form, when, under what conditions, and at what terms of trade. Most important, what it offers for sale is determined not by the seller but by the buyer. The seller takes his cues from the buyer in such a way that the product becomes a consequence of the marketing effort, not vice versa.

Lag in Detroit: This may sound like an elementary rule of business, but that does not keep it from being violated wholesale. It is certainly more violated than honored. Take the automobile industry.

Here mass production is most famous, most honored, and has the greatest impact on the entire society. The industry has hitched its fortune to the relentless requirements of the annual model change, a policy

that makes customer orientation an especially urgent necessity. Consequently the auto companies annually spend millions of dollars on consumer research. But the fact that the new compact cars are selling so well in their first year indicates that Detroit's vast researches have for a long time failed to reveal what the customer really wanted. Detroit was not persuaded that he wanted anything different from what he had been getting until it lost millions of customers to other small car manufacturers.

How could this unbelievable lag behind consumer wants have been perpetuated so long? Why did not research reveal consumer preferences before consumers' buying decisions themselves revealed the facts? Is that not what consumer research is for—to find out before the fact what is going to happen? The answer is that Detroit never really researched the customer's wants. It only researched his preferences between the kinds of things which it had already decided to offer him. For Detroit is mainly product-oriented, not customer-oriented. To the extent that the customer is recognized as having needs that the manufacturer should try to satisfy, Detroit usually acts as if the job can be done entirely by product changes. Occasionally attention gets paid to financing, too, but that is done more in order to sell than to enable the customer to buy.

As for taking care of other customer needs, there is not enough being done to write about. The areas of the greatest unsatisfied needs are ignored, or at best get stepchild attention. These are at the point of sale and on the matter of automotive repair and maintenance. Detroit views these problem areas as being of secondary importance. That is underscored by the fact that the retailing and servicing ends of this industry are neither owned and operated nor controlled by the manufacturers. Once the car is produced, things are pretty much in the dealer's inadequate hands. Illustrative of Detroit's arm's-length attitude is the fact that, while servicing holds enormous sales-stimulating, profit-building opportunities, only 57 of Chevrolet's 7,000 dealers provide night maintenance service.

Motorists repeatedly express their dissatisfaction with servicing and their apprehensions about buying cars under the present selling setup. The anxieties and problems they encounter during the auto buying and maintenance processes are probably more intense and widespread today than 30 years ago. Yet the automobile companies do not *seem* to listen to or take

their cues from the anguished consumer. If they do listen, it must be through the filter of their own preoccupation with production. The marketing effort is still viewed as a necessary consequence of the product, not vice versa, as it should be. That is the legacy of mass production, with its parochial view that profit resides essentially in low-cost full production.

What Ford put first: The profit lure of mass production obviously has a place in the plans and strategy of business management, but it must always *follow* hard thinking about the customer. This is one of the most important lessons that we can learn from the contradictory behavior of Henry Ford. In a sense Ford was both the most brilliant and the most senseless marketer in American history. He was senseless because he refused to give the customer anything but a black car. He was brilliant because he fashioned a production system designed to fit market needs. We habitually celebrate him for the wrong reason, his production genius. His real genius was marketing. We think he was able to cut his selling price and therefore sell millions of $500 cars because his invention of the assembly line had reduced the costs. Actually he invented the assembly line because he had concluded that at $500 he could sell millions of cars. Mass production was the *result* not the cause of his low prices.

Ford repeatedly emphasized this point, but a nation of production-oriented business managers refuses to hear the great lesson he taught. Here is his operating philosophy as he expressed it succinctly:

"Our policy is to reduce the price, extend the operations, and improve the article. You will notice that the reduction of price comes first. We have never considered any costs as fixed. Therefore we first reduce the price to the point where we believe more sales will result. Then we go ahead and try to make the prices. We do not bother about the costs. The new price forces the costs down. The more usual way is to take the costs and then determine the price; and although that method may be scientific in the narrow sense, it is not scientific in the broad sense, because what earthly use is it to know the cost if it tells you that you cannot manufacture at a price at which the article can be sold? But more to the point is the fact that, although one may calculate what a cost is, and of course all of our costs are carefully calculated, no one knows what a cost ought to be. One of the ways of discovering ... is to name a price so low as to force everybody in the place to the highest point of efficiency.

[handwritten annotation at top:] tendency of growth industry to lose sight of mktg + the customer i.e Auto industry

The low price makes everybody dig for profits. We make more discoveries concerning manufacturing and selling under this forced method than by any method of leisurely investigation."[5]

Product provincialism: The tantalizing profit possibilities of low unit production costs may be the most seriously self-deceiving attitude that can afflict a company, particularly a "growth" company where an apparently assured expansion of demand already tends to undermine a proper concern for the importance of marketing and the customer.

The usual result of this narrow preoccupation with so-called concrete matters is that instead of growing, the industry declines. It usually means that the product fails to adapt to the constantly changing patterns of consumer needs and tastes, to new and modified marketing institutions and practices, or to product developments in competing or complementary industries. The industry has its eyes so firmly on its own specific product that it does not see how it is being made obsolete.

The classical example of this is the buggy whip industry. No amount of product improvement could stave off its death sentence. But had the industry defined itself as being in the transportation business rather than the buggy whip business, it might have survived. It would have done what survival always entails, that is, changing. Even if it had only defined its business as providing a stimulant or catalyst to an energy source, it might have survived by becoming a manufacturer of, say, fanbelts or air cleaners.

What may some day be a still more classical example is, again, the oil industry. Having let others steal marvelous opportunities from it (e.g., natural gas, as already mentioned, missile fuels, and jet engine lubricants), one would expect it to have taken steps never to let that happen again. But this is not the case. We are now getting extraordinary new developments in fuel systems specifically designed to power automobiles. Not only are these developments concentrated in firms outside the petroleum industry, but petroleum is almost systematically ignoring them, securely content in its wedded bliss to oil. It is the story of the kerosene lamp versus the incandescent lamp all over again. Oil is trying to improve hydrocarbon fuels rather than develop *any* fuels best suited to the needs of their users, whether or not made in different ways and with different raw materials from oil.

Here are some things which nonpetroleum companies are working on:

• Over a dozen such firms now have advanced working models of energy systems which, when perfected, will replace the internal combustion engine and eliminate the demand for gasoline. The superior merit of each of these systems is their elimination of frequent, time-consuming, and irritating refueling stops. Most of these systems are fuel cells designed to create electrical energy directly from chemicals without combustion. Most of them use chemicals that are not derived from oil, generally hydrogen and oxygen.

• Several other companies have advanced models of electric storage batteries designed to power automobiles. One of these is an aircraft producer that is working jointly with several electric utility companies. The latter hope to use off-peak generating capacity to supply overnight plug-in battery regeneration. Another company, also using the battery approach, is a medium-size electronics firm with extensive small-battery experience that it developed in connection with its work on hearing aids. It is collaborating with an automobile manufacturer. Recent improvements arising from the need for high-powered miniature power storage plants in rockets have put us within reach of a relatively small battery capable of withstanding great overloads or surges of power. Germanium diode applications and batteries using sintered-plate and nickel-cadmium techniques promise to make a revolution in our energy sources.

• Solar energy conversion systems are also getting increasing attention. One usually cautious Detroit auto executive recently ventured that solar-powered cars might be common by 1980.

As for the oil companies, they are more or less "watching developments," as one research director put it to me. A few are doing a bit of research on fuel cells, but almost always confined to developing cells powered by hydrocarbon chemicals. None of them are enthusiastically researching fuel cells, batteries, or solar power plants. None of them are spending a fraction as much on research in these profoundly important areas as they are on the usual run-of-the-mill things like reducing combustion chamber deposit in gasoline engines. One major integrated petroleum company recently took a tentative look at the fuel cell and concluded that although "the companies actively working on it indicate a belief in ultimate success … the

timing and magnitude of its impact are too remote to warrant recognition in our forecasts."

One might, of course, ask: Why should the oil companies do anything different? Would not chemical fuel cells, batteries, or solar energy kill the present product lines? The answer is that they would indeed, and that is precisely the reason for the oil firms having to develop these power units before their competitors, so they will not be companies without an industry.

Management might be more likely to do what is needed for its own preservation if it thought of itself as being in the energy business. But even that would not be enough if it persists in imprisoning itself in the narrow grip of its tight product orientation. It has to think of itself as taking care of customer needs, not finding, refining, or even selling oil. Once it genuinely thinks of its business as taking care of people's transportation needs, nothing can stop it from creating its own extravagantly profitable growth.

'Creative destruction': Since words are cheap and deeds are dear, it may be appropriate to indicate what this kind of thinking involves and leads to. Let us start at the beginning—the customer. It can be shown that motorists strongly dislike the bother, delay, and experience of buying gasoline. People actually do not buy gasoline. They cannot see it, taste it, feel it, appreciate it, or really test it. What they buy is the right to continue driving their cars. The gas station is like a tax collector to whom people are compelled to pay a periodic toll as the price of using their cars. This makes the gas station a basically unpopular institution. It can never be made popular or pleasant, only less unpopular, less unpleasant.

To reduce its unpopularity completely means eliminating it. Nobody likes a tax collector, not even a pleasantly cheerful one. Nobody likes to interrupt a trip to buy a phantom product, not even from a handsome Adonis or a seductive Venus. Hence, companies that are working on exotic fuel substitutes which will eliminate the need for frequent refueling are heading directly into the outstretched arms of the irritated motorist. They are riding a wave of inevitability, not because they are creating something which is technologically superior or more sophisticated, but because they are satisfying a powerful customer need. They are also eliminating noxious odors and air pollution.

Once the petroleum companies recognize the customer-satisfying logic of what another power system can do they will see that they have no more choice about working on an efficient, long-lasting fuel (or some way of delivering present fuels without bothering the motorist) than the big food chains had a choice about going into the supermarket business, or the vacuum tube companies had a choice about making semiconductors. For their own good the oil firms will have to destroy their own highly profitable assets. No amount of wishful thinking can save them from the necessity of engaging in this form of "creative destruction."

I phrase the need as strongly as this because I think management must make quite an effort to break itself loose from conventional ways. It is all too easy in this day and age for a company or industry to let its sense of purpose become dominated by the economies of full production and to develop a dangerously lopsided product orientation. In short, if management lets itself drift, it invariably drifts in the direction of thinking of itself as producing goods and services, not customer satisfactions. While it probably will not descend to the depths of telling its salesmen, "You get rid of it; we'll worry about profits," it can, without knowing it, be practicing precisely that formula for withering decay. The historic fate of one growth industry after another has been its suicidal product provincialism.

Dangers of R&D

Another big danger to a firm's continued growth arises when top management is wholly transfixed by the profit possibilities of technical research and development. To illustrate I shall turn first to a new industry—electronics—and then return once more to the oil companies. By comparing a fresh example with a familiar one, I hope to emphasize the prevalence and insidiousness of a hazardous way of thinking.

Marketing shortchanged: In the case of electronics, the greatest danger which faces the glamorous new companies in this field is not that they do not pay enough attention to research and development, but that they pay *too much* attention to it. And the fact that the fastest growing electronics firms owe their eminence to their heavy emphasis on technical research is completely beside the point. They have vaulted to affluence on a sudden crest of unusually strong general receptiveness to new technical ideas. Also, their success has been shaped in the virtually guaranteed market of military subsidies and by military orders that in many cases actually preceded the existence of facilities to make the products.

Their expansion has, in other words, been almost totally devoid of marketing effort.

Thus, they are growing up under conditions that come dangerously close to creating the illusion that a superior product will sell itself. Having created a successful company by making a superior product, it is not surprising that management continues to be oriented toward the product rather than the people who consume it. It develops the philosophy that continued growth is a matter of continued product innovation and improvement.

A number of other factors tend to strengthen and sustain this belief:

1. Because electronic products are highly complex and sophisticated, managements become top-heavy with engineers and scientists. This creates a selective bias in favor of research and production at the expense of marketing. The organization tends to view itself as making things rather than satisfying customer needs. Marketing gets treated as a residual activity, "something else" that must be done once the vital job of product creation and production is completed.

2. To this bias in favor of product research, development, and production is added the bias in favor of dealing with controllable variables. Engineers and scientists are at home in the world of concrete things like machines, test tubes, production lines, and even balance sheets. The abstractions to which they feel kindly are those which are testable or manipulatable in the laboratory, or, if not testable, then functional, such as Euclid's axioms. In short, the managements of the new glamour-growth companies tend to favor those business activities which lend themselves to careful study, experimentation, and control—the hard, practical realities of the lab, the shop, the books.

What gets shortchanged are the realities of the *market*. Consumers are unpredictable, varied, fickle, stupid, shortsighted, stubborn, and generally bothersome. This is not what the engineer-managers say, but deep down in their consciousness it is what they believe. And this accounts for their concentrating on what they know and what they can control, namely, product research, engineering, and production. The emphasis on production becomes particularly attractive when the product can be made at declining unit costs. There is no more in-

viting way of making money than by running the plant full blast.

Today the top-heavy science-engineering-production orientation of so many electronics companies works reasonably well because they are pushing into new frontiers in which the armed services have pioneered virtually assured markets. The companies are in the felicitous position of having to fill, not find markets; of not having to discover what the customer needs and wants, but of having the customer voluntarily come forward with specific new product demands. If a team of consultants had been assigned specifically to design a business situation calculated to prevent the emergence and development of a customer-oriented marketing viewpoint, it could not have produced anything better than the conditions just described.

Stepchild treatment: The oil industry is a stunning example of how science, technology, and mass production can divert an entire group of companies from their main task. To the extent the consumer is studied at all (which is not much), the focus is forever on getting information which is designed to help the oil companies improve what they are now doing. They try to discover more convincing advertising themes, more effective sales promotional drives, what the market shares of the various companies are, what people like or dislike about service station dealers and oil companies, and so forth. Nobody seems as interested in probing deeply into the basic human needs that the industry might be trying to satisfy as in probing into the basic properties of the raw material that the companies work with in trying to deliver customer satisfactions.

Basic questions about customers and markets seldom get asked. The latter occupy a stepchild status. They are recognized as existing, as having to be taken care of, but not worth very much real thought or dedicated attention. Nobody gets as excited about the customers in his own backyard as about the oil in the Sahara Desert. Nothing illustrates better the neglect of marketing than its treatment in the industry press.

The centennial issue of the *American Petroleum Institute Quarterly*, published in 1959 to celebrate the discovery of oil in Titusville, Pennsylvania, contained 21 feature articles proclaiming the industry's greatness. Only one of these talked about its achievements in marketing, and that was only a pictorial record of how service station architecture has changed. The issue also contained a special section on "New

Horizons," which was devoted to showing the magnificent role oil would play in America's future. Every reference was ebulliently optimistic, never implying once that oil might have some hard competition. Even the reference to atomic energy was a cheerful catalogue of how oil would help make atomic energy a success. There was not a single apprehension that the oil industry's affluence might be threatened or a suggestion that one "new horizon" might include new and better ways of serving oil's present customers.

But the most revealing example of the stepchild treatment that marketing gets was still another special series of short articles on "The Revolutionary Potential of Electronics." Under that heading this list of articles appeared in the table of contents:

- "In the Search for Oil"
- "In Production Operations"
- "In Refinery Processes"
- "In Pipeline Operations"

Significantly, every one of the industry's major functional areas is listed, *except* marketing. Why? Either it is believed that electronics holds no revolutionary potential for petroleum marketing (which is palpably wrong), or the editors forgot to discuss marketing (which is more likely, and illustrates its stepchild status).

The order in which the four functional areas are listed also betrays the alienation of the oil industry from the consumer. The industry is implicitly defined as beginning with the search for oil and ending with its distribution from the refinery. But the truth is, it seems to me, that the industry begins with the needs of the customer for its products. From that primal position its definition moves steadily back-stream to areas of progressively lesser importance, until it finally comes to rest at the "search for oil."

Beginning & end: The view that an industry is a customer-satisfying process, not a goods-producing process, is vital for all businessmen to understand. An industry begins with the customer and his needs, not with a patent, a raw material, or a selling skill. Given the customer's needs, the industry develops backwards, first concerning itself with the physical *delivery* of customer satisfactions. Then it moves back further to *creating* the things by which these satisfactions are in part achieved. How these materials are created is a matter of indifference to the customer, hence the particular form of manufacturing, processing, or what-have-you cannot be considered as a vital aspect of the industry.

Finally, the industry moves back still further to *finding* the raw materials necessary for making its products.

The irony of some industries oriented toward technical research and development is that the scientists who occupy the high executive positions are totally unscientific when it comes to defining their companies' overall needs and purposes. They violate the first two rules of the scientific method—being aware of and defining their companies' problems, and then developing testable hypotheses about solving them. They are scientific only about the convenient things, such as laboratory and product experiments.

The reason that the customer (and the satisfaction of his deepest needs) is not considered as being "the problem" is not because there is any certain belief that no such problem exists, but because an organizational lifetime has conditioned management to look in the opposite direction. Marketing is a stepchild.

I do not mean that selling is ignored. Far from it. But selling, again, is not marketing. As already pointed out, selling concerns itself with the tricks and techniques of getting people to exchange their cash for your product. It is not concerned with the values that the exchange is all about. And it does not, as marketing invariably does, view the entire business process as consisting of a tightly integrated effort to discover, create, arouse, and satisfy customer needs. The customer is somebody "out there" who, with proper cunning, can be separated from his loose change.

Actually, not even selling gets much attention in some technologically minded firms. Because there is a virtually guaranteed market for the abundant flow of their new products, they do not actually know what a real market is. It is as if they lived in a planned economy, moving their products routinely from factory to retail outlet. Their successful concentration on products tends to convince them of the soundness of what they have been doing, and they fail to see the gathering clouds over the market.

Conclusion

Less than 75 years ago American railroads enjoyed a fierce loyalty among astute Wall Streeters. European monarchs invested in them heavily. Eternal wealth was thought to be the benediction for anybody who could scrape a few thousand dollars together to put into rail stocks. No other form of transportation could compete with the

railroads in speed, flexibility, durability, economy, and growth potentials.

As Jacques Barzun put it, "By the turn of the century it was an institution, an image of man, a tradition, a code of honor, a source of poetry, a nursery of boyhood desires, a sublimest of toys, and the most solemn machine—next to the funeral hearse—that marks the epochs in man's life."[6]

Even after the advent of automobiles, trucks, and airplanes, the railroad tycoons remained imperturbably self-confident. If you had told them 30 years ago that in 30 years they would be flat on their backs, broke, and pleading for government subsidies, they would have thought you totally demented. Such a future was simply not considered possible. It was not even a discussable subject, or an askable question, or a matter which any sane person would consider worth speculating about. The very thought was insane. Yet a lot of insane notions now have matter-of-fact acceptance—for example, the idea of 100-ton tubes of metal moving smoothly through the air 20,000 feet above the earth, loaded with 100 sane and solid citizens casually drinking martinis—and they have dealt cruel blows to the railroads.

What specifically must other companies do to avoid this fate? What does customer orientation involve? These questions have in part been answered by the preceding examples and analysis. It would take another article to show in detail what is required for specific industries. In any case, it should be obvious that building an effective customer-oriented company involves far more than good intentions or promotional tricks; it involves profound matters of human organization and leadership. For the present, let me merely suggest what appear to be some general requirements.

Visceral feel of greatness: Obviously the company has to do what survival demands. It has to adapt to the requirements of the market, and it has to do it sooner rather than later. But mere survival is a so-so aspiration. Anybody can survive in some way or other, even the skid-row bum. The trick is to survive gallantly, to feel the surging impulse of commercial mastery; not just to experience the sweet smell of success, but to have the visceral feel of entrepreneurial greatness.

No organization can achieve greatness without a vigorous leader who is driven onward by his own pulsating *will to succeed*. He has to have a vision of grandeur, a vision that can produce eager followers in vast numbers. In business, the followers are the customers.

In order to produce these customers, the entire corporation must be viewed as a customer-creating and customer-satisfying organism. Management must think of itself not as producing products but as providing customer-creating value satisfactions. It must push this idea (and everything it means and requires) into every nook and cranny of the organization. It has to do this continuously and with the kind of flair that excites and stimulates the people in it. Otherwise, the company will be merely a series of pigeonholed parts, with no consolidating sense of purpose or direction.

In short, the organization must learn to think of itself not as producing goods or services but as *buying customers*, as doing the things that will make people *want* to do business with it. And the chief executive himself has the inescapable responsibility for creating this environment, this viewpoint, this attitude, this aspiration. He himself must set the company's style, its direction, and its goals. This means he has to know precisely where he himself wants to go, and to make sure the whole organization is enthusiastically aware of where that is. This is a first requisite of leadership, for *unless he knows where he is going, any road will take him there.*

If any road is okay, the chief executive might as well pack his attaché case and go fishing. If an organization does not know or care where it is going, it does not need to advertise that fact with a ceremonial figurehead. Everybody will notice it soon enough.

Retrospective commentary

Amazed, finally, by his literary success, Isaac Bashevis Singer reconciled an attendant problem: "I think the moment you have published a book, it's not any more your private property.... If it has value, everybody can find in it what he finds, and I cannot tell the man I did not intend it to be so." Over the past 15 years, "Marketing Myopia" has become a case in point. Remarkably, the article spawned a legion of loyal partisans—not to mention a host of unlikely bedfellows.

Its most common and, I believe, most influential consequence is the way certain companies for the first time gave serious thought to the question of what businesses they are really in.

The strategic consequences of this have in many cases been dramatic. The best-known case, of course, is the shift in think-ing of oneself as being in the "oil business" to being in the "energy business." In some instances the payoff has been spectacular (getting into coal, for example) and in others dreadful (in terms of the time and money spent so far on fuel cell research). Another successful example is a company with a large chain of retail shoe stores that redefined itself as a retailer of moderately priced, frequently purchased, widely assorted consumer specialty products. The result was a dramatic growth in volume, earnings, and return on assets.

Some companies, again for the first time, asked themselves whether they wished to be masters of certain technologies for which they would seek markets, or be masters of markets for which they would seek customer-satisfying products and services.

Choosing the former, one company has declared, in effect, "We are experts in glass technology. We intend to improve and expand that expertise with the object of creating products that will attract customers." This decision has forced the company into a much more systematic and customer-sensitive look at possible markets and users, even though its stated strategic object has been to capitalize on glass technology.

Deciding to concentrate on markets, another company has determined that "we want to help people (primarily women) enhance their beauty and sense of youthfulness." This company has expanded its line of cosmetic products, but has also entered the fields of proprietary drugs and vitamin supplements.

All these examples illustrate the "policy" results of "Marketing Myopia." On the operating level, there has been, I think, an extraordinary heightening of sensitivity to customers and consumers. R&D departments have cultivated a greater "external" orientation toward uses, users, and markets—balancing thereby the previously one-sided "internal" focus on materials and methods; upper management has realized that marketing and sales departments should be somewhat more willingly accommodated than before, finance departments have become more receptive to the legitimacy of budgets for market research and experimentation in marketing, and salesmen have been better trained to listen to and understand customer needs and problems, rather than merely to "push" the product.

A mirror, not a window

My impression is that the article has had more impact in industrial-products compa-nies than in consumer-products companies—perhaps because the former had lagged most in customer orientation. There are at least two reasons for this lag: (1) industrial-products companies tend to be more capital intensive, and (2) in the past, at least, they have had to rely heavily on communicating face-to-face the technical character of what they made and sold. These points are worth explaining.

Capital-intensive businesses are understandably preoccupied with magnitudes, especially where the capital, once invested, cannot be easily moved, manipulated, or modified for the production of a variety of products—e.g., chemical plants, steel mills, airlines, and railroads. Understandably, they seek big volumes and operating efficiencies to pay off the equipment and meet the carrying costs.

At least one problem results: corporate power becomes disproportionately lodged with operating or financial executives. If you read the charter of one of the nation's largest companies, you will see that the chairman of the finance committee, not the chief executive officer, is the "chief." Executives with such backgrounds have an almost trained incapacity to see that getting "volume" may require understanding and serving many discrete and sometimes small market segments, rather than going after a perhaps mythical batch of big or homogeneous customers.

These executives also often fail to appreciate the competitive changes going on around them. They observe the changes, all right, but devalue their significance or underestimate their ability to nibble away at the company's markets.

Once dramatically alerted to the concept of segments, sectors, and customers, though, managers of capital-intensive businesses have become more responsive to the necessity of balancing their inescapable preoccupation with "paying the bills" or breaking even with the fact that the best way to accomplish this may be to pay more attention to segments, sectors, and customers.

The second reason industrial products companies have probably been more influenced by the article is that, in the case of the more technical industrial products or services, the necessity of clearly communicating product and service characteristics to prospects results in a lot of face-to-face "selling" effort. But precisely because the product is so complex, the situation produces salesmen who know the product more than they know the customer, who are more adept at explaining what they have and what it can do than learning what the customer's needs and problems are. The result has been a narrow product orientation rather than a liberating customer orientation, and "service" often suffered. To be sure, sellers said, "We have to provide service," but they tended to define service by looking into the mirror rather than out the window. They *thought* they were looking out the window at the customer, but it was actually a mirror—a reflection of their own product-oriented biases rather than a reflection of their customers' situations.

A manifesto, not a prescription

Not everything has been rosy. A lot of bizarre things have happened as a result of the article:

• Some companies have developed what I call "marketing mania"—they've become obsessively responsive to every fleeting whim of the customer. Mass production operations have been converted to approximations of job shops, with cost and price consequences far exceeding the willingness of customers to buy the product.

• Management has expanded product lines and added new lines of business without first establishing adequate control systems to run more complex operations.

• Marketing staffs have suddenly and rapidly expanded themselves and their research budgets without either getting sufficient prior organizational support or, thereafter, producing sufficient results.

• Companies that are functionally organized have converted to product, brand, or market-based organizations with the expectation of instant and miraculous results. The outcome has been ambiguity, frustration, confusion, corporate infighting, losses, and finally a reversion to functional arrangements that only worsened the situation.

• Companies have attempted to "serve" customers by creating complex and beautifully efficient products or services that buyers are either too risk-averse to adopt or incapable of learning how to employ—in effect, there are now steam shovels for people who haven't yet learned to use spades. This problem has happened repeatedly in the so-called service industries (financial services, insurance, computer-based services) and with American companies selling in less-developed economies.

"Marketing Myopia" was not intended as analysis or even prescription; it was intended as manifesto. It did not pretend to take a balanced position. Nor was it a new idea—Peter F. Drucker, J. B. McKitterick, Wroe Alderson, John Howard, and Neil Borden had each done more original and balanced work on "the marketing concept." My scheme, however, tied marketing more closely to the inner orbit of business policy. Drucker—especially in *The Concept of the Corporation* and *The Practice of Management*—originally provided me with a great deal of insight.

My contribution, therefore, appears merely to have been a simple, brief, and useful way of communicating an existing way of thinking. I tried to do it in a very direct, but responsible fashion, knowing that few readers (customers), especially managers and leaders, could stand much equivocation or hesitation. I also knew that the colorful and lightly documented affirmation works better than the tortuously reasoned explanation.

But why the enormous popularity of what was actually such a simple preexisting idea? Why its appeal throughout the world to resolutely restrained scholars, implacably temperate managers, and high government officials, all accustomed to balanced and thoughtful calculation? Is it that concrete examples, joined to illustrate a simple idea and presented with some attention to literacy, communicate better than massive analytical reasoning that reads as though it were translated from the German? Is it that provocative assertions are more memorable and persuasive than restrained and balanced explanations, no matter who the audience? Is it that the character of the message is as much the message as its content? Or was mine not simply a different tune, but a new symphony? I don't know.

Of course, I'd do it again and in the same way, given my purposes, even with what more I now know—the good and the bad, the power of facts and the limits of rhetoric. If your mission is the moon, you don't use a car. Don Marquis's cockroach, Archy, provides some final consolation: "an idea is not responsible for who believes in it."

Notes

1. Jacques Barzun, "Trains and the Mind of Man," *Holiday*, February 1960, p. 21.

2. For more details see M. M. Zimmerman, *The Super Market: A Revolution in Distribution* (New York, McGraw-Hill Book Company, Inc., 1955), p. 48.

3. Ibid., pp. 45–47.

4. *The Affluent Society* (Boston, Houghton Mifflin Company, 1958), pp. 152–160.

5. Henry Ford, *My Life and* Work (New York, Doubleday, Page & Company, 1923), pp. 146–147.

6. Jacques Barzun, "Trains and the Mind of Man," *Holiday*, February 1960, p. 20.

At the time of the article's publication, Theodore Levitt was lecturer in business administration at the Harvard Business School. He is the author of several books, including The Third Sector: New Tactics for a Responsive Society *(1973) and* Marketing for Business Growth *(1974).*

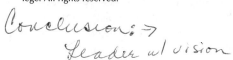

Conclusion: →
  Leader w/ vision

Why Customer Satisfaction
Starts with HR

There's convincing evidence that HR drives customer satisfaction—and corporate revenues—by careful attention to who is hired, how they are trained, how they are coached, and how they are treated on the job.

By Patrick J. Kiger

In a conference room at Philadelphia-based Rosenbluth International, one of the country's most successful travel agencies, a dozen new employees are participating in a customer-service training exercise. What's astonishing is that the new company associates are practicing how to provide *bad* customer service.

One group is asked to dream up the rudest ways a motor-vehicle bureau staff member could treat a hapless customer who comes in to apply for a driver's license. After a few minutes of preparation, the associates perform a skit for an audience of other new employees. The trainee who plays the customer arrives at the ersatz office and stands in line. Just as he reaches the counter, the trainee portraying the clerk posts a sign proclaiming that he'll be back in 15 minutes. Other trainees make the hands move on a fake clock to simulate the wait stretching to 20 minutes, then 30, then 40. As the customer pleads for service, the clerk—who is sitting behind the counter, reading a magazine and loudly cracking gum—berates him for his impatience. The ultimate indignity comes when the customer proceeds to the license-photo area and learns that the camera is broken.

Rosenbluth's HR team uses the exercise because it's fun, but mainly to focus trainees on a serious lesson: Customer service arguably is the most critical factor in an organization's long-term success and even survival.

There was a time when customer service was seen as the responsibility of sales managers and tech-support team leaders. Today that attitude is as dated as rotary telephones at corporate call centers. Increasingly, companies are recognizing that HR plays a seminal role in building a customer-friendly culture. Throughout the business world, HR departments are focusing their efforts on improving customer satisfaction. They're using HR activities—hiring, training, coaching, and evaluation pro-

grams—to give employees the tools and support they need to develop and nurture positive, lasting relationships with clients.

The evidence is compelling that HR practices can promote customer satisfaction—and, in the process, improve corporate revenues. A landmark 1999 analysis of 800 Sears Roebuck stores, for example, demonstrated that for every 5 percent improvement in employee attitudes, customer satisfaction increased 1.3 percent and corporate revenue rose a half-percentage point.

Most service-quality gurus say that hiring is not only the first, but the most critical step in building a customer-friendly company.

Moreover, subtle changes in hiring or training sometimes can produce major improvements in customer happiness. One of this year's *Workforce* Optimas Award winners, NCCI Holdings Inc., discovered in a survey last year that its customers wanted more help in using the company's insurance-data software products. As a result, NCCI created a training initiative to give its customer-service reps more technical expertise. By the fourth quarter, the surveys were showing that customers were much more favorably impressed with the reps' technical abilities. Apparently as a result, the overall customer-satisfaction rating rose 33 percent during that period, from 6 to 8 on a 10-point scale.

A company with strong customer satisfaction and loyalty can survive and prosper even when faced with a tough economy or an unforeseen disaster. The salient example: Southwest Airlines, which consistently ranks first among airlines in customer satisfaction. Following the September 11 terrorist attacks, which pushed many airline companies to the brink of demise, Southwest actually managed to post a profit in the fourth quarter of 2001, and was confident enough about the future to add new routes.

Conversely, a company that provides lousy service may have trouble hanging on to its customers over time, and thus may be forced to continually replace lost accounts that have fled in frustration. The cost of acquiring new customers is five times higher than the expense of servicing existing ones, says Michael De-Santo, a consultant for Walker Information, an Indianapolis-based business research firm. At that rate, chronically dysfunctional customer service becomes a monster that can devour whatever gains a company is making in other areas. If that company runs into a stalled economy or an aggressive competitor, its bad customer karma can prove fatal.

For proof, you only have to look at Kmart, the once-mighty discount retailer that went bankrupt in January, at least in part because it couldn't compete with the famously courteous folks at Wal-Mart. (A recent study by MOHR Learning, a New Jersey-based consulting firm, found that 20 percent of customers will immediately walk out of a store when confronted by bad service, and 26 percent will warn their friends and neighbors not to shop there.) Last year, the Dow Jones News Service reported that customer dissatisfaction was costing the McDonald's chain a breathtaking $750 million in lost business annually.

Identifying employees with customer-satisfaction potential

Most service-quality gurus say that hiring is the first and most critical step in building a customer-friendly company. "You need to be selective," says Ron Zemke, president of the consulting firm Performance Research Associates, located in Minneapolis. "It's a lot easier to start with people who've got the right personality qualities to work with customers than it is to struggle to teach those skills to whoever walks in the door."

"We don't want people who are mavericks or into self-aggrandizement. We're looking for a person who plays nicely with others."

Zemke says the key indicator of customer-service potential is a high level of what mental-health professionals call "psychological hardiness"—qualities such as optimism, flexibility, and the ability to handle stressful situations or criticism without feeling emotionally threatened. Those are, of course, good qualities for many jobs. But experts note that the personality of a customer-service maven may be markedly different from those of achievers in other business venues. Verbal eloquence and

persuasiveness, for example, aren't as important as the ability to listen.

"The great customer-relationship person has a very even-handed view of things, a strong sense of fairness," says Dianne Durkin, who teaches customer-satisfaction techniques at Loyalty Factor, an HR consulting firm in New Castle, New Hampshire. "This is a person who tends to balance his or her own interests and the company's interests with the customer's interests."

Ruth Cohen, Rosenbluth's director of HR/learning and development, says her company doesn't want "people who are mavericks or into self-aggrandizement. We're looking for a person who plays nicely with others."

Five HR Tips for Improving the Customer Relationship
tools

- **Look for customer-pleasing personalities**. The ability to empathize with others, flexibility, and emotional resilience under pressure are qualities that aren't easy to teach. Design a structured, situational interviewing process to find those special people.

- **Don't be afraid to emphasize the negative**. Good service isn't always noticed, but bad service invariably is. Use role-playing exercises and encourage trainees to discuss their own experiences as mistreated customers to help them understand the impact on the company's fortunes when they don't make a good impression.

- **Give employees tools for understanding their customers**. Your training program should include training in techniques such as "active listening" and advice on how to interpret customers' verbal cues.

- **Don't neglect "hard" skills**. A nice smile and polite telephone manners aren't enough when a customer needs advice on which hardware to pick or help with a product that isn't working. Make sure your customer-service people have a good working knowledge of whatever you're selling.

- **Promote a service-oriented culture from the top**. A company's customer relationships are heavily influenced by the tone of the management/employee relationship. Sell your top leaders on the importance of company rituals that emphasize service as a core value—for example, an employee tea or luncheon where executives do the serving.

—*PJK*

What's the best way to distinguish those who are the most likely to please customers from a raft of applicants? Some companies have tried standardized psychological tests. But many consultants and HR professionals say that it's more effective to observe an applicant at work. At Rosenbluth, the scrutiny begins the moment that a job-seeker walks in the door for an interview. "We're looking for a person who shows the same courtesy to everyone he or she encounters," says Cecily Carel, company vice president for HR. "Our receptionist, who's been with the company 20 years, is a pretty good judge of character.

One time she called me from her desk to say, 'This person is not polite.' That applicant wasn't hired."

Patrick Wright, director of the Center for Advanced HR Studies at Cornell University, recommends a carefully structured, situational interview process like the one he helped develop for Whirlpool. "You want to present an applicant with a series of potential scenarios that he might face on the job, and ask him what he would do," Wright says. "Just because a person gives a good answer, of course, doesn't ensure that he's going to actually do that when he becomes an employee. But you want to make sure you've got a person who at least has the right instincts, which you can reinforce through training."

Talent+, Inc., an HR consulting firm in Lincoln, Nebraska, has designed a system for evaluating job applicants that compares their answers in an open-ended interview to analyses of the traits of top performers in that particular field. The company's managing director, Lisa French, says the process can predict a candidate's job performance 80 to 85 percent of the time. In the case of customer service, she says, one of the key determinants is a strong sense of values. A good customer-service performer will work hard on a customer's behalf, not with the hope of getting a raise or a promotion, but because it's the right thing to do. "This is the sort of person who will go down fighting for his or her customers," she says.

Talent+ started working with Ritz-Carlton in 1992, when the rate of "customer defects"—people who complained about the service—had reached a disturbing 27 percent. The consultants helped Ritz-Carlton overhaul its interview and hiring practices, with a focus on identifying applicants with the best customer-service potential. With the new system in place, complaints dropped steadily. By 2000, they had dropped to 1 percent. At the same time, annual job turnover at Ritz-Carlton also decreased from 75 percent to 25 percent.

Turning the knack for niceness into skilled service

Service-quality consultants and HR professionals from service-conscious companies say that even an employee with the right personality traits needs guidance on how to channel positive qualities into developing good customer relationships. At a time of economic uncertainty, when many companies may try to cut costs by scrimping on customer-service training, it's all the more crucial for HR to make a strong case for its vital importance.

One of the most basic steps in teaching good customer-service skills is fostering employees' self-awareness, Durkin says. "You're not going to be good at customer relations unless you first understand yourself. You have to know how you come across to other people, how you react under stress, what your communication style is."

To help an employee become more self-aware, a company may want to use an assessment tool. The Myers-Briggs Type Indicator, for example, helps an employee see her own personality style, such as whether she is a "thinker," a methodical person; a "sensor," one who learns through observation; an "intuitor,"

who is enthusiastic and excitable; or a "feeler," who tends to avoid conflict. With training, a customer-service employee also can learn more about identifying customers' personality types.

Another crucial area of customer-service training is communication skills. "Research shows that only 7 percent of the impact of your communication with another person is in the words you use," Durkin says. "Thirty-eight percent is in the tone of voice. The remaining 55 percent of the message comes from physical appearance, mannerisms, eye contact, and so on." Because so much of communication is nonverbal, customer-service employees who have to deal with customers primarily over the phone find themselves at a major disadvantage in getting across their message—or, conversely, in understanding the customer's need.

One way to compensate for the lack of human contact is by teaching customer-service employees the technique of "active listening"—restating and summarizing what the customer tells them. This not only helps understanding but also conveys a message of attentiveness and concern. Employees also can be taught to notice and respond to subtle cues in a customer's speech.

A big part of achieving great customer service turns out to be keeping customer-service employees happy.

Rosenbluth takes a slightly different approach. The travel agency focuses on educating its customer-service associates to use what it calls "elegant language"—words and phrases intended to create a tone of courtesy, respect, and attentiveness to detail. A company associate uses the word "certainly" instead of "yeah" or "sure," and after helping a customer with a problem, reflexively responds, "It has been my pleasure." And they always, always ask for permission—and wait for the response—before putting a customer on hold. "We think this gives customers a message about how much attention we pay to little details," Cecily Carel says. "It's subtle, but important."

But good customer service requires more than just "soft," or non-technical, skills. Customer-service consultant Zemke notes that organizations frequently neglect to give their customer-service employees adequate product training. "If I order something and it doesn't work, I want somebody who knows the product and can help me, not somebody who's been trained to smile at the right times." Companies such as NCCI have successfully used surveys to find out what kind of technical knowledge and assistance customers most need, and incorporate the information into customer-service training.

Supervising to build a customer-friendly environment

In order for carefully selected, well-trained employees to build great relationships with customers, a company must develop its own good internal relationships, HR professionals say.

Discovering and Fixing Customer-Service Ills

business results

When Don Frye joined Process Software as a manager of technical support and management information systems in August 2001, he quickly found himself in the midst of a customer-service crisis. The company's meal ticket is a narrow technological niche: Internet-related software for business and university computer servers running the VMS platform.

"Basically, we compete against a product that Compaq gives away for free," Frye says. "That's why for us, customer service is really crucial. We need to demonstrate on a daily basis that we treat people well, so that they'll be motivated not only to purchase our product but also to purchase tech support services from us."

But when Frye received the results of an annual customer-satisfaction survey, he was disheartened to see a number of clients who rated their experience with Process as below their expectations. "I contacted every one of those people, to see what was the matter with us," he says. "It wasn't the quality of the product. Basically, the problem was account management. Those customers told me that they felt forgotten, out of the loop. They were frustrated about having to call repeatedly to get updates on their cases."

Hiring new people with better customer skills wasn't an option for Frye, because the company's veteran tech-support staff had accumulated crucial knowledge that wasn't easily replaceable. Instead, he brought in an outside consultant, Loyalty Factor, to analyze the staff's customer woes and develop an individualized prescription for fixing them.

In addition to using the Myers-Briggs test to give employees insight about their own personalities and style of relating to customers, the consultant helped Frye make subtle but important adjustments to the team's communication with customers. A third of contact with customers was through e-mail, a mode that, because it strips away facial expressions, tone of voice, and other nonverbal cues, conveys only about 7 percent of the intended message.

To reduce the number of misunderstandings, employees were coached to choose their words more carefully and to utilize emotions. To lessen customer frustration, the staff studies "active listening" techniques, learning to repeat and summarize what customers told them. "One of the big benefits is that it shows people that you're paying attention to their problems," Frye says. Follow-up and continuity were other problems that emerged in the analysis, so the staff learned to take more thorough and systematic case notes on calls. "That way, when the customer called back, whoever answered the phone could immediately pick up their service without missing a beat."

The fix worked, even better than Frye had hoped. Within a month of tech-support completing its training, complaints were down by more than 50 percent. More important, one of the company's most critical indicators, the renewal rate for customers, actually rose 2 percent over the previous year.

—*PJK*

Walker Information's Michael DeSanto says that he's noticed an intriguing phenomenon: customers' and employees' relationships with companies tend to have striking parallels.

Research at Cornell University's Center for Advanced HR Studies and at other institutions indicates that there's a strong link between customer and employee satisfaction. "The really crucial issues are retention and, more important, loyalty," DeSanto says. "Both of them tend to operate in a three- to five-year cycle. Brand-new employees tend to love you, because they're still learning new skills and have the potential to move up in the company. New customers love you because you'll do anything to keep them happy." Three years down the road, both the employee and customer relationships with the company suddenly are different, he notes. "The employee may feel like he's buried in the organization. Chances are, he's already got whatever training you're going to give him. He's hearing from headhunters. And the customer is in a similar rut. He's being taken for granted, and he's already learned about the business from you, so maybe he doesn't need you as much."

Strong relationships between employees and customers may actually keep both from fleeing the company. "Good customer relationships may actually be a factor in employee retention," DeSanto says.

A large part of achieving great customer service is keeping the employees happy. Service-quality experts say that customer-service employees tend to model externally the treatment they receive from management. An intensely top-driven, autocratic corporate culture with spotty internal communication leads to tense, confused customer relations. A company with a collegial atmosphere and good channels of communication will be a lot better at keeping its customers happy.

There are many things HR can do to help create an environment that nurtures good service and customer relationships. Rosenbluth International has developed a culture that encourages associates to seek one another's help in solving customer problems, and emphasizes its concern for the customer with "elegant language." CEO Hal Rosenbluth often personally serves tea and cookies to new associates at the completion of their training. "It's a little corporate ritual that sets the mood," Carel says. At the same time, it helps Rosenbluth talk with new employees about what they can do to serve customers.

Rosenbluth's HR team has discovered an important truth. Just as subtle qualities such as a facial expression, choice of words, or a nuance of etiquette can help make a good impression on a customer, any comprehensive HR strategy for customer satisfaction depends on attention to detail. In designing hiring, training, evaluation, and other programs, nothing should be left to chance.

Patrick J. Kiger is a freelance writer in Washington, D.C. E-mail editors@workforce.com to comment.

Start With the Customer

At top-performing service companies, the customer always comes first.

By Stephen W. Brown

THIS COLUMN IS THE first in a series of three that will explore the best practices of truly excellent service companies like Disney, Southwest Airlines, Marriott, and Harley-Davidson Motor Co. The second column in the series will focus on "The Employee Experience" and the last will focus on "The Leadership Experience."

These best practices represent the business fundamentals of firms that are masterful at exceeding customer expectations. Deceptively simple yet highly effective for attracting and retaining customers, they can be applied to both service and non-service firms alike. The columns are derived in part from the recent article, "Delivering Excellent Service: Lessons from the Best Firms" by Robert Ford, Cherrill Heaton, and Stephen Brown, which appeared in the Fall 2001 issue of *California Management Review.*

The common ground between all truly excellent service firms is they know it "all starts with the customer" and they look first to the customer to define quality and value. Any company—whether they're primarily a product, service, or distri-

bution company—can benefit from applying these essential best practices of top-performing service companies.

Think and act in terms of the entire customer experience. There's more to a customer's experience than the product itself. Leading companies realize that every interaction with the customer can make or break the relationship. Harley-Davidson customers don't simply buy a motorcycle; they buy into a brand experience and a way of life. Successful firms know how to emulate Harley's ability to create an experience around a product or service. These organizations look beyond the core product or service to also carefully study the "where" and "how" of the customer experience.

For example, benchmark service organizations have learned that if the physical environment is not in keeping with the rest of the experience, customer satisfaction diminishes. The "servicescape" extends from ambient temperature and lighting that affect the physiological responses of customers to the character and feel of the experience. Dis-

ney spends considerable time, thought, and money designing the optimal environment for the experiences it provides customers. One example is the diligence of the Main Street painters. Their only responsibility, all year long, is to start at one end of Main Street and paint all the buildings and structures until they get to the other end and then start all over again. This high level of cleanliness and upkeep supports the guests' fantasies of the Disney image.

A good example of managing the "how" of the customer experience is looking at the ways great companies manage wait time. Disney is the master of this. It knows the exact relationship between wait times at the parks and customer satisfaction and makes sure it has sufficient attractions, food service, and merchandise available to handle the number of guests in the park without unacceptable waits. Disney knows guests want to be kept informed, so it posts the estimated wait times. It also sends mobile entertainment teams to entertain people in long lines.

Continuously improve all parts of the customer experience. Although "continuous improvement" is a mantra for many organizations, benchmark service organizations feature two important aspects to this concept. First, they start with the customer and find out what the customer expects to be improved. Second, they consider all parts of the customer experience as potential areas for improvement. These firms not only try to improve the product and service itself, but also the setting in which the product is delivered and the quality of the delivery system.

Even small, low-cost changes based on customer feedback can produce higher levels of customer retention. Disney's customers indicated that the Tower of Terror—a ride designed to simulate the feeling of an elevator dropping—seemed like it was over too quickly. By making some adjustments to the sequencing of the drops, the customers felt the ride time was just long enough without Disney changing the actual length of the ride.

Empower customers to help co-produce their own experience. Outstanding organizations know customer involvement leads to a number of positive organizational benefits. First, whatever customers can do for themselves, the organization does not have to do for them. This outcome can have a cost and convenience benefit to customers as well. Second, the organization knows that the more customers are involved in producing their own ser-

vice experience, the greater the likelihood the experience will meet each customer's expectations. If the experience does not, the customer bears part of the responsibility. It's hard to find fault with a physician if you fail to follow the treatment plan for an illness or injury. Third, the organization can gain loyalty from participating customers who think of themselves as part of the organization's family.

A great example of creating a "family feeling" is Southwest Airlines. Southwest invites its frequent flyers to help interview new flight attendants. This involvement not only brings customer expertise to the selection process, but also sends a strong message to the customers participating—you're so important to us that we want you to help us pick the people you think can best serve your needs.

Build-a-Bear Workshop, a growing national retailer, engages customers of all ages in creating customized stuffed animals, including naming, dressing, and accessorizing each animal. Research I've been involved with in information technology services also demonstrates the effectiveness of customer co-production in B2B settings.

Treat all customers like guests. Disney insists on everyone using the term guest instead of customer for their millions of visitors. Looking at a customer as a genuine guest changes everything the organization

and its employees do. Creating a hospitable experience instead of merely selling a product or service is an important way to turn customers into loyal patrons or repeat guests. It's cheaper to retain loyal customers than it is to recruit new ones, and repeat business is the key to long-term profitability. Although treating customers as guests is a simple sounding lesson, it represents a major challenge that organizations have to master in order to compete successfully in an increasingly customer-driven marketplace.

In short, the benchmark service organization has a key lesson to teach companies of all types: The customer experience is the key element to consider when shaping your business practices. The time and energy spent on accurately understanding the totality of your customer's needs and wants and finding cost-effective ways to address those factors will be rewarded with greater levels of customer retention—the ultimate driver of long-term profitability.

About the Author

Stephen W. Brown holds the Edward M. Carson Chair in Services Marketing and is a professor of marketing at Arizona State University and director of ASU's Center for Services Leadership. He may be reached at stephen.brown@asu.edu. For more information on ASU's Center for Services Leadership visit, www.cob.asu.edu/csl.

From *Marketing Management*, January/February 2003, pp. 12-13. © 2003 by the American Marketing Association. Reprinted by permission.

What Drives Customer Equity

A company's current customers provide the most
reliable source of future revenues and profits.

By Katherine N. Lemon, Roland T. Rust, and Valarie A. Zeithaml

Consider the **issues** facing a typical brand manager, product manager, or marketing-oriented CEO: How do I manage the brand? How will my customers react to changes in the product or service offering? Should I raise price? What is the best way to enhance the relationships with my current customers? Where should I focus my efforts?

Business executives can answer such questions by focusing on customer equity—the total of the discounted lifetime values of all the firm's customers. A strategy based on customer equity allows firms to trade off between customer value, brand equity, and customer relationship management. We have developed a new strategic framework, the Customer Equity Diagnostic, that reveals the key drivers increasing the firm's customer equity. This new framework will enable managers to determine what is most important to the customer and to begin to identify the firm's critical strengths and hidden vulnerabilities. Customer equity is a new approach to marketing and corporate strategy that finally puts the customer and, more important, strategies that grow the value of the customer, at the heart of the organization.

For most firms, customer equity is certain to be the most important determinant of the long-term value of the firm. While customer equity will not be responsible for the entire value of the firm (eg., physical assets, intellectual property, and research and development competencies), its current customers provide the most reliable source of future revenues and profits. This then should be a focal point for marketing strategy.

Although it may seem obvious that customer equity is key to long-term success, understanding how to grow and manage customer equity is more complex. How to grow it is of utmost importance, and doing it well can create a significant competitive advantage. There are three drivers of customer equity—value equity, brand equity, and relationship equity (also known as retention equity). These drivers work independently and together. Within each of these drivers are specific, incisive actions,

or levers, the firm can take to enhance its overall customer equity.

Value Equity

Value is the keystone of the customer's relationship with the firm. If the firm's products and services do not meet the customer's needs and expectations, the best brand strategy and the strongest retention and relationship marketing strategies will be insufficient. Value equity is defined as the customer's objective assessment of the utility of a brand, based on perceptions of what is given up for what is received. Three key levers influence value equity: quality, price, and convenience.

EXECUTIVE
briefing

Customer equity is critical to a firm's long-term success. We developed a strategic marketing framework that puts the customer and growth in the value of the customer at the heart of the organization. Using a new approach based on customer equity—the total of the discounted lifetime values of all the firm's customers—we describe the key drivers of firm growth: value equity, brand equity, and relationship equity. Understanding these drivers will help increase customer equity and, ultimately, the value of the firm.

Quality can be thought of as encompassing the objective physical and nonphysical aspects of the product and service offering under the firm's control. Think of the power FedEx holds in the marketplace, thanks, in no small part, to its maintenance of high quality standards. Price represents the aspects of "what is given up by the customer" that the firm can influence. New e-world entrants that enable customers to find the best price (e.g., www.mysimon.com) have revolutionized the power of price as a marketing tool. Convenience relates to actions that help reduce the customer's time costs, search costs, and efforts to do business with the firm. Consider Fidelity Investments' new strategy of providing Palm devices to its best customers to enable anytime, anywhere trading and updates—clearly capitalizing on the importance of convenience to busy consumers.

Brand Equity

Where value equity is driven by perceptions of objective aspects of a firm's offerings, brand equity is built through image and meaning. The brand serves three vital roles. First, it acts as a magnet to attract new customers to the firm. Second, it can serve as a reminder to customers about the firm's products and services. Finally, it can become the customer's emotional tie to the firm. Brand equity has often been defined very broadly to include an extensive set of attributes that influence consumer choice. However, in our effort to separate the specific drivers of customer equity, we define brand equity more narrowly as the customer's subjective and intangible assessment of the brand, above and beyond its objectively perceived value.

The key actionable levers of brand equity are brand awareness, attitude toward the brand, and corporate ethics. The first, brand awareness, encompasses the tools under the firm's control that can influence and enhance brand awareness, particularly marketing communications. The new focus on media advertising by pharmaceutical companies (e.g., Zyban, Viagra, Claritin) is designed to build brand awareness and encourage patients to ask for these drugs by name.

Second, attitude toward the brand encompasses the extent to which the firm is able to create close connections or emotional ties with the consumer. This is most often influenced through the specific nature of the media campaigns and may be more directly influenced by direct marketing. Kraft's strength in consumer food products exemplifies the importance of brand attitude—developing strong consumer attitudes toward key brands such as Kraft Macaroni and Cheese or Philadelphia Cream Cheese. The third lever, corporate ethics, includes specific actions that can influence customer perceptions of the organization (e.g., community sponsorships or donations, firm privacy policy, and employee relations). Home Depot enhanced its brand equity by becoming a strong supporter of community events and by encouraging its employees to get involved.

Relationship Equity

Consider a firm with a great brand and a great product. The company may be able to attract new customers to its product with its strong brand and keep customers by meeting their expectations consistently. But is this enough? Given the significant shifts in the new economy—from goods to services, from transactions to relationships—the answer is no. Great brand equity and value equity may not be enough to hold the customer. What's needed is a way to glue the customers to the firm, enhancing the stickiness of the relationship. Relationship equity represents this glue. Specifically, relationship equity is defined as the tendency of the customer to stick with the brand, above and beyond the customer's objective and subjective assessments of the brand.

The key levers, under the firm's control, that may enhance relationship equity are loyalty programs, special recognition and treatment, affinity programs, community-building programs, and knowledge-building programs. Loyalty programs include actions that reward customers for specific behaviors with tangible benefits. From airlines to liquor stores, from Citigroup to Diet Coke, the loyalty program has become a staple of many firms' marketing strategy. Special recognition and treatment refers to actions that recognize customers for specific behavior with intangible benefits. For example, US Airways' "Chairman Preferred" status customers receive complimentary membership in the US Airways' Club.

Affinity programs seek to create strong emotional connections with customers, linking the customer's relationship with the firm to other important aspects of the customer's life. Consider the wide array of affinity Visa and MasterCard choices offered by First USA to encourage increased use and higher retention. Community-building programs seek to cement the customer-firm relationship by linking the customer to a larger community of like customers. In the United Kingdom, for example, soft drink manufacturer Tango has created a Web site that has built a virtual community with its key segment, the nation's youth.

Finally, knowledge-building programs increase relationship equity by creating structural bonds between the customer and the firm, making the customer less willing to recreate a relationship with an alternative provider. The most often cited example of this is amazon.com, but learning relationships are not limited to cyberspace. Firms such as British Airways have developed programs to track customer food and drink preferences, thereby creating bonds with the customer while simultaneously reducing costs.

Determining the Key Drivers

Think back to the set of questions posed earlier. How should a marketing executive decide where to focus his or her efforts: Building the brand? Improving the product or service? Deepening the relationships with current customers? Determining what is the most important driver of customer equity will often depend on characteristics of the industry and the market, such as market maturity or consumer decision processes. But determining the critical driver for your firm is the first step in building the truly customer-focused marketing organization.

When Value Equity Matters Most

Value equity matters to most customers most of the time, but it will be most important under specific circumstances. First, value equity will be most critical when discernible differences exist between competing products. In commodity markets, where products and competitors are often fungible, value equity is difficult to build. However, when there are differences between competing products, a firm can grow value equity by influencing customer perceptions of value. Consider IBM's ThinkPad brand of notebook computers. Long recognized for innovation and advanced design, IBM has been able to build an advantage in the area of value equity by building faster, thinner, lighter computers with advanced capabilities.

Second, value equity will be central for purchases with complex decision processes. Here customers carefully weigh their decisions and often examine the trade-offs of costs and benefits associated with various alternatives. Therefore, any company that either increases the customer benefits or reduces costs for its customers will be able to increase its value equity. Consider consumers contemplating the conversion to DSL technology for Internet access. This is often a complex, time-consuming decision. DSL companies that can reduce the time and effort involved in this conversion will have the value equity advantage.

Third, value equity will be important for most business-to-business purchases. In addition to being complex decisions, B2B purchases often involve a long-term commitment or partnership between the two parties (and large sums of money). Therefore, customers in these purchase situations often consider their decisions more carefully than individual consumers do.

Fourth, a firm has the opportunity to grow value equity when it offers innovative products and services. When considering the purchase of a "really new" product or service, customers must carefully examine the components of the product because the key attributes often may be difficult to discern. In many cases, consumers make one-to-one comparisons across products, trying to decide whether the new product offers sufficient benefits to risk the purchase. New MP3-type devices that provide consumers with online access to music are examples of such innovative products and services. Consumers will seek out substantial information (e.g., from the Web, friends, and advertisements) to determine the costs and benefits of new products. Firms that can signal quality and low risk can grow value equity in such new markets.

Finally, value equity will be key for firms attempting to revitalize mature products. In the maturity stage of the product life cycle, most customers observe product parity, sales level off, and, to avoid commoditization, firms often focus on the role of the brand. But value equity also may grow customer equity. By introducing new benefits for a current product or service, or by adding new features to the current offering, firms can recycle their products and services and grow value equity in the process. Consider the new Colgate "bendable" toothbrush. It seeks to revitalize the mature toothbrush market with a new answer to an age-old problem. The success of this new innovation increases Colgate's value equity.

Clearly then, the importance of value equity will depend on the industry, the maturity of the firm, and the customer decisionmaking process. To understand the role of value equity within your organization, ask several key customers and key executives to assess your company using the set of questions provided in the Customer Equity Diagnostic on the following page.

When Brand Equity Matters Most

While brand equity is generally a concern, it is critical in certain situations. First, brand equity will be most important for low-involvement purchases with simple decision processes. For many products, including frequently purchased consumer packaged goods, purchase decisions are often routinized and require little customer attention or involvement. In this case, the role of the brand and the customer's emotional connection to the brand will be crucial. In contrast, when product and service purchase decisions require high levels of customer involvement, brand equity may be less critical than value or relationship equity. Coca-Cola, for example, has been extremely successful making purchases a routine aspect of consumer's shopping trips by developing extremely strong connections between the consumer and the brand.

Second, brand equity is essential when the customer's use of the product is highly visible to others. Consider Abercrombie & Fitch, the home of in-style gear for the "Net Generation." For A&F aficionados, the brand becomes an extension of the individual, a "badge" or statement the individual can make to the world about himself or herself. These high-visibility brands have a special opportunity to build brand equity by strengthening the brand image and brand meanings that consumers associate with the brand.

Third, brand equity will be vital when experiences associated with the product can be passed from one individual or generation to another. To the extent that a firm's products or services lend themselves to communal or joint experiences (e.g., a father teaching his son to shave, shared experiences of a special wine), the firm can build brand equity. The Vail ski resort knows the value of this intergenerational brand value well. The resort encourages family experiences by promoting multigenerational visits.

Fourth, the role of the brand will be critical for credence goods, when it is difficult to evaluate quality prior to consumption. For many products and services, it is possible to "try before you buy" or to easily evaluate the quality of specific attributes prior to purchase. However, for others, consumers must use different cues for quality. This aspect of brand equity is especially key for law firms, investment banking firms, and advertising agencies, which are beginning to recognize the value of strong brand identities as a key tool for attracting new clients.

Customer Equity Diagnostic

How much do your customers care about value equity?

❑ Do customers perceive discernible differences between brands? Do they focus on the objective aspects of the brand?

❑ Do you primarily market in a B2B environment?

❑ Is the purchase decision process complex in your industry?

❑ Is innovation a key to continued success in your industry?

❑ Do you revitalize mature products with new features and benefits?

How are you doing?

❑ Are you the industry leader in overall quality? Do you have initiatives in place to continuously improve quality?

❑ Do your customers perceive that the quality they receive is worth the price they paid?

❑ Do you consistently have the lowest prices in your industry?

❑ Do you lead the industry in distribution of your products and services?

❑ Do you make it most convenient for your customers to do business with you?

How important is brand equity?

❑ Are the emotional and experiential aspects of the purchase important? Is consumption of your product highly visible to others?

❑ Are most of your products frequently purchased consumer goods?

❑ Is the purchase decision process relatively simple?

❑ Is it difficult to evaluate the quality of your products or services prior to consumption or use?

❑ Is advertising the primary form of communication to your customers?

How are you doing?

❑ Are you the industry leader in brand awareness?

❑ Do customers pay attention to and remember your advertising and the information you send them?

❑ Are you known as a good corporate citizen? Active in community events?

❑ Do you lead your industry in the development and maintenance of ethical standards?

❑ Do customers feel a strong emotional connection to the brand?

How does relationship equity weigh in?

❑ Are loyalty programs a necessity in your industry?

❑ Do customers feel like "members" in your community?

❑ Do your customers talk about their commitment to your brand?

❑ Is it possible to learn about your customers over time and customize your interactions with them? Do your customers perceive high switching costs?

❑ Are continuing relationships with customers important?

How are you doing?

❑ Do customers perceive that you have the best loyalty program in your industry?

❑ Do you lead the industry in programs to provide special benefits and services for your best customers?

❑ To what extent do your customers know and understand how to do business with you?

❑ Do customers perceive you as the leader in providing a sense of community?

❑ Do you encourage dialogue with your customers?

Therefore, brand equity will be more important in some industries and companies than others. The role of brand equity will depend on the level of customer involvement, the nature of the customer experience, and the ease with which customers can evaluate the quality of the product or service before buying it. Answering the questions in the Customer Equity Diagnostic will help determine how important brand equity is for your organization.

When Relationship Equity Matters Most

In certain situations, relationship equity will be the most important influence on customer equity. First, relationship equity will be critical when the benefits the customer associates with the firm's loyalty program are significantly greater than the actual "cash value" of the benefits received. This "aspirational value" of a loyalty program presents a solid opportunity for firms to strengthen relationship equity by creating a strong incentive for the customer to return to the firm for future purchases. The success of the world's frequent flyer programs lies, to some extent, in the difference between the "true" value of a frequent flyer mile (about three cents) and the aspirational value—the customer's perception of the value of a frequent flyer mile ("I'm that much closer to my free trip to Hawaii!").

Second, relationship equity will be key when the community associated with the product or service is as important as the product or service itself. Certain products and services have the added benefit of building a strong community of enthusiasts. Customers will often continue to purchase from the firm to maintain "membership" in the community. Just ask an active member of a HOG (Harley-Davidson Owners Group) to switch to a Honda Gold Wing; or ask a committed health club member to switch to an alternate health club. Individuals who have become committed to brand communities tend to be fiercely loyal.

Third, relationship equity will be vital when firms have the opportunity to create learning relationships with customers. Often, the relationship created between the firm and the customer, in which the firm comes to appreciate the customer's preferences and buying habits, can become as important to the customer as the provision of the product or service. Database technology has made such "learning" possible for any company or organization willing to invest the time and resources in collecting, tracking, and utilizing the information customers reveal. For example, Dell has created learning relationships with its key business customers through Dell's Premier Pages—customized Web sites that allow customers to manage their firm's purchases of Dell computers. The benefit: It becomes more difficult for customers to receive the same personal attention from an alternative provider without "training" that new provider.

Finally, relationship equity becomes crucial in situations where customer action is required to discontinue the service. For many services (and some product continuity programs), customers must actively decide to stop consuming or receiving the product or service (e.g., book clubs, insurance, Internet service providers, negative-option services). For such products and services, inertia helps solidify the relationship. Firms providing these types of products and services have a unique opportunity to grow relationship equity by strengthening the bond with the customer.

As with value and brand equity, the importance of relationship equity will vary across industries. The extent to which relationship equity will drive your business will depend on the importance of loyalty programs to your customers, the role of the customer community, the ability of your organization to establish learning relationships with your customers, and your customer's perceived switching costs. Answer the questions in the Customer Equity Diagnostic framework to see how important relationship equity is to your customers.

A New Strategic Approach

We have now seen how it is possible to gain insight into the key drivers of customer equity for an individual industry or for an individual firm within an industry. Once a firm understands the critical drivers of customer equity for its industry and for its key customers, the firm can respond to its customers and the marketplace with strategies that maximize its performance on elements that matter.

Taken down to its most fundamental level, customers choose to do business with a firm because (a) it offers better value, (b) it has a stronger brand, or (c) switching away from it is too costly. Customer equity provides the diagnostic tools to enable the marketing executive to understand which of these three motivators is most critical to the firm's customers and will be most effective in getting the customer to stay with the firm, and to buy more. Based on this understanding, the firm can identify key opportunities for growth and illuminate unforeseen vulnerabilities. In short, customer equity offers a powerful new approach to marketing strategy, replacing product-based strategy with a competitive strategy approach based on growing the long-term value of the firm.

Additional Reading

Aaker, David A. (1995), *Managing Brand Equity*. NY: The Free Press.

Dowling, Grahame R. and Mark Uncles (1997), "Do Customer Loyalty Programs Really Work?" *Sloan Management Review*, 38 (Summer), 71–82.

Keller, Kevin L. (1998), *Strategic Brand Management: Building, Measuring and Managing Brand Equity*. NJ: Prentice-Hall.

Newell, Frederick (2000), *Loyalty.com: Customer Relationship Management in the New Era of Internet Marketing*. NY: McGraw-Hill.

Rust, Roland T., Katherine N. Lemon, and Valarie A. Zeithaml (2000), *Driving Customer Equity: How Customer Lifetime Value Is Reshaping Corporate Strategy*. NY: The Free Press.

Zeithaml, Valarie A. (1988), "Consumer Perceptions of Price, Quality and Value: A Means-End Model and Synthesis of Evidence," *Journal of Marketing*, 52 (July), 2-22.

About the Authors

Katherine N. Lemon is an assistant professor at Wallace E. Carroll School of Business, Boston College. She may be reached at katherine.lemon@bc.edu.

Roland T. Rust holds the David Bruce Smith Chair in Marketing at the Robert H. Smith School of Business at the University of Maryland, where he is director of the Center for E-Service. He may be reached at rrust@rhsmith.umd.edu.

Valarie A. Zeithaml is professor and area chair at the Kenan-Flagler Business School of the University of North Carolina, Chapel Hill. She may be reached at valariez@unc.edu.

Services communications: from mindless tangibilization to meaningful messages

Banwari Mittal

Professor of Marketing, Northern Kentucky University, Highland Heights, Kentucky, USA

Abstract *Service businesses face a unique challenge: how to effectively communicate the necessarily intangible benefits of their service offering. Their attempts to tangibilize the service are often ill-designed, making service benefits more rather than less obscure. This article presents a scheme that identifies the communication task at various states of consumer decision making and then matches appropriate communication strategies. Rather than embracing misguided tangibilization, the recommended strategies handle the intangibility challenge without necessarily using any tangible props.*

Keywords *Services marketing, Intangible assets, Marketing communications, Advertising, Consumer behaviour*

Introduction

An advertisement from Aprisma, an IT infrastructure technology firm, shows a large photo shot of a ten-year old boy in baseball gear sitting on the curbside of a now deserted baseball field, waiting for his ride. The short copy at the bottom reads: "when everyone is counting on you, you need an IT infrastructure with intelligent technology that helps you to monitor and manage the things that really matter... And that is exactly what Aprisma develops and delivers—solutions as reliable as you." Imprinted on the picture shot is a bold headline: "What's your technology missing?" (*Business Week,* March 5, 2001, p. 25). A reader can quickly interpret the photo: the boy's parent is late, and he or she also did not attend the game—missing something that ought to be important to every parent. It humanizes the oth-

erwise drab and complex technology. And it tangibilizes the intangible service. That much is good. But as readers, we still do not know what our IT infrastructure actually does miss, and how exactly Aprisma manages it.

This is a key problem with services advertising. Because services are intangible, it is a challenging task to effectively communicate about them (Berry, 1980; Lovelock, 1996; Zeithaml and Bitner, 1996). A constant advice from services scholars has been to tangibilize the service (e.g. Berry and Parasuraman, 1991; Day, 1992). However, while a thoughtful approach to tangibilizing the service works effectively (Berry and Clark, 1986; Stafford, 1996), many approaches seen in practice (such as the one adopted in the Aprisma ad) often fail to capture and communicate the core service benefit, or even make it worse. The purpose of this paper is to examine the service communication task and to identify communication strategies to circumvent or manage intangibility throughout the consumer decision-making process.

The intangibility problem

Webster's New World Dictionary (1994) defines intangibility as "that which cannot be touched or grasped, is incorporeal, is impalpable." The essential meaning and nature of intangibility is incorporeal existence—intangible entities do not have physical bodies and do not exist in physical space; they cannot therefore, be sensed by physical senses. Impalpability concerns understanding something in the mind (as different from physical sensing), and is therefore not an inherent quality of intangibility, the *Dictionary* definition, notwithstanding. Often, though, service advertisers communicate intangibles in such a fashion as to make them mentally impalpable; and also more abstract rather than concrete (e.g., an insurance company promising "peace of mind"), more general rather than specific (e.g. service is "speedy" rather than "in less than 20 minutes"), and non-searchable (e.g., "highly-skilled surgeons"). These "pitfall" properties are not inevitable for intangibles (Mittal, 1999) but absent a tangible product or tangible benefit to show, conveying the intangible service benefits and at the same time avoiding these problem properties requires special communication savvy, the subject of this paper.

Service communication strategies

What is the repertoire of message content and creative approaches available to accomplish the service communication task? The academic services literature has identified the following creative approaches: physical representation, performance documentation, performance episode, service consumption documentation, and service consumption episode (see George and Berry, 1981; Legg and Baker, 1987; Mittal, 1999). Physical representation entails showing physical components of the service delivery system to represent a service brand (e.g. UPS vans delivering packages). Performance documentation entails presenting objectively documented data on past performance (e.g. the punctuality record of an airline). In the performance episode strategy, the service firm depicts a typical service delivery incidence (e.g. a Fedex employee going out of his or her way to deliver a package to a hapless customer). Service consumption documentation requires featuring testimonials from customers about some aspect of service (e.g. show a customer letter praising the service). Finally, service consumption episode strategy depicts a typical customer experiencing the service (e.g. show a consumer witnessing the fast download speed of some Web content and being thrilled with it).

Note that the last four strategies do not necessarily entail featuring any tangible components of the service delivery system. They deploy, instead, either documentation (objectively documented benefits) or episodes (word and picture narratives of service events). Each can be presented either from the service company's perspective (namely, performance documentation

and performance episode) or from the customer's standpoint, featuring the benefit claim or service delivery as the customer actually experiences it (consumption documentation and consumption episode). See Mittal (1999) for a fuller exposition. To these five strategies construed specifically for services, we add two basic strategies common to both products and services:

1. Direct benefit statement—the communication makes a direct statement of the benefit, e.g. "gives fresh breath" or "4 percent interest rate"; and
2. use of logos and icons, as symbols of the service, e.g. McDonalds' golden arch.

These two latter approaches can be used within or without the preceding, services-specific, approaches. A key question is how to deploy this repertoire of approaches to address various services communication tasks. As we shall see, some of the above strategies are more appropriate for some communication tasks and some less appropriate; moreover, the problem of intangibility is handled differently by different strategies.

Consumer decision stages and communication tasks

A consumer moves through a sequence of stages comprising:

- problem-recognition;
- evoked and consideration set formation;
- pre-purchase evaluation;
- acquisition and use; and
- post-use evaluation (Fisk, 1981).

The communication task is different at every stage, and accounting for these differences becomes particularly challenging both because a service product is multi-faceted (Mittal and Baker, 1998), and because many of these facets and outcomes are intangible. Below we match the aforementioned communication strategies to different service communication tasks at various consumer decision stages.

Problem recognition. At the problem recognition stage, the consumer senses a problem in his/her life and looks for a solution. Advertising at this stage has to make a connection in the consumer mind between the consumer problem and the service category *per se* as its solution. For new services, problem recognition may simply entail making the consumer aware of what the service does, and how this can be of use to the consumer, i.e. by a direct benefit statement. Often the new service benefit, even if it is intangible, is easily understood by consumers (e.g. the benefits of home delivery of groceries or a high speed DSL Internet connection). The task of problem recognition is, however, more demanding when the direct benefit of the new service is not immediately valued by target customers. These customers need a demonstration of the second-order benefit of the service. In the DSL example, where high speed by itself does not draw a customer, the second-order benefit of, say, faster online trade execution might be appealing; and this can be conveyed, for example, simply by a side-by-side comparison of two customers trading online with a slow versus a fast connection, and the DSL customer delighted with the faster execution and therefore a more favorable trade price (a consumption episode strategy). There is no need to mindlessly tangibilize the benefit, for example, by showing, side-by-side, a cargo train and a European bullet train, and labeling the two respectively as "your present connection" and "high speed Internet connection"—such ill-advised "concretization", makes the intangible service benefit more, not less, obscure.

Evoked and consideration set placement. Once the problem is recognized, the next task is to place the brand into the consumer's evoked and consideration sets. In the case of the DSL service, for instance, someone viewing an ad could buy into the basic idea but then patronize a competing DSL service provider. Advertising helps create brand awareness and brand evocation, but this is made difficult if the brand does not have a clear identity. Brand identity is created by associating a brand's name with some sensory image, i.e. a symbol, logo, graphics, or other visual form. For physical products, the form of the product itself, along with the associated visual forms, easily and usually does the job. For services, symbols alone have to carry the entire burden. These symbols must at the minimum be unique in visual form, but many services fail even on this minimum requirement (e.g. Embassy Suites' stylized "E" is unique but Radisson's font style is not).

Uniqueness will however enable, at best, a brand identity but not placement into consideration set. The latter would require service differentiation which in turn requires that symbols be connotative as well (i.e. they capture the core meaning of the service). Merrill Lynch's bull or Traveler's umbrella are often cited as exemplary, and indeed they are both tangible and connotative. So is the equally effective (but still intangible) unique and connotative Delta symbol for its namesake airline, or the dab of the red paint ring for Lucent Technologies signifying energy and innovation.

Physical representation also serves brand identity but only if the service system has unique visual form (e.g. brown vans of UPS as opposed to indistinct service vans of most local utility companies). In addition, if the physical system components have connotative overtones, the brand evocation is also served well (e.g. the networked globe icon on UPS vehicles). Absent any uniqueness (let alone any connotativeness), physical representation (while delivering tangibilization) does nothing for brand identity and evocation (e.g. "hey, that ad which showed black jack tables, which casino was that ad for?").

An even more potent tool for consideration set placement is a core value proposition statement that differentiates the service brand. For services, often the core value is intangible; its communication however, need not suffer from the intangibility's "pitfall" properties of generality or abstractness. "Dreams made real"—the tagline in Agilent Technologies ads, when viewed without the accompanying stories, suffers from generality; in contrast, "we are custodians of your financial dreams" (a Charles Schwab value proposition) is intangible but still free from generality or abstractness. The core value proposition

(which is a direct benefit strategy) should be phrased not broadly—which would make it general and abstract—but in a concrete and meaningful way.

Pre-purchase evaluation. Basically, the issue at this stage is: what criteria do target customers use in pre-purchase evaluation? A service's end product is typically intangible, but many components of its service delivery system are tangible. The choice of a tangible or an intangible feature in advertising should depend on which attributes are "determinant"—those which the customer employs in evaluating an option, and on which the brand is not at parity. Communicating an intangible feature is more challenging, but that is no excuse for diverting advertising to a tangible feature, if the determinant attribute in a particular case is an intangible one (e.g. better cabin service rather than more comfortable seats for an airline).

Now, an attribute (whether tangible or intangible) can be communicated by linking it to relevant tangible elements of the service delivery system; or alternatively, by linking it to even more intangible outcomes. To illustrate, for wireless services, freedom from dropped calls (a pervasive annoyance to customers, and consequently a key determinant attribute) can be communicated as a tangible simply by citing the objective and documented call drop rates (performance documentation strategy) or by consumers' testimonials of few if any calls dropped (consumption documentation strategy). Alternatively, the "dropped calls" feature can also be communicated by linking it to a more intangible benefit, such as in "you will never annoy a sales prospect due to a dropped call." This can be communicated by showing, for example, a salesperson able to get to speak, after months of networking, to a high level executive in the customer firm, and then losing him in the middle of the conversation, never again to get him back (i.e. consumption episode strategy). Likewise, although not applicable to the "dropped calls" case, an intangible execution of other determinant attributes can also be communicated by a performance episode where a service firm is shown meticulously delivering that attribute, e.g. a Fedex employee making a difficult delivery to a hapless customer.

At least for some target audiences, such intangible executions may be more appealing than corresponding tangible execution. In and of itself, the latter strategy (of making an intangible even more so) is not less effective. What makes an ad ineffective is failing to diligently avoid the pitfall properties of intangibility. Make vague claims of reliability of wireless connection (e.g. "Our name stands for reliability and service"), and the intangible appeal becomes inflicted with generality and also non-searchability. But document call-drop rate history (performance documentation strategy), or present customer testimonials of uninterrupted calls (consumption documentation strategy) and the intangible attribute becomes specific and "searchable." Resort to a mere direct statement about "never lose out on that important sales pitch again" and the bland intangible has none of the impact of a tangible benefit, and no persuasive power. Capture it, instead, in a vivid narrative of the emotional experience of uninterrupted and successfully concluded conversation with a significant other (a consumption ep-

Table I. Services communication tasks and recommended strategies

Consumer decision stage	Communication task	Communication strategy	Example
Problem recognition	Establish service as solution	Direct benefit statement	DSL: high-speed connection
		Second-order benefit depiction via consumption episode	DSL: Better trade price due to high-speed order transmission
Evoked and consideration set placement	Service brand identity	Unique and connotative brand icons	Delta symbol for Delta Airlines
	Service evocation/differentiation	Physical representation if unique	UPS brown vans
		Value proposition: concrete and meaningful phrasing	Charles Schwab: "Custodian of your financial dreams"
Pre-purchase evaluation	Determinant service attributes (technical rather than functional; reliability and assurance rather than empathy and responsiveness)	Performance documentation	Wireless: "dropped calls" record
		Consumption documentation	Wireless: customer testimonials
		Consumption episode featuring "determinant" attributes	A wireless customer successfully concluding calls
		Performance episode	Fedex: difficult package delivery instance
Acquisition and consumption	Performance appreciation	Service process visibility	Car-repair: visible service bays
		Customer education via: POP literature; Personal selling	Car repair: "what and how" charts displayed
			Car mechanics debriefing the customer
Post-purchase evaluation	"Total experience"	Consumption documentation	Customers raving about the quality of the service they received from a firm
		Consumption episode	A CIO enjoying a weekend worry-free since he/she installed the advertised brand of process monitoring IT infrastructure

pre-purchase Benefit - goal they seek [handwritten]

isode strategy), and the intangible becomes more powerful than even a tangible.

Service acquisition and consumption. It is during the service consumption stage that the customer assesses service performance. Perceived performance depends on actual performance, but the latter is not always obvious to the service recipient. Therefore, perception shaping is an important communication task at this stage. One strategy, suggested in prior literature, is to bring service work from below to above "the line visibility" (Legg and Baker, 1987). For example, when car repair customers can watch the arduous work of balancing and mounting a tire, they appreciate why they have to pay five (or eight) extra dollars. When bringing such transparency to service work by physical relocation is not feasible, the task is then to educate the customer by communications. Such communications can take the form of point-of-purchase (POP) information displays (e.g. detailed process charts placed in customer waiting rooms of care repair services), or personal, educational "selling," (e.g. the car mechanic debriefing the customer, reviewing the details of the service performed). Giving the service process transparency via physical location restructuring, POP materials, or personal debriefing—these exemplify use of channels other than mass media advertising. In other words, integrated marketing communications (IMC), rather than just advertising, is required for performance appreciation.

Post-purchase evaluation. Post-purchase evaluation differs from pre-purchase evaluation in one key respect. In the services marketing literature, researchers have identified several dimensions of perceived service quality, such as reliability, assurance, empathy, responsiveness, etc. (e.g. Parasuraman *et al.,* 1988). This literature does not imply (nor should we assume) that all of these will be the dimensions of service quality evaluations be-

fore the purchase. They might well be, but they all need not be. Logically, pre-purchase evaluation criteria come predominantly from one's purchase goals, i.e. the benefits the consumer seeks from a purchase. From a hair salon, for example, he/she wants a good hairstyle. Typically, he or she does not go to a hair salon to socialize with a smiling and courteous hair stylist, or even to receive a "memorable experience." But once he/she has chosen a salon, and after he/she has been there, the quality of the haircut plus the courtesy of the stylist and everything else the customer experienced while at the salon become an input in service quality evaluation. That is, the post-purchase evaluation takes into account the totality of the service experience. In contrast, at the pre-purchase evaluation stage, the consumer focuses on a limited set of "determinant" service attributes.

Accordingly, pre-purchase communications should not unnecessarily burden consumers with claims of all dimensions of service quality or depictions of a total experience, but focus merely on "determinant" service attributes. Advertising should depict a total experience (use of consumption episode strategy) only if such an experience itself is the principal purchase goal (e.g. as in a leisure cruise). In other situations, when purchase goals are more limited and not experiential, pre-purchase advertising should feature only the purchase goals, which would typically entail only technical (rather than functional) quality, and only reliability and assurance rather than empathy (or even responsiveness). In sharp contrast, post-purchase communication, directed at retention of current customers (via such channels as direct mail, Web site visits by registered customers, and more directed advertising) should feature functional qualities and "total experience." Two communication strategies are especially suited for this task:

1. consumption documentation—since satisfied customers talk about their experiences, customers' live testimonials (a cus-

tomer actually narrating on-camera) about their service experience can make an effective communication; and
2. consumption episode—where current and recent customers are shown experiencing the delight of the service.

These strategies were of course included also at the pre-purchase evaluation stage; the difference is that at the post-purchase evaluation stage, these approaches have to feature "total consumption experiences," centered around the functional and empathy and responsiveness dimensions of service quality.

Table 1 summarizes these communication tasks and corresponding recommended communication strategies.

Summary and conclusion

If, by tangibilization, one means using a physical/material prop, then such tangibilization can hinder rather than aid services communication. Except physical representation (which helps brand identity and evocation but only if unique and connotative), all other aforementioned communication strategies rely largely on intangible, i.e. non-physical executions. Intangible service benefits can be effectively communicated as intangibles (i.e. without physical props), by strategies that avoid the probable but not inherent pitfall properties of intangibility, as do the aforementioned strategies. They do it by "documentation"—which delivers specificity and searchability, or by narrative "episodes"—which overcome abstractness and mental impalpability, as the consumer understands them well intuitively by drawing on his/her repertoire of similar life-experiences.

The Aprisma ad is indeed a "consumption episode" execution; unfortunately, that consumption is drawn from a domain entirely unrelated to the service benefit. Be depicting a ten year-old child waiting for a ride from a parent who was unable to keep his/her priorities in "personal life" straight, the ad draws attention away from the task priorities in "business processes" that the prospective customers' IT infrastructure might be missing. Consequently, the ad makes the intangible Aprisma service more, not less, obscure and mentally impalpable. The consumption episode needed to be drawn from the relevant slice-of-life of its customers (i.e. chief information or technology officers), experiencing the breakdown-free technology infrastructure. Of course, a "consumption episode" strategy itself may not be called for, since the communication task for this new company at this stage is perhaps "problem recognition" and "evoked and consideration set placement," not post-purchase positive evaluation. For these communication goals, "physical representation" and "performance documentation" or even "performance episode" strategies might be more suitable. Aprisma and other services advertisers need to diligently delineate the exact communication task facing them, and then adopt a matching communication strategy as described in this paper. These strategies may or may not entail physical representation, and they may or may not use a physical prop, but they commu-

nicate the intangible benefits of service just as well by steering clear of the pitfall properties of intangibles. Making the service benefit understood should be the goal of service communications managers, not mindless tangibilization. Mindless tangibilization draws attention away from the core benefits of the service. Sensible tangibilization seeks to make intangibles understood by staying close to the domain of service benefits itself, and by portraying the role of the service in that domain compellingly, by "documentation" and "episode" strategies as argued in this paper.

References

Berry, L. L. (1980), "Services marketing is different," *Business,* Vol. 30, May–June, pp. 24–9.

Berry, L. L. and Clark, T. (1986), "Four ways to make services more tangible," *Business,* Vol. 36, October–December, pp. 53–4.

Berry, L. L. and Parasuraman, A. (1991), *Marketing Services: Competing Through Quality,* Free Press, New York, NY.

Day, E. (1992), "Conveying service quality through advertising", *Journal of Services Marketing,* Vol. 6, Fall, pp. 53–61.

Fisk, R. P. (1981), "Toward a consumption/evaluation process model for services", in Donnelly, J. H. and George, W. R. (Eds), *Marketing of Services,* American Marketing Association, Chicago, IL, pp. 191–5.

George, W. R. and Berry, L. L. (1981), "Guidelines for the advertising of services", *Business Horizons,* Vol. 24, July–August, pp. 52–6.

Legg, D. and Baker, J. (1987), "Advertising strategies for service firms", in Suprenant, C. (Ed.), *Add Value to Your Service,* American Marketing Association, Chicago, IL, pp. 163–8.

Lovelock, C. (1996), *Services Marketing,* 3rd ed., Prentice-Hall, Upper Saddle River, NJ.

Mittal, B. (1999), "The advertising of services: meeting the challenge of intangibility", *Journal of Service Research,* Vol. 2 No. 1, pp. 98–116.

Mittal, B. and Baker, J. (1998), "The services marketing system and consumer psychology", *Psychology and Marketing,* Vol. 15 No. 8, pp. 727–34.

Parasuraman, A., Zeithaml, V. A. and Berry, L. L. (1988), "SERVQUAL: a multiple-item scale for measuring consumer perceptions of service quality", *Journal of Retailing,* Vol. 64, Spring, pp. 12–40.

Stafford, M. R. (1996), "Tangibility in services advertising: an investigation of verbal versus visual cues", *Journal of Advertising,* Vol. 25 No. 3, pp. 13–26.

Zeithaml, A. and Bitner, M. J. (1996), *Services Marketing,* McGraw-Hill, New York, NY.

I benefited greatly from comments from Marla R. Stafford, the guest editor, on an earlier version of the paper.

Ban Mittal is a Professor of Marketing at Northern Kentucky University, visiting professor at University of New South Wales, Australia, and author of *Valuespace: Winning the Battle for Market Leadership* (McGraw Hill, 2001). The present paper is part of his long-standing interest in bringing consumer understanding to improving marketing communications. He can be reached via his web site www.myvaluespace.com.

WHY SERVICE STINKS

Companies know just how good a customer you are—and unless you're a high roller, they would rather lose you than take the time to fix your problem

By Diane Brady

When Tom Unger of New Haven started banking at First Union Corp. several years ago, he knew he wasn't top of the heap. But Unger didn't realize just how dispensable he was until mysterious service charges started showing up on his account. He called the bank's toll-free number, only to reach a bored service representative who brushed him off. Then he wrote two letters, neither of which received a response. A First Union spokeswoman, Mary Eshet, says the bank doesn't discuss individual accounts but notes that customer service has been steadily improving. Not for Unger. He left. "They wouldn't even give me the courtesy of listening to my complaint," he says.

And Unger ought to know bad service when he sees it. He works as a customer-service representative at an electric utility where the top 350 business clients are served by six people. The next tier of 700 are handled by six more, and 30,000 others get Unger and one other rep to serve their needs. Meanwhile, the 300,000 residential customers at the lowest end are left with an 800 number. As Unger explains: "We don't ignore anyone, but our biggest customers certainly get more attention than the rest."

As time goes on, that service gap is only growing wider. Studies by groups ranging from the Council of Better Business Bureaus Inc. to the University of Michigan vividly detail what consumers already know: Good service is increasingly rare (charts). From passengers languishing in airport queues to bank clients caught in voice-mail hell, most consumers feel they're getting squeezed by Corporate America's push for profits and productivity. The result is more efficiencies for companies— and more frustration for their less valuable customers. "Time

saved for them is not time saved for us," says Claes Fornell, a University of Michigan professor who created the school's consumer satisfaction index, which shows broad declines across an array of industries. Fornell points to slight improvements in areas like autos and computers.

FLYING

Canceled flight? No problem. With top status, you're whisked past the queue, handed a ticket for the next flight, and driven to the first-class lounge. The rest can cross their fingers and come back tomorrow

Andrew Chan's experience with Ikea is typical. The Manhattan artist recently hauled a table home from an Ikea store in New Jersey only to discover that all the screws and brackets were missing. When he called to complain, the giant furniture retailer refused to send out the missing items and insisted he come back to pick them up himself, even though he doesn't own a car. Maybe he just reached the wrong guy, says Tom Cox, customer-service manager for Ikea North America, noting that the usual procedure is to mail small items out within a couple of days.

NO ELEPHANT? Life isn't so tough for everyone, though. Roy Sharda, a Chicago Internet executive and road warrior is a "platinum" customer of Starwood Hotels & Resorts World-

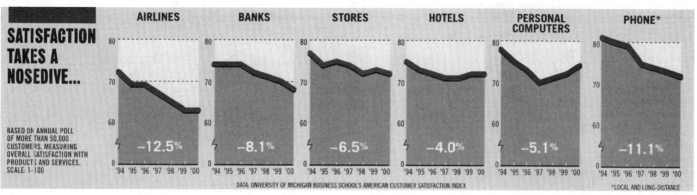

SATISFACTION TAKES A NOSEDIVE...

BASED ON ANNUAL POLL OF MORE THAN 50,000 CUSTOMERS, MEASURING OVERALL SATISFACTION WITH PRODUCTS AND SERVICES. SCALE: 1-100

AIRLINES −12.5%
BANKS −8.1%
STORES −6.5%
HOTELS −4.0%
PERSONAL COMPUTERS −5.1%
PHONE* −11.1%

DATA: UNIVERSITY OF MICHIGAN BUSINESS SCHOOL'S AMERICAN CUSTOMER SATISFACTION INDEX

*LOCAL AND LONG-DISTANCE

CHARTS BY RAY VELLA/BW

wide. When he wanted to propose to his girlfriend, Starwood's Sheraton Agra in India arranged entry to the Taj Mahal after hours so he could pop the question in private. Starwood also threw in a horse-drawn carriage, flowers, a personalized meal, upgrades to the presidential suite, and a cheering reception line led by the general manager. It's no wonder Sharda feels he was "treated like true royalty."

Welcome to the new consumer apartheid. Those long lines and frustrating telephone trees aren't always the result of companies simply not caring about pleasing the customer anymore. Increasingly, companies have made a deliberate decision to give some people skimpy service because that's all their business is worth. Call it the dark side of the technology boom, where marketers can amass a mountain of data that gives them an almost Orwellian view of each buyer. Consumers have become commodities to pamper, squeeze, or toss away, according to Leonard L. Berry, marketing professor at Texas A&M University. He sees "a decline in the level of respect given to customers and their experiences."

More important, technology is creating a radical new business model that alters the whole dynamic of customer service. For the first time, companies can truly measure exactly what such service costs on an individual level and assess the return on each dollar. They can know exactly how much business someone generates, what he is likely to buy, and how much it costs to answer the phone. That allows them to deliver a level of service based on each person's potential to produce a profit—and not a single phone call more.

BILLING
Big spenders can expect special discounts, promotional offers, and other goodies when they open their bills.
The rest might get higher fees, stripped-down service, and a machine to answer their questions

The result could be a whole new stratification of consumer society. The top tier may enjoy an unprecedented level of personal attention. But those who fall below a certain level of profitability for too long may find themselves bounced from the customer rolls altogether or facing fees that all but usher them out the door. A few years ago, GE Capital decided to charge $25 a year to GE Rewards MasterCard holders who didn't rack up at least that much in annual interest charges. The message was clear: Those who pay their bills in full each month don't boost the bottom line. GE has since sold its credit-card business to First USA. Others are charging extra for things like deliveries and repairs or reducing service staff in stores and call centers.

Instead of providing premium service across the board, companies may offer to move people to the front of the line for a fee. "There has been a fundamental shift in how companies assess customer value and apply their resources," says Cincinnati marketing consultant Richard G. Barlow. He argues that managers increasingly treat top clients with kid gloves and cast the masses "into a labyrinth of low-cost customer service where, if they complain, you just live with it."

Companies have always known that some people don't pay their way. Ravi Dhar, an associate professor at Yale University, cites the old rule that 80% of profits come from 20% of customers. "The rest nag you, call you, and don't add much revenue," he says. But technology changed everything. To start, it has become much easier to track and measure individual transactions across businesses. Second, the Web has also opened up options. People can now serve themselves at their convenience at a negligible cost, but they have to accept little or no human contact in return. Such huge savings in service costs have proven irresistible to marketers, who are doing everything possible to push their customers—especially low-margin ones—toward self-service.

FRONT-LOADING ELITE. That's a far cry from the days when the customer was king. In the data-rich new millennium, sales staff no longer let you return goods without question while rushing to shake your hand. And they don't particularly want to hear from you again unless you're worth the effort. How they define that top tier can vary a lot by industry. Airlines and hotels love those who buy premier offerings again and again. Financial institutions, on the other hand, salivate over day traders and the plastic-addicted who pay heavy interest charges because they cover only the minimum on their monthly credit-card bills.

Almost everyone is doing it. Charles Schwab Corp.'s top-rated Signature clients—who start with at least $100,000 in assets or trade 12 times a year—never wait longer than 15 seconds

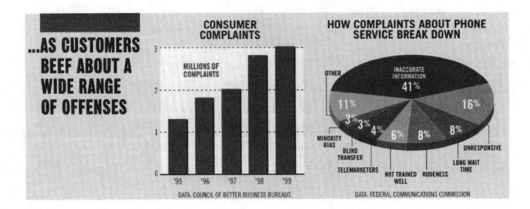

...AS CUSTOMERS BEEF ABOUT A WIDE RANGE OF OFFENSES

CONSUMER COMPLAINTS

MILLIONS OF COMPLAINTS

'95 '96 '97 '98 '99

DATA: COUNCIL OF BETTER BUSINESS BUREAUS

HOW COMPLAINTS ABOUT PHONE SERVICE BREAK DOWN

OTHER 11%
INACCURATE INFORMATION 41%
16%
3% 3% 4% 6% 8% 8%
MINORITY BIAS
BLIND TRANSFER
TELEMARKETERS
NOT TRAINED WELL
RUDENESS
LONG WAIT TIME
UNRESPONSIVE

DATA: FEDERAL COMMUNICATIONS COMMISSION

to get a call answered, while other customers can wait 10 minutes or more. At Sears, Roebuck & Co., big spenders on the company's credit card get to choose a preferred two-hour time slot for repair calls while regular patrons are given a four-hour slot. Maytag Corp. provides premium service to people who buy pricey products such as its front-loading Neptune washing machines, which sell for about $1,000, twice the cost of a top-loading washer. This group gets a dedicated staff of "product experts," an exclusive toll-free number, and speedy service on repairs. When people are paying this much, "they not only want more service; they deserve it," says Dale Reeder, Maytag's general manager of customer service.

BANKING
There's nothing like a big bank account to get those complaints answered and service charges waived every time. Get pegged as a money-loser, and your negotiating clout vanishes

Of course, while some companies gloat about the growing attention to their top tier, most hate to admit that the bottom rungs are getting less. GE Capital would not talk. Sprint Corp. and WorldCom Inc. declined repeated requests to speak about service divisions. Off the record, one company official explains that customers don't like to know they're being treated differently.

Obviously, taking service away from the low spenders doesn't generate much positive press for companies. Look at AT&T, which recently agreed to remove its minimum usage charges on the 28 million residential customers in its lowest-level basic plan, many of whom don't make enough calls to turn a profit. "To a lot of people, it's not important that a company make money," says AT&T Senior Vice-President Howard E. McNally, who argues that AT&T is still treated by regulators and the public as a carrier of last resort. Now, it's trying to push up profits by giving top callers everything from better rates to free premium cable channels.

SERIAL CALLERS. Is this service divide fair? That depends on your perspective. In an era when labor costs are rising while prices have come under pressure, U.S. companies insist they simply can't afford to spend big bucks giving every customer the hands-on service of yesteryear. Adrian J. Slywotzky, a partner with Mercer Management Consulting Inc., estimates that gross margins in many industries have shrunk an average of 5 to 10 percentage points over the past decade because of competition. "Customers used to be more profitable 10 years ago, and they're becoming more different than similar" in how they want to be served, he says.

The new ability to segment customers into ever finer categories doesn't have to be bad news for consumers. In many cases, the trade-off in service means lower prices. Susanne D. Lyons, chief marketing officer at Charles Schwab, points out that the commission charged on Schwab stock trades has dropped by two-thirds over the past five years. Costs to Schwab, meanwhile, vary from a few cents for Web deals to several dollars per live interaction. And companies note that they're delivering a much wider range of products and services than ever before—as well as more ways to handle transactions. Thanks to the Internet, for example, consumers have far better tools to conveniently serve themselves.

Look at a company like Fidelity Investments, which not only has a mind-boggling menu of fund options but now lets people do research and manipulate their accounts without an intermediary. Ten years ago, the company got 97,000 calls a day, of which half were automated. It now gets about 550,000 Web site visits a day and more than 700,000 daily calls, about three-quarters of which go to automated systems that cost the company less than a buck each, including development and research costs. The rest are handled by human beings, which costs about $13 per call. No wonder Fidelity last year contacted 25,000 high-cost "serial" callers and told them they must use the Web or automated calls for simple account and price information. Each name was flagged and routed to a special representative who would direct callers back to automated services—and tell them how to use it. "If all our customers chose to go through live reps, it would be cost-prohibitive," says a Fidelity spokeswoman.

ENTITLED? Segmenting is one way to manage those costs efficiently. Bass Hotels & Resorts, owners of such brands as Holiday Inn and Inter-Continental Hotels, know so much about individual response rates to its promotions that it no longer bothers sending deals to those who did not bite in the past. The result: 50% slashed off mailing costs but a 20% jump in response rates. "As information becomes more sophisticated, the whole area of customer service is becoming much more complex," says Chief Marketing Officer Ravi Saligram.

'WE'RE SORRY, ALL OF OUR AGENTS ARE BUSY WITH MORE VALUABLE CUSTOMERS'

	CODING	ROUTING	TARGETING	SHARING
Companies have become sophisticated about figuring out if you're worth pampering—or whether to just let the phone keep ringing. Here are some of their techniques:	Some companies grade customers based on how profitable their business is. They give each account a code with instructions to service staff on how to handle each category.	Based on the customer's code, call centers route customers to different queues. Big spenders are whisked to high-level problem solvers. Others may never speak to a live person at all.	Choice customers have fees waived and get other hidden discounts based on the value of their business. Less valuable customers may never even know the promotions exist.	Companies sell data about your transaction history to outsiders. You can be slotted before you even walk in the door, since your buying potential has already been measured.

Consumers themselves have cast a vote against high-quality service by increasingly choosing price, choice, and convenience over all else. Not that convenience always takes the sting out of rotten service—witness priceline.com Inc., the ultimate self-service site that lets customers name their own price for plane tickets, hotels, and other goods. Many consumers didn't fully understand the trade-offs, such as being forced to stop over on flights, take whatever brand was handed to them, and forgo the right to any refund. And when things went wrong, critics say, no one was around to help. The results: a slew of complaints that has prompted at least one state investigation. Priceline.com responds that its revamping the Web site and intensifying efforts to improve customer service. While many consumers refuse to pay more for service, they're clearly dismayed when service is taken away. "People have higher expectations now than two or three years ago because we have all this information at our fingertips," says Jupiter Communications Inc. analyst David Daniels.

Indeed, marketers point to what they call a growing culture of entitlement, where consumers are much more demanding about getting what they want. One reason is the explosion of choices, with everything from hundreds of cable channels to new players emerging from deregulated industries like airlines and telecom companies. Meanwhile, years of rewards programs such as frequent-flier miles have contributed to the new mindset. Those who know their worth expect special privileges that reflect it. Says Bonnie S. Reitz, senior vice-president for marketing, sales, and distribution at Continental Airlines Inc.: "We've got a hugely educated, informed, and more experienced consumer out there now."

For top-dollar clients, all this technology allows corporations to feign an almost small-town intimacy. Marketers can know your name, your spending habits, and even details of your personal life. Centura Banks Inc. of Raleigh, N.C., now rates its 2 million customers on a profitability scale from 1 to 5. The real moneymakers get calls from service reps several times a year for what Controller Terry Earley calls "a friendly chat" and even an annual call from the CEO to wish them happy holidays.

No wonder attrition in this group is down by 50% since 1996, while the percentage of unprofitable customers has slipped to 21% from 27%.

LODGING

Another day, another upgrade for frequent guests. Sip champagne before the chef prepares your meal. First-time guest? So sorry. Your room is up three flights and to the left

Even for the lower tier, companies insist that this intense focus on data is leading to service that's better than ever. To start with, it's more customized. And while executives admit to pushing self-help instead of staff, they contend that such service is often preferable. After all, many banking customers prefer using automated teller machines to standing in line at their local branch. American Airlines Inc., the pioneer of customer segmentation with its two-decade-old loyalty program, says it's not ignoring those in the cheap seats, pointing to the airline's recent move to add more legroom in economy class. Says Elizabeth S. Crandall, managing director of personalized marketing: "We're just putting more of our energies into rewarding our best customers."

MARKED MAN. This segmentation of sales, marketing, and service, based on a wealth of personal information, raises some troubling questions about privacy. It threatens to become an intensely personal form of "redlining"—the controversial practice of identifying and avoiding unprofitable neighborhoods or types of people. Unlike traditional loyalty programs, the new tiers are not only highly individualized but they are often invisible. You don't know when you're being directed to a different telephone queue or sales promotion. You don't hear about the benefits you're missing. You don't realize your power to negotiate with everyone from gate agents to bank employees is predetermined by the code that pops up next to your name on a computer screen.

HOW TO IMPROVE YOUR PROFILE

Even if you're not a big spender, there are ways to improve your standing with companies in order to command better service. The key is to recognize that your spending habits, payment history, and any information you volunteer can be used for or against you. What's more, if you do think you're being pegged at a low tier, there are ways to get the recognition you feel you deserve.

The first step in fighting segmentation is to be stingy with the information you give out—especially if it's unlikely to help your status. Don't fill our surveys, sweepstakes forms, or applications if you're not comfortable with how the information might be used. Be wary when a company asks if it can alert you to other products and services. A yes may permit them to sell data that you don't want distributed.

PIGEONHOLING. The Consumers Union points out that it's unnecessary to fill out surveys with warranty cards. Just send in a proof of purchase with your name and address. "Protecting your privacy is a significant tool to prevent yourself from being pigeonholed as undesirable," says Gene Kimmelman, Washington co-director for the CU. It's equally important to recognize what kind of information companies are looking for. If you don't live in an upmarket Zip Code, consider using your work address for correspondence. Be optimistic when estimating your income or spending: The better the numbers look, the better you'll be treated.

Still, it's tough to keep personal information to yourself, especially when companies are compiling data on the business they do with you. A critical concern for all consumers is their actual payment record. Donna Fluss, a vice-president at the technology consultants Gartner Group Inc., advises pulling your credit history at least once a year to check if there are any liens or mistakes. "You may discover that you're listed as having missed a payment that you thought you made on time," she says. The three main reporting bureaus—Experian, Trans Union, and Equifax—charge a small fee for a copy of your credit history. If, however you have recently been denied credit, employment, or insurance, such a report is free from all three companies. The largest bureau is Equifax, which has data on 190 million Americans, but all three may have slightly different records based on who reports to them.

Multiple credit cards can be a mistake, especially if they're the no-frills variety that are frequently offered to less desirable

MAKING THE GRADE

How to get better service

CONSOLIDATE YOUR ACTIVITIES Few things elevate status and trim costs like spending big in one place. Be on the lookout for packages or programs that reward loyal behavior.

PROTECT YOUR PRIVACY Avoid surveys and be frugal with releasing credit-card or Social Security information. The less companies know, the less they can slot you.

JUMP THE PHONE QUEUE If you want to reach a live human, don't admit to having a touch-tone phone at the prompt. Or listen for options that are less likely to be handled automatically.

FIGHT BACK If you feel badly treated, complain. Make sure management knows just how much business you represent and that you're willing to take it elsewhere.

candidates. Not only can they drain the credit you might need for other activities, but they're also unlikely to propel you into a higher category. Using a spouse's card or account is also to be avoided, because it robs you of a chance to build your own credit history. If a mistake is made on your account, fight it.

Pros disagree on tactics for bypassing the service maze. One customer representative argues that when calling a service center it's better to punch in no account number if you're a low-value customer. The reason? Without proper identification, he says, a live person has to get on the line. "Pretend you're calling from a rotary phone," he advises. But another tactic may be to punch zero or choose an option that's likely to get immediate attention.

In the end, resistance may be futile, and the best strategy for beating the system may be to join it. Shop around for the best company, and try to consolidate your business there. These days, the best way to ensure good service is to make yourself look like a high-value, free-spending customer.

By Diane Brady in New York

When the curtain is pulled back on such sophisticated tiering, it can reveal some uses of customer information that are downright disturbing. Steve Reed, a West Coast sales executive, was shocked when a United Airlines Inc. ticketing agent told him: "Wow, somebody doesn't like you." Not only did she have access to his Premier Executive account information but there was a nasty note about an argument he had had with a gate agent in San Francisco several months earlier. In retrospect, he feels that explained why staff seemed less accommodating following the incident. Now, Reed refuses to give more than his name for fear "of being coded and marked for repercussions." United spokesman Joe Hopkins says such notes give agents a more complete picture of passengers. "It's not always negative infor-

mation," says Hopkins, adding that the practice is common throughout the industry.

Those who don't make the top tier have no idea how good things can be for the free-spending few. American Express Co. has a new Centurion concierge service that promises to get members almost anything from anywhere in the world. The program, with an annual fee of $1,000, is open by invitation only. "We're seeing a lot of people who value service more than price," says Alfred F. Kelly Jr., AmEx group president for consumer and small-business services. Dean Burri, a Rock Hill (S.C.) insurance executive, found out how the other half lives when he joined their ranks. Once he became a platinum customer of Starwood Hotels, it seemed there was nothing the hotel operator wouldn't do for him. When the Four Points Hotel in Lubbock, Tex., was completely booked for Texas Tech freshman orientation in August, it bumped a lower-status guest to get Burri a last-minute room. Starwood says that's part of the platinum policy, noting that ejected customers are put elsewhere and compensated for inconvenience. With the right status, says Burri, "you get completely different treatment."

RETAILING

Welcome to an after-hours preview for key customers where great sales abound and staff await your every need. Out in the aisles, it's back to self-service

The distinctions in customer status are getting sliced ever finer. Continental Airlines Inc. has started rolling out a Customer Information System where every one of its 43,000 gate, reservation, and service agents will immediately know the history and value of each customer. A so-called intelligent engine not only mines data on status but also suggests remedies and perks, from automatic coupons for service delays to priority for upgrades, giving the carrier more consistency in staff behavior and service delivery. The technology will even allow Continental staff to note details about the preferences of top customers so the airline can offer them extra services. As Vice-President Reitz puts it: "We even know if they put their eyeshades on and go to sleep." Such tiering pays off. Thanks to its heavy emphasis on top-tier clients, about 47% of Continental's customers now pay higher-cost, unrestricted fares, up from 38% in 1995.

Elsewhere, the selectivity is more subtle. At All First Bank in Baltimore, only those slotted as top customers get the option to click on a Web icon that directs them to a live service agent for a phone conversation. The rest never see it. First Union, meanwhile, codes its credit-card customers with tiny colored squares that flash when service reps call up an account on their computer screens. Green means the person is a profitable customer and should be granted waivers or otherwise given white-glove treatment. Reds are the money losers who have almost no negotiating power, and yellow is a more discretionary category in between. "The information helps our people make decisions on fees and rates," explains First Union spokeswoman Mary Eshet.

Banks are especially motivated to take such steps because they have one of the widest gaps in profitability. Market Line Associates, an Atlanta financial consultancy, estimates that the top 20% of customers at a typical commercial bank generate up to six times as much revenue as they cost, while the bottom fifth cost three to four times more than they make for the company. Gartner Group Inc. recently found that, among banks with de-posits of more than $4 billion, 68% are segmenting customers into profitability tranches while many more have plans to do so.

Tiering, however, poses some drawbacks for marketers. For one thing, most programs fail to measure the potential value of a customer. Most companies can still measure only past transactions—and some find it tough to combine information from different business units. The problem, of course, is that what someone spends today is not always a good predictor of what they'll spend tomorrow. Life situations and spending habits can change. In some cases, low activity may be a direct result of the consumer's dissatisfaction with current offerings. "We have to be careful not to make judgments based on a person's interaction with us," cautions Steven P. Young, vice-president for worldwide customer care at Compaq Computer Corp.s' consumer-products group. "It may not reflect their intentions or future behavior."

PAY NOT TO WAIT? Already, innovative players are striving to use their treasure trove of information to move customers up the value chain instead of letting them walk out the door. Capital One Financial Corp. of Falls Church, Va., is an acknowledged master of tiering, offering more than 6,000 credit cards and up to 20,000 permutations of other products, from phone cards to insurance. That range lets the company match clients with someone who has appropriate expertise. "We look at every single customer contact as an opportunity to make an unprofitable customer profitable or make a profitable customer more profitable," says Marge Connelly, senior vice-president for domestic card operations.

In the future, therefore, the service divide may become much more transparent. The trade-off between price and service could be explicit, and customers will be able to choose where they want to fall on that continuum. In essence, customer service will become just another product for sale. Walker Digital, the research lab run by priceline.com founder Jay S. Walker, has patented a "value-based queuing" of phone calls that allows companies to prioritize calls according to what each person will pay. As Walker Digital CEO Vikas Kapoor argues, customers can say: "I don't want to wait in line—I'll pay to reduce my wait time."

For consumers, though, the reality is that service as we've known it has changed forever. As Roger S. Siboni, chief executive of customer-service software provider E.piphany Inc., points out, not all customers are the same. "Some you want to absolutely retain and throw rose petals at their feet," Siboni says. "Others will never be profitable." Armed with detailed data on who's who, companies are learning that it makes financial sense to serve people based on what they're worth. The rest can serve themselves or simply go away.

With bureau reports

TRUST
IN THE
MARKETPLACE

**John E. Richardson and
Linnea Bernard McCord**

Traditionally, ethics is defined as a set of moral values or principles or a code of conduct.

> ... Ethics, as an expression of reality, is predicated upon the assumption that there are right and wrong motives, attitudes, traits of character, and actions that are exhibited in interpersonal relationships. Respectful social interaction is considered a norm by almost everyone.
> ... the overwhelming majority of people perceive others to be ethical when they observe what is considered to be their genuine kindness, consideration, politeness, empathy, and fairness in their interpersonal relationships. When these are absent, and unkindness, inconsideration, rudeness, hardness, and injustice are present, the people exhibiting such conduct are considered unethical. A genuine consideration of others is essential to an ethical life. (Chewning, pp. 175–176).

An essential concomitant of ethics is of trust. Webster's Dictionary defines trust as "assured reliance on the character, ability, strength or truth of someone or something." Businesses are built on a foundation of trust in our free-enterprise system. When there are violations of this trust between competitors, between employer and employees, or between businesses and consumers, our economic system ceases to run smoothly. From a moral viewpoint, ethical behavior should not exist because of economic pragmatism, governmental edict, or contemporary fashionability—it should exist because it is morally appropriate and right. From an economic point of view, ethical behavior should exist because it just makes good business sense to be ethical and operate in a manner that demonstrates trustworthiness.

Robert Bruce Shaw, in *Trust in the Balance*, makes some thoughtful observations about trust within an organization. Paraphrasing his observations and applying his ideas to the marketplace as a whole:

1. Trust requires consumers have confidence in organizational promises or claims made to them. This means that a consumer should be able to believe that a commitment made will be met.

2. Trust requires integrity and consistency in following a known set of values, beliefs, and practices.

3. Trust requires concern for the well-being of others. This does not mean that organizational needs are not given appropriate emphasis—but it suggests the importance of understanding the impact of decisions and actions on others—i.e. consumers. (Shaw, pp. 39–40)

Companies can lose the trust of their customers by portraying their products in a deceptive or inaccurate manner. In one recent example, a Nike advertisement exhorted golfers to buy the same golf balls used by Tiger Woods. However, since Tiger Woods was using custom-made Nike golf balls not yet available to the general golfing public, the ad was, in fact, deceptive. In one of its ads, Volvo represented that Volvo cars could withstand a physical impact that, in fact, was not possible. Once a company is "caught" giving inaccurate information, even if done innocently, trust in that company is eroded.

Companies can also lose the trust of their customers when they fail to act promptly and notify their customers of problems that the company has discovered, especially where deaths may be involved. This occurred when Chrysler dragged its feet in replacing a safety latch on its Minivan (Geyelin, pp. A1, A10). More recently, Firestone and Ford had been publicly brought to task for failing to expeditiously notify American consumers of tire defects in SUVs even though the problem had occurred years earlier in other countries. In cases like these, trust might not just be eroded, it might be destroyed. It could take years of painstaking effort to rebuild trust under these circumstances, and some companies might not have the economic ability to withstand such a rebuilding process with their consumers.

A *20/20* and *New York Times* investigation on a recent *ABC 20/20* program, entitled "The Car Dealer's Secret" revealed a sad example of the violation of trust in the marketplace. The investigation divulged that many unsuspecting consumers have had hidden charges tacked on by some car dealers when purchasing a new car. According to consumer attorney Gary Klein, "It's a dirty little secret that the auto lending industry has not owned up to." (*ABC News 20/20*)

The scheme worked in the following manner. Car dealers would send a prospective buyer's application to a number of lenders, who would report to the car dealer what interest rate the lender would give to the buyer for his or her car loan. This interest rate is referred to as the "buy rate." Legally a car dealer is not required to tell the buyer what the "buy rate" is or how much the dealer is marking up the loan. If dealers did most of the loans at the buy rate, they only get a small fee. However, if they were able to convince the buyer to pay a higher rate, they made considerably more money. Lenders encouraged car dealers to charge the buyer a higher rate than the "buy rate" by agreeing to split the extra income with the dealer.

David Robertson, head of the Association of Finance and Insurance Professionals—a trade group representing finance managers—defended the practice, reflecting that it was akin to a retail markup on loans. "The dealership provides a valuable service on behalf of the customer in negotiating these loans," he said. "Because of that, the dealership should be compensated for that work." (*ABC News 20/20*)

Careful examination of the entire report, however, makes one seriously question this apologetic. Even if this practice is deemed to be legal, the critical issue is what happens to trust when the buyers discover that they have been charged an additional 1–3% of the loan without their knowledge? In some cases, consumers were led to believe that they were getting the dealer's bank rate, and in other cases, they were told that the dealer had shopped around at several banks to secure the best loan rate they could get for the buyer. While this practice may be questionable from a legal standpoint, it is clearly in ethical breach of trust with the consumer. Once discovered, the companies doing this will have the same credibility and trustworthiness problems as the other examples mentioned above.

The untrustworthiness problems of the car companies was compounded by the fact that the investigation appeared to reveal statistics showing that black customers were twice as likely as whites to have their rate marked up—and at a higher level. That evidence—included in thousands of pages of confidential documents which *20/20* and *The New York Times* obtained from a Tennessee court—revealed that some Nissan and GM dealers in Tennessee routinely marked up rates for blacks, forcing them to pay between $300 and $400 more than whites. (*ABC News 20/20*)

This is a tragic example for everyone who was affected by this markup and was the victim of this secret policy. Not only is trust destroyed, there is a huge economic cost to the general public. It is estimated that in the last four years or so, Texas car dealers have received approximately $9 billion of kickbacks from lenders, affecting 5.2 million consumers. (*ABC News 20/20*)

Let's compare these unfortunate examples of untrustworthy corporate behavior with the landmark example of Johnson & Johnson which ultimately increased its trustworthiness with consumers by the way it handled the Tylenol incident. After seven individuals, who had consumed Tylenol capsules contaminated by a third party died, Johnson & Johnson instituted a total product recall within a week costing an estimated $50 million after taxes. The company did this, not because it was responsible for causing the problem, but because it was the right thing to do. In addition, Johnson & Johnson spearheaded the development of more effective tamper-proof containers for their industry. Because of the company's swift response, consumers once again were able to trust in the Johnson & Johnson name. Although Johnson & Johnson suffered a decrease in market share at the time because of the scare, over the long term it has maintained its profitability in a highly competitive market. Certainly part of this profit success is attributable to consumers believing that Johnson & Johnson is a trustworthy company. (Robin and Reidenbach)

The e-commerce arena presents another example of the importance of marketers building a mutually valuable relationship with customers through a trust-based collaboration process. Recent research with 50 e-businesses reflects that companies which create and nurture trust find customers return to their sites repeatedly. (Dayal.... p. 64)

In the e-commerce world, six components of trust were found to be critical in developing trusting, satisfied customers:

- State-of-art reliable security measures on one's site
- Merchant legitimacy (e.g., ally one's product or service with an established brand)
- Order fulfillment (i.e. placing orders and getting merchandise efficiently and with minimal hassles)
- Tone and ambiance—handling consumers' personal information with sensitivity and iron-clad confidentiality
- Customers feeling that they are in control of the buying process
- Consumer collaboration—e.g., having chat groups to let consumers query each other about their purchases and experiences (Dayal..., pp. 64–67)

Additionally, one author noted recently that in the e-commerce world we've moved beyond brands and trademarks to "trustmarks." This author defined a trustmark as a

... (D)istinctive name or symbol that emotionally binds a company with the desires and aspirations of its customers. It's an emotional connection—and it's much bigger and more powerful than the uses that we traditionally associate with a trademark.... (Webber, p. 214)

Certainly if this is the case, trust—being an emotional link—is of supreme importance for a company that wants to succeed in doing business on the Internet.

It's unfortunate that while a plethora of examples of violation of trust easily come to mind, a paucity of examples "pop up" as noteworthy paradigms of organizational courage and trust in their relationship with consumers.

In conclusion, some key areas for companies to scrutinize and practice with regard to decisions that may affect trustworthiness in the marketplace might include:

- Does a company practice the Golden Rule with its customers? As a company insider, knowing what you know about the product, how willing would you be to purchase it for yourself or for a family member?
- How proud would you be if your marketing practices were made public.... shared with your friends....

or family? (Blanchard and Peale, p. 27)

- Are bottom-line concerns the sole component of your organizational decision-making process? What about human rights, the ecological/environmental impact, and other areas of social responsibility?

- Can a firm which engages in unethical business practices with customers be trusted to deal with its employees any differently? Unfortunately, frequently a willingness to violate standards of ethics is not an isolated phenomenon but permeates the culture. The result is erosion of integrity throughout a company. In such cases, trust is elusive at best. (Shaw, p. 75)

- Is your organization not only market driven, but also value-oriented? (Peters and Levering, Moskowitz, and Katz)

- Is there a strong commitment to a positive corporate culture and a clearly defined mission which is frequently and unambiguously voiced by upper-management?

- Does your organization exemplify trust by practicing a genuine relationship partnership with your customers—*before, during, and after* the initial purchase? (Strout, p. 69)

Companies which exemplify treating customers ethically are founded on a covenant of trust. There is a shared belief, confidence, and faith that the company and its people will be fair, reliable, and ethical in all its dealings. *Total trust is the belief that a company and its people will never take opportunistic advantage of customer vulnerabilities*. (Hart and Johnson, pp. 11–13)

References

ABC News 20/20, "The Car Dealer's Secret," October 27, 2000.

Blanchard, Kenneth, and Norman Vincent Peale, *The Power of Ethical Management*, New York: William Morrow and Company, Inc., 1988.

Chewning, Richard C., *Business Ethics in a Changing Culture* (Reston, Virginia: Reston Publishing, 1984).

Dayal, Sandeep, Landesberg, Helen, and Michael Zeissner, "How to Build Trust Online," *Marketing Management*, Fall 1999, pp. 64–69.

Geyelin, Milo, "Why One Jury Dealt a Big Blow to Chrysler in Minivan-Latch Case," *Wall Street Journal*, November 19, 1997, pp. A1, A10.

Hart, Christopher W. and Michael D. Johnson, "Growing the Trust Relationship," *Marketing Management*, Spring 1999, pp. 9–19.

Hosmer, La Rue Tone, *The Ethics of Management*, second edition (Homewood, Illinois: Irwin, 1991).

Kaydo, Chad, "A Position of Power," *Sales & Marketing Management*, June 2000, pp. 104–106, 108ff.

Levering, Robert; Moskowitz, Milton; and Michael Katz, *The 100 Best Companies to Work for in America* (Reading, Mass.: Addison-Wesley, 1984).

Magnet, Myron, "Meet the New Revolutionaries," *Fortune*, February 24, 1992, pp. 94–101.

Muoio, Anna, "The Experienced Customer," *Net Company*, Fall 1999, pp. 025–027.

Peters, Thomas J. and Robert H. Waterman Jr., *In Search of Excellence* (New York: Harper & Row, 1982).

Richardson, John (ed.), *Annual Editions: Business Ethics 00/01* (Guilford, CT: McGraw-Hill/Dushkin, 2000).

_____, *Annual Editions: Marketing 00/01* (Guilford, CT: McGraw-Hill/Dushkin, 2000).

Robin, Donald P., and Erich Reidenbach, "Social Responsibility, Ethics, and Marketing Strategy: Closing the Gap Between Concept and Application," *Journal of Marketing*, Vol. 51 (January 1987), pp. 44–58.

Shaw, Robert Bruce, *Trust in the Balance*, (San Francisco: Jossey-Bass Publishers, 1997).

Strout, Erin, "Tough Customers," *Sales Marketing Management*, January 2000, pp. 63–69.

Webber, Alan M., "Trust in the Future," *Fast Company*, September 2000, pp. 209–212ff.

Dr. John E. Richardson is Professor of Marketing in the Graziadio School of Business and Management at Pepperdine University, Malibu, California

Dr. Linnea Bernard McCord is Associate Professor of Business Law in the Graziadio School of Business and Management at Pepperdine University, Malibu, California

A MATTER OF TRUST

In the aftermath of highly publicized corporate scandals, all eyes are on company executives and the way they do business. Here's how some are leveraging their salespeople as the first line of defense against skeptics

BY JENNIFER GILBERT

Gary Welch was hoping his early December meeting with a prospective business partner, a local builder, would go well. What he didn't expect was that he'd all but closed the deal in that one meeting on the strength of his company's ethical reputation.

"We were just wanting to build a relationship with him where we would act as his exclusive lender," says Welch, vice president of HomeBanc Mortgage Corporation, an Atlanta-based retail mortgage lender. For HomeBanc, prospective business partners are essentially prospective customers. When a deal is signed, HomeBanc becomes a builder's preferred lender—allowed to put marketing materials in the builder's homes and offices, and recommended to the builder's home buyers.

What sealed the deal in the meeting wasn't some knock 'em dead presentation—it was an article the builder had read in *The Atlanta Journal-Constitution* the previous day about HomeBanc's new chief people officer, Dwight "Ike" Reighard, an ordained minister. HomeBanc hired Reighard in December to maintain the quality of its workforce as the company expands.

"The builder said that if HomeBanc was willing to invest its money and its human capital in keeping employees happy, he had no questions as to how we would treat his customers," Welch says.

Such an example supports Welch's belief that customers do care about companies' ethical standards—and that it's in a company's best interest to have salespeople make such standards known. "That value has been heightened by all the negative things that have happened; it's a growing appreciation," Welch says. "If you can provide people with service and trust, they are willing to pay for that."

It's an issue that's coming up more and more during sales calls: An increasing number of sales managers are telling their reps to address the issues of ethics, corporate responsibility, and even financial viability in interactions with clients. In this business climate, some experts say, touting ethics during sales meetings is a golden opportunity to bolster a company's image.

While most companies have ethics codes already in place, some are taking a second look at them, says John Boatright, professor of business ethics at Loyola University Chicago and executive director of the Society for Business Ethics, in Chicago.

"But they're also looking at the need to increasingly focus on the code and use that code in decision making."

One potential use of the code, Boatright says, is "to make customers aware of it and to transmit this through the sales force. If companies are failing to do this, they are missing a good opportunity, because it increases the credibility of the company."

According to a recent *SMM*/Equation Research survey, 83 percent of 220 respondents said they train their reps to sell their companies' ethics and integrity along with their products and services. Nearly 70 percent said they believe their clients consider a company's ethical reputation when deciding whether to make a purchase. And while 48 percent said their companies haven't changed their emphasis on ethics and values in this economic climate, another 48 percent said they are placing somewhat more or much more emphasis on ethics.

"If corporations are not trying to promote, advertise, and sell their integrity through customers, employees, investors, and potential investors, then they are really missing a tremendous opportunity," says W. Michael Hoffman, executive director of the Center for Business Ethics at Bentley College, in Waltham, Massachusetts. Companies that develop strategies to convince those stakeholders to trust them will have a major competitive advantage over those that cannot, he says. "We are in an economic environment in which trust is at a premium. It's like air: When it's present, you don't think about it. When it's not present, you think about it all the time," Hoffman says. "We're in a financial market where there isn't a lot of air."

Speaking Up

Salespeople today are being told by their managers that a company's integrity can be as much of a selling point as low prices. So they talk about it.

HomeBanc's salespeople, for example, like to speak at length with customers about the company's commitment to keeping its employees happy. They hope that in every interaction, clients ask, "Why should we do business with you?" Welch says. HomeBanc's mission statement is: "To enrich and

Employee Treatment

DENS OF INIQUITY

What aspects of corporate culture foster unethical behavior among employees, particularly salespeople?

An environment in which employees don't have a clear understanding of what is expected of them "The ideal approach is for an organization to have a written code of conduct that everyone receives and reads," says Jim Eskin, a public affairs consultant in San Antonio, Texas. It doesn't have to be formal; expectations regarding ethical conduct can be effectively communicated in meetings, orientation, bulletins, and e-mail. "The employer is asking for trouble when there is no communication at all," he says.

A communication breakdown Employees need to feel comfortable talking to supervisors. Otherwise, they will be less inclined to report ethics violations.

Rules dictated from the top down Smart employers bring their people together to talk about common issues such as gifts and entertainment, and the use of e-mail and other company resources. "The most effective rules result from employee input and feedback," Eskin says.

A win-at-any-price attitude from management Management leads by example, and if executives send signals that grabbing short-term profits is desirable regardless of the consequences, workers throughout the organization will reflect that attitude in their behavior.

A commission-centric environment Commissions can be tricky and run the risk of distorting judgment, especially when they put salespeople's personal interests at odds with those of the customer or client.

The cog-in-the-wheel trap If employees are proud of their organization and feel a sense of loyalty, their conduct is far more likely to be ethical. "But if they feel management is making profits at their expense, there could be a mindset of getting even," Eskin says.

—*J.G.*

fulfill lives by serving each other, our customers and communities… as we support the dream of homeownership." The company's list of values includes, "We have integrity—do the right thing, always!" and "We deliver world-class service—serve all customers as they wish to be served." The company's mission and values are printed on cards that marketing materials sales associates carry with them to pass out to potential customers, and HomeBanc's marketing packages include reprints of newspaper articles high-lighting the company's ethical initiatives.

Welch, who manages 10 salespeople and also engages in direct selling, says he has experienced a customer's appreciation for a company's integrity and ethical reputation and how that affects his or her buying decision. "There's been a real awakening to the question of, 'Who can we trust?'" in the wake of recent corporate scandals, he says. "What we're finding is that as people learn and see us live by our mission statement, they are attracted to doing business with us, because we fall in line with what their mission statement is."

Nancy Sparks, vice president of sales and marketing for Marietta, Georgia–based builder Homes by Williamscraft Inc., says her company chose HomeBanc as its exclusive lender for

that reason. "We wanted to be associated with just them," she says. "They deliver as promised."

Sparks says HomeBanc also promotes itself positively in the community through its advertising and salespeople and clearly sends the message that it is a well-established, reputable company. "In the corporate climate that we're in right now, any kind of business is suspect," she says. "Companies have to get out there every day and prove themselves. You don't want to be associated with any company that might not be doing that."

A big part of HomeBanc's ethical agenda is keeping employees honest and satisfied. It's on the right track, at least according to one expert: "The best indicator of how sales organizations are going to treat their clients is how they treat their employees," says Brian Clapp, managing principal of the mid-Atlantic region for Right Management Consultants, based in Philadelphia.

HomeBanc stages day-long orientation programs for new salespeople, during which reps learn about how to best treat customers—by providing service guarantees and full refunds for unsatisfactory services, for example. Training is a seven-week process that teaches salespeople how to identify the best loans for customers. And to make sure all reps are behaving ethically, HomeBanc set up a hotline eight years ago that salespeople can use to report behavior that would reflect negatively on the company.

"We've been Atlanta's number-one mortgage lender for eleven straight years and if we weren't ethically responsible, I don't think we'd be here," HomeBanc's Chief People Officer Reighard says.

Another company, Memphis, Tennessee–based Inventory Locator Service (ILS), also tries to promote its ethical standards—inside and out. "When I saw some of our new dot-com competitors come out in 1999, one of the things I developed for our sales team was a white paper that focused on integrity, because at the time, the competitors were using less-than-ethical business practices," says James Sdoia, vice president of sales and service at the company, which runs an electronic marketplace for the aviation, marine, and industrial gas turbine industries and the U.S. Department of Defense.

Salespeople give the two-page sheet to customers. It addresses ILS's fiscal integrity, data integrity, and client integrity, Sdoia says, and has been "quite effective in several cases—even more so when the competitors started using high-pressure tactics such as those you'd get from a door-to-door salesman."

Recently revised, the two-pager details the company's new products and services and has been reformatted into a question-and-answer structure. The handout answers questions such as, "What makes up your financial strength and stability?" And while his company's business-to-business customer base hasn't been rocked by corporate scandals reported in the news to the extent that he believes consumers have, Sdoia insists that his salespeople address the issue of ethics.

"Certainly, the corporate integrity of any company should be reflected by the salespeople when they talk about the company," he says. "You don't have to come out and say 'Our company's trustworthy'; you show how long you've been in business, that you are financially stable, and that you have long-term relationships with clients. Salespeople should say those things in pitches."

Bill Morales, president of Tracer Corporation, a Milwaukee-based aircraft parts company, says he's proud to be a 10-year ILS customer because of its ethical and professional reputation. "They back up what they say they can do," he says. "From an ethics standpoint, they are extremely open and forward-thinking. They are willing to stand behind their product."

Uphill Battle

WorldCom is one company working overtime to show its customers that it has a soul. The bankrupt Clinton, Mississippi-based telecommunications company has been rebuilding itself following the admission of multibillion-dollar accounting fraud in summer 2002 and the investigation into its accounting and management practices.

Despite WorldCom's initiative to put new people in place, including a new CEO, and a renewed commitment to integrity, Chris Atkins, director of global corporate practice at New York-based public relations firm Ketchum, thinks the telecom giant has a steep climb ahead. "It's going to take years before people stop thinking of WorldCom as an unethical institution," he says. "On the other hand, I'm often surprised by how short America's memory really is."

WorldCom is banking on that short-term memory—and an overhaul of internal practices. In its quest to reinvent its image, the sales organization has become a critical vehicle for relaying the company's new commitment to customers and financial integrity in both words and action, says Jonathan Crane, president of U.S. sales, marketing, and services.

"We are probably the safest company in the U.S. right now because of what we've done internally and what's been done to us externally" by the courts, Crane says. He has led the charge to address ethics and corporate responsibility within the sales ranks via such programs as town-hall meetings. He also enforces the company's zero-tolerance ethics policy.

As part of sales training, all employees are asked to read, sign, and abide by the ethics policy or risk termination, Crane says. And WorldCom's commitment to integrity "is something salespeople want to make sure they get out on the table," he says.

Salespeople tell customers about new ethics programs, the independent ethics office, the new board structure and corporate governance, the hiring of a new corporate controller, and the expansion of its internal department audit staff.

"We tell people exactly what we're doing," Crane says. Salespeople also provide customers with written materials, and WorldCom posts detailed information regarding its efforts on its Web site. "We have to convince our client base that there will not be a reoccurrence of this behavior," Crane says. That

has to be a priority, he says, because customers care about WorldCom's integrity more than that of other companies.

"Because we are the company accused of perpetrating the largest fraud in the history of American business, customers are asking, 'Well, what are you doing to make sure it doesn't happen again in the future?'" Crane says. "As we enter this new year, we get a sense from our client base that our approach to this has helped us. We're starting to see an opening up of buying decisions."

Loose Lips Sink Ships?

Some experts, of course, caution managers against having their salespeople talk too much about their company's integrity and ethical responsibility in pitches, advocating a show-don't-tell approach. Broaching the subject, they argue, can actually backfire and raise suspicion.

"The least effective way to be seen as trustworthy is to say, 'I'm trustworthy.' You have to behave in a way that inspires confidence," Atkins says, rather than say, "'We're really honest.' It sounds a little disingenuous."

Like Atkins, Bill Cook, vice president of sales at Santa Clara, California-based Sun Microsystems, is an advocate of the actions-speak-louder-than-words philosophy. A 17-year alumnus of Sun's sales team, Cook says his company's ethical reputation has been built over time through its employees' actions.

Indeed, it's the small stuff that often means more to customers than words, Right's Clapp says. These include following up on commitments, not being cavalier, honoring noncompetes, and not selling empty promises.

Still, Cook acknowledges that the latest corporate scandals have shed new light on the issues of corporate and financial responsibility. Last October, Sun rolled out the Fiduciary Boot Camp, a special training program for all senior-level managers worldwide. The boot camp is designed to educate executives on the new rules and regulations included in the Sarbanes-Oxley Act of 2002, which holds companies to higher corporate governance standards, and informs them of Sun's view of ethical leadership. Executives who attend share the lessons with salespeople.

Sun's boot camp has boosted reps' recognition of the issues. But salespeople still interact with customers as they always have, Cook says. Customers do perceive Sun to be an ethical company with which to do business, Cook says, but that's because of the way its salespeople conduct themselves. "You just show it, day in and day out," he says. "We tell our customers about our products and offerings, and then we make sure we deliver against those. It's part of Sun's culture."

Senior Editor Jennifer Gilbert can be reached at jgilbert@salesandmarketing.com

UNIT 2

Research, Markets, and Consumer Behavior

Unit Selections

Key Points to Consider

• As marketing research techniques become more and more advanced, and as psychographic analysis leads to more and more sophisticated models of consumer behavior, do you believe marketing will become more capable of predicting consumer behavior? Explain.

• Where the target population lives, its age, and its ethnicity are demographic factors of importance to marketers. What other demographic factors must be taken into account in long-range market planning?

• Psychographic segmentation is the process whereby consumer markets are divided into segments based upon similarities in lifestyles, attitudes, personality type, social class, and buying behavior. In what specific ways do you envision psychographic research and findings helping marketing planning and strategy in the next decade?

 **Links: www.dushkin.com/online/**
These sites are annotated in the World Wide Web pages.

Canadian Innovation Centre
http://www.innovationcentre.ca/company/Default.htm
CBA.org: Research and Develop
http://www.cba.org/CBA/National/Marketing/research.asp
Industry Analysis and Trends
http://www.bizminer.com/market_research.asp
Marketing Intelligence
http://www.bcentral.com/articles/krotz/123.asp
Maritz Marketing Research
http://www.maritzresearch.com
USADATA
http://www.usadata.com
WWW Virtual Library: Demography & Population Studies
http://demography.anu.edu.au/VirtualLibrary/

If marketing activities were all we knew about an individual, we would know a great deal. By tracing these daily activities over only a short period of time, we could probably guess rather accurately that person's tastes, understand much of his or her system of personal values, and learn quite a bit about how he or she deals with the world.

In a sense, this is a key to successful marketing management: tracing a market's activities and understanding its behavior. However, despite the increasing sophistication of market research techniques, this task is not easy. Today a new society is evolving out of the changing lifestyles of Americans, and these divergent lifestyles have put great pressure on the marketer who hopes to identify and profitably reach a target market. At the same time, however, each change in consumer behavior leads to new marketing opportunities.

The writings in this unit were selected to provide information and insight into the effect that lifestyle changes and demographic trends are having on American industry.

The first unit article in the Market Research subsection provides some insight into why well-focused brainstorming sessions are a key in new product development. The next article describes how a popular research technique helps marketers and consumers get what they really want. The last article in this subsection shows how common testing mistakes can derail a promising new product launch.

The five articles in the Markets and Demographics subsection examine the importance of demographic data, geographic settings, economic forces, and age considerations in making marketing decisions. In the first article, "A Beginner's Guide to Demographics," Berna Miller provides a helpful background for understanding demographics. The remaining four articles scrutinize some unique demographic and psychographic considerations to be reckoned with for various "generational" and multicultural groupings.

The three articles in the final subsection examine how consumer behavior, social attitudes, cues, and quality considerations, and online communities will have an impact on the evaluation and purchase of various products and services for different consumers.

A Different Approach for Developing New Products or Services

BY ROBERT BRASS

"When all else fails, ask your customer!" At first utterance, this advice seems to make sense. But it assumes two things:

- A group of potential customers can effectively describe their needs in terms of new products or services.
- These same customers can then rank those needs in terms of importance to offer guidance to development teams.

Both of these "beliefs" have a history of ineffectiveness. Of all new products, 80 to 90 percent fail, and there is no proof that traditional market research techniques would have altered that fact.

Does that mean that market research is useless? The answer is, "No, it doesn't." However, it points to some problems with traditional market research.

INHERENT PROBLEMS WITH TRADITIONAL MARKET RESEARCH

The standard approach to market research is to ask customers in a focus group or one-on-one to describe what they would like to have in a new product or service. Typically, then, after multiple sessions using this approach, the information is sifted, condensed and clarified. To address priorities, a follow-up survey based on a distillation of the discussions is done to quantify the "wants" of the customer. The result is then treated as the basis for defining the features and functions for new products or services.

All problems are not created equal so prioritizing is essential.

The problem with this approach is that it rejects the reality of our lives. If we are to identify the things that make us unhappy, we can usually be precise. On the other hand, if we are asked to formulate the products or the services that would relieve our problems, in most cases, we struggle. However, if you still are tempted to use this old approach, recall the old saying: a camel is a horse designed by a committee.

A DIFFERENT APPROACH

Is there a methodology that would work? The answer is "Yes." Experience demonstrates that the one common denominator for almost all successful products is that they solve high-priority problems in a cost-effective and easy-to-understand manner! Given this clue, there is a process to follow that leverages this wisdom:

1. Find out what problems there are with an existing product or service that you are attempting to improve or replace.
2. Use an objective method to prioritize those problems.
3. Present the results to a very creative individual or to a creative group in a simple and unambiguous manner. Charge them with the goal of developing the actual products or services that would solve the high-priority problems.
4. Create prototypes and implement a preliminary but very different "concept test." Don't ask customers if they like the new product or service. Instead, ask a carefully selected group how well the proposed solution addresses those high priority problems that it was intended to solve.
5. If it passes the test of being an effective solution and it is cost effective, launch it as a new product or service.

PAINSTORMING, NOT BRAINSTORMING

Instead of using brainstorming to get ideas for new products or services, use "painstorming" to identify problems. The key to success in this process is identification of the major problems. All problems are not created equal, so prioritizing is essential. Develop a survey, but don't ask customers to rate the importance of each problem.

First, the human decision process is extremely complex, and the importance or priority of any element varies with circumstances. A totally satisfied customer who has no problems with a new car will have a very different set of priorities from one who needs to go to the dealer every week for repairs. Second, since virtually every purchase decision is emotional, we often consciously or unconsciously support our decisions with rationalizations that may have no real relationship to the actual reason for the decision.

SO IF YOU CAN'T ASK ABOUT IMPORTANCE, THEN WHAT?

Suppose you were designing luggage that would be convenient for traveling. During various focus groups and one-on-one interviews, numerous items continually surface as problems. Among those might be weight, the ability of the luggage to fit under the airline seat, the need to totally unpack to get at all of the clothes, the wrinkling of clothing in the luggage, identification of the luggage on the luggage transport at an airport, and so forth.

> True out-of-the-box thinking is a scarce commodity, but is usually the roadmap to successful products or services.

To obtain a good survey sample, you would randomly choose several hundred travelers who matched the market you were interested in. The survey would ask these respondents to express their satisfaction with their current luggage with respect to each of the individual items identified as problems.

Implicit, but subtly buried within the results from all of the surveys, is the actual common complex decision process. What is needed is a method of extracting it. Fortunately, analysis techniques exist that do precisely that, including one based on Neural Networks. As a test of validity, if the results of the overall assessment of a person's current luggage can be predicted knowing only the survey respondents' opinions of their satisfaction with the problem areas, then you will have figured out the decision process. Our experience with Neural Network analysis has demonstrated that over 90 percent of the time it meets that test. Using this model and testing each problem independently allows a clear quantification of the importance of each problem area related to luggage. So, instead of asking for importance, analytical techniques derive the hierarchical irritation level of problems.

DEVELOP CREATIVE SOLUTIONS

Once the problems have been defined and quantified, give the information to the most creative group you know. Let it come up with the solution. You want an unexpected solution. True out-of-the-box thinking is a scarce commodity, but is usually the roadmap to successful products or services. With each potential solution, however, one more task remains: define the savings that accrue. Some may be financial or even personal, but the value needs to be defined.

THE WEAKNESS OF THE CLASSIC CONCEPT TEST

Now you are at the stage where several alternative products or services have been developed. It is time to subject the solutions to a reality test. The Concept Test is a favorite tool of market research. It presents one or more products or services to a group and attempts to obtain their likes, dislikes and general opinions. The skill of the moderator, the choice of the participants and the interpretation of the results of the group are all elements of subjectivity that can inject major biases into the conclusions. The problem with this process stems from the question being asked of the group, which is "What do you think of this concept?" What's missing is the phrase "Compared to what?"

This subtle but important point of view leads to a change in the normal process to create a methodology we call "The Concept Assessment." It leverages our innate and proven ability to identify problems, as opposed to our questionable capability for evaluating solutions. The methodology uses the objective list of prioritized problems that the creative individuals used to develop the products or services. This list then can be considered the answer to the question "Compared to what?"

PRIORITIZE PROBLEMS

We do not ask the group what it likes. Instead, the group is asked to assess how well the various products or services solve the prioritized problems. Participants are chosen for their expertise in the field, not because they are a favorite or knowledgeable customer, and the moderator now has a much less influential role in biasing the conclusions. The group focuses on identifying weaknesses in the products or services with respect to the prioritized problems instead of selecting their favorite solution.

Robert Brass is president of Development II, a market research, survey and new product development company based in Woodbury, CT (www.development2.com).

From *M World*, Winter 2003, pp. 35-36. © 2003 by the American Management Association, www.amanet.org. Reprinted by permission.

Product by Design

An increasingly popular research technique helps marketers and consumers get what they really want.

BY DAVID J. LIPKE

This past November, the Lands' End Web site launched "My Personal Shopper," a recommendation engine for customers who want help sorting through the retailer's vast selection of sweaters, skirts, and button-downs. Big whoop, you say—Amazon's been doing this for years. But unlike companies that use past purchases to proffer suggestions to cyber-browsers, Lands' End is the first apparel retailer to use a technique called conjoint analysis. In a brief survey, six pairs of outfits are shown to the shopper, who chooses a preferred outfit among each pair. Through analysis of these six simple choices, and the answers to a few other questions, the site sorts through 80,000 apparel options and presents the most suitable ones to the busy shopper.

While the use of conjoint analysis by Lands' End is unique, the methodology itself is not. It's a research technique that has been around for three decades, but which is increasing in popularity as software developments and the Internet make it easier to use, as well as more powerful and flexible. Understanding how conjoint analysis works, and the innovative ways it's now being used, provides a good opportunity

for any company to increase its chances of giving consumers more of what they want, and less of what they don't. "Use of this method will increase as more marketers realize what it can do, and how well it can work," says John Seal, senior analytical consultant at Burke, Inc., a Cincinnati-based research firm.

So what is conjoint analysis? The rationale underlying the technique is that consumers weigh all the many elements of a product or service—such as price, ingredients, packaging, technical specifications, and on and on—when choosing, say, a sweater, airline ticket, or stereo system. While this may seem obvious to anyone who's faced a wall of DVD players at Circuit City, figuring out how to leverage this concept in the marketing arena can be difficult. Conjoint analysis does this by breaking products down into their many elements, uncovering which ones drive consumer decisions and which combination will be most successful. But rather than directly asking survey respondents to state the importance of a certain component *à la* traditional surveys, participants judge hypothetical product profiles, consisting of a range of defining characteristics called "el-

ements." Their responses are run through an analytical process that indirectly identifies the importance and appeal of each element, based upon their pattern of preferences for the element groups.

If this process sounds more complicated than a traditional survey, it is. And it tends to be more expensive as well. But, as the saying goes, you get what you pay for. While traditional surveys can gauge interest in product features, the results can be misleading. This is because it can be difficult for respondents to directly relate how valuable a particular product feature will be to them. "If you ask respondents how much they are willing to pay for a certain feature, they often can't or won't answer truthfully," says Tom Pilon, a Carrollton, Texas-based consultant who specializes in conjoint research projects. "They'll tend to say they're interested in all the new features." They wouldn't be lying, but they might not actually pay for those features when the product comes to the market. Similarly, focus groups are a good way to draw out consumer opinion on new products, but it's difficult to accurately quantify how a product will perform in the marketplace from this data.

A BRIEF HISTORY OF CONJOINT

1964
The fundamental theories for conjoint analysis are laid out in a paper by R. D. Luce and J. W. Tukey, "Simultaneous Conjoint Measurement: A New Type of Fundamental Measurement," in the *Journal of Mathematical Psychology*.

1971
Conjoint is introduced to market research firm by Professors Paul Green and V. R. Rao, in the guide "Conjoint Measurement for Quantifying Judgemental Data," in the *Journal of Marketing Research*. First commercial use of conjoint analysis is conducted.

1980
Approximately 160 conjoint research projects are completed by market research firms, according to a survey of 17 firms known to conduct this type of research by Professors Philippe Cattin and Richard Wittink. In total, 700 projects are completed from 1971 through 1980.

1983
Choice-based conjoint is introduced to the market research industry by J. J. Louviere and G. G. Woodworth, in an article in the *Journal of Marketing Research*.

1985
Bretton-Clark introduces the first commercial, full-profile conjoint system, called Conjoint Designer.
Sawtooth Software introduces ACA, a software package for adaptive conjoint analysis. It is now the most widely used software for this type of research.

1989
Professors Cattin and Wittink find that 1,062 conjoint research projects have been completed since 1984, and estimate that close to 2,000 conjoint research projects will be conducted that year.

1990
SPSS introduces a full-profile conjoint analysis software package for the computer.

1993
Sawtooth Software introduces the first commercial choice-based conjoint software for the computer.

Source: Sawtooth Software: The Journal of Marketing, Summer 1982: The Journal of Marketing, July 1989; The Journal of Marketing Research, Fall 1995.

"Conjoint mimics the way that consumers actually think," says Joel Greene, director of database marketing at Akron, Ohio-based Sterling Jewelers. Greene first used conjoint research last spring, and is impressed with the results. Fed up with consumers tossing his mailings into the trash, Greene hired White Plains, New York-based market research firm Moscowitz Jacobs Inc. (MJI) to figure out a way to make them more appealing. Using a proprietary research tool called IdeaMap, MJI worked with Greene to systematically break down the brand image and communication efforts of Shaw's (a division of Sterling Jewelers) into bite-size elements. These factors were culled through focus groups and brainstorming sessions that examined previous marketing efforts and possible new approaches. Well over a hundred elements were part of the tested pool, which included different ways to convey messages about Shaw's stores, merchandise, brand differentiation, and emotional appeals. "We wanted to cast a wide net, because we didn't know what would work," says Greene.

MJI recruited a group of more than a hundred survey respondents to its testing facilities in Chicago and White Plains. Seated at computers, they were systematically exposed to the different elements, grouped as words, phrases, and pictures. For each random grouping of elements, the respondent would rate the appeal of the group as a whole. From an analysis of the pattern of ratings, MJI was able to give a utility score to each element. Using these scores, Shaw's could then create marketing messages from this universe of elements appealing to the widest group of customers, or to specific segments. The words, phrases, and pictures (i.e. elements) that scored highest for each segment were then used to create new mailings. And the glittering result? The creative geared toward each segment resulted in significantly higher rates of response, as well as increased dollar sales per response.

Understanding how conjoint analysis works is a good way for any company to increase its chances of giving consumers more of what they want, and less of what they don't.

The effectiveness with which conjoint can be used to understand precisely which aspects and features of a product are driving sales is especially crucial in an industry such as consumer electronics. With an increase in digital convergence, and with hybrid electronic products coming to the market—think refrigerators connected to the Internet, and cameras as MP3 players—the question arises: Will consumers actually pay for these products, and how much? "We really have to avoid the 'if you build it, they will come' pitfall," says Maria Townsend-Metz, a marketing manager at Motorola.

Heeding this warning, Townsend-Metz used conjoint analysis while working on enhancing Motorola's popular TalkAbout two-way radios. "We couldn't put all the different options we were thinking about on the radio, so we needed to know which ones were going to be of most value to the consumer, and help sell the most radios," says Townsend-Metz. Because of the complexity of creating and modeling well-run conjoint studies, she brought in Boise, Idaho-based research firm POPULUS, Inc. In six markets across the U.S., the company conducted conjoint surveys of consumers who participated in activities, such as camping and biking, where a two-way radio would be a natural accessory. POPULUS tested 18 attributes, covering technical specifications, price points, and the appearance of the devices.

Using a conjoint methodology was especially appropriate because all the attributes were interdependent—different features, for example, would affect the look of the radio, as well as the price. "The goal was to find the combination of features that would maximize interest at the lowest production cost," says John Fiedler of POPULUS. The resulting product was right on consumers' wavelength, and the TalkAbout now leads the market for recreational and industrial two-way radios.

CONJOINT ANALYSIS IN A NUTSHELL

Conjoint analysis presents a way for researchers to understand which specific elements (i.e. parts or features) of a product, package design, or marketing message are most valued by consumers when making a decision to purchase. It involves placing a series of product concepts, composed of different elements, in front of survey respondents. The respondents express their preferences for the different concepts, and the importance of each element is determined by analyzing the pattern of the respondents' choices. The elements tested are "attributes" (such as color, brand, and price) and "levels" within those attributes (such as blue or red, Ford or Honda, $100 or $150). After the survey, "utility scores" are calculated for each level showing which ones were most preferred, and which were most important in the hypothetical purchase decision. Many researchers have created their own unique methodology for conducting this type of research, but there are three main types of conjoint analysis:

TYPE	DESCRIPTION	PROS & CONS
TRADITIONAL (a.k.a.: full-profile; preference-based; ratings-based; card-sort)	Respondents are given a series of product profiles to rate. Each profile is composed of one level for each attribute being tested (e.g. How likely are you to buy a blue Ford that costs $150?)	• Easy, straightforward design process • Can be administered on paper or by computer • Encourages respondents to evaluate the product individually, rather than in comparison to others • Because full profiles are used (a level for each attribute is included in every profile), large numbers of attributes can confuse respondents. Respondents can begin to ignore some attributes to simplify the process. This limits the number of attributes that can be successfully tested.
CHOICE-BASED (a.k.a.: discrete choice)	Respondents are given two or more profiles at once and asked to choose the one they prefer, or none (e.g., Which would you purchase: a blue Ford that costs $100 or a red Honda that costs $150, or neither?).	• Allows for measurement of "special effects" (complex interactions between utility scores across attributes and levels in certain types of analysis). • Some researchers believe this method better re-creates the real-life shopping experience, in which consumers choose among products. • Other researchers don't believe consumers always make these side-by-side comparisons and prefer the traditional conjoint rating system. • Comparisons of side-by-side full profiles, with large numbers of attributes, can lead respondents to ignore some attributes, as in traditional conjoint methods.
ADAPTIVE (a.k.a.: Sawtooth Software's ACA)	This technique is divided into three main phases. Respondents first rate or rank the levels within an attribute (e.g., Rank these brands in order of preference: Sony, Toshiba, Compaq). Second, they rate how important a certain attribute is to them (e.g., How important is brand in considering this purchase?). Respondents then rate partial profiles (two to three attributes at a time) that are chosen to test those attributes that mattered most to them.	• Because only "partial profiles" are tested, it can be easier for respondents to make accurate preference choices between the different profiles. • More attributes can be tested in the first phase, and then the questions can hone in on the most important attributes. • Software, such as ACA, makes the design and administration of these surveys easier. • Can only be administered on a computer. • Some researchers dislike the adaptive methodology, as it depends largely on the first questions being answered accurately. If they are not, subsequent questions can focus on the wrong product attributes. • Cannot directly measure certain "special effects."

Source: Information compiled from reports by Maritz Marketing Research; Sawtooth Software, POPULUS, Moscowitz Jacobs, and DSS Research.

The popularity of conjoint research was greatly increased by the development of software in the 1980s that made it easier to design and run these types of studies. The leader in this field is Sequim, Washington-based Sawtooth Software, whose ACA brand of conjoint is the most widely used in the world. Other software suppliers include SPSS Inc. and SAS Systems. Prior to computer-assisted research, conjoint surveys were conducted using cards that had groups of attributes printed on them, and which were sorted by preference. The number of attributes that could be tested in this manner was severely limited, as was the concluding analysis.

The trend toward conducting survey research on the Web will further increase the use of conjoint, according to experts in the field. The Web provides an easy way to present respondents with groups of attributes, something that was much more difficult to do over the phone (people can only remember so many features at once). Fuji Film, for one, has used conjoint Web surveys to uncover the effects of price, brand, and package configurations (i.e. the number of rolls in a package) on sales. "Film is a low-involvement category, the product is standardized, and the effects of price and packaging are significant," says Doug Rose, president of Austin, Texas-based DRC Group, who worked on conjoint projects last year for Fuji.

By showing respondents side-by-side attribute profiles of different brand, price, and packaging configurations, Fuji was able to analyze their patterns of preference, and deduce what was driving their choices. The film manufacturer was further able to estimate exactly what effect a certain price point on a particular package of film would have on market share. This conjoint study was so accurate that its estimates perfectly matched ACNielsen data on price elasticity in the film sector, which appeared after the Fuji study.

One research firm taking conjoint analysis a step further on the Web is Burlingame, California-based Active Research. Its proprietary "Active Buyer's Guide" is a powerful research tool for marketers, disguised as a shopping search engine for consumers. Licensed to over 70 popular sites, such as Lycos and MySimon, it helps Web shoppers find the computers, appliances, and financial services (135 categories in all) that most closely match their needs, both online and offline. By filling out a conjoint survey that hones in on what features, price points, and attributes they are looking for, the Guide delivers a list of products that are most likely to interest the shopper.

But Active Research doesn't do this just to help out consumers. By answering the questions required by the search engine, shoppers are providing the company with a gold mine of continuous information on what kind of products they want, and at what price. In effect, Active Research is compiling 1.5 million surveys a month. What's more, these surveys are from people who are providing the most accurate information possible and are in the market, at that moment, to buy a particular product. By compiling and analyzing this data, Active Research provides up-to-the-minute information for clients such as Ford, GE, and Sony on which aspects of a product are driving consumer decisions, which demographic segments are driving sales, and who's interested in different features.

In addition, clients of Active Research can create hypothetical products and measure what their likely market share would be. Using the conjoint-produced utility scores of different product features, marketers can preview how a new product will sell in the marketplace, without the time and cost of a test launch. Because of the size of its sample, Active Research can slice-and-dice hypothetical products in an array of categories, demographics, and configurations. "It's not an exaggeration to say that what they are doing is an absolutely unique way to do primary research," says client Suzanne Snygg, futures product manager at Palm, Inc. The dual nature of their service is highlighted by the fact that Snygg herself has used Active Research data not only to shape product concepts for Palm but also to find the best mini-stereo system for her home. As the Web makes conjoint analysis more popular, it's important to note that conjoint research is still more complicated to conduct than straightforward survey research. To produce worthwhile results, it is crucial to create a pool of attributes that actually influences consumer choice. This requires careful and creative brainstorming. Researchers have to choose the correct conjoint method (there are several types, with many researchers creating their own unique variants). They have to show groupings of elements to respondents that cover many possible combinations, in a balanced and useful way. The final results are only as good as the design and analysis of the research, which can be complicated. Keith Chrzan, director of marketing sciences at Maritz Marketing Research, goes so far as to say that "a lot of people are using conjoint who shouldn't be," due to the easy-to-use software.

That said, the effectiveness and accuracy of conjoint techniques make them powerful tools for marketers who use them properly. Says Tom Pilon, the Texas-based consultant, "once a company has done it once, they always come back for more."

SURVIVING Innovation

Common testing mistakes can derail a promising new product launch.

By Kevin J. Clancy and Peter C. Krieg

Watching the sports coverage on Monday after Sunday's loss, any knowledgeable fan can spot the quarterback's mistakes and see what he might have done to exploit the other team's weaknesses. In the same way, once a new product has failed, any informed marketing executive usually can spot the company's slip-ups.

Take Cottonelle Fresh Rollwipes, "America's first and only disposable, pre-moistened wipe on a roll." Kimberly-Clark announced this "breakthrough product" in January 2001. According to the corporation's press release, "It is the most significant category innovation since toilet paper first appeared in roll form in 1890." Cottonelle Fresh Rollwipes "deliver the cleaning and freshening of pre-moistened wipes with the convenience and disposability of toilet paper."

The corporation was certain a market existed. Its market research had established that 63% of Americans had experimented with a wet "cleansing method" and that one out of four uses a moist wipe daily. Most of these people are using a baby wipe, but baby wipes usually can't go into a septic system. Kimberly-Clark had been selling tubs containing sheets of "disposable" moistened toilet paper for years, and the growth of this product convinced the company to invest research money into finding a more convenient delivery mechanism.

It came up with a refillable beige plastic dispenser that clips to the standard toilet paper spindle and holds both a roll of dry toilet paper and the wet Fresh Rollwipes. The dispenser with four starter rolls was to sell for $8.99; a refill pack of four rolls was $3.99. Kimberly-Clark, which says it spent $100 million on research for the project, protected the product and dispenser with 30 patents.

EXECUTIVE briefing

New product and service introductions have a startlingly high rate of failure, largely because they weren't tested properly before launch. Even a great new product or service can fail if marketers don't do their homework first. Avoiding some common mistakes in testing concepts and marketing plans can help companies make sure their products enjoy a long and healthy life in the marketplace.

In making the January 2001 announcement, the corporation said that the U.S. toilet paper market was $4.8 billion a year. Kimberly-Clark expected first-year Fresh Rollwipes sales to reach at least $150 million and $500 million within six years. Even better, those sales would expand the total U.S. toilet paper market because moistened toilet paper tends to supplement dry toilet paper rather than replace it.

But by October, 10 months later, Kimberly-Clark was blaming the economy for poor sales. According to Information Resources Inc., Cottonelle Fresh Rollwipes sales were about one-third of the forecasted $150 million. In our experience, however, if consumers are interested in a product, a weak economy won't depress sales so badly. Something had to be wrong with Kimberly-Clark's marketing, and in April 2002, *The Wall Street Journal* reported some of the corporation's missteps.

Start with the premature announcement. Although Kimberly-Clark rolled out the publicity and advertising in January, it was not ready to ship the product to stores until July. This is like heating a home in the summer expecting it to remain warm in winter. The late arrival of manufacturing equipment may have been responsible for "a good part" of the delay, but by July, most shoppers had forgotten about the hype. "I know I've heard something about it. I can't recall if it was a commercial or a comedian making fun of it," said Rob Almond, who purchases paper goods as director of housekeeping services for Richfield Nursing Center, in Salem, Va., one of the markets where Rollwipes are available.

Then there was the ineffective advertising. Granted Kimberly-Clark was trying to promote the advantages of a product that few people can talk about without embarrassment, but it never explained to consumers what the product does in its advertising and promotions. The ads, which cost $35 million, carried the slogan, "sometimes wetter is better" and feature shots from behind of people splashing in water. A print ad was an extreme close-up of a sumo wrestler's behind. Analysts criticized the ads for not clearly explaining the product—or helping create demand. Also, Kimberly-Clark ran the ads nationally when (a) the product was not available and (b) when it was finally available but only in certain Southern markets.

No more than 10% of all new products or services are successful— that is, still on the market and profitable after three years.

If there was ever a product suitable for a sampling campaign, this was it. But Rollwipes weren't produced in small trial sizes, which meant no free samples. Instead, Kimberly-Clark scheduled a mobile restroom tour to stop at public places so people could try out the product in the Southeast in mid-September 2001. It was just bad luck the road trip got canceled after September 11.

Production design posed yet another problem. Unlike the wipes in boxes that bashful consumers can hide under the bathroom sink, Rollwipes' beige plastic dispenser is immediately visible. The dispenser clips onto the spindle of the regular toilet tissue but is about the size of two rolls on top of one other. Not every bathroom has space for the dispenser, and not every consumer wants beige plastic. As Tom Vierhile, president of Marketing Intelligence services, a firm that tracks new product introductions, told *The Wall Street Journal*, "You do not want to have to ask someone to redecorate their bathroom."

A year and a half after Kimberly-Clark's big announcement, Fresh Rollwipes were in one regional market and executives said sales are so weak they are not financially material.

The Cost of Failure

While Monday morning quarterbacking can be instructive for marketers, it certainly hasn't helped improve anyone's chances of launching a successful new product or service or prevented the waste of millions— even billions of dollars—on failing efforts.

Industry speakers generally say 80% to 90% of new products succeed, and a recent Nielsen BASES and Ernst & Young study put the failure rate of new U.S. consumer products at 95% and new European consumer products at 90%. Based on research at Copernicus, we believe that no more than 10% of all new products or services are successful—that is, still on the market and profitable after three years. This is true for consumer package goods, financial services, pharmaceuticals, consumer durables, telecommunications services, Hollywood movies, and more.

And failure costs companies a tremendous amount of money. One way to calculate exactly how much is to take the average cost to develop and introduce a new product and multiply it by the number of failures.

Edward F. Ogiba, president of Group EFO Limited, a new product development consulting company, has written that the cost of introducing a national brand can easily exceed $20 million. "The going budget for creative development and market research alone now reportedly exceeds $500,000 per project, a 150% increase in two years."

The editor of *New Product News* has written "it probably costs $100 million to introduce a truly new soft drink nationally and it costs $10,000 to introduce a new flavor of ice cream in Minneapolis. Somewhere in between is a worthless 'average' cost to introduce a new product." He added that with the help of media experts, the magazine built an "ideal" national introductory advertising/consumer promotion/trade promotion-marketing plan for a major new product. The total expenditure was roughly $54 million and did not include product development, package design, sales force contribution, or brand management costs.

A marketing research manager at the Best Foods Division of CPC International recently told us that, based on what he believed to be several conservative assumptions, the total marketing dollars spent by manufacturers for failed new food products in a single year ranged from $9 billion to $14 billion, a figure we believe understates reality.

Now compare these estimates of development and launch costs with a stunning analysis done a few years ago by SAMI/Burke data that found fewer than 200 products of the thousands introduced in a 10-year period had more than $15 million in sales, and only a handful produced more than $100 million in sales. Very few new products and services are returning a positive return on investment, let alone one large enough to justify the allocation of limited time and resources in the first place.

But it doesn't have to be this way. The key to improving the odds of launching successful new products and services is to avoid making critical marketing mistakes in the first place. Doing this requires new ways of creating new product ideas, testing new concepts, testing product and service formulations in terms of consumer acceptance, testing advertising and promotions, and finally testing entire marketing plans. In this article, we will focus on two of the possible reasons for failure: concept testing that falls short and break-downs in marketing plans.

Concept Testing Falls Short

New ideas for products and services come from everywhere. They fly into people's heads in the middle of the night. Or the company has the opportunity to license or buy the rights to something from another country (e.g., Häagen-Daz has had enormous success with dulce de leche ice cream, which began life in South America; Clorox, with Brita water purification systems that origi- nated in Europe; and Red Bull with an energy drink from Thailand). Or the firm has actually generated some new product ideas through one-on-one interviews, focus groups, or customer observations followed by intensive brainstorming sessions.

At some point in the process, the idea turns into a concept, often described in one or two paragraphs, sometimes with a name and price. And if the marketer is smart, this concept is tested among a cross-section of prospective buyers in a category. After all, why waste precious time and dollars to develop a product or service if customers don't want to buy it?

Concept testing the way it is most frequently done today, however, is plagued with problems. Almost every marketer has done one (if not hundreds) of these tests, yet such tests often raise as many questions as they answer. We hear marketing executives ask questions like, "Is 14% in the top box ["definitely will buy"] a good score?" Or they say, "We studied three pricing variations. How could they all get 10% in the top box? Is there a fourth variation we should offer?" Or, "If we change the price (or formulation or the packaging), how much would trial increase? Would it go to 30%?" Traditional concept tests are fraught with problems, which we list here:

Sample limitations. Marketers contract with research companies that generally employ small (75 to 150), non-projectable groups of men and women wandering through shopping malls and willing to answer questions for the research. Further, they tend to use only about three non-representative malls and markets for a given study.

Data collection. Concept tests by phone and via the Web also have drawbacks. On the phone, an interviewer

Exhibit 1
Eleven-point purchase probability scale

Purchase probability	Percentage
Certain	99%
Almost certain	90%
Very probably	80%
Probably	70%
Good possibility	60%
Fairly good possibility	50%
Fair possibility	40%
Some possibility	30%
Slight possibility	20%
Very slight possibility	10%
No chance	0%

- More discriminating
- More reliable
- Enhance serious thinking by respondents
- Clear interpretation across respondents
- Reminds us to deal in probabilities (not "top-box" cutoffs)
- Greater validity

reads a description of the concept to respondents. Because they're reading and because people forget the first sentence by the time they hear the second, researchers must shorten the concept and distill it down to its bare bones. The bare bones sometimes can be as short as a sentence. The distilled concept is then coupled with rating scales with typically fewer points (i.e., less discrimination) than would be employed in a personal interview or Web-based survey. On the phone, the respondent has to remember a rating scale and give this stranger a number.

Though it allows more visual capabilities, the Web can be just as dangerous as the phone. Many marketers don't realize there are two broad methods of internet data collection: databases and panels. According to Greg McMahon, a senior vice president at international market research firm Synovate, making this distinction between the methods is critical: "Only research firms with true Internet panels maintain detailed demographic (and other) information about their panel members and balance their samples so they match U.S. Census statistics. Without this balance, there is a very high risk survey results will not measure what they are supposed to and lack study-to-study consistency." Also, the average response rate to a Web survey is less than 1%, making it even less likely to get a reliable read on the potential of a new product.

Alternative possibilities. Few marketers are able to efficiently ask "What if?" questions concerning variations in a concept's features and benefits. For example, an insurance company considering a concept for a new car insurance product might wonder, "What if we provided preferred access to a car repair shop? What if we take care of the whole registration process for a small fee? For free?"

Ignorance of costs. In our experience, marketing managers seldom know the fixed and variable manufacturing and marketing costs of a new product or service, and they certainly never pass this kind of information along to their researchers. But without knowing costs, a manager cannot estimate profitability.

Limited models. Finally, few research companies offer a valid model of the marketing mix into which they can feed concept scores to predict sales and profitability. Researchers present concept scores to marketers as if they were discrete pieces of information in themselves: "This one got a 33% top two box score, beating the control concept by almost two to one." That's nice, but will it sell? And if it sells, will it be profitable? Blank stares from the researcher.

The Quick Fix

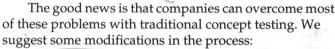

The good news is that companies can overcome most of these problems with traditional concept testing. We suggest some modifications in the process:

Larger samples. Instruct researchers to use a larger, more projectable sample of prospective buyers (300 to 500) in more locations than is traditionally used. These people should be serious respondents, recruited via random-digit dialing and then brought to a central location—not the first warm bodies willing to stand still in a shopping mall.

Balance phone and Web data collection. Mail a concept description and scoring scale to a respondent before the phone call. Do some one-on-one interviews to balance the results from a Web survey. Check to make sure the Internet research firm uses a panel.

Full descriptions. Expose the sample to the big idea—a full description of the concept, complete with the name, positioning, packaging, features, and price (in our experience, we've consistently been surprised by how many concept tests ignore price). Present the concept in its competitive context, that is, with competing products sold in the market at their actual prices. The more a test mirrors reality, the more accurate the forecast. Even so, most concept testing ignores the competitive frame.

Measure purchase probability. Have consumers rate the concept in terms of purchase probability using a scale superior to traditional 3-, 5-, or 7-point purchase intention scales for predicting likely market response. We've discovered through extensive experimentation that an 11-point scale better predicts real world behavior, especially for mixed and high-involvement decisions.

Yet even this 11-point scale overstates the actual purchasing that takes place. People don't do exactly what they say. For one thing, the research environment assumes 100% awareness and 100% distribution—in other words, all are aware of it and able to find it easily—

which never happens in the real world. Even taking this into consideration, the overstatement problem remains.

We have closely examined the relationship between people's reports on the 11-point scale and actual buyer behavior (among people who were aware of the product or service and for whom it was available to be purchased) for numerous companies in consumer and B2B categories. As Exhibit 2 indicates, usually no more than 75% of the people who claim they definitely will buy actually do so. This figure declines as self-reported purchase probability declines, but the ratio is not constant. This leads to a set of adjustments for each level of self-report, which converts questionnaire ratings into estimates of likely behavior.

Usually no more than 75% of the people who claim they definitely will buy actually do so.

These adjustments, as an aside, vary by the consumer's (or industrial buyer's) level of "involvement" in a category. The higher their involvement, the more faith we can have in what people say and the lower the need for overstatement adjustment. Needless to say, by taking purchase probabilities and involvement into account, it's possible to produce a reasonably valid estimate of actual sales (i.e., the percentage of consumers who would buy the product at least once).

While the traditional methods of concept testing remain the most common way to investigate new product concepts, traditional methods do not ipso facto represent the best approach. The goal of traditional tests is to find the concept that produces the highest level of buyer appeal, but they often fail to address what a company really needs. Computer-aided new product/service design is an alternative to traditional methods. It begins with a modified multiple trade-off analysis using either conjoint measurement or choice modeling methodologies. These approaches offer several advanced features: they predict real-world behavior and sales for a constellation of alternative concepts; use a nonlinear optimization algorithm to identify the most profitable concepts; allow the marketer to play out "what if" scenarios; and offer targeting and positioning guidance.

The Trouble With Test Markets

Once the concept is selected, perfected, and ready to go, the next step for most marketers is a test market, essentially a small-scale dry run with the new product or service and its marketing campaign. But like traditional concept testing methods, traditional test markets are also fraught with problems. Often the company selects a test market because it's easy to manage or because a retailer in the market will cooperate. It often fails to select the market that best represents the target the company wants to reach.

■ Exhibit 2
Self-reported probability and actual behavior

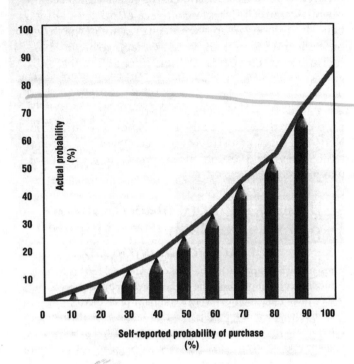

Self-reported probability of purchase (%)

Traditional test markets have four major defects. First of all, they're expensive. They can cost as little as $3 million, but typically run more. Costs include the research, the media, and the effort throughout the organization to control and check the test. Second, they take a long time. Waiting a year, 18 months, or two years for results is simply not feasible in today's competitive environment.

A third problem with traditional test markets is that competitors often have the opportunity to sabotage results. Even modest efforts by competitors can spoil the company's ability to read the test market outcome. Competitors have undermined tests by having their salespeople pull the new products off retail shelves, turn them sideways, or move them to other shelves where shoppers will not notice them. Meanwhile, these same competitors scramble to devise a similar new product or service to counter a national introduction.

Finally, traditional test markets usually don't tell marketers what they need to know. While a product failing in a test market is not as painful as one failing in a national rollout, it's often difficult to determine why it failed. Was it a problem with the way the company executed the idea or was the idea simply too small? Was the problem with the marketing program or with the competitive response? What part of the marketing program wasn't working? Could the company have done something to turn a modest failure into a roaring success? Conversely, if the test was successful, is there anything that could have made the product or service even more profitable?

A simulated test market (STM) is both an alternative and a complement to traditional methods. Today's better simulated test marketing systems capture every important component in the marketing mix and assess the effect of any plan on product awareness, trial, repeat rates, market share, profitability, and more. These STMs test any plan the marketer wants to consider—even a competitor's. The marketer enters plan details into a PC program, and the model forecasts what is likely to occur month by month in the real world.

Do Something Different

If all you do is what you've done, then all you'll get is what you've got. Most companies haven't gotten much in terms of new product/service success in the past two decades. Companies need to do something different.

A growing number of companies embrace the sentiments of Harvard economists John McArthur and Jeffrey Sachs, who said, "Innovation is no mere vanity plate on the nation's economic engine. It trumps capital accumulation and allocation of resources as the most important contributor to growth." The time is now for companies to take advantage of computer-aided design technologies and simulated test marketing to improve the performance of marketing programs for new products and services. The technologies can help marketers find the best product and service concept and discover the marketing plan, within or without a given budget, that will stimulate demand and grow the bottom line.

About the Authors

Kevin J. Clancy is chairman and CEO and **Peter C. Krieg** is president and COO of Copernicus Marketing Consulting and Research. They are currently working on a new book on technologies for improving new product/service success rates. Clancy may be reached at kclancy@copernicusmarketing.com and Krieg may be reached at pkrieg@copernicusmarketing.com.

From *Marketing Management*, March/April 2003, pp. 14-20. © 2003 by the American Marketing Association. Reprinted by permission.

A BEGINNER'S GUIDE TO
Demographics

Who are your customers?
Where do they live?
How many are there?

Answering these and similar questions can help you sharpen your marketing strategy.

BERNA MILLER
WITH AN INTRODUCTION BY PETER FRANCESE

Whatever you sell, customer demographics are important to your business. Demographics can tell you who your current and potential customers are, where they are, and how many are likely to buy what you are selling. Demographic analysis helps you serve your customers better by adjusting to their changing needs. This article provides a review of the basic concepts used in such analysis.

The most successful use of demographic analysis identifies those population or household characteristics that most accurately differentiate potential customers from those not likely to buy. The second part of using demographics is finding those geographic areas with the highest concentrations of potential customers. Once potential customers are described and located, and their purchase behavior analyzed, the next step is to determine their media preferences in order to find the most efficient way to reach them with an advertising message.

It wasn't always this complicated. Until fairly recently everyone practiced mass marketing, dispersing one message via media—newspapers, radio, broadcast television—that presumably reached everyone. No special effort was made to ensure that the message would appeal to (or even reach) the most likely customers.

The result: A great deal of money was spent pitching products and services to sections of the audience who didn't want or need them. In buying a prime-time spot for its television ads, a motorcycle company would be paying to
(continued)

The most important marketing question a business faces is: "Who are my customers?" And the first **demographic*** question a business must ask about its product or service is whether it is to be sold to an individual or a **household**. Refrigerators, for example, are household products; and most households have only one or two refrigerators. On the other hand, everyone within the household has their own toothbrush and dozens of other personal-care products.

There are more than 261 million individuals in the United States and nearly 100 million households. Those classified as "**family** households" include married couples with **children** (26 percent), married couples without children (29 percent), single parents living with their children (9 percent), and brothers and sisters or other related family members who live together (7 percent). "**Nonfamily** households" include people who live alone (24 percent) and cohabiting couples and other unrelated roommates (5 percent).

Different types of households are more prevalent among certain age groups. For instance, the majority of women who live alone are over age 65, while the majority of men who live alone are under age 45. Household types differ between **generations** as well. Younger people today are much more likely to live in the other type of nonfamily household because they are moving out of their parents' *reach the housebound elderly as well as the young adults for whom their product was designed. A swimsuit manufacturer that ran an ad in a national magazine would pay a premium to reach the inhabitants of Nome, Alaska, as well as Floridians. Gradually it was recognized that the "shotgun" approach is not an efficient use of marketing dollars.*

Mass marketing has since given way to target marketing, whose guiding principle is Know Thy Customers. How old are they? Where do they live? What are their interests, concerns, and aspirations? Knowing the answers to questions like these gives you insight into the marketing approaches most likely to appeal to your customers—and whether you're even shooting for the right customers in the first place! (Sometimes there is more than one set of customers: for example, research shows that low-fat frozen dinners are purchased by young women wishing to stay slim and by much older retired people who just want a light meal.)

Let's say that you find out that your customers are predominantly college graduates, and that you know in which zip codes your existing customers reside. How do you use this information?

The first step is to obtain a tabulation of the number of college graduates by zip code, which is available through an information provider (see the American Demographics Directory of Marketing Information Companies for names and numbers) or the Census Bureau. Then, for any metropolitan area that you serve, establish the percent of all college graduates in the metropolitan area who reside in each zip code. Calculate the percent of existing customers who reside in each zip code. By dividing the percent of college graduates in zip 12345 by percent of customers (and multiplying by 100), we get an index of penetration for each zip code. If the index of penetration is 100 or above, the market is being adequately served. If it is below 100, there is more potential, which can be realized through direct mail to those specific zip codes.

This analysis can be done using any group of geographic areas that sum to a total market area, such as counties within a state or metropolitan areas within a region. The object is to compare the percent of customers who should be coming from each sub-market area against the percent who are actually coming from there. The resulting indexes essentially measure marketing performance zip by zip or county by county.

Not so long ago, demographic information came printed on reams of paper or rolls of computer tape. With the tremendous advances in technology in recent years, it is now readily available on your personal computer. Demographic statistics can be obtained on CD-ROM or via the Internet, complete with software for accessing the data.

Information providers can analyze these data for you, as well as provide customized data, such as how many pairs of shoes people own and how often they shop for new ones. Census demographics can't tell you how many times a week people use floor cleaners, but it does have basic demographic characteristics that will help determine who your market is, how many of them there are, and where they live. Information providers can help you take these data and merge them with customer data to form a clearer picture of your market and its potential.

—Peter Francese

Peter Francese is founding president of American Demographics Inc., and publisher of American Demographics *and* Marketing Tools *magazines.*

homes before marriage and living with friends or lovers; such living arrangements being more acceptable today, younger people are much more likely than earlier generations to do so.

The U.S. can no longer be effectively treated as a mass market, because Americans and their lifestyles have changed dramatically.

Everyone in the United States except for the homeless lives in either a household or **group quarters**. Many businesses ignore group-quarter populations, reasoning that nursing-home patients and prison inmates probably are not doing much shopping. However, if your market is computers, beer, pizza, or any number of products that appeal to young adults or military personnel, you cannot afford to overlook these populations. This is especially important when marketing a product in a smaller area where a college or military base is present. People who live in these situations may have different wants and needs from those who live in households; in addition, the area may have a much higher rate of population turnover than other **places** do.

Refining Your Customer's Profile

Once you have determined whether you want to market to households or people, the next step is to find out which segment of households or of the population would be most likely to want your product or service. Demographics allow you to refine your conception of who your market is, who it can or should be, and how it is likely to change over time. People have different needs at different ages and lifestages, and you need to factor that into your customer profile. In addition, there are both primary and secondary markets. For instance, if you were marketing baby food, you would first target married couples with young children and single parents, and then possibly grandparents.

This level of refinement was made necessary by the massive social, economic, and technological changes of the past three decades. The United States can no longer be effectively treated as a mass market, because the people who live here and their lifestyles have changed dramatically. Due to increasing divorce rates, increasing cohabitation, rising number of nonmarital births, and increased female participation in the labor force, married couples with one earner make up only 15 percent of all households. Dual-earner households have become much more common—the additional income is often necessary for the family to pay their bills. Thus, the stereotypical family of the 1950s has been replaced by two harried, working parents with much less time available.

At the same time, there has been an explosion in the number of products available to the American public, each of which, either by design or default, tends to appeal to the very different segments of the population.

Another important trend is the increasing diversity of that population. The United States has always been an immigrant nation. However, large numbers of immigrants from Latin America and Asia have increased the proportion of minorities in the country to one in four, up from one in five in 1980.

This increasing diversity is particularly noticeable in the children's market. Minorities are overrepresented in the younger age brackets due to the higher fertility and the younger population structure of these recent immigrants. The result: one in three children in the United States is black, **Hispanic**, or Asian. Nearly all of today's children grow up in a world of divorce and working mothers. Many are doing the family shopping and have tremendous influence over household purchases. In addition, they may simply know more than their elders about products involving new technology, such as computers.

The recent influx of Hispanics, who may be of any **race**, has important implications for understanding the demographic data you have on your customers. "Hispanic" is an ethnicity, not a race; a person who describes himself as Hispanic must also choose a racial designation: white, black, Asian/Pacific Islander, American Indian/Eskimo/Aleut, or "other." Confusion on this score… can result in accidentally counting Hispanics twice, in which case the numbers won't add up.

Income and education are two other important demographic factors to consider when refining your customer profile. As a general rule, income increases with age, as people get promoted and reach their peak earning years. Married couples today often have the higher incomes because they may have two earners. Married couples may also have greater need for products and services, because they are most likely to have children and be homeowners.

Income is reported in several different ways, and each method means something very different in terms of consumer behavior. Earnings, interest, dividends, royalties, social security payments, and public assistance dollars received before taxes and union dues are subtracted are defined in the **census** as money income. **Personal** income, as reported by the Bureau of Economic Analysis, is money income plus certain noncash benefits (such as food stamps and subsidized housing). **Disposable** income is the money available after taxes, while **discretionary** income is the money available after taxes and necessities (food, shelter, clothing) have been paid for.

All of these are useful measures as long as their differences are fully understood. For example, discretionary income of $30,000 has much more potential for businesses than does a personal income of $30,000. But none of these statistics measures wealth, which includes property owned. Ignoring wealth may provide a skewed picture: a 70-year-old woman with a personal income of $15,000 who must pay rent is much less able to afford additional items than a woman of the same age and income who owns a fully paid-for house, which she could sell if she needed to.

Income can be reported for people or households; household income is the most commonly used measure in business demographics since it provides the best picture of the overall situation of everyone in the household. Income is often reported as **mean income**. But mean income can be distorted by very large or small incomes, called "outliers," which are very different from most of the other values. Thus multimillionaires skew the mean income upward, overestimating the income of the population in question. Using a measure called **median** income can avoid this bias and is more widely used as a measure of income in demographics. The mean income of all United States households is $41,000. The median income is $31,200—almost $10,000 lower than the mean.

It is important to not only identify today's customers, but to predict how their wants and needs will change tomorrow.

Education is another very important and commonly used demographic characteristic—in today's increasingly technological and highly skilled economy, education makes a big difference in occupation and thus in earning power. Education is most often measured as number of years of schooling or in terms of level of education completed. Today's adults are better educated than ever before; however, only one in four adults older than age 24 has a college degree or higher. Another 23 percent have attended college. Eight in ten American adults have a high school diploma. One reason for the low percentages of college graduates is that many older people did not attend college. Therefore, we should expect to see the percentage of college graduates and attendees increase substantially in the future.

College-educated people are one of the most lucrative markets, but you may have to work extra hard to get and keep them as customers. They are more open to technology and innovation, but they are also less brand loyal, since they are more able financially to take risks. They are more likely to read and less likely to watch television than those without any college education. They like to make informed decisions about purchases; hence, they are the most likely group to request product information.

Segmenting the Market

All of these demographic data are available in easy-to-understand packages called **cluster systems** (also known as **geodemographic** segmentation systems), which are available from information providers. Cluster systems take many demographic variables and create profiles of different individual or household characteristics, purchase behaviors, and media preferences. Most cluster systems have catchy, descriptive names, such as "Town and Gown" or "Blue Blood Estates," making it easier to identify the groups most likely to be interested in what you have to sell.

Cluster systems are especially powerful when used in conjunction with business mapping. Sophisticated mapping software programs easily link demographics to any level of geography (a process called geocoding). Some software can pinpoint specific households within neighborhoods from your customer data and then create schematic maps of neighborhoods by cluster concentrations. Geocoding can be done for **block group,** counties, zip codes, or any other market area. Businesses can integrate knowledge of customer addresses and purchase decisions with basic demographic data based on geography and come up with a clearer, more informative picture of customers—and where they can be found.

Cluster analysis is sometimes confused with **psychographics**, but the two are very different. Cluster systems are based on purchase decisions and demographics that cover physical characteristics like age, sex, income, and education. Psychographics measure motivations, attitudes, **lifestyles**, and feelings, such as openness to technology or reluctance to try new products. Both demographics and psychographics need to be taken into account.

Looking to the Future

It is not only important to identify who your customers are and how many of them there are today, but how many of them there will be in five or ten years, and whether their wants and needs will change.

Projections of population or households by **marital status**, age, or income can be very useful in determining the potential of a market a few years down the road. All projections start with the assumption that the projected population will equal the current population plus births minus deaths and plus net **migration**. For example, let's take projections at the household level. New household configurations occur through in-migration of residents or through the formation of a household due to the separation of an already existing household (such as when a child moves out of a parent's home or a divorce occurs). Household losses occur when existing households are combined due to marriage, when a child moves back home, etc., or when the residents in a household move away from the area (out-migration).

Projections can vary greatly, so it is important to ask about the methodology and assumptions behind them and make sure you fully understand why these assumptions were made. Accurate demographic data can be very valuable, but data that are flawed or biased can be seriously misleading.

In general, the future population of a larger area of geography, such as the United States or a particular state, is much easier to **estimate** accurately than populations for small areas, such as neighborhoods, which often experience greater population fluctuations. In addition, the shorter the time period involved, the more accurate the projections are likely to be, because there's less time for dramatic changes to take place. There will be factors in 15 years that we cannot begin to include in our assumptions, because they do not exist yet.

You can have more confidence in your educated guesses about the future if you know a little about past population trends in the United States, especially the **baby boom** and **baby bust** cycle. It is also important to understand the difference between a generation and a **cohort**.

The events for which generations are named occur when their members are too young to remember much about them (i.e., the Depression generation includes people born during the 1930s). That's why cohort is often the more useful classification for marketers; it provides insight into events that occurred during the entire lifetimes of the people in question.

To illustrate, let's look at the baby boomers, who were born between 1946 and 1965. In their youth, they experienced a growing economy, but they also dealt with competition and crowding in schools and jobs due to the sheer number of cohort members. Their lives were shaped by events like the civil rights movement, the Vietnam conflict, the women's movement, and Watergate. Baby boomers have seen increasing diversity and technology. They're living longer, healthier lives than the cohorts that came before them.

All these factors make baby boomers very different from 32-to-51-year-olds of 20 years ago. Traditional ideas concerning the preferences of 50-year-olds versus 30-year-olds are no longer accurate; age-old adages such as "coffee consumption increases with age, and young people drink cola" are no longer as valid as they once were—people who grew up on cola often continue to drink it. The same is true for ethnic foods and a host of other products.

The received wisdom will have to change constantly to reflect new sets of preferences and life experiences. For example, baby boomers remember when the idea of careers for women was considered pretty radical. Not so for younger Generation X women; most of them work as a matter of course, just like their own mothers. As a result, ideas about marriage, family, and jobs are changing and will continue to do so.

If you are marketing a product to a certain age range, be aware that the people who will be in that range in five or ten years will not be the same as the ones who are there now. A strategy that has worked for years may need to be rethought as one cohort leaves an age range and another takes its place.

Therein lies the challenge in contemporary marketing: the fact that it is no longer advisable to treat a market as an undifferentiated mass of people with similar fixed tastes, in-

Define Your Terms

A GLOSSARY OF DEMOGRAPHIC WORDS AND PHRASES

Demographic terms consist of fairly common words and phrases, but each one has a highly specific meaning. Study them carefully to ensure that when you discuss demographics with someone, you're both talking about the same thing.

demography: derived from two Greek words meaning "description of" and "people," coined by the French political economist Achille Guillard in 1855. Sometimes a distinction is drawn between "pure" demography (the study of vital statistics and population change) and "social" demography, which gets into socioeconomic characteristics. Business demography is also often understood to include consumer attitudes and behavior.

POPULATION COMPONENTS

The three things that add to or subtract from population are:

• **fertility:** having to do with births. There are several measures of fertility, mostly different kinds of annual rates using different base populations.

• **mortality:** otherwise known as death. There are different death rates, as there are for births.

• **migration:** the movement of people into or out of a defined region, like a state. It typically refers only to moves that cross county lines.

A related term is **mobility**, meaning change of residence. This usually refers to how many people move any distance in a given period of time, even if they just move across town.

HOUSEHOLDS/FAMILIES/ MARITAL STATUS

household: one or more people who occupy a housing unit, as opposed to group quarters (dorms, hospitals, prisons, military barracks, etc.). The vast majority of Americans live in households.

householder: formerly called "head of household," the householder is the one adult per household designated as the reference person for a variety of characteristics. An important thing to check when looking at demographics of households (such as age or income) is to see whether the information pertains to the householder or to the entire household. *Household composition is determined by the relationship of the other people in the household to the householder.*

family: a household consisting of two or more people in which at least one person is related to the householder by blood, marriage, or adoption. The major types of families are **married** couples (these may be male- or female-headed and with or without children), and **families without a spouse present**, which may also be headed by a man or a woman. The latter category includes single parents as well as other combinations of relatives, such as siblings living together or grandparents and grandchildren. Note that seemingly single parents may live with a partner or other adult outside of marriage.

nonfamily: households consisting of persons living alone, or multiple-person households in which no one is related to the householder, although they may be related to each other. This includes unmarried and gay couples, as well as roommates, boarders, etc.

children: The United States Census Bureau makes a distinction between the householder's own children under age 18 (including adopted and stepchildren), and other related children, such as grandchildren or children aged 18 and older. Other surveys may define children differently.

marital status: this is an individual characteristic, usually measured for people aged 15 and older. The four main categories are never married; married; divorced; and widowed. The term "single" usually refers to a person who has never married, but may include others not currently married. Likewise, the term "ever-married" also includes widowed and divorced people. "Married" includes spouse present and spouse absent. "Spouse absent" includes couples who are separated or not living together because of military service.

RACE/ETHNICITY

race: white, black, Asian and Pacific Islander, and native American (includes American Indians, Eskimos, and Aleutian Islanders). That's it. The government does not use the term African American, but many others do.

Hispanics: the only ethnic origin category in current use. NOT A RACE. Most Hispanics are actually white. Used to be called Spanish Origin. The term Latino is becoming popular, but is currently not used by the government. It is becoming more common to separate out Hispanics from race categories and talk about non-Hispanic whites, blacks, etc. This way, the numbers add up to 100 percent.

Note: The Office of Management and Budget is considering revamping the racial categories used in federal data collection, including the addition of a mixed-race group. This may happen in time for use in the 2000 census.

GENERATIONS/COHORTS

cohort: a group of people who share an event, such as being born in the same year, and therefore share a common culture and history. The most commonly used cohorts are birth cohorts, although there are also marriage cohorts, etc.

generations: more loosely defined than cohorts, typically refers to people born during a certain period of time. These examples are not definitive:

• **GI Generation:** born in the 1910s and 1920s, served in WWII. Today's elderly.
• **Depression:** born in the 1930s. Boomers' parents. Now aged 56 to 65.
• **War Babies:** born during WWII, now aged 50 to 55. Sometimes lumped with the Depression group as the "silent generation."
• **Baby Boom:** born between 1946 and 1964, now aged 31 to 49. Further introductions are probably unnecessary.
• **Baby Bust:** born 1965 to 1976. Today's twentysomethings, although the oldest turned 30 this year. Also called **Generation X**.
• **Baby Boomlet:** or Echo Boom. Born 1977 to 1994. Today's children and teens.

EDUCATION

• **attainment:** completed education level, typically measured for adults

(continued)

aged 25 and older because it used to be the case that virtually everyone was finished with school by then. This is less true today, with one-third of all college students over age 25. Until 1990, attainment was measured by years completed rather than actual degrees earned. The new categories include no high school, some high school but no diploma, high school graduate, some college but no degree, associate's degree, and other types of college degrees.

INCOME

Income can be measured for households, persons, or even geographic areas. When you look at income figures, make sure you know which kind is being referred to!

disposable: after-tax (net) income. In other words, all the money people have at their disposal to spend, even if most of it goes for things we have little choice about, like food, electric bills, and kids' braces.

discretionary: income left over after necessities are covered. This is extremely tough to measure: Who's to say what's necessary for someone else? It's generally accepted that very few of the poorest households have any discretionary income at all, but also that the level of necessary expenses rises with income.

personal and **per capita:** aggregate measures for geographic areas such as states and counties. Personal income is total income for all people in an area, and per capita divides it equally by total population, regardless of age or labor force status.

mean income: the average of all income in the population being studied.

median income: the midway point, at which half of the people being studied have higher incomes and half have lower incomes.

ESTIMATES/PROJECTIONS

census: complete count of a population.

survey: the process of collecting data from a sample, hopefully representative of the general population or the population of interest.

estimate: calculation of current or historic number for which no census or survey data are available. Usually based on what's known to have happened.

projection: calculation of future population or characteristic, based on assumptions of what might happen—a "what if" scenario. Two related terms are **prediction** and **forecast**. Both refer to a "most likely" projection—what the forecaster feels may actually happen.

MEDIA/MARKETING TERMS

The following are not defined by the government, so there are no real standards.

mature: an age segment, usually defined as those 50- or 55-plus, although some go so far as to include those in their late 40s. This is often seen as an affluent and active group, but it actually consists of several age segments with vastly diverse economic and health status. Related terms include:

- **elderly:** usually 65 and older, although sometimes narrowed down to very old (85 and older).
- **retired:** not necessarily defined by age; although most retirees are older people, not all older people are retired.

middle class: This is one of the most widely used demographic terms. it is also perhaps one of the most statistically elusive: If you ask the general public, the vast majority will claim to be middle class. It might be most sensible to start with the midpoint—that is, median income ($31,200 for households in 1993)—and create a range surrounding it (e.g., within $10,000 of the median) until you come up with a group of households that says "middle class" to you.

affluent: most researchers used to consider households with annual incomes of $50,000 or more as affluent, although $60,000 and $75,000 thresholds are becoming more popular. Upper-income households are sometimes defined more broadly as those with incomes of $35,000 or more. As of the mid-1990s, this merely means they are not lower income, suggesting that there is no middle class.

lifestyles/psychographics: these terms are somewhat interchangeable, but **psychographics** usually refers to a formal classification system such as SRI's VALS (Values and Lifestyles) that categorizes people into specific types (Achievers, Belongers, etc.). **Lifestyle** is a vaguer term, and many 'lifestyle' types or segments have been defined in various market studies. Generally speaking, these systems organize people according to their attitudes or consumer behavior, such as their involvement with and spending on golf. These data may seem soft, but they often use statistical measures such as factor analysis to derive the segments.

cluster systems/geodemographic segmentation: developed by data companies to create meaningful segments based on residence, and the assumption that people will live in areas where there are a lot of other people just like them. This geographic element is one thing that distinguishes clusters from psychographic segments. Another difference is that cluster categories are virtually always based on socioeconomic and consumer data rather than attitudinal information. Each system has at least several dozen clusters. The four major cluster systems are: Claritas's PRIZM, National Decision Systems' MicroVision, CACI's ACORN, and Strategic Mapping's ClusterPlus 2000.

GEOGRAPHIC TERMS

Census geography: areas defined by the government.

- **regions:** Northeast, Midwest, South, and West.
- **divisions:** there are nine Census Statistical Areas: Pacific, Mountain, West North Central, East North Central, West South Central, East South Central, New England, Middle Atlantic, and South Atlantic.
- **states:** note: data about states often include the District of Columbia for a total of 51. Congressional district: subdivision of a state created solely for Congressional representation; not considered a governmental area by the Census Bureau.
- **enumeration district:** census area with an average of 500 inhabitants, used in nonmetropolitan areas.
- **counties:** the U.S. had over 3,000 counties as of 1990.
- **places:** these include cities, towns, villages, and other municipal areas.
- **tracts:** these are subcounty areas designed to contain a roughly homogeneous population ranging from 2,500 to 8,000.
- **blocks** and **block groups:** blocks are what they sound like: an administrative area generally equivalent to a city block and the smallest unit of geography for which census data are published. Block groups are groups of blocks with average populations of 1,000 to 1,200 people; they are approximately equal to a neighborhood.

(continued)

- **metropolitan areas:** these are defined by the Office of Management and Budget, and are built at the county level. Each consists of at least one central city of the appropriate size (usually at least 50,000), its surrounding "suburban" territory within the same county, and any adjacent counties with strong economic ties to the city. Metros may have one or more central cities and/or counties. Stand-alone metros are called **MSAs** (Metropolitan Statisical Areas). Metros that are right next to each other are called **PMSAs** (Primary MSAs), and the larger areas that they make up are called **CMSAs** (Consolidated MSAs). The U.S. currently has over 300 metros (depending on how you count PMSAs and CMSAs) that include about three-fourths of the nation's population.
- **NECMA**s are New England Metropolitan Areas and are similar to MSAs.
- **central city:** largest city in the MSA and other cities of central character to an MSA.

zip code: subdivision of an area for purposes of delivering mail; not a census area.

Two related terms are **urban** and **rural** The essential difference between "metropolitan" and "urban" is that metros are defined at the county level, while urbanized areas are more narrowly defined by density. An **urban area** has 25,000 or more inhabitants, with urbanized zones around the central city comprising 50,000 or more inhabitants. This means that the outlying portions of counties in many metropolitan areas are considered rural. Oddly enough, suburbs are commonly defined as the portions of metro areas outside of central cities and have nothing to do with the urban/rural classification system.

—*Diane Crispell*

Diane Crispell is executive editor of American Demographics *magazine, and author of* The Insider's Guide to Demographic Know-How.

terest, and needs. In the age of target marketing, it is imperative to know who the customers are and how to reach them. When the customer's needs change, it's essential to know that, too, so you can adjust your marketing efforts accordingly. A working knowledge of demographics will keep you on top of the situation. It's a piece of marketing know-how that no one can afford to ignore.

*For definitions for this and other terms in **bold-faced type**, see the [article] glossary.

Berna Miller is a contributor to American Demographics *magazine.*

Handwritten notes in top margin:
Cars - "almost rich"
$4 Starbucks
$6 Tuscan sandwich (Panera)

"democratization of luxury"

Viking Range Corp.
Jaguar → X-type sedan
Mercedes

Defining Luxury:

OH, THE GOOD LIFE

Despite the recession, Americans' income has shown some remarkable resilience. A larger proportion of Americans today have higher earnings than in years past. Now, more than ever, understanding how different demographic groups define "luxury" is paramount to selling them a piece of the good life.

BY REBECCA GARDYN

In September, the U.S. Census Bureau announced that median household income dipped slightly in 2001—the first decline since 1991. Amid such gloomy reports, however, there was some good news: The number of households with an annual income of $100,000 or more has been growing steadily during the past decade. Today, there are 15.1 million U.S. households that earn $100,000 or more, up from 8.7 million in 1990. What's more, the upper middle class (defined as those who earn $75,000 to $99,999) numbers 11.8 million households today, up from 8.9 million in 1990.

While it's true that the recession has cut into income levels this past year, it's also true that a larger proportion of Americans today have higher incomes than in years past. In fact, the percentage of households with incomes of $100,000 or more has grown to 14 percent in 2001 from 9 percent in 1990. That growth has not gone unnoticed by luxury marketers. While the primary purchasers of traditional luxury goods (think Gucci) and services (think at-home seaweed wrap) are highly affluent Americans (those making $200,000 or more), businesses have begun to infuse elements of luxury in even the most ordinary of categories (think $4 Starbucks latte).

In fact, over the past decade, brands that were once available exclusively to the wealthiest among us have created more affordable product extensions, giving a far broader range of consumers a taste of the good life. Jaguar, for instance, recently launched its X-type sedan, which starts at $30,000 and is meant for the "almost rich" consumer who aspires to live in luxury. Tiffany promotes $50 sterling silver key chains in addition to its $100,000 diamond engagement rings.

Some call the increasing availability of luxury products and services at lower price points—and Americans' increasing ability to purchase those products—the "democratization of luxury." Upscale kitchen appliance company Viking Range Corporation, based in Greenwood, Miss., for example, has expanded its product line over the past decade to include everything from cookware to cutlery at various prices, in an effort to interest more of these almost-rich consumers in the luxury lifestyle, says Terry Tanner, vice president and media director at The Ramey Agency in Ridgeland, Miss., which handles the Viking account. "A consumer may not be able to afford a Viking range [about $8,000], but she can afford a carving knife," says Tanner. "Even if they aren't super rich, many consumers aspire to be, and we want to provide an opportunity for everyone with the desire to live the luxury lifestyle to get a taste of it through using our products."

With more money in more people's hands, luxury companies are wise to reach out to the "mass affluent," upper-middle-class and middle-class targets, says Michael J. Silverstein, head of the worldwide consumer and retail group at the Boston Consulting Group in Chicago. Despite today's recession—and perhaps even because of it—consumers are looking for more affordable luxuries, or what Silverstein calls "new luxury" products.

"New luxury goods range in price from a $6 Tuscan chicken sandwich at Panera to a $26,000 Mercedes CLK," he says. "What they have in common is that they enable less affluent consumers to trade up to higher levels of quality, taste and aspiration. These are the luxuries that continue to sell even when the economy is shaky, because they often meet very powerful emotional needs."

WHAT'S IT TO YOU?

White consumers are more likely to define "luxury" as something "prestigious" or "exclusive" than are blacks or Hispanics (53 percent, compared with 43 percent and 41 percent, respectively). On the other hand, minorities are almost twice as likely as whites to define luxury as "trendy" or "fashionable" (30 percent of blacks and 33 percent of Hispanics, compared with 18 percent of whites).

WHICH OF THE FOLLOWING ADJECTIVES DO YOU ASSOCIATE WITH THE TERM "LUXURY"?

	MEN	WOMEN	18–34	35–54	55+	BLACK	HISPANIC	WHITE
Glamourous/Classic/Elegant	67%	73%	72%	66%	74%	69%	64%	72%
Comforting/Relaxing/Pampering	55%	54%	52%	56%	54%	38%	51%	58%
Status symbol/Exclusive/Prestigious	51%	51%	39%	50%	57%	43%	41%	53%
Wasteful/Unnecessary/Extravagant	27%	19%	19%	28%	19%	32%	14%	23%
Trendy/Fashionable/"In"	21%	23%	26%	19%	24%	30%	33%	18%
Flashy/Gaudy/Elitist	28%	12%	37%	22%	10%	**	31%	16%
Practical/Quality/Enduring	14%	18%	**	15%	20%	**	**	18%

**Sample size too small

Note: Columns do not sum to 100 percent because more than one answer was allowed.

Source: *American Demographics*/E-Poll

NOT ONLY IS THE NUMBER OF PEOPLE WITH THE MEANS FOR MAKING LUXURY PURCHASES TODAY MUCH LARGER, IT IS A MORE DEMOGRAPHICALLY VARIED GROUP.

In fact, a new attitude toward luxury—one that values substance over style and quality over conspicuous consumption—seems to have intensified over the past year, as the recession and uncertainty about the attacks on Sept. 11 have caused consumers to think more carefully about where they spend their dollars. Whether because of tight budgets or guilt about extravagant spending, people are feeling they have to rationalize their purchasing even more today. "In the past, many people would buy according to status and brand, but now it's more about relevancy," says Brenda G. Saget, publisher of the upscale shelter magazine *House & Garden*. "Marketers today need to explain better what exactly makes their products so wonderful and what benefits having them will bring to a person's life."

Understanding what consumers are looking for from luxury products and services is increasingly important today. "In the late 1990s, when the luxury sector was strong and sales were high, things were pretty steady. You could do consumer research yearly and see very little change," says Christopher Owens, account planning director for the Dallas-based ad agency The Richards Group, whose accounts include Sub-Zero Freezer Company and The Home Depot Expo Design Center.

"Today, between stock market plunges and terrorist threats, we're seeing week-to-week shifts in attitudes and behaviors,"

says Owens. "It has become so much more important to know your customer."

Indeed, demographic and psychographic factors as well as life stage all play a part in the type of "luxury consumer" businesses attract these days. Not only is the number of people with the means for making luxury purchases today much larger, it is a much more demographically varied group than ever before. For instance, the percentage of minority households with $100,000 or more in annual income increased to 16 percent in 2001, from 11 percent in 1990. In a post-Sept. 11 climate of uncertainty, where consumer attitudes shift as quickly as the headlines, it's critical for businesses to know how different consumers define "luxury" and the value propositions that motivate each consumer to purchase such products and services.

Pam Danziger, president of Unity Marketing in Stevens, Pa., recently conducted a series of focus groups among luxury purchasers for *House & Garden* magazine and was surprised to find how much the definition of luxury varied among different consumers. "Going into this, I really thought luxury purchasing was all about brand names, but many consumers don't even recognize brands," she says. "Luxury today is really about the ability to pursue one's own passions, and those passions are very different for everyone."

GENERATION $

In September, *American Demographics* commissioned an exclusive survey to uncover some of these passions and motivations. Encino, Calif.-based online research firm E-Poll conducted the survey among a nationally representative sample of 876 adults. The findings: There are significant differences in consumers' definition of luxury by gender, race and age. For instance, and contrary to popular belief, women are actually less brand conscious than their male counterparts: while 39 percent

Shopping Attitudes by Life Stage

Marketing luxury is not necessarily about marketing to the affluent but about marketing to those most predisposed to buying luxury products.

In addition to demographics and psychographics, businesses must think about their consumers' life stage when developing marketing strategies. For instance, it isn't enough to target "single women," because there are at least five different types of single women. As the chart below shows, a savvy career woman like "Elizabeth," and an upscale mature woman like "Virginia," both have quite a bit of money to spend, but they have very different attitudes toward spending. They may both be a good customer for certain luxury goods, but the sales pitch necessarily must differ to resonate with each. The chart below illustrates the subtle differences in shopping attitudes across five types of single-female-headed households. For this analysis, New York City-based Simmons Market Research Bureau, using a tool called Cohorts, analyzed data from its spring 2002 survey. We have limited this chart to the 1,310 female households in the "affluent" and "middle class" cohorts, as defined by SMRB.

—RG

SHOPPING ATTITUDES, BY INDEX*:

CONSUMER DESCRIPTION:	ELIZABETH SAVVY CAREER WOMEN	VIRGINIA UPSCALE MATURE WOMEN	ALLISON EDUCATED WORKING WOMEN, NO KIDS	ANDREA SINGLE WORKING MOMS	BERNICE ACTIVE GRANDMAS
MEDIAN AGE	41	60	33	39	61
MEDIAN INCOME	$166,425	$69,605	$49,789	$48,916	$35,431
I am very happy with my life as it is	94	103	87	92	95
I enjoy entertaining people at home	108	112	92	98	103
It is worth paying extra for quality goods	115	127	76	75	79
Home decor is a particular interest	131	139	103	123	123
I can't resist expensive perfume/cologne	172	**	151	218	**
I like other people to think I'm rich	116	98	91	97	83
I tend to spend money without thinking	143	81	121	132	102
Most everything I wear is the highest quality	150	121	86	124	101
I spend more than I can afford for clothes	201	**	164	136	127
I plan far ahead to buy expensive items	93	95	109	100	97
Price isn't most important, what's most important is getting what I want	120	108	84	101	103
Options on a car impress me	111	75	84	121	71
I prefer driving a luxury car	106	95	59	83	70
I try to keep up with changes in style/fashion	152	101	114	125	111

*An index of 100 is the national average. For example, an index of 125 means that members of that consumer group are 25 percent more likely to agree with the statement than the average adult is.

**Sample size too small

Source: Simmons Market Research Bureau

Still in the Lap of Luxury

Research shows that the recession and Sept. 11 have had a negligible impact on spending by the wealthiest Americans.

Money cannot buy happiness, it cannot buy immunity from the emotional effects of the past year, and contrary to popular belief, it cannot buy a bubble in which to live out the current recession. Certainly, luxury spending by the more affluent income groups has been less affected by the economic downturn and by Sept. 11 than that of lower income groups. In fact, according to an August survey of luxury consumers by Unity Marketing for *House & Garden* magazine, 67 percent of consumers with household incomes of $200,000 or more say that their spending on luxury items and services has been only slightly affected or not at all affected by the recession, and 85 percent of them say Sept. 11 has not affected their spending, compared with 60 percent and 77 percent, respectively, of those in the $50,000 to $75,000 income group.

Even so, the attitudes of the wealthy toward shopping and the types of luxury items on which they choose to drop their dough has shifted somewhat. "What is different about today's affluent consumers versus those in the past is that today they have much less debt, so they are more insulated from economic downturns than they were from past recessions," says Henry Welt, president of H. Welt & Co., a consultancy for the luxury market.

Even if some of the most affluent consumers' portfolios have gone down a little, it has not had a heavy impact on their spending, says Welt. "What is different, though, is that affluent people are looking for different kinds of qualities from their products and services. Today they are looking for things that give them privacy, more experiences, more time at home."

American Demographics compared findings from New York City-based Mediamark Research Inc.'s Spring 2001 and 2002 surveys, each of which polled about 4,500 adults with incomes of $100,000 or more. Interestingly, spending by this group on fine jewelry ($1,000 or more in the past year), home computers ($3,000 or more), domestic vacations ($3,000 or more), and foreign vacations ($3,000 or more) remained flat. Yet the percentage of affluent Americans who spent $30,000 or more on their last vehicle actually increased to 14 percent in 2002, from 12 percent in 2001, and the share who spent $5,000 or more on home remodeling also grew, to 10 percent in 2002, from 8 percent in 2001.

But knowing where the money has gone is only half the story. The charts below show that purchasing habits and attitudes have shifted.

—RG

HEY, BIG SPENDER

Almost all Americans with household incomes of $200,000 or more (97 percent) say they have purchased at least one luxury* product in the past year. Of those, 45 percent have bought luxury beauty products.

	HOUSEHOLD INCOME		
	$100K+	$150K+	$200K+
Any luxury product	89%	92%	97%
Any luxury service	85%	87%	93%
Electronics (computers, home entertainment, etc)	56%	59%	66%
Fragrance & beauty products	43%	46%	45%
Apparel & accessories	41%	44%	49%
Furniture & floor coverings	35%	39%	48%
Jewelry & watches	34%	40%	56%
Fabrics, wall & window coverings	28%	33%	45%
Automobiles	27%	35%	44%
Travel	57%	64%	68%
Housecleaning or maid service	37%	45%	63%
Spa, massage, beauty treatments, or cosmetic surgery	31%	37%	**

*The definition of what constituted a "luxury" product or service was self-defined by the respondent. ** Sample size too small

Note: Survey was conducted in August 2002 with 343 adults with incomes of $100k+
Source: Unity Marketing/House & Garden

of men define luxury by the brand name of a product, just 28 percent of women do. Men are also more likely to say they aspire to live a lifestyle of luxury (45 percent) than are women (38 percent). Even so, 51 percent of men, compared with 38 percent of women, say they have recently cut back on luxury purchases.

The reasons for purchasing luxury items also differ slightly by gender. Overwhelmingly, both men and women say their most recent luxury purchase was made because "I wanted to treat myself to something special" (68 percent of men versus 72 percent of women), or because "I liked the quality of the merchandise" (45 percent versus 43 percent, respectively). However, women are much more likely than men to say they bought their last luxury purchase because "It made me feel good about myself" (36 percent versus 23 percent, respectively).

THEN AND NOW

Seventy-four percent of Americans making $250,000 or more say they enjoy entertaining at home, compared with just 57 percent who said so prior to Sept. 11 and the start of the recession.

PERCENTAGE OF AMERICANS WHO AGREE WITH THE FOLLOWING, BY HOUSEHOLD INCOME:	HHI $100K–$150K		HHI $150K–$250K		HHI $250K+	
	PRE-RECESSION/ 9/11	TODAY	PRE-RECESSION/ 9/11	TODAY	PRE-RECESSION/ 9/11	TODAY
I enjoy entertaining people at home	52%	60%	54%	62%	57%	74%
I indulge my kids with little extras	46%	44%	45%	44%	49%	55%
I'm looking for new ideas to improve my home	52%	53%	47%	55%	45%	57%
I often buy clothes I don't need	23%	24%	22%	23%	26%	32%
I can afford to buy expensive designer clothes	18%	20%	22%	26%	32%	41%
I prefer driving a luxury vehicle	28%	28%	34%	36%	44%	47%

Note: "Pre-Recession/ 9/11" data is from SMRB's Fall 2001 Survey (Fielded October 2000–September 2001, with 6,392 adults with HHI $100K+).
"Today" data is from SMRB's Spring 2002 Survey (Fielded January 2002–May 2002, with 2,433 adults with HHI $100K+)

Source: Simmons Market Research Bureau

When it comes to defining luxury goods, race and ethnicity do matter. Black and Hispanic consumers are almost twice as likely to look at a label as are white consumers, according to the *American Demographics*/E-Poll survey. Almost half of blacks (48 percent) and Hispanics (47 percent) say that "luxury is defined by the brand of a product," compared with just 27 percent of white consumers. Interestingly, Hispanics are more likely than either blacks or whites to say that they aspire to live a lifestyle of luxury (49 percent, compared with 37 percent of blacks and 40 percent of whites). They are also the most likely to agree that "luxury means high status" (63 percent, compared with 49 percent of blacks and 47 percent of whites).

A consumer's age also influences how he or she defines luxury. Older consumers (here defined as those age 55 and older) are the biggest fans of luxury products. Fully 74 percent of them say they associate "luxury" with "elegance." And while 37 percent of the Gen X/Y group (in this study, 18 to 34) and 22 percent of Baby Boomers (in this study, 35 to 54) define luxury as being "flashy" or "elitist," just 10 percent of the older consumer group says the same.

In fact, the supposed "Me Generation," Baby Boomers are actually the most likely to think of luxury as being "wasteful" or "unnecessary." Over a quarter (28 percent) of Boomers say so, compared with 19 percent of each of the other two age groups. Gen X/Y on the other hand, seems to be in awe of the lap of luxury. Fully 61 percent of the youngest group aspire to live a "lifestyle of luxury," while only 38 percent of Boomers and 36 percent of the older consumers have similar aspirations. Interestingly, almost a quarter of Gen X/Y (23 percent) already think they live a luxurious lifestyle, more than twice the percentage of Boomers who think the same (10 percent).

PSYCHOGRAPHICS OF LUXURY CONSUMERS

A consumer's motivation for luxury spending has as much to do with personality and state of mind as with his or her demographics. Three distinct mind-sets drive the majority of luxury spending, according to SRI Consulting Business Intelligence (SRIC-BI), a Menlo Park, Calif.-based firm that analyzes consumer psychographics. Each group responds to different value propositions and marketing messages, says Kristen Thomas, an SRIC-BI consultant. SRIC-BI breaks its consumers out into three groups.

Luxury Is Functional. These consumers tend to buy luxury products for their superior functionality and quality. Consumers in this segment, the largest of the three, tend to be older and wealthier, and are willing to spend more money to buy things that will last and have enduring value. These consumers buy a wide array of luxury goods, from luxury automobiles to artwork to vacations. They conduct extensive prepurchase research and make logical decisions rather than emotional or impulsive decisions. Messages that highlight product quality and are information-intensive are powerful with this group.

A CONSUMER'S MOTIVATION FOR LUXURY SPENDING HAS AS MUCH TO DO WITH PERSONALITY AND STATE OF MIND AS WITH HIS OR HER DEMOGRAPHICS. THREE MIND-SETS DRIVE LUXURY SPENDING.

Luxury Is a Reward. These consumers tend to be younger than the first group but older than the third group. They often use luxury goods as status symbols or to say "I've made it." The desire to be successful and to demonstrate their success to others motivates these consumers to purchase conspicuous luxury items, such as luxury automobiles and homes in exclusive communities. Luxury brands that have widespread recognition are popular with this segment. And yet, this segment is also concerned that owning luxury goods might make them appear lavish or hedonistic, especially in these economic times. They want to purchase "smart" luxury that demonstrates their importance, while not leaving them open to criticism. Marketing messages that communicate acceptable exclusivity resonate with this group.

Luxury Is Indulgence. This group is the smallest of the three, and tends to include younger consumers and slightly more males than the other two groups. To these consumers, the purpose of owning luxury is to be extremely lavish and self-indulgent. This group is willing to pay a premium for goods that express their individuality and make others take notice. These consumers are not overly concerned with product quality or longevity, or with the possibility that others might criticize their purchases. Rather, they enjoy luxury for the way it makes them feel—if a product makes them feel good, they will likely make the purchase. These consumers have a more emotional approach to luxury spending, and are more likely than the other two groups to make impulse purchases. They respond well to messages that highlight the unique and emotional qualities of a product.

"As consumers face emotional and economic stresses, they may modify some specific behaviors—for instance, delaying the purchase of a second home or new car—but their fundamental personalities don't change," says SRIC-BI's Thomas. "The different facets of luxury goods that consumers found attractive before the recession will continue to appeal to them during this recession and into recovery."

Emailing Aging Boomers vs. "Seniors"

Over 90% of US boomers use email—and studies show they love it.

But they're a tough sell: they're generally considered to be more vocal and more demanding consumers, who will not be content with standard offers that may have worked with older generations of the past, says Jean Van Ryzin, editor of *Selling to Seniors*.

Quick Boomer Demographic Basics

Baby boomers can be generally described as anyone born between 1946 and 1964. "Leading-edge" or "first-wave" boomers are those in their fifties. A typical leading-edge boomer:

- expects a lifestyle at least as good as his parents;
- is nervous about the economy, and expects to work into retirement;
- is part of the "sandwich generation," with kids in college and elderly parents who may need caretaking;
- is healthier, more active, and has a longer expected lifespan than earlier generations;
- is more interested in financial issues than healthcare issues;
- is comfortable with computer technology and uses email;
- has unusually strong ties with their mothers (males in particular.)

According to Bob Kesner, President of Evergreen Direct, these boomers (or Bloomers, as he calls them) are also "idealistic and have a wacky, tumultuous past. They don't like to feel they've sold out."

What's the difference? Aging boomers vs. "Seniors"

Though boomers are edging up on senior status, there are big distinctions in marketing to the two groups, says Kesner. Some major differences include:

- Boomers want financial independence; seniors want physical independence.
- Seniors trust the email process but not the Internet as a whole; boomers trust both.
- Boomers want endorsements and industry ratings; seniors want testimonials.
- Boomers like options; seniors prefer things that are prepackaged.

Marketing through boomers to seniors

Plus, you may end up marketing through boomers to reach seniors because a common thread among baby boomers is the reality of taking care of elderly parents. "We've marketed some products that appeal to the senior population, but we try to involve the caregiver," says Kesner.

This can be tricky, since seniors can be touchy about their age and independence issues. On the other hand, a caretaker has found herself in the position of discovering her parents are not invincible. She is looking for reassurance, and wants a personal touch.

(And yes, we say "she" on purpose—a study done by the Metropolitan Insurance Company shows that 82% of caregivers are female.)

To walk the fine line between the needs of boomer caregivers and their senior parents, it's important to use first person and be conversational but polite—not condescending. Let them know that you understand the issues they're facing, that you're on their team.

It's hard to go too far with the personal touch when reaching out to boomer caregivers. "We've even seen slight increases when using the word 'Mom' rather than 'Mother,'" says Steve Hardman of seniormag.com.

Eight Tips on Emailing Boomers

You can maximize your email efforts to boomers by taking the following considerations into account. Here's what it all boils down to:

#1. Use wording that lets them maintain their idealistic dreams.

As part of the Woodstock generation, they don't want to feel they've sold out in any way. References to JFK, Woodstock, the "summer of love," civil rights, can all help boomers recapture the past. According to Kesner, "Words boomers may remember include Barbie doll, black hole, flower children, microwave oven, mini skirt, zip codes, hippies."

But don't overdo it. They'll see right through you.

#2. Focus on the financial and calm their potential fears.

Boomers are pre-retirement and, with an uncertain economy, they're feeling financially uncertain themselves. Give assurances. Talk about portfolios, bonuses, fast-track retirement.

Unlike seniors, healthcare issues are not their main concern.

#3. Emphasize convenience.

Boomers are busy. They have kids, jobs, elderly parents, second families, lots of responsibility. Make it easy for them.

#4. Avoid scare tactics.

They're too savvy to be taken in. "It's negative advertising, and it's just a bad idea," says Kesner.

#5. Use statistics.

Cynical as a group, boomers need to be convinced of your credibility. Establish it early on in a message, to set up a trusting relationship at the outset. Statistics, testimonials from named individuals, and press clippings can help. Hype-laden copy will hurt.

#6. Give them options.

This audience wants to feel in charge of their decisions. Offer them a variety of choices, and a variety of ways to respond. So, include a phone number as well as a hotlink.

#7. It's not all about HTML.

"Counter-intuitively, we mix up our HTML and text," says Nancy Cathey, VP of emarketing/investments for Phillips Investment Resources. This audience, she says, favors letter-like messages rather than splashy images.

You can also get away with more text with this audience—in fact it may come across as more sincere, honest and trustworthy.

#8. Use personal or cultural references.

This group is more likely to open an email if the subject line references current events.

"These tactics work," says Cathey. "It's just enough to get attention, as long as it's contextual and current, like a story in the news."

You can also try using the customer's name in the subject line for a personal touch.

Most of all, remember:

Baby boomers are at the peak of their earning power, they're financially savvy, they're socially aware—and they're in love with email as a communications medium. They're open to hearing from you: just make sure you know their needs.

From *ConsumerMarketingBiz*, Marketing Sherpa, May 12, 2003. © 2003 by Marketing Sherpa Inc.

RACE, ETHNICITY AND THE WAY WE SHOP

Understanding the different attitudes and behaviors of Asian, black, Hispanic and white consumers.

BY REBECCA GARDYN AND JOHN FETTO

They may be outnumbered at the shopping mall, but minority consumers and their buying power should not be underestimated. In 2002, blacks, Hispanics and Asians wielded significant discretionary income: $646 billion, $581 billion and $296 billion, respectively, according to the Selig Center for Economic Growth at the University of Georgia, which defines "buying power" as the total personal income available, after taxes, for spending on goods and services—that is, disposable income. And while whites continue to account for the majority of total consumer spending ($6.3 trillion), their market share is dwindling. In 1990, whites represented 87 percent of the total consumer marketplace, but they accounted for 82 percent by 2002, according to the Selig Center. By 2007, analysts expect white consumers' share to shrink to 80 percent of all U.S. consumer spending.

whites continue to account for the majority of consumer spending, $6.3 trillion, but their market share is dwindling.

As the buying power of blacks, Hispanics and Asians increases, understanding the differences between these groups in terms of how, when, where and why they shop for goods and services becomes even more important to businesses' bottom lines. Here, we highlight some of the more interesting differences between the attitudes and behaviors of Asian, black, Hispanic and white Americans. The data was culled from a Simmons Market Research study of about 22,000 consumers (18,542 whites; 1,444 blacks; 1,349 Hispanics; and 640 Asians) fielded between January and May 2002.

35 percent of Asians have made an Internet purchase in the past year. They are also more than twice as likely as the average consumer to use the Internet to help plan their shopping.

asians

How do you say "shop till you drop" in Japanese or Korean? Not only are Asian consumers the most frequent shoppers of all racial and ethnic groups, they are also the most brand-conscious. Almost half (43 percent) say that they always look for a brand name when they shop. Yet, interestingly, they are also the least brand-loyal. Fully a quarter of Asians say they change brands often, compared with 22 percent of Hispanics, 20 percent of blacks and 17 percent of whites. Asian consumers are also the most concerned about keeping up appearances. More than a quarter (26 percent) say they buy what they think their neighbors will approve of, compared with 12 percent each of Hispanics and blacks and just 10 percent of whites. Asians also do not like to shop alone: 31 percent say they prefer shopping with their friends, compared with 25 percent each of Hispanics and blacks, and 23 percent of whites. And Asians never leave home without a plan. They are 125 percent more likely than the average consumer to rely on the Internet to help them plan their shopping trips.

by the numbers

The facts and figures below show how shopping behaviors and motivations differ by race and ethnicity.

frequent shoppers

White shoppers are the most likely of all racial and ethnic groups to have visited a home improvement store at least five times in the past three months. But they are the least likely to have made frequent trips to electronics and home furnishings stores.

INDEX* OF AMERICANS WHO HAVE GONE TO THE FOLLOWING TYPE OF STORE FIVE OR MORE TIMES IN THE PAST THREE MONTHS, BY RACE AND ETHNICITY.

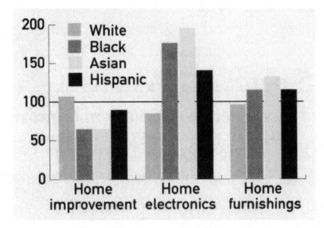

*The national average is 100. For example, Asians are significantly more likely than the average American to have made five or more trips to a home electronics store in the past three months, but they are less likely to have shopped at a home improvement store as frequently.

Source: Simmons Market Research, 2002

dressed to impress

Minority consumers are far more likely than whites to say they enjoy wearing the latest fashions.

	WHITE	BLACK	ASIAN	HISPANIC
I like to dress in the latest fashions	36%	58%	46%	46%
I like to impress people with my lifestyle	17%	20%	28%	20%
I'm very likely to buy new technology products and services	41%	42%	49%	39%
I like to look in hardware or automotive stores	46%	40%	44%	45%

Source: Mediamark Research, Inc., 2002

on the cheap

Americans of all colors like a bargain, but whites are the most likely of all racial and ethnic groups to shop at discount stores. Many Asians also look for a discount, but they are the most likely to buy their clothes, housewares and cosmetics at a traditional department store.

PERCENT OF AMERICANS WHO HAVE SHOPPED AT LEAST ONCE IN THE PAST THREE MONTHS AT DEPARTMENT STORES OR DISCOUNT STORES FOR THE FOLLOWING TYPES OF PRODUCTS, BY RACE AND ETHNICITY:

	WHITE	BLACK	ASIAN	HISPANIC
CLOTHING AND ACCESSORIES				
Department store	47%	43%	51%	48%
Discount store	60%	50%	54%	57%
FOOTWEAR				
Department store	15%	16%	18%	20%
Discount store	24%	15%	19%	21%
HOUSEWARES AND FURNITURE				
Department store	8%	5%	10%	6%
Discount store	20%	14%	18%	17%
COSMETICS				
Department store	6%	5%	8%	7%
Discount store	21%	11%	16%	19%

Source: Simmons Market Research, 2002

joining in on the fun

In 1998, whites were almost twice as likely as blacks or Hispanics to have made an online purchase. Today, the share of Hispanics and whites going online to shop is the same, and almost half of all blacks do so as well.

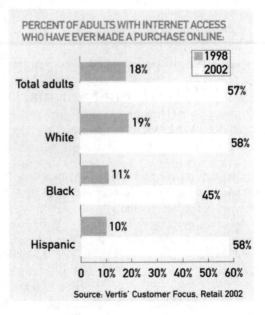

PERCENT OF ADULTS WITH INTERNET ACCESS WHO HAVE EVER MADE A PURCHASE ONLINE:

Source: Vertis' Customer Focus, Retail 2002

diversified dollars

Black, Asian and Hispanic consumers' buying power is growing while the whites' share is shrinking. By 2007, whites are expected to make up 80 percent of the consumer marketplace, down from 87 percent in 1990.

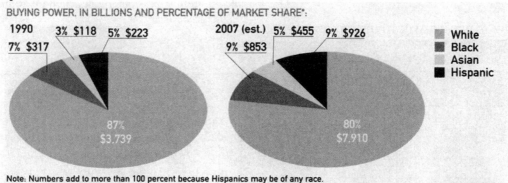

BUYING POWER, IN BILLIONS AND PERCENTAGE OF MARKET SHARE*:

1990   3% $118   5% $223
7% $317
87%
$3.739

2007 (est.)   5% $455   9% $926
9% $853
80%
$7.910

White
Black
Asian
Hispanic

Note: Numbers add to more than 100 percent because Hispanics may be of any race.

Source: Selig Center for Economic Growth, The University of Georgia

whites

Whites may make up the majority of the shopping hordes, but they are the least likely to enjoy the process. Just 35 percent of white consumers say that they enjoy shopping, even when they don't buy anything, compared with almost half (47 percent) of Asian, 43 percent of black and 42 percent of Hispanic shoppers who say the same. Almost two-thirds (62 percent) of white consumers say they go shopping only when they absolutely need something, versus 57 percent of Asians, 54 percent of Hispanics and 47 percent of blacks who say they do the same. And nearly half of white consumers don't stick around to browse: 49 percent say that when they do go shopping, they usually just get what they want and leave. Interestingly, white consumers are the most likely to say they make spur-of-the-moment purchases (41 percent, versus 37 percent of Hispanics, 35 percent of Asians and 34 percent of blacks). Yet they are also more likely (59 percent) to plan far ahead to buy expensive items than are Asians (53 percent), Hispanics (52 percent) or blacks (44 percent).

know your customer

The principal shopper in a black household is likely to be single, divorced or widowed.

PERCENT OF HOUSEHOLDS IN WHICH THE PRINCIPAL SHOPPER* IS...

	WHITE	BLACK	ASIAN	HISPANIC
Married	65%	43%	70%	64%
Single	15%	32%	19%	21%
Divorced/ separated	12%	18%	6%	12%
Widowed	7%	7%	5%	3%

*"Principal shopper" refers to the person responsible for making the majority of the everyday purchases (groceries and household necessities) for the family.

Source: Mediamark Research, Inc., 2002

black consumers make 19 trips to convenience stores each year.

charge it

More than 1 in 10 Asians (12 percent) say they have used their credit card 20 times or more in the prior month, compared with only 2 percent of blacks who say the same.

HOW MANY TIMES IN THE PAST 30 DAYS HAVE YOU USED A CREDIT CARD?

	WHITE	BLACK	ASIAN	HISPANIC
1–5	47%	28%	49%	39%
6–19	21%	9%	27%	15%
20 or more	8%	2%	12%	5%

*Note: Numbers do not add to 100 percent because some people had not used a credit card at all in the prior 30 days, and others did not answer the question.

Source: Simmons Market Research, 2002

hispanics

Hispanics, who may be of any race, tend to make shopping a family affair. More than a third (36 percent) say they prefer shopping with their families and 30 percent report they like shopping with their children, compared with 29 percent and 26 percent, respectively, of the total population. A quarter of Hispanics say their kids have a significant impact on the brands they buy. Hispanics are almost twice as likely as white consumers to go out of their way to find new stores (13 percent versus 7 percent). And they would rather shop at national chains than at local mom-and-pop stores. Just 26 percent of Hispanics

everyday needs

Warehouse clubs, like Costco and Sam's Club, depend heavily on Asian and Hispanic consumers. The typical Asian shopper, for example, makes 14 trips a year to such stores, whereas blacks report that they shop at a warehouse club just eight times a year.

NUMBER OF TRIPS MADE ANNUALLY TO THE FOLLOWING VENUES, BY RACE AND ETHNICITY:

	WHITE	BLACK	ASIAN	HISPANIC
Grocery stores	72	70	65	67
Drugstores	15	17	16	15
Mass merchants	24	20	21	24
Supercenters	19	16	12	15
Warehouse clubs	10	8	14	12
Gas/convenience stores	14	19	6	11
Dollar stores	10	16	7	10

Source: ACNielsen

shopping by proxy

Asians are the least likely to buy merchandise by phone or mail order, but they are the most likely to buy things over the Internet.

PERCENT OF AMERICANS WHO HAVE MADE ANY PURCHASE IN THE PAST YEAR OVER THE PHONE OR BY MAIL, OR VIA THE INTERNET:

	WHITE	BLACK	ASIAN	HISPANIC
Phone or mail order	39%	32%	28%	29%
Internet	28%	14%	35%	20%

Source: Simmons Market Research, 2002

say they would rather shop at a local store than at a national chain, compared with 28 percent of blacks and 30 percent each of Asians and whites.

blacks

Blacks are the most fashion-conscious of all racial and ethnic groups. In fact, 34 percent of black consumers say they like to keep up with changes in trends and fashion, compared with 28 percent of Asians, 27 percent of Hispanics and 25 percent of whites. Blacks are the most likely of all groups to be willing to travel an hour or more to shop at their favorite store and almost twice as likely as the average consumer to go out of their way

to find new stores, especially if a bargain is to be had. The Simmons study found that a third (34 percent) of the black respondents will travel an hour or more to shop at a factory outlet store, compared with 27 percent of all consumers. And once they get there, black consumers, more than anyone else, prefer conquering the sales racks alone, rather than with friends. Indeed, blacks simply enjoy shopping, even for something as mundane as the groceries.

it's in the mail

Across most product categories, black consumers are more likely than the average American to buy items based on direct mail advertisements.

INDEX* OF AMERICANS WHO HAVE PURCHASED THE FOLLOWING TYPES OF PRODUCTS IN THE PAST YEAR IN RESPONSE TO DIRECT MAIL ADVERTISING, BY RACE AND ETHNICITY:

	WHITE	BLACK	ASIAN	HISPANIC
New/used car	87	144	112	126
CDs/tapes/records	91	132	93	119
Children's clothing	89	139	105	128
Computer hardware	94	117	151	104
Computer software	97	125	131	83
Cosmetics/perfume/skin care products	95	119	94	108
Fast food	100	110	91	91
Furniture	91	146	109	109
Groceries	105	103	89	73
Mattress	91	140	101	109
Women's lingerie	94	132	98	104
Women's sportswear	110	89	73	61

*An index of 100 is the national average. For example, black consumers are 44 percent more likely than the average American to have bought a new or used car as a result of direct mail advertising, but they are 11 percent less likely to have bought women's sportswear as a result of direct mail.

Source: Scarborough Research

Asian-American consumers as a unique market segment: **fact or fallacy?**

Keywords *Consumer behavior, Market segmentation, Consumer marketing, Ethnic groups*

Abstract *The Asian-American consumer group is thought to be the fastest-growing market in the USA. Asian-Americans are thought to be well-educated, generally affluent, and geographically concentrated. However, significant cultural and language differences among Asian subgroups are often overlooked. These include patterns of information gathering, use of promotional media, and methods of household decision making. This article presents a comparative marketing examination of the similarities and differences among five of the largest Asian-American groups and develops implications for marketing strategies.*

Carol Kaufman-Scarborough
Associate Professor of Marketing, School of Business,
Rutgers University—Camden, New Jersey, USA

Introduction

Fastest growing population

Marketers today are attracted by the Asian-American consumer market as growing numbers of Asians emigrate to the USA. In fact, Asian-Americans are the fastest growing population in the USA, with a 99 percent increase since the 1980 census (Paisano, 1993). Currently, they account for 9.8 million of the US population. By the year 2050, they are expected to account for 10 percent of the total US population. If the Asian-American population in the USA were viewed as a separate country, it would be ranked the 85th largest country out of 220 nations (*Marketing Review*, 1994). With spending power estimates of over $200 billion, and tendencies toward brand loyalty, Asian-American consumers form a desirable market (Edmondson, 1997).

Some analysts, particularly in the popular press, have suggested that this group of consumers can be treated as one large segment, without analyzing the key acculturation issues that may be particular to each specific subgroup. Others have focused on each specific market without identifying the similarities among them that are useful to marketers. Still others have argued that Asian-Americans are over-stereotyped in ads, overemphasizing business settings, while downplaying home settings and family relationships (Taylor and Stern, 1997). Industry's eagerness to capitalize on their substantial spending power may compromise the need to identify and examine areas in which the Asian-American "market" is really composed of numerous submarkets, with neglected similarities and critical differences to take into account (Campanelli, 1995).

Similarities and differences

The present paper will present an examination of the similarities and differences among five of the largest Asian-American segments with a focus on key consumer behaviors. These groups are Chinese, Filipino, Asian Indian, Japanese, and Korean-Americans. Numerous background sources on each group's homeland consumer behaviors and immigration consumer behaviors are examined to present a summary of areas which likely to require specific subgroup attention. In addition, key similarities will also be derived, and recommendations for marketing to Asian-Americans as a unified group will be discussed.

Method of investigation

The goals of the present article are:
1. to compare and contrast existing "definitions" of Asian-Americans;
2. to summarize prevalent misconceptions in marketing regarding Asian-Americans;
3. to investigate and present some of the under-represented household aspects of consumer behavior; and
4. to describe key areas of consumer behavior and media use which are thought to differentiate one Asian subcultural group from another.

Factors which impact cultural influence

Key concepts: socialization, consumer acculturation and traditional assimilation

Many Asian-Americans have lived in the USA for numerous years and have blended their households with persons from the USA and from other cultures. Over time, second- and third-generation families have emerged, with their own particular blends of traditional and "new" consumer habits. Asian-Americans are thought to learn and use US culture in relation to the length of time they have been in the USA and their level of involvement in the workforce. Motivation for moving to the new culture or reason for being influenced by the new culture (e.g. fleeing the takeover of one's home country, searching for the "good life" in another country, traveling to acquire education or as part of one's employment) are also thought to impact cultural influence (Wallendorf and Reilly, 1983).

Less need to assimilate

Assimilation. Assimilation is generally known as the process of transforming aspects of a nondominant (in this case, immigrant Asian) culture into a status of relative adjustment to the form of the dominant culture. Changes in behavior may be deliberately undertaken, as each new generation of immigrant attempts to better fit into the dominant host culture. A critical point when considering Asian-Americans is that, given their familiarity with US life from travel, education, and global communications, they may not feel the need to assimilate in the same ways that prior generations of European immigrants did. Moreover, their ability to live in ethnically dominant Asian communities makes it possible to retain one's home country behaviors, habits, and preferences.

Socialization. Socialization occurs when people learn socially relevant behaviors from their surrounding environment. This initial "view of the world" is called primary socialization. However, as new environments are encountered, individuals learn new ways through "secondary" socialization (Penaloza, 1989). Immigrants gradually learn a new culture as they increase their contact with it; this is called the "traditional assimilation model" (Wallendorf and Reilly, 1983).

Acculturation. Acculturation can be defined as the process of learning and adopting cultural traits, different from the ones with which the person was originally reared (Berelson and Steiner, 1967; Ownbey and Horridge, 1997; Sturdivant, 1973; Valencia, 1985). New symbols and new customs are experienced, new foods are consumed, and new ways of thinking are learned. Social and cultural changes occur when people from different cultures come in direct contact with each other. That is, they learn each other's behaviors and customs.

Shaping consumer behavior

Consumer acculturation. As part of these processes, people acquire skills, knowledge, and attitudes relevant to their functioning as consumers in the marketplace. This is called consumer acculturation (Penaloza, 1989). New ways of shopping are tried, and new products are encountered. Several possibilities are thought to occur in shaping the consumer behavior that emerges. Consumers can learn and adopt all new consumer behaviors, they can maintain their consumer practices from their homeland or heritage, or they can form completely new patterns of behavior that are hybrids of both homeland and the new culture (Wallendorf and Reilly, 1983).

Contradictory themes

Misconceptions regarding the Asian-American consumer segment

Several misconceptions and contradictory themes are sometimes found in the popular press in their discussions of marketing to Asian-Americans. These misconceptions appear to overgeneralize on certain similarities among Asian-Americans, while apparently overlooking the differences which occur because of national origin, language habits, level of acculturation, reason for immigration, and so forth. While this list is not exhaustive, it is thought to be representative of some of the overly simplistic approaches which can create problems, rather than efficiencies, in marketing to Asian-American consumers. Eight misconceptions are identified as follows:

Misconception 1: Asian-Americans can be grouped together into a single segment. In this review, I argue that such an overall grouping can be useful for some aspects of consumer behavior, but may cause the manager to overlook other key differences.

Misconception 2: Since English is a common language across Asian-American subgroups, translating an English message into an Asian language will communicate the intended message. While English may be relatively common as a second language, its use, idioms, and meanings are not likely to be conceptually equivalent nor appropriate for all Asian-American groups.

Misconception 3: Since English is a common language across Asian-American subgroups, it is efficient and effective to advertise to them in English, with adjustments and inclusion of specific Asian themes. Such an approach is likely to miss the significant numbers of Asian-Americans who are not fluent in "consumer English."

Misconception 4: Asian-Americans constitute too small a percentage of the US population to target for specific messages. The overall Asian-American group is growing rapidly and will continue to do so.

Significant media differences

Misconception 5: Targeting the Asian-American market is not necessary because they can be reached through the mass media. Significant media differences are found across Asian-American subgroups.

Misconception 6: There are too many Asian-American cultures and languages to create different marketing strategies for each. Different strategies may not be necessary in all product areas; many common needs can be found. Moreover, while over 800 Asian languages are thought to exist, dominant tongues do occur within each subgroup.

Misconception 7: There are numerous similarities among Asian-American cultures; common advertising themes are always desirable. Researchers have identified both similarities and differences among preferred and acceptable themes across Asian groups.

Misconception 8: There are numerous differences among Asian-American cultures; common advertising themes aimed at Asian-Americans will not be possible. Researchers have identified both similarities and differences among preferred and acceptable themes across Asian groups.

Classification of Asian groups

Just who is an Asian-American?

There are numereous similarities that characterize persons of Asian descent. These include a strong emphasis on family and education, ties to the homeland, geographic concentration in the USA, and relative affluence in relation to the general population. However, it is often unclear just which Asian groups are included in the term "Asian-American." Several studies were consulted in identifying commonly-used methods of classification.

Problems with definitions

Depending on which study is consulted, Asian-Americans include over 30 ethnic groups who trace their roots to Asia and the islands located in the Pacific Ocean. Some definitions include a different combination of countries than others. The inconsistency in definitions creates a research nightmare, since it is essential to create a consistent understanding across researchers about which national groups are actually under consideration. Table I summarizes five different definitions that are found in the literature.

Growth of population

General characteristics

The Asian-American population has grown from 3.8 million in 1980, to 7.3 million, which is an increase of 95 percent, comprising 3 percent of the US population. The US Census Bureau statistics as of August 1, 1997, estimate that the Asian-American population is over 10 million, which constitutes 3.8 percent of the total US population. By the years 2010 and 2050, it is estimated that Asian-Americans will number over 12 million and 40 million respectively, equal to 6 percent and 10 percent of the total projected population (Natividad and Gall, 1996).

According to Ho (1997), Asians may actually be underrepresented in the annual US census. Reasons cited for this problem include:

Table I. Selected definitions used in Asian-American classification schemata

1. Persons whose ancestors came from one of over 20 Asian nations: Bangladesh, Bhutan, Cambodia (including Hmong), China (including Hong Kong or Taiwan), India, Indonesia, Japan, Korea, Laos, Malaysia, Mongolia, Myanmar (Burma), Nepal, Pakistan, the Philippines, Singapore, Sri Lanka, Thailand, and Vietnam (Baron and Gall, 1996).

2. A member of one of over 30 ethnic groups from different parts of Asia: Cambodia, China, India, Indonesia, Japan, Korea, Malaysia, Pakistan, the Philippines, Singapore, Vietnam, American Samoa, Northern Mariana Islands, Micronesia, Guam, Marshall Islands, Palau, and Hawaii (Natividad and Gall, 1996).

3. The Census Bureau's category Asian and Pacific Islander covers more than 17 countries. The Immigration and Naturalization Service counts people from more than 29 countries, ranging from the Middle East to Taiwan (Edmondson, 1997).

4. Asian-Americans are defined as persons whose ancestry is rooted in any Asian country, other than of the Indian Subcontinent (Cohen, 1992).

5. Asian-American is a term that is used to describe people who were born in the USA such as American-born Chinese, and those people who emigrated from Asian countries long ago (Ho, 1997).

1. Asian groups may distrust information collected by the government;
2. Asian persons may be unwilling to divulge personal information on black and white official forms (even if they are in their native language); and
3. illegal immigrants tend to avoid census-takers, but are still part of the consumer market.

Geographical concentration

Asian-Americans also tend to be concentrated geographically. The ten states that have the largest Asian-American population are: California, New York, Hawaii, Texas, Illinois, New Jersey, Washington, Florida, and Massachusetts. In addition, Asian-Americans tend to locate in or near major metropolitan centers. The ten cities with the largest Asian-American population are Los Angeles, New York, Honolulu, San Francisco, Oakland, San Jose, Orange County, Chicago, San Diego, and Washington D.C.

Household characteristics

Asian-Americans are recognized and often stereotyped as being technically competent, hardworking, serious, well assimilated, with a high value on education and family (Taylor and Lee, 1994; Taylor and Stern, 1997; Natividad and Gall, 1996). They have a higher average income, education, and occupational status than the average American. Of Asian-Americans 38 percent have achieved

a bachelor's degree or higher by 1990, versus 20 percent of the total population.

Of Asian households 53 percent have at least two earners, which is a higher proportion than other racial groups. The median household income of Asian-Americans is higher than that of the overall market: $38,540 versus $29,943. In contrast, their poverty rate is also higher than the national average, given at 14 percent versus 13 percent.

Strong cultural ties

Asian-Americans have strong ties to their native cultures and continue to keep their identities within the host culture of the USA. One force, which appears to link all of the Asian cultures, is Confucian ethics, which can be represented by two terms: filial piety and loyalty to authority. These are manifested in the family structure that is strong throughout each group (Larson and Kleiner, 1992). For instance, Asian-American marriages are less than half as likely to end in divorce compared to the national average (Braun, 1991).

Asian-Americans hold their families in high regard, which is a value strongly held in the homelands. Family is a source of individual identity, and a strong sense of connectedness to heritage and tradition is maintained. Asian Americans value achievement, since achievements will reflect well on one's family and group. Traditional household decision making attempts to consider the relative roles of husband and wife in understanding how purchase decisions are made, or not made. Since children and teenagers may be the dominant English-speakers in Asian-American households, their roles may be more influential than those of children/teens in US households.

Significant language differences

Language

Language is possibly one of the most significant areas of difference. Experts report that there are 800 or more different languages used in Southeast Asia. While many Asian-Americans do share the English language in common, their own native tongues are often used in a variety of situations. Because of improvements in technology, worldwide educational programs, and the ease and frequency of international travel, recent immigrants are not finding the need to assimilate into US culture, as they had in the past. Fifty-six percent of the 4.1 million Asian-Americans five years old and older do not speak English fluently, nor do they use English in everyday situations. Approximately 35 percent of those are "linguistically isolated." That is, they live in homes where no one over age 14 speaks English (Fisher, 1994). Such a situation might significantly alter the role of children in household decision making.

In many Asian-American families, younger family members use English as their primary language, whereas parents or older relatives are likely to use their native tongues as primary. Thus, when they interact, conversations are likely to be a mixture of English and the native tongue. As a result, many younger Asian-Americans can understand their native language, and can respond to it in English, but they themselves cannot speak it (Ho, 1997). In addition, many Asian-Americans prefer to use their native tongues in many situations, such as reading, entertainment, and making consumer evaluations. In fact, more than half of Asian-Americans are more comfortable speaking their native language, and 24 percent primarily use their native language.

Attraction to brand names

Brands and consumer behavior

Asian-American consumers are intensely brand-loyal and cost-conscious (Cohen, 1992). They will not buy the cheapest item, but the best item for the cheapest price. Doing business with an Asian-American means establishing a relationship. Basically, Asian-Americans do business with people, not with product attributes (Ho, 1997). A recent survey of 1,600 Asian-Americans showed that this group has a strong attraction to brand names, with 72 percent reporting that brand names are a strong influence on their purchase decisions, in contrast with 34 percent of

the general population. They also like to purchase premium products (Berkowitz, 1994). Automobiles, for instance, represent status to Asian-Americans, and they are more likely to own autos in the $20,000 to $30,000 price range.

Different motivations for coming to USA

Key similarities and differences among the five Asian-American subgroups

Although Asian-Americans come from the same area of the world, their subgroups vary in the usual ways that nationalities vary from each other. Asian Americans come from countries which differ in languages, cultural values, traditions, beliefs, religions, personality characteristics, occupational skills, and so forth. In addition, many of the Asian groups had different motivations in their move to the USA, which often has affected their desire and need to assimilate. The issues investigated across the five cultures were consumer spending and price sensitivity, household purchase decisions, language use, and advertising habits and preferences.

Chinese-Americans

About 1.6 million Chinese people live in the USA; four out of ten Chinese-Americans live in California. There are concentrations in major cities: for example, most live in New York, San Francisco, and Los Angeles. They are a hard-working people, operating numerous small businesses, and owning and developing real estate. Chinese-Americans are somewhat older than the national average. However, the China-born, compared to the American-born, are less likely to have a regular income. Seven out of ten Chinese immigrants are foreign-born. Chinese immigrants were among the first Asians to enter the USA and to establish distinct cultural communities, staying mainly on the West Cost. These "Chinatowns," as they have come to be known, have served to preserve the culture, tradition and lifestyle of China.

Chinese-American society has historically emphasized family, societal interests, and collective actions, while de-emphasizing personal goals and accomplishments (Zhang and Gelb, 1996). Immigrants from several years ago and students can be characterized by "Americanized" household decision making, in which both husband and wife participate in the decision. This is also true of recent immigrants from Hong Kong and Taiwan, but newcomers from Mainland China still practice traditional decision making, with the husband deciding large purchases (Pounds, 1998). A mid-range possibility also occurs, in which the wife makes suggestions, but the husband makes the final purchase.

Prefer ethnic markets

Chinese shoppers are typically price-sensitive, and tend to prefer ethnic markets. However, since they are bargain seekers, Chinese-Americans will shop in American discount stores as well. They often use coupons from direct mail. Moreover, they rely on advertising to provide straightforward information. Belittling or disparaging other competitors' products may be considered to be unlawful or at least unacceptable (Zhou and Belk, 1993).

Language use and learning is also a complex issues. Eighty-three percent report wanting in-language advertising, yet the language issue is quite complex. For instance, recent immigrants regularly read and watch in-language media, reinforcing both reading and hearing their homeland tongues. In contrast, US-born Chinese speak the language but do not read or write it. Thus, print messages provided in Chinese may be confusing for those born in the USA, while audio ads may be effective. While the Chinese population has several distinct language groups and dozens of dialects, Cantonese is the most accepted form of Chinese in the USA.

Racial and cultural mix

Filipino-American

Approximately 1.4 million Filipino-Americans reside in the USA, primarily in California. Los Angeles, Chicago, and New York-Newark are major cities. Filipinos may be of Chinese, Spanish, or Malayan lineage, which determines physical characteristics and subsequently influences choice and purchases of cosmetics and other appearance-related items. Lineage is also thought to determine food tastes, art and decorative preference. Thus, a variety of learned preferences is found across Filipino-Americans.

The history of the Philippines shows a nation that has been dominated by other nations for hundreds of years. The Spanish, the Americans and the Japanese have ruled over the Filipinos. Other influences include the Germans and the Chinese. Thus, there is a significant racial and cultural mix in the Philippines that is not easily captured into one uniform group of cultural behaviors. There are three major ethnolinguistic groups, which are each well-represented in the USA, as well as several smaller ones.

Acculturation is a key factor in which Filipino-Americans are likely to buy. A Filipino's level of integration into the American mainstream is greatly determined by the social class that his family belonged to back in the homeland. Class distinctions in the Philippines are similar to those underlying social class in the USA. Those who lived in large cities in the Philippines are likely to be fluent in English before coming to the USA. They are also likely to have established patterns of shopping in large department stores and be knowledgeable regarding brands (Pounds, 1998).

Like other Asian-Americans, Filipinos place a high value on education and family. However, unlike other segments, Filipinos lack a "visible and cohesive community" (Larson and Kleiner, 1992). In families with medium to high acculturation, and where the wife also works, the wife will make most purchase decisions. Large purchases are decided jointly with the husband. Children may dominate American food and toy purchases. Newcomers with lower acculturation may depend on input from relatives or friends who have been in the USA for a while.

An interesting point is that Filipino-Americans will tend to look for the "made in the USA" mark on products while shopping in their homeland (Pounds, 1998). This can be explained by the presence of factories in the Philippines that contract the manufacturing of top name brands such as Nike and Lacoste. The Phillipine-made products are cheaper than the US-made counterparts, so Filipinos tend to prefer the US-made versions as a sign of status. Upon migrating to the USA, they tend to continue this pattern and seek products made in the USA, as assurances of quality and status. Filipinos feel that promotional efforts to their group should still include in-language media, even though a majority of them read and write English. Sixty-six percent prefer in-language media advertising. Filipino-Americans are very price-sensitive, since they often have low income and low spending power in the USA. They tend to comparison shop for quality and for bargains. They frequent discount-type stores.

Varying food shopping preferences

Filipino food shopping preferences are related to their level of acculturation. Those who have a low level of acculturation, perhaps coming from rural Philippine provinces and speaking little English, tend to avoid US grocery stores in favor of oriental food and specialty stores. Those with high acculturation prefer the convenience of one-stop shopping at American supermarkets, but will visit oriental food stores for those items that they cannot find elsewhere.

Most affluent group

Asian-Indians

Over 1 million Asian-Indians are estimated to live in the USA, with concentrations on the Eastern seaboard and the West Coast. The top three states are California, New York, and New Jersey. Metro areas such as New York, Chicago, and Los Angeles are popular. Asian-Indians are the most affluent of the five groups considered in this manuscript, and can be analyzed in terms of three identifiable periods of immigration proposed by Arun Jain of SUNY-Buffalo (Edmondson, 1997). The first group, who came to the USA in the 1960s, are generally well-educated successful men, with homemaker wives and adult children. The second group came in the 1970s and are also well-educated. However, both the husband and wife are employed, and they typically have young children. The third group is generally less-educated, and typically own motels and convenience stores (Mogelonsky, 1995).

India is a country of diverse classes with many ethnic subgroups. Indian society is characterized by a distinct division between the upper and lower classes. Because labor is cheap, most households in India can afford live-in domestic help. Since they are accustomed to conveniences in the home, products that promise to be labor-saving are popular with Indian customers who migrate to the USA. Asian-Indians are typically interested in comparison shopping, seeking to attain security, financial stability, and good value. They prefer to shop in areas that are convenient.

Importance of education

Asian-Indians believe highly in education for their children, and thus invest in computers and technological items. They traditionally value money and wealth, and thus invest in stocks, bonds, CDs, and insurance. Since banking and savings are high in importance, they seek banks and investment firms which will cater specifically to them and offer the best value. They also tend to invest in businesses, paying particular heed to franchise businesses, such as gas stations and convenience stores.

Older immigrant families adhere to traditional Indian custom, in which the male head of household makes most of the purchase decisions. Newcomers to the USA, in contrast, tend to follow a more typical American style of decision making, in which both husband and wife are eligible to take part in the decision. Thus marketing campaigns that appeal to traditional norms are likely to miscommunicate with some Asian-Indian groups.

Acceptability of English in advertising

In contrast to Chinese and Filipinos, Asian Indians find English to be highly acceptable for advertising. However, they also welcome use of the Indian language in promotional messages, with 55 percent preferring in-language media. Word-of-mouth is also important in transmitting consumer information. Given these preferences, the marketer must also consider both acceptable and unacceptable thematic presentations. For instance, advertisements to Indians should avoid sales arguments, which may be interpreted as confrontational or highly impolite. Ads should also avoid trying to motivate the consumer by using psychological appeals. Direct, clear information is best, with an emphasis on verbal messages. India is a country that does not place much emphasis on using visual information in advertising (Zandapour, 1994).

Japanese-Americans

The Japanese originally began to immigrate to the USA in the late nineteenth century due to hard economic times in Japan at that time. When Japan relaxed emigration laws in the early twentieth century and allowed women to emigrate, many Japanese families moved to the USA. As a result, a large portion of Japanese-Americans are older and better established than other Asian-Americans. Many Japanese immigrants own and operate their own businesses, from large corporations to small stores. They value land ownership and investment in real estate.

The 1990 Census states that about 850,000 Japanese Americans live in the USA, with the top states being California, Hawaii and New York. Many Japanese-Americans, especially in California, come for experience, training, or education. They do not plan to stay in the USA, but instead leave once their goals are complete. Thus, learning behaviors and norms of US cultures is not as important as it is to those who plan to stay permanently in the USA. An important characteristic of these "temporary" Japanese-Americans is that the husband usually speaks English, while the wife does not speak English. Since their stay is considered short-term, the wife often does not consider it to be necessary that she learn English. That is, the traditional assimilation model breaks down under conditions of short-term residence plus isolation from mainstream culture.

Distinct cultural characteristics

The Japanese have many distinct cultural characteristics that are thought to shape their behavior. They value conformity, as expressed in the statement *hitonami consciousness*, which roughly translates to "aligning oneself with other people." They are also reserved and extremely polite. The household decision roles are somewhat more complex. The wife typically researches products and ads, making suggestions of what to buy. However, the husband generally makes the final decision on major purchases.

Emphasis on quality

Quality is a must for the Japanese shopper. They look for signals of quality in packaging and branding, and shop at specialty stores to obtain what they want. For example, they loyally patronize Asian food stores for their cooking ingredients, gadgets, small appliances, and other items and brands from Japan. They insist on products such as noodles, dried fish and seaweed, and various types of fish and fish parts for their traditional recipes.

Like ads in their native Japan, Japanese-American consumers prefer short ads that include humor, celebrities, and indirect messages (Di Benedetto *et al.*, 1992). Important themes include the company's loyalty to the customers, with product quality being less emphasized. Product quality is taken for granted. In-language media are preferred by 42 percent, especially on Asian television and in print. Japanese consumers prefer to see young people in ads, for any product or service.

Indirectness, subtlety, and symbolism have always been important in Japanese cultures (Graham *et al.*, 1993). Printed material is considered to be impersonal and perhaps insincere. Although there is a definitive preference in US advertisements for critical, realistic impressions, this is not the case with the Japanese-American consumers. The Japanese-American consumers are likely to have developed expectations that advertisements should resemble those from their home country that are typified by illustrations and cartoon figures.

Three pillars of marketing in Japan

Marketers in the USA may also want to consider incorporating themes of ads that occur in Japan. For instance, as much as 70 percent of all Japanese print ads mention the price of the advertised item (Javalgi *et al.*, 1994). In addition, emotional rather than informational appeals are used (Lin, 1993). Customer service along with product quality and after-sales service are the three pillars of marketing and selling in Japan. It would be reasonable to assume that careful attention and detail must be paid to quality and service when targeting Japanese-American consumers.

More homogeneous group

Korean-American consumers

In contrast to several of the other Asian-American groups, Koreans are homogeneous and consider themselves to be one big family. They speak only one language and, interestingly, there are only 25 predominant surnames. The overwhelming majority of Korean immigrants, 82 percent, were foreign-born, with most having immigrated since 1965. Unlike other groups, Koreans are largely Christian. The churches serve a dual purpose of a religious center and that of a center for maintaining the Korean social and cultural bonds. Over 800,000 Korean-Americans live in the USA, according to the 1990 Census, with 44 percent living in the West, 23 percent in the

Northwest, 19 percent in the South, and 14 percent in the Midwest. They are possibly one of the most geographically-diverse of the Asian Americans groups under consideration.

Husband and wife roles in household decision making tend to vary by age. Thus, younger Koreans tend to make purchases independently, while older Korean-Americans are more traditional, with the male head of household making major purchase decisions. Children tend to influence their fathers in American food and toys. While the male tends to make most of the decisions, Korean-American couples tend to shop together.

Korean-Americans have a strong interest in quality products and in well-established brand names. They shop with the goal of getting the most for their money, using top-of-the-line products and services. Korean-Americans indicate a preference for in-language advertising. Many ignore mainstream media altogether. Ads are most popular which feature young to middle-aged males, unless the product is specifically for females. Korean-Americans appreciate participation in their communities by companies.

Easy to reach

Managerial implications and applications

Asian-Americans consumers represent a growing market, with spending power and identifiable purchasing and media habits. They are generally easy to reach, since they concentrate in major metropolitan markets. Asian-American media rates are generally less expensive than mainstream media. Newer media, such as Asian-American Web sites, attempt to address the needs of several Asian groups, while maintaining the cultural identities of each. In addition, many Asian-Americans live in extended family situations. Influence throughout the family helps to extend advertising reach. Communicating with immigrants who have settled permanently in the USA is critical since they become influencers to newly-arrived immigrants who are unaware and unsure of which brand to purchase.

Common set of variables

When attempting to counter the misconceptions listed above, there are no absolute rules of thumb that can be confidently applied to Asian-American consumers. Instead, there is a common set of variables that can affect whether it is appropriate to try to reach "the" Asian-American group as a whole, or whether subgroups or even an individual group needs to be targeted independently. The issue of language, similarly, becomes an "it depends" issue, based on the level of assimilation and acculturation of the subgroups or parts of subgroups whose needs are being addressed. The following list presents a summary of guidelines:

1. Asian-Americans have been over-stereotyped in promotional media. Numerous other common characteristics have been overlooked, such as extended household cohesiveness and interaction. Use of these themes can be beneficial in presenting accurate images of Asian-American households (Taylor and Stern, 1997).
2. Desire to assimilate and degree of cultural learning are related to the reason for migration and intended length of stay in the USA.
3. While, on the average, all Asian-American groups are similar in preferring to receive advertising in their own languages (Wiesendanger, 1993), those who are more highly-acculturated and those who are second- and third-generation often prefer English messages.

Acceptable themes in advertising

4. Acceptable themes in advertising to Asian-Americans are related to acceptable interpersonal interaction and inherent "truthworthiness" of certain types of media.
5. Shopping gender roles and shopping opinion leadership are related to length of time in the USA and to consumers' acculturation levels (Ownbey and Horridge, 1997).
6. Certain Asian-American groups are composed of various subgroups and subclasses, which determine rank and privilege in their homeland societies. While less familiar in the USA, there are carried-over shared feelings that may affect behavior.

Shared needs

7. Certain needs are shared among Asian-American groups. For instance, all groups are likely to need to contact families in their homelands. Thus, long-distance service, Internet providers, and airlines are strong contenders for the Asian-American business. Messages may require adjustments for specific subgroups.
8. Other needs are specific to any given Asian-American subgroup. Food ingredients and preparation methods may be native to a specific subgroup, although there may be some cross-over of foods with other Asian-American subgroups.

Marketing to Asian-Americans requires careful balance. There are often parts of a specific marketing process that can target Asian-Americans as a mass market, and other parts in which a specific subgroups' needs must emerge. When needs are common, creating a standardized advertising campaign can be possible. However, the decision process and household interaction may differ among subgroups. Similarly, the purpose for immigration and consequent degree of acculturation are likely to affect the language used and the media selected.

References

Baron, D. and Gall, S. (Eds.) (1996), *Asian-American Chronology*, UXL, New York, NY.

Berelson, B. and Steiner, G. A. (1967), *Human Behavior: An Inventory of Scientific Findings*. Harcourt, Brace, Jovanovich, New York, NY.

Berkowitz, H. (1994), "Concerning a market," *Newsday*, December 5, p. 4.

Braun, H. D. (1991), "Marketing to minority consumers," *Discount Merchandiser*, February, pp. 44–6.

Campanelli, M. (1995), "Asian studies," *Sales and Marketing Management*, March, Vol. 147, No. 3, Part 1, p. 51.

Cohen, J. (1992), "White consumer response to Asian models in advertising," *Journal of Consumer Marketing*, Vol. 9, Spring, pp. 17–27.

Di Benedetto, C. A., Tamate, M. and Chandran, R. (1992), "Developing creative advertising strategy for the Japanese marketplace," *Journal of Advertising Research*, January/February, Vol. 32, No. 1, pp. 39–48.

Edmondson, B. (1997), "Asian Americans in 2001," *American Demographics*, Vol. 19, No. 2, pp. 16–17.

Fisher, C. (1994). "Marketers straddle Asian-American curtain," *Advertising Age*, Vol. 65, No. 47, pp. 2, 18.

Graham, J. L., Kamis, M. A. and Oetomo, D. (1993), "Content analysis of German and Japanese advertising and print media from Indonesia, Spain, and the USA," *Journal of Advertising*, June, Vol. 22 No. 2, pp. 5–15.

Ho, B. (1997), "Communicating with the Asian-American traveler," unpublished manuscript.

Javalgi, R., Cutler, B. D. and White, S. D. (1994), "Print advertising in the Pacific Basin: an empirical investigation," *International Marketing Review*, Vol. 11, No. 6, pp. 48–64.

Larson, H. H. and Kleiner, B. H. (1992), "Understanding and effectively managing Asian employees," *Equal Opportunity International*, pp. 18–22.

Lin, C. A. (1993), "Cultural differences in message strategies: a comparison between American and Japanese television commercials," *Journal of Advertising Research*, July/August. Vol. 33 No. 4, pp. 40–8.

Marketing Review (1994), Vol. 50, pp. 6–18, 22–5.

Mogelonsky, M. (1995), "Asian-Indian Americans," *American Demographics*, Vol. 17, No. 8. pp. 32–6+.

Natividad, I. and Gall, S. B. (Eds) (1996), *Asian-American Almanac*, UXL, Detroit, MI.

Ownbey, S. F. and Horridge, P. E. (1997), "Acculturation levels and shopping orientations of Asian-American consumers," *Psychology and Marketing*, Vol. 14, No. 1, January, pp. 1–18.

Paisano, E. L. (1993). *We the Americans: Asians*, US Department of Commerce, Bureau of the Census, Washington, DC.

Penaloza, L. (1989), "Immigrant consumer acculturation," *Advances in Consumer Research*, Vol. 16, pp. 110–18.

Sturdivant, F. D. (1973), "Subculture theory: poverty, minorities and marketing," in Ward, S. and Robertson, T. S. (Eds), *Consumer Behavior: Theoretical Sources*, Prentice-Hall. Englewood Cliffs, NJ.

Taylor, C. R. and Lee, J. Y. (1994), "Not in vogue: Portrayals of Asian-Americans in US advertising," *Journal of Public Policy and Marketing*, Vol. 13, Fall, pp. 239–45.

Taylor, C. R. and Stern, B. B. (1997), "Asian-Americans: television advertising and the 'model minority' stereotype," *Journal of Advertising*, Vol. 26, No. 2, pp. 47–61.

Valencia, H. (1985), "Developing an index to measure Hispanicness," in Hirschman, E. and Holbrook, M. (Eds), *Advances in Consumer Research*, Vol. 12, Association for Consumer Research, Ann Arbor, MI, pp. 118–21.

Wallendorf, M. and Reilly, M. D. (1983), "Ethnic migration, assimilation, and consumption," *Journal of Consumer Research*, Vol. 10, December, pp. 292–302.

Weisendanger, B. (1993), "Asian-Americans: the three biggest myths," *Sales and Marketing Management*, September, pp. 86–8, 101.

Zandapour, F. (1994), "Global reach and local touch: achieving cultural fitness in television advertising," *Journal of Advertising Research*, September/October, Vol. 34, No. 5, pp. 35–63.

Zhang, Y. and Gelb, B. D. (1996), "Matching advertising appeals to culture: the influence of product use conditions," *Journal of Advertising*, Fall, Vol. 25, No. 3, pp. 29–46.

Zhou, N. and Belk, R. (1993), "China's advertising and the export marketing learning curve: the first decade," *Journal of Advertising Research*, November/December, Vol. 33, No. 6, pp. 50–66.

The author wishes to extend appreciation to Bryan Ho, Darwin Lacorte, William Mason, Celeste Pounds, Karen Parikh, and Meredith Roash for detailed literature reviewing and integration.

Defining Moments: Segmenting by Cohorts

Coming of age experiences influence values, attitudes, preferences, and buying behaviors for a lifetime.

By Charles D. Schewe, Geoffrey E. Meredith, and Stephanie M. Noble

Cohorts are highly influenced by the external events that were happening when they were "coming of age" (generally between the years 17–23). For example, those now in their late seventies and early eighties lived through the Great Depression while baby boomers witnessed the assassination of JFK, saw other political assassinations, shared the Vietnam War, and lived through the energy crisis. Such shared experiences distinguish one cohort from another.

Today, many call marketing to birth groups generational marketing. Generations differ from cohorts. Each generation is defined by its years of birth. For example, a generation is usually 20 to 25 years in length, or roughly the time it takes a person to grow up and have children. But a cohort can be as long or short as the external events that defines it. The cohort defined by World War II, for example, is only six years long.

Consider how different cohorts treat spending and saving. Today's Depression cohort, those ages 79 to 88 in 2000, began working during the Great Depression. Their conduct with respect to money is very conservative. Having experienced the worst of economic times, this age group values economic security and frugality. They still save for that "rainy day." Those, however, in the 55 to 78 age category today were influenced by the Depression, but also experienced the boom times of the Post-World War II period. This group has attitudes toward saving that are less conservative; they are more willing to spend than the older group. In sharp contrast to the "Depression-scarred" is the free-wheeling generation that grew up during the "hippie revolution." Russell (1993) calls this birth group the "free agents," since its members defied the establishment, sought individualism, and were skeptical of everything. This cohort can be characterized as "buy now, pay later" and its members will carry this value into the century ahead as they journey through middle age and on into old age.

Cohort effects are life-long effects. They provide the communality for each cohort being targeted as a separate market segment. And since these cohorts can be described by the ages of their constituents, they offer an especially efficient vehicle for direct marketing campaigns.

Six American Cohorts

In 2000, American adults can be divided into six distinct cohorts, or market segments, ranging in age from the Depression cohort (age 79–88) to what many people are calling Generation X (age 24–34). This division is based on intensive content analysis of a wide range of publications and studies scanned over a 10-year period. The roughly 4 million people who are age 89 and older are not included for two reasons. First, this group is much smaller than other cohorts. Also, much of their consumption behavior is controlled by physical need. There also are more than 72 million persons under the age of 24. This newly emerging cohort can be referred to as the "N-Gen," since the impact of the internet revolution appears to be the key defining moment shaping this group's values. Yet it is too early to know their "defining moment-driven" values, preferences, and attitudes because external forces take some time to influence values. A brief description of each of the six cohorts follows.

The Depression Cohort

This group was born between 1912 and 1921, came of age from 1930 to 1939, and is age 79–88 today. Currently this cohort contains 13,054,000 people, or 7% of the adult U.S. population.

This cohort was defined by the Great Depression. Maturing, entering the workforce, trying to build and support families during the '30s had a profound influence on this cohort in so many areas, but most strongly in finances: money and savings. To many of today's business managers, the Depression seems like ancient history, almost apocryphal, like the Great Flood. Yet to this cohort, it was all too real. To put the Depression in perspective, the S&P 400 (the broadest measure of the economy as a whole available at that time) declined 69% between 1929 and 1932 in a relentless and agonizing fall. It wasn't until 1953—24 years and a World War later—before the S&P index got back to where it had been in 1929! People starting out in this environment were scarred in ways they carry with them today. In particular, financial security still rules their thinking as reflected in the following example.

A Depression Cohort Marketing Example. One savings and loan bank on the West Coast took a cohort perspective to boost deposits from this cohort. They used an icon familiar to this age group, George Feneman (Groucho Marx's television sidekick on *You Bet Your Life*), who assured this cohort of the safety of their money. He stressed that the financial institution uses their money for mortgages. "We build houses," he says, which is just what this cohort can relate to, since preserving their homes was central to the financial concerns of this age group.

EXECUTIVE
briefing

Cohorts are groups of individuals who are born during the same time period and travel through life together. They experience similar external events during their late adolescent/early adulthood years. These "defining moments" influence their values, preferences, attitudes, and buying behaviors in ways that remain with them over their lifetime. We can identify six known American cohorts that include those from age 88 to those coming of age in 2000. While generational cohorts are far from the final solution for marketers, they are certainly a relevant dynamic. Marketers should seriously consider targeting these age groupings, especially in their marketing communications.

The World War II Cohort

Born 1922–1927, this cohort came of age from 1940 to 1945. Its members are age 73–78 today. Currently 9,465,000 people, it represents 5% of our adult population.

World War II defined this cohort. Economically it was not a boom time (the S&P 500 gained 50% from 1940 to 1945, but it was still only half of what it had been in 1929), but unemployment was no longer a problem. This cohort was unified by a common enemy, shared experiences, and especially for the 16 million in the military, a sense of deferment and delayed gratification. In World War I, the average duration of service was less than 12 months; in World War II, the average was 33 months. Marriages, careers, and children were all put on hold until the war was over.

This sense of deferment made the World War II cohort an intensely romantic one. The yearning for loved ones left behind, and for those who left to fight is reflected in the music and literature and movies of the time (e.g., *I've Got My Love to Keep Me Warm*, *Homesick*, *That's All*, *'Til Then*, and *You'd Be So Nice to Come Home To*). And, while for many the war was an unpleasant experience, for many others it was the apex of their lives. They had a defined role (frequently more important in status than any other they would ever have), a measure of freedom from their particular social norms, and an opportunity to travel, some to exotic foreign shores, others just away from the towns and cornfields of their youth. The horrors and heroism experienced by our soldiers imbedded values that stay with them still. And this influence was clearly depicted in the award-winning and highly acclaimed movies of 1998: *Saving Private Ryan* and *The Thin Red Line*.

A World War II Cohort Marketing Example. Using cohort words, symbols, and memories can bring substantial rewards for marketers. A direct marketing campaign designed for a cable television provider to increase subscriptions is just such an example. Postage stamp-sized pictures of Douglas McArthur were put on the corner of the envelope with the copy "If you remember V-J Day, we've got some new programs you're going to love." This attention-getter immediately communicated that the content is for members of the targeted cohort. When this approach was used, subscription response rates surged from 1.5% to more than 10%.

The Post-War Cohort

Members of this cohort were born from 1928 to 1945, came of age from 1946 to 1963, and are age 55 to 73 in 2000. Currently 42,484,000 people, 22.7% of the adult population are Post-Wars.

This cohort is a very long one—18 years span the youngest to the oldest members. They were the beneficiaries of a long period of economic growth and relative social tranquility. Economically the S&P 500, which had struggled until 1953 just to get back to where it had been before the Depression, then tripled over the next 10 years. There were dislocations during this time—the Korean War in the early '50s, Sputnik in 1957, the first stirrings of the civil rights movement, a brief recession in 1958—but by and large, at least on the surface, things were pretty quiet.

The tenor of the times was conservative, seeking the comfortable, the secure, and the familiar. It was a time that promoted conformity and shrank from individual expression, which is why the overt sexuality of Elvis and the rebellion of James Dean were at once popular and scandalous.

A Post-War Cohort Marketing Example. The Vermont Country Store, highly successful marketers of nostalgic products difficult to find, uses cohort images and memories to target market segments. To capture the attention of Post-War cohort customers, it peppers its catalog with pictures from the '50s and value-reflective copy along the outside of various pages such as:

"When I was young, I knew kids who were allowed in their living rooms only on special occasions—and usually under adult supervision. Now, instead of a chilly room used only to entertain on holidays, we can really relax in our living rooms."
and
"In high school, buying clothes was easy. The more we dressed according to the conventions of the day, the better. If we'd known then what we know now, we could have looked every bit as good—and been a lot more comfortable. But then, that wasn't the point of being a teenager."

Boomers—I

The Baby Boom is usually defined as the 76 million people born between 1946 and 1964, since this is indeed when the annual birthrate bulged to more than 4 million per year. However there are two boomer cohorts. The first of these are the leading-edge boomers and they are 32,531,000 people strong, 17.4% of the adult population. They were born from 1946 to 1954, and came of age from 1963 to 1972. They are age 46 to 54 today.

Due to their numbers, the baby boomers as a whole have dominated marketing in America since they first appeared on the scene. When they were truly babies, they made Dr. Spock's *Infant and Child Rearing* the second best-selling book in the history of the world, after the Bible. As pre-teens, they dominated the media in shows like *Leave It to Beaver* and in merchandising with fads like Davy Crockett caps and Hula Hoops. As teens they propelled Coke, McDonald's, and Motown into corporate giants, and ensured the success of Clearasil.

The "Boomer I" cohort began coming of age in 1963, the start of a period of profound dislocations that still haunt our society today. It ended shortly after the last soldier died in Vietnam. The Kennedy presidency seemed like the natural extension of continued good times, of economic growth and domestic stability. It represented a liberated and early transfer of power from an older leader to a much younger one.

The Kennedy assassination, followed by that of Martin Luther King and Robert Kennedy, signaled an end to the status quo and galvanized a very large boomer cohort just entering its formative years. Suddenly the leadership (LBJ) was no longer 'theirs,' the war (Vietnam) was not their war, and authority and the establishment which had been the bedrock of earlier cohorts disintegrated in the melee of the 1968 Democratic National Convention in Chicago.

However, the Boomer I cohort continued to experience economic good times. Despite the social turmoil, the economy as a whole, as measured by the S&P 500, continued an upward climb. The Boomer I cohort wanted a lifestyle at least as good as they had experienced as children in the '50s, and with nearly 20 years of steady economic growth as history, they had no reason not to spend whatever they earned or could borrow to achieve it.

The Boomer I cohort still heavily values its individualism (remember, they were and are the "Me Generation,") indulgence of self, stimulation (a reflection of the drug culture they grew up with), and questioning nature. Marketing to this cohort demands attention to providing more information to back up product claims and to calm skeptical concerns. And these boomers prize holding on to their youth as the following example shows.

A Boomer I Cohort Marketing Example. The California Prune Board recommended to its plum producers that they plant many more trees, since large numbers of baby boomers were turning 50 and the 50+ age bracket (indeed, the 65+) was the heaviest consumer of prunes. However, boomers did not relate to prunes; they did not come of age with prunes as part of their consumption lives. Why, then, would they eat prunes in later life? In fact, prunes reflect cohort preferences of their parents—those same parents boomers did not want to trust ("Don't Trust Anyone Over 30").

Research into the chemical composition of prunes, however, found that they naturally stimulate the body's production of testosterone and estrogen... just the ingredients aging boomers desire to hold on to their sexual vitality and sense of youth. Clinical studies to provide advertising claim support for the estrogen and testosterone benefits were being undertaken. This approach could lead to, for example, a radio or television commercial featuring Adam and Eve in the Garden of Eden. Eve requests some fruit for sustenance, since they have a big night ahead populating the earth. She is delighted to receive a platter including one lonely prune (no apples, please). Her comment as she gulps the prune: "Well, this should get us through Asia, at least!"

Boomers II

The trailing-edge boomers were born between 1956 and 1965, came of age from 1973 to 1983, and are age 35 to 45 today. Currently 46,794,000 people are Boomer II's, 26% of the adult population.

The external events that separate the Boomer I from the Boomer II cohort were less dramatic than The Depression or World War II, but were just as real. They were composed of the stop of the Vietnam War (it never really ended—just stopped), Watergate (the final nail in the coffin of institutions and the establishment), and the Arab Oil Embargo that ended the stream of economic gains that had continued largely uninterrupted since 1945.

By 1973, something had changed for a person coming of age in America. While faith in institutions had gone, so had the idealist fervor that made the Boomer I cohort so cause-oriented. Instead, those in the Boomer II cohort exhibited a narcissistic preoccupation with themselves which manifested itself in everything from the self-help movement (*I'm OK—You're OK*, and various young and aging gurus imported from India) to self-deprecation (*Saturday Night Live, Mary Hartman, Mary Hartman*).

The change in economic fortunes had a more profound effect than is commonly realized. Throughout their childhood and as they came of age, the Boomer I cohort members experienced good times; their expectations that these good times would continue were thus reinforced, and the cohort mindset formed at that time can be seen today in a persistent resistance to begin saving for retirement. Things had been good, and they were going to stay good—somehow.

For the Boomer II cohort, the money mindset was much different. The Oil Shock of 1973 sent the economy tumbling: the S&P 500 lost 30% of its value between 1973 and 1975! At the same time, inflation began to resemble that of a banana republic. During this period, the real interest rate (Prime minus the CPI) hit a record low of -4%. In those circumstances, debt as a means of maintaining a lifestyle makes great economic sense. And a cohort with a 'debt imprint' will never lose it. Boomers II are spenders just like the Boomer Is, but for a different reason. It's not because they expect good times, but because they assume they can always get a loan, take out a second mortgage on the house, get another credit card, and never have to "pay the piper."

A Boomer II Cohort Marketing Example. A major finance company is currently aggressively promoting home equity loans with radio advertising directly oriented toward this cohort mindset. The commercial in essence states "Everyone else has a BMW, or a new set of golf clubs, and they're not any better than you are. Even if you don't think you can afford them, you can have them, now—with a home equity loan from XYZ company. And, while you're at it, why not take the

Hawaiian vacation, too—you deserve it!" The copy brings on severe anxiety attacks for the World War II and Depression cohorts, but it makes perfect sense to the Boomer IIs.

Generation X

Born 1966–1976, Gen Xers came of age from 1984 to 1994. They are age 24 to 34 today. Currently 41,119,000 people, they represent 21.9% of the adult population.

Much has been written about Generation X, most of it derogatory in tone: "Slackers" (from the movie of that name); "Whiners"; "a generation of aging Bart Simpsons," "armed and possibly dangerous." That seems to be unfair. The generation of F. Scott Fitzgerald was widely characterized as "Lost," and that describes Generation X. This cohort has nothing to hang on to—not the institutions of the Post-War cohort, not the Boomer I's idealism and causes and institutions to resist, not the narcissism of the Boomer IIs. These were the children of divorce and daycare, latch-key kids of the 1980s; no wonder they exhibit so little foundation. The fact that they are searching for anchors can be seen in their seemingly contradictory "retro" behavior—the resurgence of proms, coming-out parties, and fraternities that Boomers rejected.

It can be seen in their political conservatism, which is also motivated by a "What's in it for me?" cynicism that repudiates liberal redistribution tendencies. And they feel alienated, reflected in the violence and brutal sex of the popular culture, and resigned to a world that seems to have little hope of offering them the lifestyles of their parents.

A Generation X Cohort Marketing Example. So how does a marketer reach a cohort with no defining moments? One way is with irreverent, rebellious, self-mocking, and sassy portrayals—which helps explain the popularity of South Park, the Simpsons, and the infamous Married With Children. Commercials like Maybelline's ad for Expert Eyes Shadow with Christy Turlington also exemplifies this sassiness. The ad shows the stunning model with beautifully made-up eyes illuminated by moonlight. A voice-over says: "Was it a strange celestial event… that gave her such bewitching eyes?" Then Turlington, sitting on her living room sofa, laughs and says, "Get over it."

Managerial Implications

Cohort segmentation provides a most intriguing additional method for separating consumer markets. Age has long been a segmentation variable, but this innovative approach shows it is defining moments that shape mindsets and provide the true value of age targeting. While not a key behavior driver for all product categories, cohort segmentation is particularly appropriate for food, music, apparel, automotive, financial and insurance, as well as entertainment products. Product creation and management over its life cycle is clearly ripe for cohort implementation.

Cohort analysis can help in designing communication campaigns. Determining music, movie stars, or other icons that cohorts identified with in their past is an effective selling technique. These tactics work because they rely on nostalgia marketing, that is, tapping deep, pleasurable memories of what seemed simpler, better times. They also work by calling out the target in an implicit way. "This message is for you!" Many companies have already engaged in this tactic as evidenced by the growing number of songs, logos, and actual commercial footage from the past.

Additionally, the changing nature of values across cohorts has important implications for marketers. As new cohorts enter the marketplace, organizations need to keep apprised of their changing value structures. In particular, as the age distribution in the United States changes, so will consumers' wants and needs. A cohort analysis can help track and forecast these wants and needs. In the 1980s, for example, the age segment of 50–65 years was comprised mostly of Depression and World War II cohort consumers. Today, it is made up mostly of the Post-War cohort and in 2010 it will be all Boomers. The demographic age segmentation—age 50 to 65—is the same, but the composition of that segment is constantly changing. It's a moving target.

Final Thought

Cohort segmentation works in the United States. But what about outside of the United States? Would cohorts be the same as here? Our research has found cohort values derived from defining moments indeed do exist abroad. Germany, for example, witnessed no Depression as Hitler's war effort energized the economy. In Brazil, the 1970s found a dictatorship imposing severe censorship, which created the need for personal freedoms in individuals coming of age during that time. In Jordan,

the Six-Day War in 1967 dramatically displaced Jordanians from their homeland and they now long for stability in maintaining a place to live. As these examples illustrate, cohort segmentation offers a rich opportunity here… and around the world.

Additional Reading

Meredith, Geoffrey and Charles D. Schewe (1994), "The Power of Cohorts," *American Demographics*, December, 22–31.

Rentz, Joseph O. and Fred D. Reynolds (1991), "Forecasting the Effects of an Aging Population on Product Consumption: An Age-Period-Cohort Framework," *Journal of Marketing Research*, 28, (3), 355–60.

——, ——, and Roy G. Stout (1983), "Analyzing Changing Consumption Patterns With Cohort Analysis," *Journal of Marketing Research*, 20, 12–20.

Russell, Cheryl (1993), *The Master Trend: How the Baby Boom Generation Is Remaking America*, Plenum, New York.

Schewe, Charles D. and Stephanie M. Noble (forthcoming), "Market Segmentation by Cohorts: The Value and Validity of Cohorts in America and Abroad," *Journal of Marketing Management* (Scotland).

Schuman, Howard and Jacqueline Scott (1989). "Generations and Collective Memories," *American Sociological Review*, 54, (3), 359–381.

Smith, J. Walker and Ann Clurman (1997), *Rocking the Ages*, Harper Business, New York.

Strauss, William and Neil Howe (1997), *The Fourth Turning*, Broadway Books, New York.

About the Authors

Charles D. Schewe is professor of marketing at the University of Massachusetts and a principal in Lifestage Matrix Marketing. Focusing on the marketing implications of the aging process, Schewe has advised such companies as Coca-Cola, Kellogg's, Kraft General Foods, Time-Life, Lucky Stores, Grand Metropolitan, and K-Mart. He may be reached at schewe@mktg.umass.edu.

Geoffrey E. Meredith is president of Lifestage Matrix Marketing, located in Lafayette, Calif. Formerly a senior vice president at Olgivy & Mather, Ketchum Communications, and Hal Riney and Partners, he also spent two years with Age Wave (see V1,N3 MM). He may be reached at Lifestage@aol.com.

Stephanie M. Noble is a doctoral candidate at the University of Massachusetts. She may be reached at smevans@som.umass.edu.

From *Marketing Management*, Fall 2000, Vol. 9, No. 3, pp. 48–53. © 2000 by the American Marketing Association. Reprinted by permission.

what are your customers saying?

Online communities shed a light on consumer behavior.

By Eric L. Lesser and Michael A. Fontaine

How does a small, employee-owned business with a commodity product survive in an era of mega brands and price-sensitive customers? King Arthur Flour (KAF), a leading seller of flour and baking supplies, has tapped into its customers' energy and devotion by launching its Baking Circle, an online community for professional and home bakers. The site provides an opportunity for KAF to interact directly with thousands of its customers. It's designed to help members become better bakers and at the same time provide KAF with valuable insights about how its customers use the company's products and services.

Organizations are always looking for ways to learn about customers' preferences, wants, and needs and to educate customers about their products and services. Over the last few years, organizations have added community functions to their traditional e-commerce sites to help customers make connections and build relationships with each other. Through our research with the IBM Institute for Knowledge-Based Organizations, we've found that online communities can provide a number of valuable learning opportunities for both customers and the organizations that sponsor them.

Online Communities

Recent interest in fostering customer communities in an online environment has been fueled by a number of forces. First is the need to attract repeat visitors by adding value during the Web experience. As the number of individuals connected online continues to the rise, many of them are using the Internet to reach out to others with similar needs and interests. An October 31, 2001, study by the Pew Internet & American Life Project (Horrigan, John B., *Online Communities: Networks that Nurture Long-Distance Relationships and Local Ties*) found that approximately 23 million Americans participate in at least one online group several times per week. When asked what types of online groups they participated in, more than 50% said they were involved in trade and professional organizations or groups that shared a hobby or interest.

EXECUTIVE briefing

Organizations are always looking for ways to learn more about their customers. At the same time, they're searching for ways to boost their online presence and attract repeat traffic to their Web sites. To address both needs, organizations are using the online community environment to bring together customers with common interests. By paying attention to what customers are saying online, organization can leverage online communities to gain new customer insights and reinforce customer loyalty.

Many firms, recognizing this opportunity, have begun to provide a virtual "space" where individuals can connect and engage with others around shared concerns. By providing an additional source of value for visitors to their Web sites, many organizations have been able to increase both the number of repeat visitors and the average amount of time spent per visitor during any single visit. For example, McKinsey and Co. recently found that users of community features represented about one-third of all visitors to leading e-tailing sites, but generated two-thirds of the sites' overall sales.

Online communities are also driven by the need to create effective customer learning and communication channels. While the advent of CRM systems has produced a glut of data about customer transactions, many organizations are still wrestling with the challenge of actually learning about their customers. Online communities can provide a forum for engaging with customers and learning from these interactions. By conducting extended dialogues with individuals within the community, observing conver-

Exhibit 1

Community Web sites

Organization	Target Audience	URL
Agilent	Users of testing and measurement devices	www.measurement.tm.agilent.com/appcentral.html
Cabela's	Users of camping and outdoors equipment	www.cabelas.com
Compaq	Owners of Compaq computer equipment	www7.compaq.com/forum
Hallmark	Individuals willing to discuss life events	private community
King Arthur Flour	Professional and home bakers	www.bakingcircle.com
Mercury Interactive	Software developers and users	private community
Palm	Palm personal digital assistant users	http://www.palm.com/community/
SAP	Software developers and users	www.sap.com/community
Sony	Video game (Playstation) enthusiasts	www.scea.com/underground
Sun	Software developers and users	www.sun.com/forums

sations between participants, and reviewing frequently asked questions and discussion postings, firms are finding new windows into customer preferences and behaviors.

One company that has been using online communities as a vehicle for learning is Hallmark, which has been observing the online conversations of 200 consumers on its "Idea Exchange" Web site. As Faith Keenan reported in the July 9, 2001, issue of *Business Week,* Hallmark researchers are reviewing and participating in these conversations to identify different types of events and audiences that reflect potential greeting card subjects and trends. Based on these dialogues, Hallmark has developed new ideas for cards, such as mother-in-law cards and sympathy cards for the anniversary of a death.

On a larger scale, Compaq Computers has set up an online community that has attracted more than 92,000 registered users in its first years. As Bob Tedeschi reported in a February 11, 2002, *New York Times* article, Compaq has leveraged the questions and answers posted in the community space to identify software glitches, alter product designs, and adjust promotional campaigns.

The need to provide effective customer service in a cost-effective manner is also a factor in the growth of online communities. In these communities, customers have an opportunity to pose questions to one another, share documents, post photographs, and discuss topics of mutual interest. When faced with a particular problem, an individual can engage the collective wisdom of hundreds of others, rather than a few employees within a company's customer support organization. Enabling

customers to answer each other's questions can significantly reduce an organization's overall support costs. A presentation at the Horizons 2002 World Conference highlighted the case of Mercury Interactive, a provider of enterprise testing and performance management software. The company launched a community that provided customer support assistance in 2000. In the first quarter of 2001, it found it was 95% cheaper for a question to be answered from postings to a support forum than from a call or e-mail to the customer support center. Further, communities can allow customers to get their answers more quickly and enable the company to discover solutions to problems it hadn't previously encountered or even considered.

Customer Community Spaces

The community sites we examined demonstrated multiple opportunities for gathering data and insights that can support learning about customers. For example, during the registration process, we found that companies can obtain a great deal of information about new members, ranging from valuable demographic data to understanding an individual's specific areas of interest. Also, discussion boards provide the opportunity for customers to learn from other customers, while at the same time allowing companies to glean important insights from their conversations. Interactive events, such as synchronous chats and Web seminars, let customers connect directly with the corporation, simultaneously learning about and sharing experiences about purchasing and using the company's products and services. Each of these different learning opportunities can be leveraged to create value for both the participating customer and the sponsoring organization.

Registration. Nearly all the sites we examined require individuals to go through a registration process to participate in community activities. The first part of the process is to create a unique identity that includes a registration name and a password. This allows individuals to be recognized by other participants on the community site. Second, many of the sites ask individuals to provide demographic information and select areas of interest related to a particular product or service. This lets the organization develop rich profiles of its online users that can be used for customer segmentation. Several of the sites use this information to tailor specific content views to their members, adjusting the community experience to individual needs. By allowing members to specify their interests, these sites attempt to reduce the amount of time individuals spend searching for relevant information.

Community discussion boards. At the heart of many online communities are discussion boards, where members post questions, comments, and suggestions for others. These forums allow users to conduct organized discussions where several people can comment on a single topic. Discussion boards are useful tools for maintaining the "community memory" while providing a forum for members to express their viewpoints and ask for assistance. For example, Palm, the developer of handheld personal digital assistants, provides a community discussion board (now operated and moderated by Brighthand.com, a larger community site for handheld enthusiasts) that offers an extensive set of areas focused on general product issues, specific handheld models, and ideas for new features.

Similarly, Cabela's, an outdoor equipment retailer, provides a discussion space that engages individuals interested in hunting, fishing, and advice on the latest camping gear. This board has a section that solicits feedback on Cabela's own products and services. The company actively monitors it and provides answers to questions and concerns about its products. Virtual spaces such as those provided by Palm and Cabela's help build connections that encourage repeat visits, engage customers in dialogues that can be used to spot early trends in the market, and support customers looking for additional information.

Company-sponsored activities. In addition to using discussion boards, community members often take advantage of interactions with, and content provided by, the company itself. While these features don't directly foster discussion between individual members, they can add significant value by providing interesting and relevant content to community members. These activities, in turn, can further encourage community members to return to the site.

Synchronous chats with experts. Many customer community sites offer opportunities to engage members in online dialogues with internal experts. For example, SAP regularly holds a number of "ask-the-expert" discussions about technical and business-related topics for its com-

munity members. Such sessions allow participants to ask questions on topics such as industry trends, planned enhancements, and future product directions. These chats can then be captured and stored for individuals who can't participate in the online discussion. Interactions like these often give members a sense of having access to company "insiders" and at the same time enable the company to establish a real-time dialogue with its customers.

Web seminars. Several of the community sites provide online training courses that members can take to learn about the company's products and services. These range from very basic courses with simple instructions augmented by pictures to well-orchestrated multimedia productions with voice discussions and synchronous chat. Sun Microsystems is an example of an organization that frequently runs Web seminars conducted by its technical staff to educate interested software developers about Sun's product lines and technologies. Organizations that conduct Web seminars can help customers use their products and services more effectively, and encourage complementary purchases.

Online polling. Many community sites use online polling to both generate content for members and learn about customer ideas and preferences. Members are asked to answer short questionnaires, and the results are posted and archived for members to view when they return to the site. Sony, in its "Playstation Pulse" section, recently asked its members which characters they'd like to see matched up in its video games. The results of the survey were quickly posted on the site. Polling can be a valuable tool for engaging members and learning valuable lessons without a significant commitment of time or effort.

E-mail newsletters. E-mail newsletters are often used to send out regular updates to community members without requiring them to go to the Web site. Agilent Technologies, for example, provides e-mail updates to members of its Test and Measurement community on a range of topics, such as product support information and new developments in the world of testing and measurement equipment. Members can customize their e-mail and only receive information on topics they select as part of their profile. While e-mail newsletters themselves don't support the interaction that helps build a successful online community, they remind members to check out new content on the community site.

The Case of King Arthur Flour

KAF's online customer community, the Baking Circle, came about as the result of some of the company's initial forays into the world of e-commerce. Starting in 1997, one of the firm's first Web-based activities was to give individuals the opportunity to order its catalogue online. When individuals requested the catalogue, they were asked to complete a short online questionnaire about themselves. The firm was amazed to find that 88% of people who requested the catalogue filled out the survey, and more than 40% provided additional comments about the firm's Web site and the company in general. Recognizing that KAF had a devoted clientele in cyberspace, the company's director of MIS and Internet operations began to envision ways the Web could be used to help get closer to its customers. In previous years, the company had conducted in-person focus groups and mail surveys, but found it could never develop a true representation of its customers and their needs.

In the years before the launch of the Baking Circle, KAF had begun to establish the components of its community strategy. In November 1999 it created *The Round Table,* an e-newsletter that initially reached more than 5,000 people, but quickly grew to a distribution of 20,000 people. At the same time, it began to produce online baking classes via its Web site, using a combination of step-by-step directions and photographs.

Based on the initial success of these components, KAF decided to launch a community site in September 2001. The company created a broader community site that, in addition to the online classes, consisted of a bulletin board that could store discussion threats and an area where individuals could view recipes and store them in a personal section. Initially, KAF gave the community site only a limited amount of structure because they wanted the community members to decide what the site would look like and how it would evolve. During the site's first weekend of operation, more than 750 people sent in questions and suggestions about the site. Within the first three months of operation, more than 10,000 people had registered on the site.

Members of the firm's operating team frequently monitor and occasionally contribute to the community site. As a result, KAF has already learned a great deal about its customers. For example, it discovered more than 20% of customer inquiries were regarding sourdough bread—a development that was quickly shared with members of the firms' new product development group. Further, through the community, the firm was able to evaluate the types of stores where products were available—insights that were particularly valuable to the firm's sales and marketing teams. The firm is also beginning to look at community members' purchasing behavior on the site and is rewarding frequent purchasers with Baker's Points that are tracked online.

KAF is continually looking to upgrade its community site. Some ideas for doing this include enabling members to create profiles that others can view online and letting them post photos of themselves, display their creations, and facilitate online chats with the company's "master bakers." Each of these modifications is designed to create additional content for members, allow them to interact with one another on a regular basis, and build a greater sense of loyalty and affiliation to the site, and ultimately, to the company and its products.

As this case study demonstrates, adding community functionality to a Web site can provide real benefits for both customers and organizations. Customers use these communities to connect with individuals with similar ideas and interests, find answers to difficult questions, and learn more about an organization's products and services. At the same time, companies can leverage these communities to increase repeat site visits, reduce support costs, engage customers in dialogue about current and future products and services, and learn from community members' extended discussions with each another. Insights gained from these customer interactions can be shared and leveraged by many parts of the enterprise, ranging from customer support to new product development.

Additional Reading

Brown, Shona L., Andrew Tilton, and Dennis Woodside (2002), "The Case for Online Communities," *The McKinsey Quarterly,* (1), Web exclusive.

Cothrel, Joe and Patrick Saeger (2001), "Increasing Customer Satisfaction and Reducing Costs Through an Online Technical Support Community," paper presented at the Horizons 2002 World Conference, Savannah, GA (Oct. 2).

About the Authors

Eric L. Lesser is an executive consultant and the research manager with the IBM Institute for Knowledge-Based Organizations in Cambridge, Mass. He may be reached at ELESSER@us.ibm.com. **Michael A. Fontaine** is a senior consultant with the IBM Institute for Knowledge-Based Organizations. He may be reached at MFONTAIN@us.ibm.com.

Tough Love

In this economy, maintaining good relationships with customers is vital.
So what do you do about clients or prospects you can't stand?
Here's how to charm your five most difficult customer types

by Justin Berzon

In the booming 1990s, sales executives and their reps could afford to show pain-in-the-you-know-what customers the door. In this economic climate, losing a prospect, or worse yet, an existing account, can be devastating to the bottom line. Managers and salespeople alike are constantly reminding themselves of the old adage that the customer is always right, as they seek to please their spectrum of clients and court new business. But within that range of valued customers, there's the easy sell and there's the client from hell. When it comes to the latter, strategies exist for dealing with a difficult personality that might turn a tense initial meeting into a beautiful (and profitable) new relationship. We've broken down the tough crowd into five personality types, and we've also consulted experts and sales executives to find out how to deal with clients who roll their eyes, change their minds, and demand over-the-top treatment, all without losing your mind—or the deal.

MR. GREEDY

You've seen this guy many times before: He's the one who makes crazy demands and wants you to shower him with perks and gifts in exchange for business. He brags about what your competitors are giving him in exchange for his business and wants you to do the same. He might as well be wearing a T-shirt that reads, "What's In It for Me?"

Obviously, you have two major options with Mr. Greedy: appease him and make concessions, or refuse, stand by your product, and let him take it or leave it. Steve Rothberg, founder and president of Minneapolis-based Internet job board CollegeRecruiter.com, says he uses a system of categorizing demanding clients, first as large or small customers, and second as rude or polite. For polite clients, he'll go out of his way to meet their special requests. Catering to the de-

mands of big Mr. Greedies can often mean a big payoff. Catering to small-but-polite clients makes sense, too, Rothberg says, because there's always the chance that a small client will someday become a big client if you treat him well.

However, when it comes to clients who are not polite about making special requests for service, he handles large and small clients differently. "For larger clients, I'll grit my teeth and give them what they want," Rothberg says. "You're never going to like all of your customers, but it's still good business and good revenue." But Rothberg stops pursuing small clients who ask for special favors and aren't particularly charming about it. If they are existing customers, he lets them go when their service contracts or agreements run out.

Another way to keep Mr. Greedy in check is to preemptively offer certain bonuses and special deals so he doesn't have any ground to stand on when asking for additional perks. Ron Kern, president and general manager of the Las Vegas branch of Ferguson Enterprises, a Newport News, Virginia–based plumbing supplies wholesale distributor, says his firm takes its best clients on excursions, such as deep-sea fishing trips to Cabo San Lucas, and several golf outings each year. He uses these bonding events to keep clients in the loop year-round and alert them to special discounts and promotions before they ever have the chance to ask, making them feel that they're already getting luxury treatment. "Yeah, these guys want perks, but sometimes if it's a good client or potential client, you just have to factor that in as a cost of doing business," Kern says.

THE WAFFLER

When push comes to shove, this prospect just can't make up his mind. He lacks self-confidence, and as a result, even when the deal is ultimately signed, he'll make a million further revisions and impulsive decisions. He'll run your entire sales team ragged with his constant changes.

> **When it comes to awaiting that final purchasing decision, make sure that a waffling prospect is in fact the one responsible for making the final call. By the very nature of their indecisiveness, Wafflers are rarely the actual decision makers.**

The best way to deal with a Waffler, says Charlotte, North Carolina-based sales trainer Landy Chase, is to assign the most confident salesperson to work with him. "These folks will generally gravitate toward salespeople with a high degree of expertise, because it lowers their risk of making a bad decision," Chase says.

Wafflers often lack technical expertise or confidence, which Chase says salespeople can capitalize on if they go about it the fight way. "These people are afraid to make decisions, lest they make the wrong one. If you can step into a leadership role, they'll likely fall into a follower one," Chase says.

Rothberg, on the other hand, takes a more dismissive approach to indecisive buyers. He says he shifts such clients into a low-maintenance mode, where he follows up through e-malls, not long phone conversations. He says that he can spend up to 100 hours communicating back and forth with a major Waffler, only to get the same amount of business he would from one hour with someone who is willing and able to make a decision. "You've got to realize sometimes that spending a tremendous amount of time on this kind of a client just won't help," Rothberg says. "Sometimes they need time to procrastinate. Oh, they'll come back when it gets to be a crisis, and then they'll finally make their decision."

Joseph Rofe, president of J&A Direct, which operates the automotive Web site MisterCarHead.com, uses reverse psychology when dealing with Wafflers. He tells them they should take more time to carefully think out their decision after he's explained the deal in the most thorough terms. They usually counter by insisting they are ready to buy. It's also essential to eliminate the buyer's reluctance in advance, he says. Using an unconventional method, Rofe hands new clients a package of Smarties candy, telling them to eat a single piece whenever they feel a sense of buyer's remorse coming on or any lack of confidence that they should have made the purchase. "You'd be surprised how well it works," he says. (Such tactics might not play out well in all businesses, but Rofe insists that, they work with his particular client base.)

When it comes to awaiting that final purchasing decision, however, Chase cautions sellers to make sure that a waffling prospect is in fact the responsible for making the final call. "By the very nature of their indecisiveness, Wafflers are rarely the actual decision makers," Chase says. He recommends using this generic question to find out for sure if the Waffler is indeed the decision maker. "Assuming we were to move forward, who besides yourself would be involved?"

THE DOUBTING THOMAS

This person has had too many encounters with the stereotypical used car salesman. (Either that, or he's seen *Glengarry Glen Ross* one too many times.) He thinks salespeople are sleazy and doesn't want to give them the time of day. He won't let your reps in the door, and if he does, he makes negative comments and rolls his eyes when they tell him they want to help meet his needs.

Should you give up on Thomas? Absolutely not. In fact some managers, such as CollegeRecruiter.com's Rothberg, lure them in by giving them a free service. "I offer a free, no-strings-attached trial," Rothberg says. "That quickly separates the doubters who will try the product at no risk from the people who just simply can't make a decision. By providing this free service, I let them sell themselves on me."

Kristin Anderson, founder and president of Burnsville, Minnesota–based Say What? Consulting, warns that seeing Thomas as a lost sale can quickly become a self-fulfilling prophecy. "You think to yourself that this person is skeptical, dismissive, doesn't care what you have to say, and probably won't buy," she says. "Then you fall into the trap of giving a perfunctory sales pitch and make it all come true."

Anderson also says it's important with this type of person to demonstrate your flexibility. Make it clear that you can always come back later if he prefers, or that you are ready to work around his schedule. "If they see you as a salesperson, it isn't going to work," Anderson says. "With this customer, you've got to step out of character. Stop, laugh, reiterate that you're there to help them, but add comments like, 'Bet you've heard that a million times before' to lighten the atmosphere. You've got to be their buddy and be able to start with a friendly conversation, which should almost certainly be about something outside of work and business."

HOW TO (AMICABLY) DIVORCE YOUR CLIENT

STOP COURTING HIS BUSINESS Just let yourself discreetly fade into the background. Stop pursuing new ventures with him (but be sure to follow through on any current commitments). When his contract with you runs out, don't go out of your way to renew it. And if the two of you were in the process of exploring any new projects, you can claim to be too bogged down to work on them for now.

RECOMMEND A CHANGE IN HANDLERS With great deference, explain to your client that you don't think your firm is a good fit for him anymore. Having pored over his list of service needs, you don't think you'll be able to adequately commit the time and resources he deserves. Tell him that this would be a good time to make a clean break, and recommend a new firm that might be better able to cater to his needs. One caveat: Don't refer to a friend's firm—sending a difficult client to a fellow company or business partner could strain your relationship with that business.

BE FRANK Some people just can't take a hint. In this case, as a last resort, you may have to follow the example of Edina, Minnesota–based marketing consultant Kevin Donlin of Guaranteed Marketing. When Donlin can no longer tolerate a client, he simply tells him, "It looks like we don't have a good fit here, so I'm releasing you as a client, effective immediately. I wish you the best in moving forward."

Sound cold? "No matter how well you serve your clients, about one to three percent will never be happy no matter what you do," Donlin says. "Time isn't money—it's everything. So don't waste yours on people who don't understand or appreciate what your business does for them."

—*J.B.*

THE BEST FRIEND

These guys or gals have a hard time saying "no" because they want to be everybody's best pal. They'll go out with you and tell you that your products or services are their favorite, but meanwhile, they're telling all of your competitors the same thing.

"Tenure and time with that Best Friend is going to offer the biggest amount of ammunition against their wavering on loyalty," Ferguson's Kern says.

Chase says the main motivation of the Best Friend is that "they want to be liked and they don't want to upset anyone or be the one to give bad news." They react negatively to pressure, so try to avoid being overly aggressive or appearing exasperated, he says.

However, Kern says that after the members of your team have developed a rapport with the Best Friend, it's okay to confront him as long as it's in a positive manner. "At some point, you're within your right to make your own demands," Kern says. "If he's telling you that you're the best, you've got to ask him for the opportunity to prove it. You have to cross that bridge of talk and qualify his opinion with action."

Should you take this step, Chase suggests asking for a commitment in the form of a conditional "yes." For instance, ask the question: "If we (the company) can do this action, do we have a basis for moving forward with this deal?"

Chase says it's important to try to positively and unintrusively determine if there's any potential to actually close a deal, because your time and that of the client is very valuable.

And by all means, leave a lasting impression on the Best Friend. "When there are multiple contenders vying for this sort of fickle client's business," Chase says, "always make sure you're the last one to meet with him before he's going to make the final decision."

THE SILENT TYPE

One of the most frustrating client types, these individuals don't ask many questions and don't reveal what they are thinking through body language or other cues. Salespeople have a hard time gauging their level of interest in the product or service. Do they love your product or think it stinks?

Not to fret, though. The problem may not lie in the client's disinterest in your product—or your salesperson. Say What?'s Anderson says silence can stem from a cultural difference or even a simple issue of comprehension. "Saleswomen often think men aren't interested, but it's really because men generally give less nonverbal feedback," she says. "In other words, male clients may be very much interested in your presentation, but they are culturally less inclined to give visual responses and acknowledgement."

It may also be possible that clients don't understand the information you are presenting, Anderson says. Often they feel too insecure to ask questions, because they think it will make them look bad. They're supposed to be knowledgeable about services they already get or are considering purchasing, "The most proactive approach to dealing with this is to check in and say, 'I noticed you are quiet,' or 'I noticed you didn't have any questions. Do you understand everything?'" Anderson says.

But she also concedes that silence may be a negotiation tactic. "Silence is a powerful tool, thus that famous saying that the first one to speak is the loser," Anderson says. "They're hoping if they remain silent, it'll force you into breaking down. Maybe you'll knock off a few bucks for them."

Simma Lieberman, a Berkeley, California–based author and consultant, agrees. She says people use silence as a way of taking power and getting what they want. "If I'm being silent on the phone or in person, it's because I want more than what the person is offering me," she says. In this case, it would be up to the discretion of the salesperson, upon recognizing the prospect is using this tactic, to decide if further negotiation is in his best interest.

Kern tries to get quiet or unresponsive clients to open up by dealing with them in a more comfortable environment. For instance, he has a contractor client who used to send representatives to pick up orders and handle day-to-day relations with Ferguson. The contractor was reticent, rarely becoming too personally involved in dealings, so Kern invited him and his wife over to his house for dinner. They've since developed a more open dialogue, and the contractor has greatly increased his business with Kern. "Mind you, you can't change the stripes on an animal," Kern says. "He's still shy and removed from day-to-day dealings, but our underlying rapport has made him amenable to doing more business."

CUTTING YOUR LOSSES

Of course, there are instances when a nagging client is too much of a drain on your firm's resources (not to mention your patience), and he just isn't worth the hassle. In this case, you may want to consider discontinuing your business relationship with him. However, CollegeRecruiter. com's Rothberg cautions sales executives who drop clients to be

businesslike at all times. "You must always remember it's not the organization you have the problem with, it's the person at that organization who's your contact," Rothberg says. "Be careful not to burn bridges because difficult clients might eventually leave that firm, and then you'll have a whole new opportunity to get that firm's business."

Writer Justin Berzon can be reached at edit@salesandmarketing.com

UNIT 3
Developing and Implementing Marketing Strategies

Unit Selections

Key Points to Consider

- Most ethical questions seem to arise in regard to the promotional component of the marketing mix. How fair is the general public's criticism of some forms of personal selling and advertising? Give some examples.

- What role, if any, do you think the quality of a product plays in making a business competitive in consumer markets? What role does price play? Would you rather market a higher-priced, better-quality product or one that was the lowest priced? Why?

- What do you envision will be the major problems or challenges retailers will face in the next decade? Explain.

- Given the rapidly increasing costs of personal selling, what role do you think it will play as a strategy in the marketing mix in the future? What other promotion strategies will play increased or decreased roles in the next decade?

 **Links: www.dushkin.com/online/**
These sites are annotated in the World Wide Web pages.

American Marketing Association Homepage
   http://www.marketingpower.com
Consumer Buying Behavior
   http://www.courses.psu.edu/mktg/mktg220_rso3/sls_cons.htm
Product Branding, Packaging, and Pricing
   http://www.fooddude.com/branding.html

Marketing management objectives, the late Wroe Alderson once wrote, "are very simple in essence. The firm wants to expand its volume of sales, or it wants to handle the volume it has more efficiently." Although the essential objectives of marketing might be stated this simply, the development and implementation of strategies to accomplish them is considerably more complex. Many of these complexities are due to changes in the environment within which managers must operate. Strategies that fail to heed the social, political, and economic forces of society have little chance of success over the long run. The lead article in this section provides helpful insight suggesting a framework for developing a comprehensive marketing plan.

The selections in this unit provide a wide-ranging discussion of how marketing professionals and U.S. companies interpret and employ various marketing strategies today. The readings also include specific examples from industry to illustrate their points. The articles are grouped in four sections, each dealing with one of the main strategy areas: product, price, distribution (place), and promotion. Since each selection discusses more than one of these areas, it is important that you read them broadly. For example, many of the articles covered in the distribution section discuss important aspects of personal selling and advertising.

Product Strategy. The essence of the marketing concept is to begin with what consumers want and need. After determining a need, an enterprise must respond by providing the product or service demanded. Successful marketing managers recognize the need for continuous product improvement and/or new product introduction.

The articles in this subsection focus on various facets of product strategy. The first article provides some thoughtful ideas about making and marketing remarkable products. The second article describes how from lipsticks to cars, a growing array of products can be made to your own taste. The last article in this subsection discloses how Krispy Kreme became the hottest brand in the land.

Pricing Strategy. Few elements of the total strategy of the "marketing mix" demand so much managerial and social attention as pricing. There is a good deal of public misunderstanding about the ability of marketing managers to control prices and even greater misunderstanding about how pricing policies are determined. New products present especially difficult challenges in terms of both costs and pricing. The costs for developing a new product are usually very high, and if a product is truly new, it cannot be priced competitively, for it has no competitors.

"Kamikaze Pricing" scrutinizes the tremendous pricing pressures that companies face and suggests some ways to make better pricing decisions. In "Which Price Is Right?" the authors discuss how business is at the start of a new era of pricing. "Most Valuable Players" discloses that offering customers value-added services is often a better alternative to slashing prices to keep up with the big chains.

Distribution Strategy. For many enterprises, the largest marketing costs result from closing the gap in space and time between producer and consumer. In no other area of marketing is

efficiency so eagerly sought after. Physical distribution seems to be the one area where significant cost savings can be achieved. The costs of physical distribution are tied closely with decisions made about the number, the size, and the diversity of marketing intermediaries between producer and consumer.

The three articles in this subsection scrutinize ways that retailers can create value for their customers, the importance of designing an appropriate e-business strategy, and the dynamics of online retailing.

Promotion Strategy. The basic objectives of promotion are to inform, persuade, or remind the consumer to buy a firm's product or pay for the firm's service. Advertising is the most obvious promotional activity. However, in total dollars spent and in cost per person reached, advertising takes second place to personal selling. Sales promotion supports either personal selling and advertising, or both. Such media as point-of-purchase displays, catalogs, and direct mail place the sales promotion specialist closer to the advertising agency than to the salesperson.

The three articles in this final unit subsection cover such topics as the importance of billboards and radio advertising, suggestions for creating a good ad, and some examples of various ad campaigns.

THE VERY MODEL OF A
MODERN MARKETING PLAN

SUCCESSFUL COMPANIES ARE REWRITING THEIR STRATEGIES TO REFLECT CUSTOMER INPUT AND INTERNAL COORDINATION

SHELLY REESE

IT'S 1996. DO YOU KNOW WHERE YOUR MARKETING PLAN IS? *In a world where competitors can observe and rapidly imitate each other's advancements in product development, pricing, packaging, and distribution, communication is more important than ever as a way of differentiating your business from those of your competitors.*

The most successful companies are the ones that understand that, and are revamping their marketing plans to emphasize two points:

1. Marketing is a dialog between customer and supplier.

2. Companies have to prove they're listening to their customers by acting on their input.

WHAT IS A MARKETING PLAN?

At its most basic level, a marketing plan defines a business's niche, summarizes its objectives, and presents its strategies for attaining and monitoring those goals. It's a road map for getting from point A to point B.

But road maps need constant updating to reflect the addition of new routes. Likewise, in a decade in which technology, international relations, and the competitive landscape are constantly changing, the concept of a static marketing plan has to be reassessed.

Two of the hottest buzz words for the 1990s are "interactive" and "integrated." A successful marketing plan has to be both.

"Interactive" means your marketing plan should be a conversation between your business and your customers by acting on their input. It's your chance to tell customers about your business and to listen and act on their responses.

"Integrated" means the message in your marketing is consistently reinforced by every department within your company. Marketing is as much a function of the finance and manufacturing divisions as it is the advertising and public relations departments.

Integrated also means each time a company reaches out to its customers through an advertisement, direct mailing, or promotion, it is sending the same message and encouraging customers to learn more about the product.

WHY IS IT IMPORTANT?

The interaction between a company and its customers is a relationship. Relationships can't be reproduced. They can, however, be replaced. That's where a good marketing plan comes into play.

Think of your business as a suitor, your customers as the object of your affection, and your competitors as rivals. A marketing plan is your strategy for wooing customers. It's based on listening and reacting to what they say.

Because customers' priorities are constantly changing, a marketing plan should change with them. For years, conventional wisdom was 'prepare a five year marketing plan and review it every year.' But change happens a lot faster than it did 20 or even 10 years ago.

For that reason, Bob Dawson of The Business Group, a consulting firm in Freemont, California, recommends that his clients prepare a three year plan and review it every quarter. Frequent reviews enable companies to identify potential problems and opportunities before their competition, he explains.

ILLUSTRATION BY KELLY KENNEDY

"Preventative maintenance for your company is as important as putting oil in your car," Dawson says. "You don't wait a whole year to do it. You can't change history but you can anticipate what's going to happen."

ESSENTIAL COMPONENTS

Most marketing plans consist of three sections. The first section should identify the organization's goals. The second section should establish a method for attaining them. The third section focuses on creating a system for implementing the strategy.

Although some plans identify as many as six or eight goals, many experts suggest a company whittle its list to one or two key objectives and focus on them.

"One of the toughest things is sticking to one message," observes Mark Bilfield, account director for integrated marketing of Nissan and Infiniti cars at TBWA Chiat/Day in Los Angeles, which handles national advertising, direct marketing, public relations, and promotions for the automaker. Bilfield argues that a focused, consistent message is easier to communicate to the market place and to different disciplines within the corporation than a broad, encompassing one. Therefore, he advises, "unless there is something drastically wrong with the idea, stick with it."

SECTION I: GOALS

The goals component of your plan is the most fundamental. Consider it a kind of thinking out loud: Why are you writing this plan? What do you want to accomplish? What do you want to achieve in the next quarter? The next year? The next three years?

Like taping your New Year's resolution to the refrigerator, the goals section is a constant reminder of what you want to achieve. The key difference between a New Year's resolution and your marketing goals, however, is you can't achieve the latter alone.

To achieve your marketing goals you've got to convince your customers to behave in a certain way. If you're a soft drink manufacturer you may want them to try your company's latest wild berry flavor. If you're a new bank in town, you need to familiarize people with your name and convince them to give your institution a try. Or perhaps you're a family-owned retailer who needs to remind customers of the importance of reliability and a proven track record in the face of new competition.

The goals in each of these cases differ with the audiences. The soft drink manufacturer is asking an existing customer to try something new; the bank is trying to attract new customers; the retailer wants to retain existing customers.

Each company wants to influence its customers' behavior. The company that is most likely to succeed is the one that understands its customers the best.

There's no substitute for knowledge. You need to understand the demographic and psychographic makeup of the customers you are trying to reach, as well as the best methods for getting their attention.

Do your research. Learn as much as possible about your audience. Trade associations, trade journals and government statistics and surveys are excellent resources, but chances are you have a lot of data within your own business that you haven't tapped. Look at what you know about your customer already and find ways to bolster that information. Companies should constantly be asking clients what they want and how they would use a new product.

"If you're not asking people that use your end product, then everything you're doing is an assumption," argues Dawson.

In addition, firms should ask customers how they perceive the products and services they receive. Too often, companies have an image of themselves that they broadcast but fail to live up to. That frustrates consumers and makes them feel deceived.

Companies that claim to offer superior service often appear to renege on their promises because their definition of 'service' doesn't mesh with their customers', says Bilfield.

"Airlines and banks are prime offenders," says Bilfield. "They tout service, and when the customers go into the airport or the bank, they have to wait in long lines."

The problem often lies in the company's assumptions about what customers really want. While an airline may feel it is living up to its claim of superior service because it distributes warm towels and mints after a meal, a business traveler will probably place a higher value on its competitor's on-time record and policy for returning lost luggage.

SECTION II: THE STRATEGY

Unfortunately, after taking the time and conducting the research to determine who their audience is and what their message should be, companies often fail by zooming ahead with a plan. An attitude of, "OK, we know who we're after and we know what we want to say, so let's go!" seems to take over.

More often than not, that gung-ho way of thinking leads to disaster because companies have skipped a critical step: they haven't established and communicated an internal strategy for attaining their goals. They want to take their message to the public without pausing to get feedback from inside the company.

For a marketing plan to work, everyone within the company must understand the company's message and work cooperatively to establish a method for taking that message to the public.

For example, if you decide the goal of your plan is to promote the superior service your company offers, you'd better make sure all aspects of your business are on board. Your manufacturing process should meet the highest standards. Your financial department should develop credit and leasing programs that make it easier for customers to use

GETTING STARTED

A NINE-STEP PLAN THAT WILL MAKE THE DIFFERENCE BETWEEN WRITING A USEFUL PLAN AND A DOCUMENT THAT GATHERS DUST ON A SHELF

by Carole R. Hedden and the *Marketing Tools* editorial staff

In his 1986 book, *The Goal,* Eliyahu M. Goldratt writes that most of us forget the one true goal of our business. It's not to deliver products on time. It isn't even to manufacture the best widget in the world. The goal is to make money.

In the past, making money depended on selling a product or service. Today, that's changed as customers are, at times, willing to pay for what we stand for: better service, better support, more innovation, more partnership in developing new products.

This section of this article assumes that you believe a plan is needed, and that this plan should weave together your desires with those of your customers. We've reviewed a number of marketing plans and come up with a nine-step model. It is perhaps more than what your organization needs today, but none of the steps are unimportant.

Our model combines some of the basics of a conventional plan with some new threads that we believe will push your plan over the edge, from being satisfactory to being necessary. These include:

•Using and improving the former domain of public relations, image, as a marketing tool.
•Integrating all the business functions that touch your customers into a single, customer-focused strategic marketing plan.
•Borrowing from Total Quality theories to establish performance measures beyond

the financial report to help you note customer trends.
•Making sure that the people needed to deliver your marketing objectives are part of your plan.
•"Selling" your plan to the people whose support is essential to its success.

Taking the Plan Off the Shelf

First, let's look at the model itself. Remember that one of the primary criticisms of any plan is that it becomes a binder on a shelf, never to be seen again until budget time next year. Planning should be an iterative process, feeding off itself and used to guide and measure.

Whether you're asked to create a marketing plan or write the marketing section of the strategic plan for your business, your document is going to include what the business is trying to achieve, a careful analysis of your market, the products and services you offer to that market, and how you will market and sell products or services to your customer.

1. Describe the Business

You are probably in one of two situations: either you need to write a description of your business or you can rely on an existing document found in your annual report, the strategic plan, or a capabilities brochure. The description should include, at minimum:

•Your company's purpose;
•Who you deliver products or services to; and
•What you deliver to those customers.

Too often, such descriptions omit a discussion about what you want your business to stand for—your image.

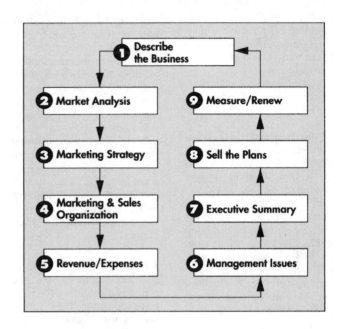

This is increasingly important as customers report they are looking for more than the product or service; they're in search of a partner. The only way to address image is to know who you want to be, who your customers think you are, and how you can bridge the gap between the two.

Part of defining your image is knowing where you are strong and where you are weak. For instance, if your current yield rate is 99.997 percent and customers rate you as the preferred supplier, then you might identify operations as a key to your company's image. Most companies tend to be their own worst critic, so start by listing all your strengths. Then identify weaknesses or the threats you face, either due to your own limitations or from the increased competency of a competitor.

The description also includes what your business delivers to its owners, be

they shareholders, private owners, or employees. Usually this is stated in financial terms: revenue, return on investment or equity, economic value added, cash generated, operating margin or earnings per share. The other measures your organization uses to monitor its performance may be of interest to outsiders, but save them for the measurement section of your plan.

The result of all this describing and listing is that you should have a fairly good idea of where you are and where you want to be, which naturally leads to objectives for the coming 6, 12, or 18 months, if not longer.

2. Analyze the Market

This is the section you probably believe you own. *Marketing Tools* challenges you to look at this as a section jointly owned by most everyone working with you. In a smaller company, the lead managers may own various pieces of this section. In a

(continued)

larger organization, you may need to pull in the ideas and data available from other departments, such as logistics, competitor intelligence, research and development, and the function responsible for quality control or quality assurance. All have two things in common: delivering value to customers, and beating the competition.

Together, you can thoroughly cover the following areas:

•**Your target markets**. What markets do you currently compete in? What do you know about them in terms of potential, dollars available, and your share of the market? Something frequently prepared for products is a life cycle chart; you might want to do the same for your market. Is it embryonic, developing, mature or in decline? Are there new markets to exploit?

•**Customer Knowledge**. Your colleagues in Quality, Distribution, Engineering, or other organizations can be helpful in finding what you need. *The customer's objectives.* What threats do your customers face? What goals does the customer have? Work with your customer to define these so you can become a partner instead of a variable component. *How is the customer addressing her or his markets?* Do you know as much about your customer's position as you know about your own? If not, find out. *How big is each customer, really?* You may find you're spending more time on a less important customer than on the customers who can break you. Is your customer growing or in decline? What plans does the customer have to expand or acquire growth? What innovations are in development? *What does your customer value?* Price, product quality,

service, innovation, delivery? The better you know what's driving your customer's purchasing decision, the better you'll be able to respond.

•**Clearly identify the alternatives your customer** has. As one customer told employees at a major supplier, "While you've been figuring out how to get by, we've been figuring out how to get by without you." Is backward integration—a situation in which the customer develops the capability in-house—possible? Is there an abundance of other suppliers? What is your business doing to avoid having your customers looking for alternatives?

•**Know your competition**. Your competitors are the obvious alternative for your customer, and thus represent your biggest threat. You can find what you need to know about your competitors through newspaper reports, public records, at trade shows, and from your customers: the size of expansions, the strengths that competitor has, its latest innovations. Do you know how your competition approaches your customers?

•**Describe the Environment**. What changes have occurred in the last 18 months? In the past year? What could change in the near future and over a longer period of time? This should include any kinds of laws or regulations that might affect you, the entry or deletion of competitors, and shifts in technology. Also, keep in mind that internal change does affect your customers. For instance, is a key leader in your business planning to retire? If so, decision making, operations or management style may change—and your customer may have obvious concerns. You can add some depth to

this section, too, by portraying several different scenarios:
•What happens if we do nothing beyond last year?
•What happens if we capitalize on our strengths?
•What might happen if our image slips?
•What happens if we do less this year than last?

3. The Marketing Strategy
The marketing strategy consists of what you offer customers and the price you charge. Start by providing a complete description of each product or service and what it provides to your customers. Life cycle, again, is an important part of this. Is your technology or product developing, mature or in decline? Depending on how your company is organized, a variety of people are responsible for this information, right down to whoever is figuring out how to package the product and how it will be delivered. Find out who needs to be included and make sure their knowledge is used.

The marketing strategy is driven by everything you've done up to this point. Strategies define the approaches you will use to market the company. For instance, if you are competing on the basis of service and support rather than price, your strategy may consist of emphasizing relationships. You will then develop tactics that support that strategy: market the company vs. the product; increase sales per client; assure customer responsiveness. Now, what action or programs will you use to make sure that happens?

Note: strategy leads. No program, regardless of how good it is, should make the

cut if it doesn't link to your business strategies and your customer.

The messages you must craft to support the strategies often are overlooked. Messages are the consistent themes you want your customer to know, to remember, to feel when he or she hears, reads, or views anything

about your company or products. The method by which you deliver your messages comes under the heading of actions or programs.

Finally, you need to determine how you'll measure your own success, beyond meeting the sales forecast. How will you know if your image takes a beating? How will you know whether the customer is satisfied, or has just given up complaining? If you don't know, you'll be caught reacting to events, instead of planning for them.

Remember, your customer's measure of your success may be quite different from what you may think. Your proposed measures must be defined by what your customer values, and they have to be quantifiable. You may be surprised at how willing the customer is to cooperate with you in completing surveys, participating in third-party interviews, or taking part in a full-scale analysis of your company as a supplier. Use caution in assuming that winning awards means you have a measurable indicator. Your measures should be stated in terms of strategies, not plaques or trophies.

4. The Marketing and Sales Organization
The most frequently overlooked element in business is something we usually relegate

(continued)

to the Personnel or Human Resources Office—people. They're what makes everything possible. Include them. Begin with a chart that shows the organization for both Marketing and Sales. You may wish to indicate any interdependent relationships that exist (for instance, with Quality).

Note which of the roles are critical, particularly in terms of customer contact. Just as important, include positions, capabilities, and numbers of people needed in the future. How will you gain these skills without impacting your cost per sale? Again, it's time to be creative and provide options.

5. Revenue and Expense

In this section, you're going to project the revenue your plan will produce. This is usually calculated by evaluating the value of your market(s) and determining the dollar value of your share of that market. You need to factor in any changes you believe will occur, and you'll need to identify the sources of revenue, by product or service. Use text to tell the story; use graphs to show the story.

After you've noted where the money is coming from, explain what money you need to deliver the projected return. This will include staff wages and benefits for your organization, as well as the cost for specific programs you plan to implement.

During this era of budget cuts, do yourself a favor by prioritizing these programs. For instance, if one of your key strategies is to expand to a new market via new technologies, products, or services,

you will need to allocate appropriate dollars. What is the payback on the investment in marketing, and when will revenues fully pay back the investment? Also, provide an explanation of programs that will be deleted should a cut in funding be required. Again, combine text and spreadsheets to tell and to show.

6. Management Issues

This section represents your chance to let management know what keeps you awake at night. What might or could go wrong? What are the problems your company faces in customer relations? Are there technology needs that are going unattended? Again, this can be a collaborative effort that identifies your concerns. In addition, you may want to identify long-term issues, as well as those that are of immediate significance.

To keep this section as objective as possible, list the concerns and the business strategy or strategies they affect. What are the short-term and long-term risks? For instance, it is here that you might want to go into further detail about a customer's actions that look like the beginnings of backward integration.

7. Executive Summary

Since most senior leaders want a quick-look reference, it's best to include a one-page Executive Summary that covers these points:

• Your organization's objectives
• Budget requirements
• Revenue projections
• Critical management issues

When you're publishing the final plan document, you'll want the executive summary to be Page One.

8. Sell the Plan

This is one of the steps that often is overlooked. Selling your plan is as important as writing it. Otherwise, no one owns it, except you. The idea is to turn it into a rallying point that helps your company move forward. And to do that, you need to turn as many people as possible into ambassadors for your marketing efforts.

First, set up a time to present the plan to everyone who helped you with information and data. Make sure that they feel some sense of ownership, but that they also see how their piece ties into the whole. This is one of those instances where you need to say your plan, show your plan, discuss your plan. Only after all three steps are completed will they *hear* the plan.

After you've shared the information across the organization, reserve some time on the executive calendar. Have a couple of leaders review the plan first, giving you feedback on the parts where they have particular expertise. Then, present the plan at a staff meeting.

Is It Working?

You may think your job is finished. It's not. You need to convey the key parts of this plan to coworkers throughout the business. They need to know what the business is trying to achieve. Their livelihood, not just that of the owners, is at stake. From their phone-answering technique to the way they process an

order, every step has meaning to the customer.

9. Measure/Renew

Once you've presented your plan and people understand it, you have to continuously work the plan and share information about it. The best way to help people see trends and respond appropriately is to have meaningful measures. In the language of Total Quality, these are the Key Result Indicators—the things that have importance to your customers and that are signals to your performance.

For instance, measure your ability to deliver on a customer request; the amount of time it takes to respond to a customer inquiry; your productivity per employee; cash flow; cycle time; yield rates. The idea is to identify a way to measure those things that are critical to you and to your customer.

Review those measurements. Share the information with the entire business and begin the process all over again. Seek new ideas and input to improve your performance. Go after more data and facts. And then renew your plan and share it with everyone—all over again.

It's an extensive process, but it's one that spreads the word—and spreads the ownership. It's the step that ensures that your plan will be constantly in use, and constantly at work for your business.

Carole Hedden is a writer and communication/planning consultant living in Elmira, New York.

your product. Finally, your customer relations personnel should be trained to respond to problems quickly and efficiently, and to use the contact as an opportunity to find out more about what customers want.

"I'm always amazed when I go into the shipping department of some company and say, 'What is your mission? What's the message you want to give to your end user?' and they say, 'I don't know. I just know I've got to get these shipments out on time,'" says Dawson.

Because the success of integrated marketing depends on a consistent, cohesive message, employees throughout the company need to understand the firm's marketing goals and their role in helping to fulfill them.

"It's very important to bring employees in on the process," says James Lowry, chairman of the marketing department at Ball State University. "Employees today are better than any we've had before. They want to know what's going on in the organization. They don't want to be left out."

HELP IS ON THE WAY

THREE SOFTWARE PACKAGES THAT WILL HELP YOU GET STARTED

Writing a marketing plan may be daunting, but there is a variety of software tools out there to help you get started. Found in electronics and book stores, the tools are in many ways like a Marketing 101 textbook. The difference lies in how they help.

Software tools have a distinct advantage: They actually force you to write, and that's the toughest part of any marketing plan. Sometimes called "MBA In a Box," these systems guide you through a planning process. Some even provide wording that you can copy into your own document and edit to fit your own business. Presto! A boiler plate plan! Others provide a system of interviewing and questioning that creates a custom plan for your operation. The more complex tools demand an integrated approach to planning, one that brings together the full force of your organization, not just Sales or Advertising.

1. Crush

Crush, a modestly named new product from a modestly named new company, HOT, takes a multimedia approach. (HOT stands for Hands-On Technology; *Crush* apparently stands for *Crushing the Competition*)

Just introduced a few months ago, *Crush* is a multimedia application for Macintosh or Windows PCs. It features the competitive analysis methods of Flegis McKenna, marketing guru to Apple, Intel and Genentech; and it features Mr. McKenna himself as your mentor, offering guidance via on-screen video. As you work through each section of a complete market analysis, McKenna provides germane comments; in addition, you can see video case studies of

marketing success stories like Intuit software.

Crush provides worksheets and guidance for analyzing your products, customers, market trends and competitors, and helps you generate an action plan. The "mentor" approach makes it a useful

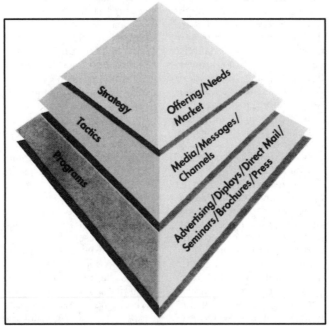

Pyramid Power: Plan Write's pyramid approach asks the user to define the messages for a business as part of the tactics.

tool for self-education; as you work through the examples and develop your company's marketing plan, you build your own expertise.

2. Marketing Plan Pro

Palo Alto's *Marketing Plan Pro* is a basic guide, useful for smaller businesses or ones in which the company leader wears a number of different hats, including marketing. It includes the standard spreadsheet capability, as well as the ability to chart numerical data. *Marketing Plan Pro* uses a pyramid process.

I liked the pyramid for a simple reason: It asks you to define messages for your business as part of your tactics. Without a message, it's easy to jump around, reacting to the marketplace instead of anticipating, leaving customers wondering what really is

significant about your company or your product.

The step-by-step process is simple, and a sample plan shows how all the information works together. The customer-focus aspect of the plan seemed a little weak, demanding only sales potential and buying capacity of the customers. Targeted marketing is increasingly important, and the user may want to really expand how this section is used beyond what the software requires.

The package displays, at a glance, your strategy, the tactics you develop for each

strategy, and the action plan or programs you choose to support the strategy. That could help when you're trying to prioritize creative ideas, eliminating those that really don't deliver what the strategy demands. Within each of three columns, you can click on a word and get help. Click on the heading program: a list of sample actions is displayed. They may not be what you're looking for, but if this is your first plan, they're lifesavers.

I also really liked *Marketing Plan Pro's* user's manual. It not only explains how the software works with your computer, it helps with business terms and provides a guide to planning, walking you through step-by-step.

3. Plan Write

Plan Write, created by Business Resource Software, Inc., is exponentially more powerful than *Marketing Plan Pro*. *Plan Write* brings together the breadth of the business, integrating information as far flung as distribution systems and image. And this software places your marketing strategy within the broader context of a business plan, the approach that tends to prove most effective.

As with *Marketing Plan Pro*, *Plan Write* provides a sample plan. The approach is traditional, incorporating a look at the business environment, the competition, the product or service mix you are offering, the way you will tell customers about that mix, pricing, delivery, and support.

Among the sections that were particularly strong was one on customer alternatives and people planning. Under the heading of customer alternatives, you're required to

(continued)

incorporate competitive information with customer information. If you don't meet the customer's needs, where could he or she go? Most often we look only at the competition, without trying to imagine how the customer is thinking. This exercise is particularly valuable to the company who leads the market.

The people part of planning too often is dumped on the personnel guy instead of being seen as a critical component of your organization's capabilities. *Plan Write* requires that you include how marketing is being handled, and how sales will be accomplished. In addition, it pushes you to define what skills will be needed in the future and where the gaps are between today and the future. People, in this plan, are viewed as a strategic component.

Plan Write offers a fully integrated spreadsheet that can import from or export to most of the popular spreadsheet programs you may already be using. Another neat feature allows you to enter numerical data and select from among 14 different graphing styles to display your information. You just click on the style you want to view, and the data is reconfigured.

Probably the biggest danger in dealing with software packages such as *Marketing Plan Pro* and *Plan Write* is to think the software is the answer. It's merely a guide.

—Carole Hedden

Employees are ambassadors for your company. Every time they interact with a customer or vendor, they're marketing your company. The more knowledgeable and helpful they are, the better they reflect on your firm.

At Nordstrom, a Seattle-based retailer, sales associates are empowered to use their best judgment in all situations to make a customer happy.

"We think our sales associates are the best marketing department," said spokeswoman Amy Jones. "We think word of mouth is the best advertising you can have." As a result, although Nordstrom has stores in only 15 states, it has forged a national reputation.

If companies regard marketing as the exclusive province of the marketing department, they're destined to fail.

"Accounting and sales and other departments have to work together hand in hand," says Dawson. "If they don't, you're going to have a problem in the end."

For example, in devising an integrated marketing campaign for the Nissan 200SX, Chiat/Day marketers worked in strategic business units that included a variety of disciplines such as engineers, representatives from the parts and service department, and creative people. By taking a broad view of the business and building inter-related activities to support its goals, Chiat/Day was able to create a seamless campaign for the 200SX that weaves advertising, in-store displays, and direct marketing together seamlessly.

"When everybody understands what the mission is, it's easier," asserts Bilfield. "It's easier to go upstream in the same direction than to go in different directions."

After bringing the different disciplines within your company on board, you're ready to design the external marketing program needed to support your goals. Again, the principle of integrated marketing comes into play: The message should be focused and consistent, and each step of the process should bring the consumer one step closer to buying your product.

In the case of Chiat/Day's campaign for the Nissan 200SX, the company used the same theme, graphics, type faces, and message to broadcast a consistent statement.

Introduced about the same time as the latest Batman movie, the campaign incorporates music and graphics from the television series. Magazine ads include an 800 number

potential customers can call if they want to receive an information kit. Kits are personalized and include the name of a local Nissan dealer, a certificate for a test drive, and a voucher entitling test drivers to a free gift.

By linking each step of the process, Chiat/Day can chart the number of calls, test drives, and sales a particular ad elicits. Like a good one-two punch, the direct marketing picks up where the national advertising leaves off, leveraging the broad exposure and targeting it at the most likely buyers.

While the elaborate 200SX campaign may seem foolproof, a failure to integrate the process at any step along the way could result in a lost sale.

For example, if a potential client were to test drive the car and encounter a dealer who knew nothing about the free gift accompanying the test drive, the customer would feel justifiably annoyed. Conversely, a well-informed sales associate who can explain the gift will be mailed to the test driver in a few weeks will engender a positive response.

SECTION III EXECUTION

The final component of an integrated marketing plan is the implementation phase. This is where the budget comes in.

How much you'll need to spend depends on your goals. If a company wants to expand its market share or promote its products in a new region, it will probably have to spend more than it would to maintain its position in an existing market.

Again, you'll need to create a system for keeping your employees informed. You might consider adding an element to your company newsletter that features people from different departments talking about the marketing problems they encounter and how they overcome them. Or you might schedule a regular meeting for department heads to discuss marketing ideas so they can report back to their employees with news from around the company.

Finally, you'll need to devise a system for monitoring your marketing program. A database, similar to the one created from calls to the 200SX's 800 number, can be an invaluable tool for determining if your message is being well received.

It's important to establish time frames for achieving your goals early in the process. If you want to increase your market share, for instance, you should determine the rate at which you intend to add new customers. Failing to achieve that rate could signal a flaw in your plan or its execution, or an unrealistic goal.

"Remember, integrated marketing is a long-range way of thinking," warns Dawson. "Results are not going to be immediate."

Like any investment, marketing requires patience, perseverance, and commitment if it is to bear fruit. While not all companies are forward thinking enough to understand the manifold gains of integrated marketing, the ones that don't embrace it will ultimately pay a tremendous price.

MORE INFO

Software for writing marketing plans:

Crush, Hands-On Technology; for more information, call (800) 772-2580 ext. 14 or (415) 579-7755; e-mail info@HOT.sf.ca.us; or visit the Web site at http://www.HOT.sf.ca.us.

Marketing Plan Pro, Palo Alto Software: for more information, call (800) 229-7526 or (503) 683-6162.

Plan Write for Marketing, Business Resource Software, Inc.: for more information, call (800) 423-1228 or (512) 251-7541.

Books about marketing plans:

Twelve Simple Steps to a Winning Marketing Plan, Geraldine A. Larkin (1992, Probus Publishing Co.)*

Preparing the Marketing Plan, by David Parmerlee (1993, NTC Business Books)*

Your Marketing Plan: A Workbook for Effective Business Promotion (Second Edition), by Chris Pryor (1995, Oregon Small Business Development Center Network)*

Your Business Plan: A Workbook for Owners of Small Businesses, by Dennis J. Sargent, Maynard N. Chambers, and Chris Pryor (1995, Oregon Small Business Development Center Network)*

Recommended reading:

Managing for Results, Peter Drucker

The One to One Future: Building Relationships One Customer at a Time, by Don Peppers and Martha Rogers, Ph.D. (1993, Currency/Doubleday)*

"Real World Results," by Don Schultz (*Marketing Tools* magazine, April/May 1994)*

* Available through American Demographics; call (800) 828-1133

Shelly Reese is a freelance writer based in Cincinnati.

IN PRAISE OF THE PURPLE COW

REMARKABLY HONEST IDEAS (AND REMARKABLY USEFUL CASE STUDIES) ABOUT MAKING AND MARKETING REMARKABLE PRODUCTS.
A MANIFESTO FOR MARKETERS

BY SETH GODIN

For years, marketers have talked about the "five *P*s" (actually, there are more than five, but everyone picks their favorite handful): product, pricing, promotion, positioning, publicity, packaging, pass along, permission. Sound familiar? This has become the basic marketing checklist, a quick way to make sure that you've done your job. Nothing is guaranteed, of course, but it used to be that if you dotted your *i*s and paid attention to your five *P*s, then you were more likely than not to succeed.

No longer. It's time to add an exceptionally important new *P* to the list: Purple Cow. Weird? Let me explain.

While driving through France a few years ago, my family and I were enchanted by the hundreds of storybook cows grazing in lovely pastures right next to the road. For dozens of kilometers, we all gazed out the window, marveling at the beauty. Then, within a few minutes, we started ignoring the cows. The new cows were just like the old cows, and what was once amazing was now common. Worse than common: It was boring.

Cows, after you've seen them for a while, are boring. They may be well-bred cows, Six Sigma cows, cows lit by a beautiful light, but they are still boring. A Purple Cow, though: Now, that would really stand out. The essence of the Purple Cow—the reason it would shine among a crowd of perfectly competent,

even undeniably excellent cows—is that it would be *remarkable*. Something remarkable is worth talking about, worth paying attention to. Boring stuff quickly becomes invisible.

The world is full of boring stuff—brown cows—which is why so few people pay attention. Remarkable marketing is the art of building things worth noticing right into your product or service. Not just slapping on the marketing function as a last-minute add-on, but also understanding from the outset that if your offering itself isn't remarkable, then it's invisible—no matter how much you spend on well-crafted advertising.

This is an essay about what it takes to create and sell something remarkable. It is a manifesto for marketers who want to make a difference at their company by helping create products and services that are worth marketing in the first place. It is a plea for originality, for passion, guts, and daring. Not just because going through life with passion and guts beats the alternative (which it does), but also because it's the only way to be successful. Today, the one sure way to fail is to be boring. Your one chance for success is to be remarkable.

And that means you have to be a leader. You can't be remarkable by following someone else who's remarkable. One way to figure out a great theory is to look at what's working in the real world and determine what the successes have in common. With marketing, it's puzzling though. What could the Four Seasons and Motel 6 possibly have in common? Other than the fact that both companies have experienced extraordi-

NOW *THAT'S* REMARKABLE: OTIS ELEVATOR CO.

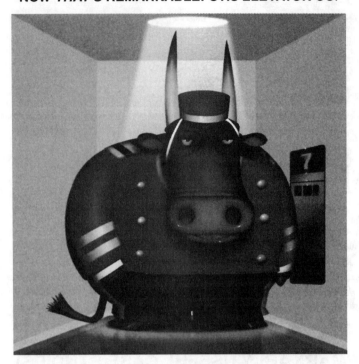

When is a bank of elevators more than a bank of elevators? When it's smart enough to tell you which elevator will provide the quickest ride to the floor you need to reach. A product *that* smart changes how people move, how buildings get designed—and how companies, in this case Otis Elevator Co., market their innovation.

NOW *THAT'S* REMARKABLE: TOMBSTONE PIZZA

It's good to be first with an innovation that the world is hungry for. Ron Simek learned that lesson when he launched the first successful line of frozen pizza. The product was a hit. Kraft bought it and advertised like mad. The rest is history. Of course, 40 years later, introducing another brand of frozen pizza seems less appetizing. Me-too products lead to also-ran companies.

nary success and growth, they couldn't be more different. Or Neiman Marcus and Wal-Mart, both growing during the same decade? Or Nokia (bringing out new hardware every 30 days or so) and Nintendo (marketing the same Game Boy for 14 years in a row)?

It's like trying to drive looking in the rearview mirror. Sure, those things worked. But do they help us predict what will work tomorrow? The thing that all of those companies have in common is that they have *nothing* in common. They are outliers. They're on the fringes. Superfast or superslow. Very exclusive or very cheap. Extremely big or extremely small.

The reason it's so hard to follow the leader is this: The leader is the leader precisely because he did something remarkable. And that remarkable thing is now taken—so it's no longer remarkable when you decide to do it.

STAND OUT FROM THE HERD I: GOING UP!

Elevators aren't a typical consumer product. They can easily cost more than a million dollars, they generally get installed when a building is first constructed, and they're not much use unless the building is more than three or four stories tall.

How, then, does an elevator company compete? Until recently, selling involved a lot of golf, dinners, and long-term relationships with key purchasing agents at major real-estate developers. No doubt that continues, but Otis Elevator Co. has

radically changed the game by developing a remarkable Purple Cow.

Every elevator ride is basically a local one. The elevator stops 5, 10, 15 times on the way to your floor. This is a hassle for you, but it's a huge, expensive problem for the building. While your elevator is busy stopping at every floor, the folks in the lobby are getting more and more frustrated. The building needs more elevators, but there's no money to buy them and no room to put them. Walk into the Times Square offices of Cap Gemini Ernst & Young, and you're faced with a fascinating solution to this problem.

Otis's insight? When you approach the elevators, you key in your floor on a centralized control panel. In return, the panel tells you which elevator is going to take you to your floor. With this simple presort, Otis has managed to turn every elevator into an express. Your elevator takes you immediately to the 12th floor and races back to the lobby. This means that buildings can be taller, they need fewer elevators for a given density of people, the wait is shorter, and the building can use precious space for people rather than for elevators. A huge win, implemented at a remarkably low cost.

Is there a significant real-estate developer in the world who is unaware of this breakthrough? Not likely. And it doesn't really matter how many ads or how many lunches the competition sponsors: Otis now gets the benefit of the doubt.

10 WAYS TO RAISE A PURPLE COW

Making and marketing something remarkable means asking new questions—
and trying new practices. Here are 10 suggestions.

1. Differentiate your customers. Find the group that's most profitable. Find the group that's most likely to influence other customers. Figure out how to develop for, advertise to, or reward either group. Ignore the rest. Cater to the customers you would choose if you could choose your customers.

2. If you could pick one underserved niche to target (and to dominate), what would it be? Why not launch a product to compete with your own that does nothing but appeal to that market?

3. Create two teams: the inventors and the milkers. Put them in separate buildings. Hold a formal ceremony when you move a product from one group to the other. Celebrate them both, and rotate people around.

4. Do you have the email addresses of the 20% of your customer base that loves what you do? If not, start getting them. If you do, what could you make for them that would be superspecial?

5. Remarkable isn't always about changing the biggest machine in your factory. It can be the way you answer the phone, launch a new brand, or price a revision to your software. Getting in the habit of doing the "unsafe" thing every time you have the opportunity is the best way to see what's working and what's not.

6. Explore the limits. What if you're the cheapest, the fastest, the slowest, the hottest, the coldest, the easiest, the most efficient, the loudest, the most hated, the copycat, the outsider, the hardest, the oldest, the newest, or just the most! If there's a limit, you should (must) test it.

7. Think small. One vestige of the TV-industrial complex is a need to think mass. If it doesn't appeal to everyone, the thinking goes, it's not worth it. No longer. Think of the smallest conceivable market and describe a product that overwhelms it with its remarkability. Go from there.

8. Find things that are "just not done" in your industry, and then go ahead and do them. For example, JetBlue Airways almost instituted a dress code—for its passengers! The company is still playing with the idea of giving a free airline ticket to the best-dressed person on the plane. A plastic surgeon could offer gift certificates. A book publisher could put a book on sale for a certain period of time. Stew Leonard's took the strawberries out of the little green plastic cages and let the customers pick their own. Sales doubled.

9. Ask, "Why not?" Almost everything you *don't* do has no good reason for it. Almost everything you don't do is the result of fear or inertia or a historical lack of someone asking, "Why not?"

10. What would happen if you simply told the truth inside your company and to your customers?

THE SAD TRUTH ABOUT MARKETING JUST ABOUT ANYTHING

Forty years ago, Ron Simek, owner of the Tombstone Tap (named for a nearby cemetery) in Medford, Wisconsin, decided to offer a frozen version of his pizza to his customers. It caught on, and before long, Tombstone Pizza was dominating your grocer's freezer. Kraft eventually bought the brand, advertised it like crazy, and made serious dough. This was a great American success story: Invent a good product that everyone wants, advertise it to the masses, earn billions.

That strategy didn't just work for pizza. It worked for most everything in your house, including aspirin. Imagine how much fun it must have been to be the first person to market aspirin. Here's a product that just about every person on earth needed and wanted. A product that was inexpensive, easy to try, and promised huge immediate benefits. Obviously, it was a big hit.

Today, a quick visit to the drugstore turns up lots of aspirin and aspirinlike products: Advil, Aleve, Alka-Seltzer Morning Relief, Anacin, Ascriptin, Aspergum, Bayer, Bayer Children's, Bayer Regimen, Bayer Women's, BC Powder, Bufferin, Cope, Ecotrin, Excedrin Extra Strength, Goody's, Motrin, Nuprin, St. Joseph, Tylenol, and, of course, Vanquish. Within each of those brands, there are variations, sizes, and generics that add up to more than 100 different products to choose from.

Think it's still easy to be an analgesics marketer today? If you developed a new kind of pain reliever, even one that was a little bit better than the ones that I just listed, what would you do? The obvious answer, if you've got money and you believe in your product, is to spend everything you've got to buy tons of national TV and print advertising.

There are a few problems that you'll face, though. First, you need people who want to buy a pain reliever. While it's a huge market, it's not for everyone. Once you find people who buy pain relievers, then you need people who want to buy a *new kind* of pain reliever. After all, plenty of people want the "original" kind, the kind they grew up with. Finally, you need to find the people who are willing to listen to what you have to say about your new pain reliever. The vast majority of folks are just too busy and will ignore you, regardless of how many ads you buy. So you just went from an audience of everyone to an audience a fraction of that size. Not only are these folks hard to find, they're picky as well. Being first in the frozen-pizza category was a good idea.

Being first in pain relievers was an even better idea. Alas, they're both taken. Which brings me to the sad truth about marketing just about anything, whether it's a product or a service, whether it's marketed to consumers or corporations: Most people *can't* buy your product. Either they don't have the money, they don't have the time, or they don't want it.

NOW *THAT'S* REMARKABLE: U.S. POSTAL SERVICE

The runaway success of "zip+4" might give new meaning to the term "going postal." This simple innovation makes it quicker for the Postal Service to deliver mail, easier for marketers to target neighborhoods, and cheaper for marketers to send bulk mail. But the innovation would never have taken hold without savvy marketing by an organization not famous for its savviness.

And those are serious problems. An audience that doesn't have the money to buy what you're selling at the price you need to sell it for is not a market. An audience that doesn't have the time to listen to and understand your pitch treats you as if you and your product were invisible. And an audience that takes the time to hear your pitch and decides that they don't want it… well, you're not going to get very far.

The old rule was this: Create safe products and combine them with great marketing. Average products for average people. *That's broken*. The new rule is: Create remarkable products that the right people seek out.

As I write this, the top song in France, Germany, Italy, Spain, and a dozen other countries in Europe is about ketchup. It's called "Ketchup," and it's by two sisters you've never heard of. The number-two movie in America is a low-budget animated film in which talking vegetables act out Bible stories. Neither is the sort of product you'd expect to come from a lumbering media behemoth.

Sam Adams beer was remarkable, and it captured a huge slice of business from Budweiser. Hard Manufacturing introduced a product that costs 10 times the average (the $9,945 Doernbecher crib) and opened up an entirely new segment of the hospital-crib market. The electric piano let Yamaha steal an increasingly larger share of the traditional piano market away from the entrenched leaders. Vanguard's remarkably low-cost mutual funds continue to whale away at Fidelity's market dominance. Bic lost tons of market share to Japanese competitors that had developed pens that were remarkably fun to write with, just as Bic had stolen the market away from fountain pens a generation or two earlier.

STAND OUT FROM THE HERD II: MAIL CALL

Very few organizations have as timid an audience as the United States Postal Service. Dominated by a conservative bureaucracy and conservative big customers, the USPS has an awfully hard time innovating. The big direct marketers are successful because they've figured out how to thrive under the current system, and they're in no mood to see that system change. Most individuals are in no hurry to change their mailing habits either.

The majority of new-policy initiatives at the USPS are either ignored or met with nothing but disdain. But "zip + 4" was a huge success. Within a few years, the USPS was able to diffuse a new idea, making the change in billions of address records in thousands of computer databases.

How? First, it was a game-changing innovation. Zip +4 makes it far easier for marketers to target neighborhoods and much faster and easier to deliver the mail. The product was a true Purple Cow, completely changing the way customers and the USPS would deal with bulk mail. It offered both dramatically increased speed in delivery and significantly lower costs for bulk mailers. That made it worth the time it took for big mailers to pay attention. The cost of ignoring the innovation would be felt immediately on the bottom line.

Second, the USPS wisely singled out a few early adopters. These were organizations that were technically savvy and that were extremely sensitive to both pricing and speed issues. These early adopters were also in a position to sneeze the benefits to other, less astute, mailers.

The lesson here is simple: The more intransigent your market, the more crowded the marketplace, the busier your customers, the more you need a Purple Cow. Half-measures will fail. Overhauling the product with dramatic improvements in things that the right customers care about, on the other hand, can have an enormous payoff.

WHY THERE ARE SO FEW PURPLE COWS

If being a Purple Cow is such an effective way to break through the clutter, why doesn't everyone do it? One reason is that people think the opposite of remarkable is "bad" or "poorly done." They're wrong. Not many companies sell things today that are flat-out lousy. Most sell things that are good enough. That's why the opposite of remarkable is "very good." Very good is an everyday occurrence, hardly worth mentioning—certainly not the basis of breakthrough success. Are you making very good stuff? How fast can you stop?

Some people would like you to believe that there are too few great ideas, that their product or their industry or their company simply can't support a great idea. That, of course, is absolute nonsense. Another reason the Purple Cow is so rare is because people are so *afraid*.

If you're remarkable, then it's likely that some people won't like you. That's part of the definition of remarkable. Nobody gets unanimous praise—ever. The best the timid can hope for is to be unnoticed. Criticism comes to those who stand out.

Playing it safe. Following the rules. They seem like the best ways to avoid failure. Alas, that pattern is awfully dangerous. The current marketing "rules" will ultimately lead to failure. In a crowded marketplace, fitting in is failing. In a busy marketplace, not standing out is the same as being invisible.

In *Marketing Outrageously* (Bard Press, 2001), author Jon Spoelstra points out the catch-22 logic of the Purple Cow. If times are tough, your peers and your boss may very well point out that you can't afford to be remarkable. There's not enough room to innovate: We have to conserve, to play it safe. We don't have the money to make a mistake. In good times, however, those very same people will tell you to relax, take it easy. There's not enough need to innovate: We can afford to be conservative, to play it safe.

So it seems that we face two choices: Either be invisible, uncriticized, anonymous, and safe or take a chance at true greatness, uniqueness, and the Purple Cow. The point is simple, but it bears repeating: Boring always leads to failure. Boring is always the riskiest strategy. Smart businesspeople realize this and work to minimize (but not eliminate) the risk from the process. They know that sometimes it's not going to work, but they accept the fact that that's okay.

STAND OUT FROM THE HERD III: THE COLOR OF MONEY

How did Dutch Boy Paint stir up the paint business? It's so simple, it's scary. They changed the can.

Paint cans are heavy, hard to carry, hard to close, hard to open, hard to pour, and no fun. Yet they've been around for a long time, and most people assumed that there had to be a reason why they were so bad. Dutch Boy realized that *there was no reason*. They also realized that the can was an integral part of the product: People don't buy paint, they buy painted walls, and the can makes that process much easier.

Dutch Boy used that insight and introduced an easier-to-carry, easier-to-pour, easier-to-close paint jug. "Customers tell us that the new Twist & Pour paint container is a packaging innovation that was long overdue," says Dennis Eckols, group vice president of the home division for Fred Meyer stores. "People wonder why it took so long for someone to come up with the idea, and they love Dutch Boy for doing it."

It's an amazing innovation. Worth noticing. Not only did the new packaging increase sales, but it also got them more distribution (at a higher retail price!).

That is marketing done right. Marketing where the marketer changes the product, not the ads.

WHY IT PAYS (BIG) TO BE A PURPLE COW

As the ability to be remarkable continues to demonstrate its value in the marketplace, the rewards that follow the Purple Cow increase. Whether you develop a new insurance policy, make a hit record, or write a groundbreaking book, the money and satisfaction that follow are extraordinary. In exchange for taking the risk, creators of a Purple Cow get a huge upside when they get it right.

Even better, you don't have to be remarkable all the time to enjoy the upside. Starbucks was remarkable a few years ago. Now they're boring. But that burst of innovation and insight has allowed them to expand to thousands of stores around the world. Compare that growth in assets to Maxwell House. Ten years ago, all of the brand value in coffee resided with them, not with Starbucks. But Maxwell House played it safe (they

thought), and now they remain stuck with not much more than they had a decade ago.

Once you've created something remarkable, the challenge is to do two things simultaneously: One, milk the Purple Cow for everything it's worth. Figure out how to extend it and profit from it for as long as possible. Two, build an environment where you are likely to invent an entirely new Purple Cow in time to replace the first one when its benefits inevitably trail off.

These are contradictory goals. The creator of a Purple Cow enjoys the profits, accolades, and feeling of omniscience that come with a success. None of those outcomes accompany a failed attempt at a new Cow. Thus, the tempting thing to do is to coast. Take no chances. Take profits. Fail to reinvest.

AOL, Marriott, Marvel Comics, Palm, Yahoo—the list goes on and on. Each company had a breakthrough, built an empire around it, and then failed to take another risk. It used to be easy to coast for a long time after a few remarkable successes. Disney coasted for decades. Milton Berle did too. It's too easy to decide to sit out the next round, rationalizing that you're spending the time and energy to build on what you've got instead of investing in the future. So here's one simple, tangible suggestion. Create two teams: the inventors and the milkers. Put them in separate buildings. Hold a formal ceremony when you move a product from one group to the other. Celebrate them both, and rotate people around.

STAND OUT FROM THE HERD IV: CHEWING MY OWN CUD

So, how does an author get his new book to stand out from all of the other marketing books? By trying to create a remarkable way to market a book about remarkable marketing. How? By not selling it in stores. Instead, a copy of the book version of *Purple Cow* is available for free to anyone reading this article. You pay for postage and handling ($5), and FAST COMPANY will send you one copy of the book-length version of this article for free (visit www.fastcompany.com/keyword/purplecow67 for details). How does this pay? Visit the site and I'll show you my entire marketing plan.

WHAT IT MEANS TO BE A MARKETER TODAY

If the Purple Cow is now one of the *Ps* of marketing, it has a series of big implications for the enterprise. In fact, it changes the definition of marketing. It used to be that engineering invented, manufacturing built, marketing marketed, sales sold, and the president managed the whole shebang. Marketing, better called "advertising," was about communicating the values of a product after it had been developed and manufactured.

That's clearly not a valid strategy in a world where product attributes (everything from service to design) are now at the heart of what it means to be a marketer. Marketing is the act of inventing the product. The effort of designing it. The craft of producing it. The art of pricing it. The technique of selling it. How can a Purple Cow company not be run by a marketer?

Companies that create Purple Cows, such as JetBlue Airways, Hasbro, Poland Spring, and Starbucks, *have* to be run by marketers. Turns out that the CEO of JetBlue made a critical decision on day one: He put the head of marketing in charge of product design and training as well. It shows. JetBlue sells a time-sensitive commodity just like American Airlines does, but somehow it manages to make a profit doing it. All of these companies are marketers at their very core.

The geniuses who managed to invent 1-800-COLLECT are true marketers. They didn't figure out how to market an existing service. Instead, the marketing is built into the product—from the easy-to-remember phone number to the very idea that MCI could steal the collect-call business from the pay-phone companies.

But isn't the same idea true for a local restaurant, a grinding-wheel company, and Citibank? In a world where anything we need is good enough and where just about all of the profit comes from the Purple Cow, we must all be marketers.

You've got a chance to reinvent who you are and what you do. Your company can reenergize itself around the idea of involving designers in marketing and marketers in design. You can stop fighting slow growth with mind-numbing grunt work and start investing in insight and innovation instead. If a company is failing, it's the fault of the most senior management, and the problem is probably this: They are just running a company, not marketing a product. And today, that's a remarkably ineffective way to compete.

Contributing editor **Seth Godin** (sgodin@fastcompany.com) has written some of FAST COMPANY's most influential articles, from "Permission Marketing" (April: May 1998) to "Unleash Your Idea Virus" (August 2000). This essay is adapted from his forthcoming book, *Purple Cow: Transform Your Business by Becoming Remarkable* (Do You Zoom, February 2003). The book is available only at www.Apurplecow.com and other select locations. Visit www.fastcompany.com/keyword/Purplecow67 for Information on how you can qualify for a free copy of the book.

Have It Your Way

From lipsticks to cars, a growing array of products can be custom-made to your own taste—and waist

By LISA TAKEUCHI CULLEN

CANDY SHORT IS A BORN SHOPPER. SHE studies every purchase with the zeal of her hound dogs sniffing out a trail. So she couldn't help herself when, while laid up with a back injury in her Southern California home last month, she chanced upon a curious offer on the Internet. A company called Reflect.com promised it could customize cosmetics for her based on information she entered on its website. Short, 33, formulated a lipstick, a moisturizer, then pretty much an entire product line. Some $500 later, she kissed mass-market makeup goodbye for good.

As a mother of two on workers' compensation, Short isn't given to excess. She would have spent about as much for mass-market makeup at a department store. "Now more than ever," she says, "it made me feel good getting something made just for me."

The custom craze is on. Once a privilege exclusive to the Park Avenue class, customization has come to hoi polloi courtesy of the Internet. A few clicks beget jeans, sneakers, shampoo, cars, candy, furniture, even vampire fangs made just for you and delivered to your door, for not a whole lot more than the mass-market equivalent. Just in time too. In the age of TiVo and iPod, consumers increasingly expect to custom-tailor their lives, and retailers are eager to comply. New manufacturing technologies and the Internet make custom service possible, and the prices, while in most cases modestly higher, are still affordable. As Dell Computer has been proving for years, tooling products individually cuts inventory expense, pleases customers and even lures new traffic.

The trend is driven by the tech-savvy young looking for something unique—and by their parents looking for something that fits. In apparel—the industry charging fastest into customization—the nation's 76 million baby boomers, with their expanding girth and shrinking patience, are fueling the trend. Bill Bass, head of e-commerce for Lands' End, knew there was pent-up demand for better-fitting casual clothing. Two years ago, in a promotional campaign, his company put a high-tech body scanner on a truck and traveled around the country to offer personalized fittings. "People loved it, but they had to stand in line and take their clothes off, and it was a hassle," says Bass.

Therein lay the problem—and the opportunity. For apparel retailers, customizing used to mean high cost and low efficiency; for consumers, the indignity of strangers' circling tape measures around ample waistlines in public storefronts. Levi's has long offered customized jeans, but the Original Spin line is not available on the Internet, and the company says it has never grown to more than a small fraction of sales. At Burberry's flagship store in New York City, custom-made trench coats start at $700 and require an hour of fitting; just 20 sell a week.

Could a virtual tailor change those dynamics? Using new software from Archetype Solutions, Lands' End launched a custom-fit service on its website last fall. Customers measure themselves, detail their style preferences and answer questions about their figure. The data yield a precise pattern that gets beamed to factories in Mexico or the Caribbean, and a pair of customized jeans arrives on the customer's doorstep three weeks later. Bass says he expected the custom-fit line would grow to 10% of sales. But a year later, nearly half of all Lands' End pants sold online are custom.

MAKING MAKEUP FOR ME

HOW IT WORKS

- On Reflect.com's website, I customize makeup, lipstick and other products for my skin and hair. I start by answering a series of questions about skin tone, hair texture, coloring and favorite fragrances

- After I supply the personal data, lab technicians in San Francisco match them with unique, active ingredients and mix those with base formulas. Finally, they inject my chosen scent

- "You're the ultimate brand," Reflect.com CEO Richard Gerstein tells us. So I make like Estee Lauder, Bobbi Brown and J. Lo, naming all my creations after myself

One of the company's happy customers is Alex von Bidder, 52. He has a wardrobe packed with $2,500 suits in which he hobnobs with guests at the Four Seasons, his famed New York City restaurant. "I'm used to the finest things in life," Von Bidder says. "Best wine, best food. Still, I never thought I'd get custom-made jeans." His $54 pair from Lands' End is "the best-fitting thing I've ever owned," swears Von Bidder, who has since ordered custom-fit chinos and shirts

SHOES
Nike iD, the shoemaker's customization website, lets you pick favorite colors and add words to personalize the treads. But it won't let you alter the basic shoe design

Custom mass-consumer products typically cost 10% to 20% more than off-the-rack items. Jupiter Research found in a recent study that more than half of consumers were willing to pay $10 extra to custom-order a pair of $50 slacks—but not much more. "The economy's bad," says Madison Riley of retail consultants Kurt Salmon Associates. "But if it's not going to stop people spending, they'll make for darn sure what they do spend is on the best quality and fit."

Take Jane Miller, 57, a retiree in Knoxville, Tenn. "I don't like to drive, and I'm not a big shopper," she says. "Most of the time you don't know what you're getting.

You make an investment, and it's a crapshoot." She tailors her purchases through Reflect.com and Lands' End and, with her MP3 player and DVD-rental club, customizes her tunes and movies online too.

Car buyers have always added features, a major profit driver for automakers and customizing shops that garners an estimated $26 billion-plus in sales each year. Gary Cowger, president of GM North America, says the trend toward personalization is evident in sales of the Hummer H2, a favorite of affluent baby boomers. Sales of accessories like running boards, brush guards and roof racks are "much better than we expected," he says.

Recession-squeezed automakers salivate at the thought of persuading even more buyers to customize by offering easy, accessible options online. In a study published this month, Forrester Research analyst Baba Sheddy found that 66% of prospective buyers customized vehicles while researching price online. In a bid to turn speculative customizers into real ones, Toyota's Scion, Honda's Element and Saturn's Ion will let customers order personalized cars on their websites with touches like aluminum pedals and gearshifts, and springs that adjust the car's height. Because young buyers "want something that says, 'I'm unique,'" says Toyota's Jim Farley, the youth-targeted Scion will offer 40 accessories.

But customization extends to gearhead items like air intakes, enhanced exhaust systems and rear spoilers. As Jill Lajdziak, a Saturn executive, notes, "Many young

buyers would rather buy an affordable vehicle and then have a couple of thousand dollars to invest in a higher level of performance."

CARS
Many automakers now let car buyers test-drive custom features online. On the Honda website, potential buyers can check out a "bug bra" for the front grille and other accessories

One thing's for sure with young buyers: custom sells. This fall American Eagle Outfitters, a clothing company, instructed its college-age buyers how to tear up T shirts and embroider jeans—and sold 12% more jeans in the process. Nike iD lets customers help design their own sneakers.

But there's a limit to how far retailers will go to let customers fiddle with their products. Jonah Peretti, 28, who works for a new-media arts group in New York, tried to order a pair of Nike iD shoes embroidered with the word sweatshop. That's a swipe at Nike's reputation as a company reliant on cheap foreign labor. Nike's response: Just forget it.

—With reporting by Joseph R. Szczesny/Detroit

The Hole Story:

How Krispy Kreme became the hottest brand in America

by Andy Serwer

THEY BEGIN LINING UP IN THE COLD DARKNESS, hours before the store opens. Some come wearing pajamas, some lug couches and TVs, others bring beer. And when dawn finally breaks and the ribbon is cut, the rabid customers bolt through the doors. Many of them, in what must be an anticipatory sugar rush, scream at the top of their lungs *"Krispy Kreme doughnuts, yowweeee!"* Last year it happened in Fargo and Philadelphia and Amarillo and dozens of other cities in North America. This year it will happen in Boston, Sydney, and elsewhere. All for a simple doughnut. Consider that for a moment: With so many companies today desperate for customers, here is a business—remember, we're talking doughnuts—that has shrieking fanatics lining up around the block in the middle of the night to buy its product.

If you've never sampled a Krispy Kreme, we should get one thing straight: These doughnuts—particularly the original glazed served hot—are amazingly good. (My older daughter says they taste like glazed fluffy clouds.) They are loved equally by 5-year-olds and 75-year-olds. By whites, blacks, Asians, and Hispanics. By New Englanders and Southerners. By Californians and New Yorkers. (Never mind by junkies and cops.) I say only three types of people claim they don't like Krispy Kremes: nutritionists (your basic glazed has 200 calories and 12 grams of fat), Dunkin' Donuts franchisees, and compulsive liars. Fortunately for the company, that's not a large group.

Sure, Krispy Kreme is still relatively small. It has just 292 stores (Dunkin' Donuts has 3,600 in the U.S. alone) and last year did $492 million in sales and earned $33 million (that includes a one-time charge of $9 million). But, boy, does it have oomph. For starters, get a load of KKD's stock: up four times since its IPO three years ago. Net income per share has compounded at more than 45% since 1998. Significantly, Krispy Kreme's same-store sales are still growing by more than 11%. It has operating margins of nearly 16%—and growing. System-

wide revenues, which include sales by franchises, were $779 million last year and should cross $1 billion this year.

Then there's the power of the Krispy Kreme brand. No, it's not as recognizable as Coke or McDonald's—yet. Still, despite the fact that it is a fraction of the size of those icons and spends zilch on national advertising (more on that later), the company's retro red, white, and green logo is rapidly becoming part of American popular culture.

No question that Krispy Kreme is hot, but is the company for real? Is it a great American growth story or merely a culinary flash in the pan? Those are not idle questions. Not for the 7,000 folks who have been hired by the company over the past three years, nor for the companies that supply Krispy Kreme, nor for those who have invested in its yeasty stock. But the question of Krispy Kreme's viability touches on something more significant than all that. It has to do with the American dream. It may seem grimly amusing that in a time of economic pain, corporate scandals, and troubles overseas, this company should be growing so explosively. But the Krispy Kreme story is about far more than comfort food—the company's wild success in this hard environment is a tale of shrewdness, original think, and brinksmanship. The yarn is part Southern gothic—as in long (try six decades) and tortured, replete with heroes and even Yankee villains—and part sophisticated yet homey marketing that helped create the hottest brand in the land (think about it: Can you name a hotter one?).

The man behind Krispy Kreme's dramatic ascent is its CEO, Scott Livengood (pronounced *Saturday Night Live*-ngood). The unassuming Livengood, who grew up in Krispy Kreme's buttoned-down hometown of Winston-Salem, N.C., has been with the company for 26 years, coming up through its human resources department. During the long, strange trip that is Krispy Kreme, Livengood, 50, has seen just about everything. Yes, he's at the helm of a high-end growth company, but to hear him

Doughnuts to Dollars

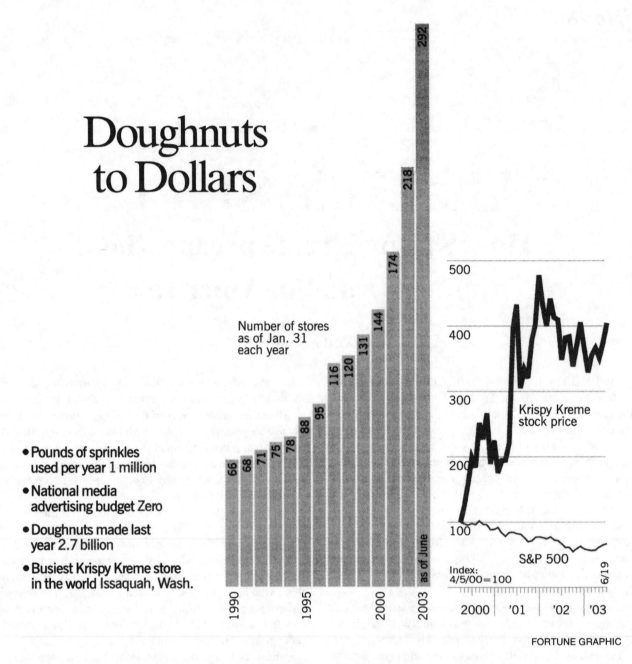

Number of stores
as of Jan. 31
each year

- Pounds of sprinkles
  used per year 1 million
- National media
  advertising budget Zero
- Doughnuts made last
  year 2.7 billion
- Busiest Krispy Kreme store
  in the world Issaquah, Wash.

66 68 71 75 78 88 95 116 120 131 144 174 218 292

1990 1995 2000 2003

Krispy Kreme
stock price

S&P 500

Index:
4/5/00 = 100

6/19

500 400 300 200 100

2000 '01 '02 '03

as of June

FORTUNE GRAPHIC

tell it, his job is actually easier now. "Running a public company growing like this—that's nothing," he says. "I'm enjoying myself." And who wouldn't be? Here is a guy coining money selling doughnuts.

It's a rainy June morning in Winston, and the Krispy Kreme faithful have gathered for the company's annual meeting in the Adam's Mark Hotel. The religious overtones are unmistakable. First of all we have doughnuts. And for lovers of this food group, KKD's annual meeting is sacred ground. There are hundreds of doughnuts laid out before you. All you can eat. (Easy! Easy! Pace yourself!) That may explain the unusual number of kids—who may or may not be shareholders—in attendance. Before long, Livengood marches through the company's financial vitals. Then the fun begins. Livengood gives a year's supply of doughnuts to the oldest and to the youngest attending shareholders, and to the shareholder who has traveled the farthest

(from Finland). But he spends even more time talking about the company's charitable works and, in long citations, singles out six employees who've helped their churches, Little Leagues, and communities. To the folks at Krispy Kreme, this isn't just about doughnuts; it's a calling.

It's also an increasingly big business that is attracting some blue-chip names. "I did a lot of homework on Krispy Kreme," says the company's newest board member, Erskine Bowles, a North Carolina banker, onetime U.S. Senate candidate in the Tar Heel state, and President Clinton's former chief of staff. "I didn't want to join a company in my home state that was going to flop. But I've got to tell you, I've never seen another company like it. It's clean, it's conservative, and I love the margins." Ah, yes, those sweet, fat margins. In part they are a reflection of how the company is run. While Coke makes money selling syrup, and McDonald's is about selling real estate, Krispy Kreme's business model is something altogether different.

On the east side of Winston-Salem, in an old industrial neighborhood that looks as if it could be the setting for a Lucinda Williams video, sits the original Ivy Avenue Krispy Kreme mix plant. Walk in the door and a sweet floury powder greets your nose and covers your clothes in a fine dust. Then you hear that sound. *Whomp! Whomp! Whomp!* Every seven seconds a 50-pound brown paper sack is filled with Krispy Kreme doughnut mix. This is the heart of the Krispy Kreme Doughnut company. The bagged mix, of course, goes to Krispy Kreme's doughnut shops, where doughnuts are made on the premises. So what's in the bag, man? "I could tell you, but I'd have to shoot you," says Fred Mitchell, head of manufacturing. Now, Fred's an affable guy, but he doesn't look as if he's kidding. In fact, the secret formula is kept in a vault upstairs from the bagging room. Mitchell later shows me the recipe—from a distance. Last year the Ivy Avenue plant was running 24 hours at 110% capacity, but since the opening of the Effingham, Ill., plant, where a bag is filled in three seconds, the Winston plant is operating only 18 hours a day.

"It's clean, it's conservative, and I love the margins," says director Erskine Bowles.

Krispy Kreme brings in money three ways. It makes 65% of its revenue selling doughnuts directly to the public through its 106 company-owned stores. Another 31% of its sales come from selling flour mix, doughnut-making machines, and sundry doughnut supplies to its 186 franchised stores. And it gets about 4% of its revenue from franchisee licenses and fees. Though the last category is tiny, it has operating margins (before corporate general and administrative costs) upwards of 74%, vs. the high teens for their bigger businesses. "This company has its act together," says Ron Paul, president of Technomic, a Chicago food consulting company. "All kinds of companies sell sweet products, but Krispy Kreme has been very smart about their operations and how they exploit their brand."

That may be true now, but for much of the company's 66-year history, "smart" and "Krispy Kreme" rarely appeared in the same sentence. The company began in the mid-1930s, when a doughnut maker named Vernon Rudolph bought a secrete recipe for yeast doughnuts from a French pastry chef out of New Orleans. (Yeast doughnuts are the fully glazed concoctions. The denser varieties are cake doughnuts.) Rudolph moved from Paducah, Ky., to Nashville to Winston-Salem and on July 13, 1937 (go ahead and celebrate the day if you want to), he opened up a wholesale business selling to local grocery stores. If you know Krispy Kreme doughnuts, you know their wafting aroma is worth ten times more than any fancy Madison Avenue ad campaign. Folks walking by Rudolph's plant began pounding on his door asking whether they could buy hot doughnuts. So Rudolph cut a hole in the factory wall and sold 'em out on to the street. *Voilá!* Krispy goes retail.

Over the next few decades Rudolph opened other stores—some his, some franchised—in the Carolinas and contiguous states, and a regional chain was born. The red, white, and green colors and the wide scripted logos were chosen, as well as the twin "walking KK" letters. (After a few cocktails Scott Livengood has been know to do a little dance number called the walking KKs, which is kind of a cross between Michael Jackson's moonwalk and the goose step.) As for the Krispy Kreme name itself, it just came on the recipe from the French chef, suggesting perhaps a language problem, since the doughnuts are neither crispy nor creamy. Most important, though, Krispy Kremes became the treat of choice for millions of Southern boys and girls. "I grew up eating Krispy Kreme doughnuts," singer and Atlanta native Gladys Knight told Rosie O'Donnell a while back. "My dad used to bring them to me at two in the morning. So now I bought stock... so I gotta eat them."

Vernon Rudolph may have been a great doughnut man, but poke around Winston-Salem—where doughnuts are quickly replacing cigarettes as a major employer (hmm)—and you hear stories about the man. That he was a heavy drinker. And a little over the top. There's one legend about Rudolph's gathering all his store managers in the basement of the long since torn-down Robert E. Lee Hotel in downtown Winston-Salem and reveling in an extended night of drinking. After hours of this, and with the contingent bleary from smoke and drink, Rudolph called for the men to push aside the big table in the middle of the room. Then ripping his shirt off, he yelled, "Come on! Let's wrassle!" And so the doughnut men did.

Rudolph died in 1973. He had a family but apparently no estate planning, so Krispy Kreme would have to be sold. It took some time, but finally Beatrice, the Chicago conglomerate that owned everything from Tropicana orange juice to Samsonite luggage, bought the company in 1976. A year later young Scott Livengood, who worked for the Winston-Salem fire department after graduating from Chapel Hill, joined the company as a trainee in personnel. "I made $1,000 a month," says Livengood, "but what I remember more than that was Krispy Kreme was a mess."

Turns out that Krispy Kreme and Beatrice made one horrible marriage. Let Livengood count the ways: "Beatrice didn't care so much if the stores made money, as long as we sold doughnuts to supermarkets," he says. "They didn't want to invest in stores or grow the company, they just wanted cash. Then they changed the logo to a tacky '70s look. And they actually messed with the doughnut formula. They made it cheaper." And there were the dreaded days when the boys from Chicago came down to go over the numbers. "There was trauma around reporting time, that's for sure," says Livengood. Beatrice soon made it clear that Krispy Kreme was for sale. That was just fine with the franchisees, who were by this time livid.

Liggett & Myers looked at the company, and so did Bowles Hollowell, Erskine Bowles's old investment banking firm, but neither struck a deal. Finally, in 1982, the franchisees themselves, led by a man named Joe McAleer of Mobile, decided to acquire the company for $24 million in a leveraged buyout. (Today the McAleer family owns 6.3% of Krispy Kreme's stock, worth $129 million.) The buyout was a welcome change.

Batting for Krispy Kreme: celebrity franchisees

TO HANK AARON, THERE ARE TWO TYPES OF doughnuts. One is the metal weight with the rubber covering that he slid over the handle of his bat in the on-deck circle. The other is Krispy Kreme. "I used to stop by the store many years ago and stuff my face with their products," says Aaron, who grew up in Mobile, Ala. Somehow Aaron's waistline never reached Ruthian proportions, but he did wind up surpassing the Babe as baseball's all-time home-run leader.

Hammering Hank still owns that record today (sorry, Barry). He also owns a Krispy Kreme franchise. "I asked them if they had anything I could do in the way of franchises," he says. "So now I have a shop in the West End of Atlanta, and I am planning on opening two more." He checks in on his store a couple of times a week before heading over to Turner Field, home of his Braves, for a workout.

Aaron joins Dick Clark of *American Bandstand* fame and Jimmy Buffett of margarita fame as Krispy Kreme celebrity franchisees. Even though he grew up in Mount Vernon, N.Y., Clark was an early adopter. He traveled through the South in the '50s with the Caravan of Stars music tour, and, he says, "the whole bus would unload whenever we saw a Krispy Kreme." So when the doughnuts went national, Clark, the host of *New Year's Rockin' Eve,* pleaded with the head office to give him a Times Square franchise in New York. That didn't happen, but CEO Scott Livengood did ask if he would be interested in being an overseas franchisee. In December 2002, Clark, along with two partners, got the rights to develop 25 Krispy Kreme franchises in Britain. The first one will open in the fall.

Like Aaron, Buffett grew up in Mobile ("those doughnuts are in my genes," he says) and knew former Krispy Kreme CEO Mack McAleer in grade school. Last year he opened a franchise in Palm Beach, and he hopes to open another in Jamaica soon. How about a doughnut with that jerk chicken and margarita?—*Melanie Shanley*

But there was bad news too. Part of it was obvious: Krispy Kreme was saddled with a ton of debt. Another bugaboo was less clear at the time: McAleer's group of purchasing franchisees numbered 21, and they decided that all votes on significant company financial matters must be determined unanimously, instead of by a simple majority. The intentions were noble, but it was a structure that later drove Scott Livengood to the brink of insanity.

The very first move under McAleer was to revert to the original formula and traditional logo. Then they started tweaking. "A lot of people think that all our traditions go way, way back, but not all of them do," says company marketing chief Stan Parker. Take the famous HOT DOUGHNUTS NOW sign. Everybody knows that when a Krispy Kreme store flips on its neon HOT DOUGHNUTS NOW sign, the doughnuts are coming right off

the line. Around 1980 the folks in Winston noticed sales at the Chattanooga store were going through the roof. HQ decided to send a man up to Chattanooga for a look-see. Turns out the store manager, Bob Glidden, had printed up an ordinary block sign that read HOT DOUGHNUTS NOW. But his customers complained he kept the sign up all the time, even when his doughnuts weren't hot. So Glidden went down to J.C. Penney and bought a window shade. When he wasn't making doughnuts he pulled the shade closed; when he was cooking, he pulled open the blind and customers streamed in. Bingo, a sales tactic was born!

By the mid-1980s Joe McAleer retired to Mobile, and his son Mack took over. "One day Mack walked in my office," recalls Livengood, "and said, 'I need a partner to run this thing, and I want it to be you.'" So as the debt was gradually paid down, Mack McAleer and Livengood focused on bringing marketing to the fore of the company. Many a long night the two men brainstormed, margaritas in hand, while listening to Jimmy Buffett, who later became a franchisee (see box).

What's in the bag? "I could tell you, but I'd have to shoot you," says Fred Mitchell.

It was Mack who came up with the concept of "doughnut theater." They put the doughnut-making equipment in stores so that people could see the doughnuts cook for exactly 115 seconds in 365-degree vegetable shortening, after which the precious confections plow through a glaze waterfall before curving 180 degrees around to the counter so that a salesperson can pluck a hot one right off the line and hand it to the drooling customer. McAleer and Livengood also decided their doughnuts were too small for retail, so they increased their size by 40%. They made the Ivy Avenue mix plant more efficient and began to expand outside the Southeast. Then came the biggest switch. "One day Mack walked in my office again and said, 'I want to go back to running stores, and I want you to be the CEO,'" says Livengood.

In 1996 Krispy Kreme opened a store in New York City, and the company pulled off a publicity coup, delivering boxes and boxes of doughnuts to the *Today Show* (this occurred during Al Roker's binging days), garnering huge national exposure. To this day the company has no traditional media advertising budget. It's simply much cheaper and more effective to give away doughnuts. Before entering a new market, such as Boston at the end of June, Krispy Kreme inundates TV and radio stations and newspapers with free doughnuts.

The company also provides millions of doughnuts at a discount to charitable organizations, which then sell them for fundraising. That is partly a reflection of Livengood's leanings (the calling part)—which are Southern-religious-progressive, á la Jimmy Carter—and partly good business, as in great exposure. And speaking of exposure, it's hard to think of a brand that's been in more movies and TV shows—*How to Lose a Guy in Ten Days, Bruce Almighty, The Sopranos, Will & Grace*—than Krispy Kreme this decade. "This is a marketing company," says

Bowles. "Scott Livengood once told me if a finance guy ever gets ahold of Krispy Kreme, sell every share."

By the late 1990s, Livengood had a major problem on his hands. Employees were clamoring for stock, while old franchisees wanted to sell out. "We looked at a private market for our stock like UPS had, but it was too clunky," he says. "We needed to go public." And here's where Joe McAleer's group of 21 franchisees and the unanimous voting protocol came back to haunt the company. Because of inheritances and gifting of stock, that group of 21 had mushroomed to 183 shareholders, each with veto power. "It was," says Livengood, grimacing, "an absolute nightmare."

The group of 183 included all sorts of people: old widows, young hotheads, ornery types, and even a few sensible folks. "Some were interested [in an IPO], some were skeptical, and some were downright hostile," recalls Livengood. "It was like getting a vote through the United Nations." By early 1999, after a year of lobbying and meetings and phone calls, Livengood finally had everyone onboard. Everyone except a single crusty stockholder with about 5,000 shares. Tension was building. Wall Street was expecting the IPO, the S-1 registration statement was drafted, and the road show was only months away. The whole offering would be torpedoed if the shareholder didn't move off the dime. "This was a person who was just saying no for the sake of saying no," Livengood says. "Finally I said, 'We are going to do this IPO whether he is with us or not,' and I just walked away." It was the ultimate game of chicken with the whole future of the company in the balance. Then the recalcitrant shareholder blinked. And Livengood never heard from him again.

"Running a company that's growing like this—that's nothing," says Livengood.

Krispy Kreme's IPO in April 2000—right at the peak of the tech boom—has been a sweet success. The stock ended the first day of trading at $9.25, split adjusted, and today sells for $37 and change. As we mentioned, that's up four times, while the market is off some 30% during the same period. Not that there haven't been a few bumps in the road. The company got major grief for entering into a $35 million synthetic lease to fund the new Illinois mixing plant back in 2001. This off-balance-sheet financing raised eyebrows during the days of Enronitis, and the company terminated the lease a year later. There have also been governance problems, like partnerships that allowed company management to invest in its stores, not enough outside directors, and loans to managers. (Those issues have since been rectified.) And Livengood has been criticized for selling some $15 million of company stock since the IPO (he still owns about a million shares).

None of that has been a big concern to those who follow this company. Instead they ask two related questions: Is the stock too high? And where does the company go from here? "This is a stock that people will always say is too expensive," says John Glass, a restaurant analyst with CIBC in Boston, "but on a P/E basis, it's priced the same as peers like Starbucks and Panera Bread." On Glass's projected 2004 earnings of $1.15, shares of KKD have a P/E of 32. Starbucks has a P/E of 30 on *Value Line*'s 2004 estimate. Significantly, though, Krispy Kreme's earnings per share are growing faster than Starbucks'. Yes, at some point growth will slow for Krispy Kreme, but probably not for a good while. "Sure there are some folks on Wall Street who want us to move faster, but we're not going to apologize for 25% [revenue] growth," says Krispy Kreme CFO Randy Casstevens. Glass of CIBC says the company could grow to 1,000 stores, and that doesn't include expansion outside the U.S., which could be significant. What about same-store sales growth? Can that stay above 10%? Not forever. But the company just rolled out its own branded roasted coffee in October. Right now coffee, a high-margin product, accounts for only 10% of sales. That number will probably rise, which down the road could lead to an intriguing run-in with Starbucks, whose founder Howard Shultz has given counsel to Livengood.

Whether you think Krispy Kreme is a buy or a sell at $27 or $37 or $57, here's the thing: Unless the fat police run riot across this land, Krispy Kreme is here to stay. It isn't some fly-by-night dot-com. There's 66 years of history here. It's a product that people not only love but understand. (Quick, what does InfoSpace do?) The world is always filled with unknown, never more so than right now. With all that's wrong out there, sometimes it's easy to lose focus on the big picture. So take a second and ask yourself: Is the American dream still alive? Is Krispy Kreme for real? Don't bet against it.

FEEDBACK *aserwer@fortunemail.com*

Kamikaze Pricing

When penetration strategies run amok, marketers can find themselves in a dive-bomb of no return.

by Reed K. Holden and Thomas T. Nagle

Price is the weapon of choice for many companies in the competition for sales and market share. The reasons are understandable. No other weapon in a marketer's arsenal can be deployed as quickly, or with such certain effect, as a price discount. The advantage is often short-lived, though, and managers rarely balance the long-term consequences of deploying the price weapon against the likely short-term gains.

Playing the price card often is a reaction to a competitor and assumes that it will provide significant gain for the firm. Usually, that's not the case. Firms start price wars when they have little to lose and much to gain; those who react to the initiators often have little to gain and much to lose. The anticipated gains often disappear as multiple competitors join the battle and negate the lift from the initial reductions.

Managers in highly competitive markets often view price cuts as the only possible strategy. Sometimes they're right. The problem is that they are playing with a very dangerous weapon in a war to improve near-term profitability that ends in long-term devastation. As the Chinese warrior, Sun Tzu, put it, "Those who are not thoroughly aware of the disadvantages in the use of arms cannot be thoroughly aware of the advantages."

If marketers are going to use low prices as a competitive weapon, they must be equally aware of the risks as well as the benefits (see "The Prisoner's Dilemma"). They also must learn to adjust their strategies to deploy alternatives when pricing alone is no longer effective. Failure to do so has put companies and entire industries into tail spins from which they never fully recover.

Pricing Options

Marketers traditionally have employed three pricing strategies: skim, penetration, and neutral. Skim pricing is the process of pricing a product high relative to competitors and the product's value. Neutral pricing is an attempt to eliminate price as a decision factor for customers by pricing neither high nor low relative to competitors. Penetration pricing is the decision to price low relative to the product's value and to the prices of similar competitors. It is a decision to use price as the main competitive weapon in hopes of driving the company to a position of market dominance.

EXECUTIVE BRIEFING

Penetration pricing is perhaps the most abused pricing strategy. It can be effective for fixed periods of time and in the right competitive situation, but many firms overuse this approach and end up creating a market situation where everyone is forced to lower prices continually, driving some competitors from the market and guaranteeing that no one realizes a good return on investment. Managers can prevent the fruitless slide into kamikaze pricing by implementing a value-driven pricing strategy for the most profitable customer segments.

All three strategies consider how the product is priced relative to its value for customers and that of similar competitors. When Lexus entered the luxury segment of the automobile industry, the car's price was high relative to

EXHIBIT 1

Experience curve effects

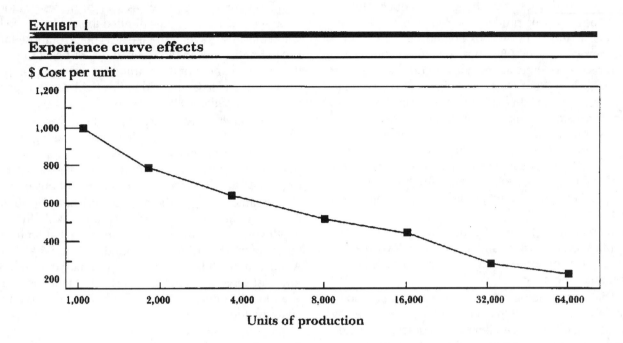

$ Cost per unit

standard vehicles but low relative to Mercedes and BMW. The penetration strategy was defined not by the price but by the price relative to the value of the vehicle and to similar competitive products.

The main ingredient to successful penetration pricing is a large segment of customers for whom price is the primary purchase motivation.

Any of these strategies can be associated with a variety of cost structures and can result in either profits or losses. To understand when each strategy is likely to be successful, managers should evaluate their current and potential cost structure, their customers' relative price sensitivities, and their current and potential competitors. All three areas must be carefully considered before employing any pricing strategy.

Penetration Strategies Can Work

If a firm has a fixed cost structure and each sale provides a large contribution to those fixed costs, penetration pricing can boost sales and provide large increases to profits—but only if the market size grows or if competitors choose not to respond. Low prices can draw additional buyers to enter the market. The increased sales can justify production expansion or the adoption of new technologies, both of which can reduce costs. And, if firms have excess capacity, even low-priced business can provide incremental dollars toward fixed costs.

Penetration pricing can also be effective if a large experience curve will cause costs per unit to drop significantly. The experience curve proposes that, as a firm's production experience increases, per-unit costs will go down. On average, for each doubling of production, a firm can expect per-unit costs to decline by roughly 20%. Cost declines can be significant in the early stages of production (see Exhibit 1).

The manufacturer who fails to take advantage of these effects will find itself at a competitive cost disadvantage relative to others who are further along the curve. This is often the case with new technologies and innovative products, where relatively small increments in units sold yield substantial decreases in unit costs. This is also the case for many new entrants to a market who are just beginning to see experience curve cost reductions.

However, the main ingredient to successful penetration pricing is a large segment of customers for whom price is the primary purchase motivation. This can be the case in business markets where original equipment commodities are sold to the production process of a customer's business, but it rarely occurs in consumer markets where image is an important part of the use of a product.

When Omega watches—once a brand more prestigious than Rolex—was trying to improve market share in the 1970s, it adopted a penetration pricing strategy that succeeded in destroying the watch's brand image by flooding the market with lower priced products. Omega never gained sufficient share on the lower price/lower image competitors to justify destroying its brand image and high-priced position with upscale buyers. Similar outcomes were experienced by the Cadillac Cimarron and Lacoste clothing.

A better strategy would have been to introduce a totally new brand as a flanking product, as Heublein did with the Popov, Relska, and Smirnoff vodka brands and Intel did with microprocessors in 1988. After the introduction of the 386 microprocessor, Intel adopted a skim price strategy for the high value and proprietary 386 chips. It also wanted to market a circuit in the 286 market that could compete with AMD and Cirrus on a nonprice, value-added basis. The 386SX was introduced as a scaled down version of the 386, but at a price only slightly higher than the 286. The net result was to migrate price sensitive customers more quickly to the proprietary 386 market with the 386SX, while still capturing increased profit from the high value users with the 386.

In its marketing of the 486, Pentium, and Pentium Pro circuits, Intel continues this flanking strategy with dozens of varieties of each microprocessor to meet the needs of various market segments.

For penetration pricing to work, there must be competitors who are willing to let the penetration pricer get away with the strategy. If a penetration price is quickly matched by a competitor, the incremental sales that would accrue from the price-sensitive segment must now be split between two competitors. As more competitors follow, smaller incremental sales advantages and lower profits accrue to both the initiator and the followers.

Fortunately, there are two common situations which often cause competitors to let penetration pricers co-exist in markets. When the penetration-pricing firm has enough of a cost or resource advantage, competitors might conclude they would lose a price war. Retailers are beginning to recognize that some consumers who are unconcerned about price when deciding which products and brands to buy become price sensitive when deciding where to buy. They are willing to travel farther to buy the same branded products at lower prices. Category killers like Toys 'R' Us use penetration pricing strategies because they are able to manage their overhead and distribution costs much more tightly than traditional department stores. Established stores don't have the cost structure to compete on this basis, so they opt to serve the high-value segment of the market.

When the penetration-pricing firm has enough of a cost or resource advantage, competitors might conclude they would lose a price war.

The second situation conducive to penetration pricing occurs when large competitors have high-price positions and don't feel a significant number of their existing customers would be lost to the penetration pricer. This was the case when People's Express entered the airline industry with low priced fares to Europe in the 1970s. The fares were justified with reduced services such as no reservations or meal service. People's also limited the ability of the high value business traveler to take advantage of those fares by not permitting advanced reservations or ticket sales. This was a key element of their strategy: Focus only on price sensitive travelers and avoid selling tickets to the customers of their competitors.

Major airlines didn't respond to the lower prices because they didn't see People's Express taking away their high value customers. It was only when People's began pursuing the business traveler that the major airlines responded and quickly put People's out of business.

The same strategy is being repeated today by Southwest Airlines in the domestic market far more skillfully. Southwest has a cost and route structure that limits the ability of major airlines to respond. In fact, when United Airlines, a much larger competitor, did try to respond with low-cost service in selected West Coast markets, it had to abandon the effort because it couldn't match Southwest's cost structure.

Penetration or Kamikaze?

An extreme form of penetration pricing is "kamikaze" pricing, a reference to the Japanese dive bomber pilots of World War II who were willing to sacrifice their lives by crashing their explosives-laden airplanes onto enemy ships. This may have been a reasonable wartime tactic (though not a particularly attractive one) by commanders who sacrificed single warriors while inflicting many casualties on opponents. But in the business world, the relentless pursuit of more sales through lower prices usually results in lower profitability. It is often an unnecessary and fruitless exercise that damages the entire dive-bombing company—not just one individual—along with the competitor. Judicious use of the tactic is advised; in as many cases as it works, there are many more where it does not.

Kamikaze pricing occurs when the justification for penetration pricing is flawed, as when marketers incorrectly assume lower prices will increase sales. This may be true in growth markets where lower prices can expand the total market, but in mature markets a low price merely causes the same customers to switch suppliers. In the global economy, market after market is being discovered, developed, and penetrated. High growth, price sensitive markets are quickly maturing, and even though customers may want to buy a low-priced product, they don't increase their volume of purchases. Price cuts used to get them to switch fail to bring large increases in demand and end up shrinking the dollar size of the market.

A prominent example is the semiconductor business, where earlier price competition led to both higher demand and reduced costs. But in recent years, total demand tends to be less responsive to lower prices, and most suppliers are well down the experience curve. The net result is an industry where participation requires huge investments, added value is immense, but because of a penetration price

The Prisoner's Dilemma

A popular exercise in seminars and executive briefings we hold is to ask executives to participate in a prisoner's dilemma pricing game. Each team must decide whether to price its products high or low compared to those of another team in 10 rounds of competition. The objective is to earn the most money; results are determined by the decision that two competitors make in comparison with each other.

The game fairly accurately simulates a typical profit/loss scenario for price competition in mature markets. The objective is to impart several lessons in pricing competition, the first being that pricing is more like playing poker than solitaire. Success depends not just on a combination of luck and how the hand is played but also on how well competitors play their hands. In real markets, outcomes depend not only on how customers respond but, perhaps more important, on how competitors respond to changes in price.

If a competitor matches a price decrease, neither the initiator nor the follower will achieve a significant increase in sales and both are likely to have a significant decrease in profits. In developing pricing strategy, managers need to anticipate the moves of their competitors and attempt to influence those moves by selectively communicating information to influence competitive behavior.

The second lesson is that managers must adopt a very long time horizon when considering changes in price.

Once started, price wars are difficult to stop. A simple decision to drop price often becomes the first shot in a war that no competitor wins. Before initiating a price decrease, managers must consider how it will affect the competitive stability of markets.

Philip Morris discovered this when it initiated a price war in the cigarette business by cutting the prices of its top brands. Competitors followed, and the net result was a $2.3 billion drop in operating profits for Philip Morris, even as the Marlboro brand increased its market share seven points to 29%. The manufacturer of Camels experienced a $1.3 billion drop in profits.

The third lesson from the prisoner's dilemma is that careful use of a value-based marketing approach can reverse a trend toward price-based marketing. This is accomplished through signaling, a nonprice competitive tactic that involves selectively disclosing information to competitors to influence their behavior. The steel and airline industries provide prominent examples of the signaling strategy's use. They often rely on announcements that conveniently appear on the front pages of the Wall Street Journal to signal competitors of pending price moves and provide them with opportunities to follow. The strategy takes time to implement, but it provides a far better long-term competitive position for marketers who employ it.

Most managers who play the prisoner's dilemma adopt a low-price strategy. This mirrors the real world, where 63% of managers who adopt an identifiable strategy use low price, according to an ongoing research project in which we are engaged. In the game, low-price teams fail to earn any profit in a majority of cases. The strategy works in round one, but competitors quickly learn to respond and both parties end up losing any chance for profit.

Executives rationalize that, if their firm can't make money, competitors shouldn't, either. Managers quickly forget that the objective of this game—and the game of business—is profit. Price cuts in the real world can be devastating. A current example is the personal computer business, where Packard Bell sets the low price standard that many competitors follow.

Packard Bell's management is less concerned with profit than with achieving a volume of sales and market share in a growing industry. But unless the company has operational characteristics that distinguish it from competitors and permit Packard Bell to deliver a quality product at those low prices, its ability to leverage market share will be limited. Analysts estimate that Packard Bell has only made $45 million in net profit over the past 10 years and is staying afloat through loans granted by suppliers and massive cash infusions from its Japanese and European co-owners.

—*Reed Holden and Thomas Nagle*

mentality, suppliers can't pull out of the kamikaze death spiral.

There was a time when large, well-entrenched competitors took a long time to respond to new low-price competitors. That is no longer true; domestic automobiles are now the low priced brands, and even AT&T has learned to respond to the aggressive price competition of Sprint and MCI. The electronics, soft goods, rubber, and steel companies that ignored low-price competitors in the 1970s and '80s have become ruthless cost and price cutters. The days of free rides from nonresponsive market leaders are gone.

Another risk comes in using penetration pricing to increase sales in order to drive down unit costs. Unfortunately, there are generally two reasons managers run into trouble when they justify price discounts by anticipated reductions in costs. First, they view the relationship between costs and volume as linear, when it actually is exponential—the cost reduction per unit becomes smaller with larger increases in volume. Initial savings are substantial, but as sales grow, the incremental savings per unit of production all but disappear (see Exhibit 2). Costs continue to decline on a per-unit basis, but the incremental cost reduction seen from each additional unit of sale becomes insignificant. Managers need to recognize that experience curve cost savings as a percentage of incremental sales volume declines with increases in volume. It works great in early growth phases but not in the later stages.

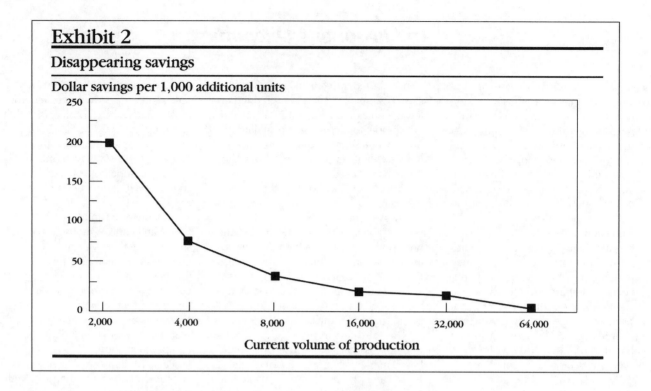

Exhibit 2

Disappearing savings

Dollar savings per 1,000 additional units

Current volume of production

Many managers believe that sales volume is king. They evaluate the success of both their sales managers and marketing managers by their ability to grow sales volume. The problem is that their competitors employ the exact same strategy. Customers learn that they can switch loyalties with little risk and start buying lower priced alternatives. Marketers find themselves stuck with a deadly mix of negligible cost benefits, inelastic demand, aggressive competition, and no sustainable competitive advantage. Any attempt to reduce price in this environment will often trigger growing losses. To make matters worse, customers who buy based on price are often more expensive to serve and yield lower total profits than do loyal customers. Thus starts the death spiral of the kamikaze pricers who find their costs going up and their profits disappearing.

Penetration pricing is overused, in large part, because managers think in terms of sports instead of military analogies. In sports, the act of playing is enough to justify the effort. The objective might be to win a particular game, but the implications of losing are minimal. The more intense the process, the better the game, and the best way to play is to play as hard as you can.

This is exactly the wrong motivation for pricing where the ultimate objective is profit. The more intense the competition, the worse it is for all who play. Aggressive price competition means that few survive the process and even fewer make reasonable returns on their investments. In pricing, the long-term implications of each battle must be considered in order to make thoughtful decisions about which battles to fight. Unfortunately, many managers find that, in winning too many pricing battles, they often lose the war for profitability.

Value Pricing

To avoid increasingly aggressive price competition, managers must first recognize the problem and then develop alternate strategies that build distinctive, nonprice competencies. Instead of competing only on price, managers can develop solutions to enhance the competitive and profit positions of their firms.

In most industries, there are far more opportunities for differentiation than managers usually consider. If customers are receiving good service and support, they are often willing to pay more to the supplier, even for commodities. A client in India produced commodity gold jewelry that was sold into the Asian market at extremely low penetration prices. Because of the client's good relationships with wholesale and retail intermediaries, we recommended a leveraging of those relationships to increase prices to a more reasonable level. Despite much anxiety, the client followed suit and major customers accepted the increases.

Opportunities to Add Value

Marketers often fail to recognize the opportunity for higher prices when they get caught up in kamikaze pricing. To avoid this, they need to understand how their customers value different product and company attributes. The objective is to identify segments of customers who have problems for which unique and cost-effective solutions can be developed. Sometimes it's as simple as a minor adjustment in packaging.

Know what customers want. Loctite Corp., a global supplier of industrial adhesives, introduced a specialty

Exhibit 3

Customer purchasing agenda

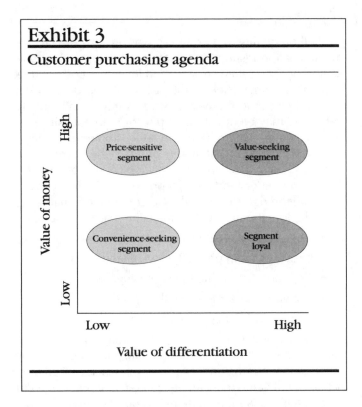

liquid adhesive in a 1-oz. bottle for use in emergency applications. Unfortunately, sales were less than spectacular. After a number of customer interviews, Loctite discovered that the liquid was difficult to apply and the bottle was difficult to carry. What customers really wanted was an easy-to-apply gel in a tube. The product was reformulated to meet these criteria and saw huge success. In the process, Loctite almost doubled the price.

Firms that attract value customers get the loyal buyer as part of the bargain and sell to the price buyer only when it is profitable and reasonable.

Managers should identify features that they can add more cost effectively than their competitors can. IBM has been under intense price pressure in the personal computer segment. Besides introducing lower-priced flanking products (with limited success), IBM also has introduced computers with more internal memory. This feature had significant appeal because of the higher memory demands of the Windows 95 operating system. The value of this feature was greater than a price cut because IBM is arguably the most cost-effective producer of random access memory in the world. It also forced low-price competitors to incur higher relative costs to match IBM, thereby undercutting their ability to price their PCs below IBM's.

In the process of adding value to their products, firms should remember that value is achieved not only from the products themselves, but from the services associated with their use. The manufacturer of a heavy-duty truck oil broke out of commodity pricing when it began analyzing the oil from its customers' trucks to determine if there were excessively high temperatures or metal in the oil that would indicate a breakdown of the internal components of engines. The service was promoted in a mailer included with each large drum of oil. The cost of this service was minimal, and a large segment of small- and owner-operator customers placed a huge value on it. This tactic helped the firm to differentiate its product with a valued service connected to the product.

Offer complete benefits. Another way to avoid downward pricing is to offer complete product benefits, which is especially useful in the early phases of a new product's life. This tactic is not as effective when products mature and customers no longer need as much service support. However, when customers are still developing their expertise, they require complete systems to achieve the maximum benefit to their organization. This is often an expensive affair that needs to be justified by the future business and profit potential that a customer represents.

When marketers correctly assess this type of situation, they often develop a sustainable competitive advantage that makes them impervious to competitive erosion. This was the strategy that Intel employed when it introduced the 8086 microprocessor to the PC industry in the early 1980s. Although the 8086 was slightly inferior technically to Motorola's 6800, Intel adopted sophisticated customer support programs that permitted new PC manufacturers to introduce new products quickly. This and other services were backed by a strong sales and marketing program that focused on specific customer adoptions. The net result was the beginning of Intel's dominance in PC microprocessors.

Understand customer agendas. Marketers make a serious mistake when they assume that all their customers are willing to sacrifice quality to obtain low prices. A few are, but most really want to get high-quality products at the lowest possible price. The seller of a high-quality product can compete against a low-price, low-quality product by recognizing that, despite the words of the purchasing agent, pricing need not be too aggressive.

Sellers who understand why customers buy their products often find that there is a fairly uniform set of reasons underlying purchasing behavior. Price is often important, but it seldom is the sole motivation. In most business situations, there are four types of agendas with regard to the pricing of products and a buyer's desired relationship with the supplying firm (see Exhibit 3). One of the best ways for marketers to avoid the trap of excessive price competition is to develop market- and customer-level strategies that reflect those behaviors.

For example, loyal customers highly value specific things that a supplier does for them, such as technical support, quality products, and customer-oriented service agents. These customers are less concerned about the price than about the care they receive. They often have a single supplier and have no intention of qualifying another. Understanding who the loyal customers are and keeping their loyalty is critical.

The purpose of sales is not to use a lower price to close a sale, but to convince the customer that the price of a product is fair.

Conversely, price buyers care little about a long-term relationship with a supplier and want the lowest possible price for products. These commodity buyers have multiple vendors and encourage them to dive into kamikaze price wars. For consumer marketers, price shoppers who switch allegiances at the drop of a coupon provide few incremental dollars to the retailers who cater to them. For business-to-business sellers, these tend to be the buyers who scream loudest and dictate pricing and selling strategies. Unfortunately, the profits they generate rarely justify the attention they demand.

The price buyer's agenda is to get products at the lowest possible prices, so he or she uses tactics that force marketers to employ kamikaze pricing tactics even when it might not be the wisest thing to do. For the marketer, the trick is only to do business with the price buyer when it is profitable to do so and when it doesn't prompt a more profitable customer to purchase elsewhere.

Convenience buyers don't care whose product they purchase, and have little regard for price. They simply want it readily available. This often is the most profitable market segment, provided marketers can deliver their products at the locations preferred by these buyers. Unfortunately, this group exhibits little brand loyalty and provides sellers with no sustainable competitive advantage beyond their distribution systems.

Offer the best deal. Value buyers evaluate vendors on the basis of their ability to reduce costs through lower prices or more efficient operations, or to make the buyer's business more effective with superior features or services. From a customer perspective, this is the place to be; while both price and loyal buying have unique costs, value buying comes with the assumption that these customers are getting the best deal possible, given all factors of consumption. From a marketing perspective, firms that attract value customers get the loyal buyer as part of the bargain and sell to the price buyer only when it is profitable and reasonable.

Organizations that employ kamikaze pricing have a poor understanding of how their products create value for customers. This lack of understanding results in excessive reliance on price to obtain orders. Successful marketers use price as a tool to reflect the value of the product and implement systems in the organization to assure that value is delivered to customers and captured in the pricing.

The Five Cs

"Sell on quality, not on price" was once a popular marketing aphorism. Unfortunately, while product quality can reduce the seller's rework and inventory costs, it does little for customers. Selling the quality of a product is often not enough because buyers have difficulty quantifying its value and may be unwilling to pay for it. By focusing on quality, we miss the opportunity for customers to understand the true value that quality brings to the buyers of our products. Instead, resolving to "sell on value, not on price" focuses on understanding how pricing really should work. To avoid the rigors of price-based competition, marketers should adopt the five "Cs" of the value-based approach:

- Comprehend what drives customer value.
- Create value in product, service, and support.
- Communicate value in advertising.
- Convince customers of value in selling.
- Capture value in pricing strategy.

How a product provides customer value and which value-creation efforts best differentiate a product from the competition must be understood by marketers. When there is additional value that can be created, marketers need to do a better job creating it in their products, service, and support activities. Once a firm provides differentiating value to its customers, the primary responsibility of the marketer is to set up a communications system, including the salesperson, that educates the customer on the components of that value.

The purpose of sales is not to use a lower price to close a sale, but to convince the customer that the price of a product, which is based on its value in the market, is fair. Of course, most sales compensation systems do just the opposite, rewarding salespeople for closing a sale, regardless of the price. Salespeople who lack an understanding of a product's value often bend to a buyer's wishes and match a lower-value competitor's price. Product prices should reflect a fair portion of their value, and they should be fixed so salespeople will have to sell on the basis of value.

Companies that approach pricing as a process rather than an event can effectively break the spiral of kamikaze pricing.

Penetration pricing gains ground in markets against competitors, but extended use of this offensive tactic inevitably leads to kamikaze pricing and calamity in markets as competitors respond, cost savings disappear, and customers learn to ignore value. Good marketers employ such weapons selectively and only for limited periods of time to build profitable market position. They learn how to draw from a broad arsenal of offensive and defensive weapons, understanding how each will affect their overall long-term market conditions, and never losing sight of the overall objective of stable market conditions in which they can earn the most sustainable profit.

Additional Reading

Darlin, Damon (1996), "The Computer Industry's Mystery Man," *Forbes*, (April 8), 42.

Nagle, Thomas and Reed Holden (1995), *The Strategy and Tactics of Pricing*. New York: Prentice Hall.

Reichheld, Frederick F. (1996), *The Loyalty Effect*. Boston: Harvard Business School Press.

Shapiro, Eileen C. (1995), *Fad Surfing in the Boardroom*. Reading, Mass.: Addison-Wesley Publishing.

Taylor, William (1993), "Message and Muscle: An Interview with Swatch Titan Nicolas Hayek," *Harvard Business Review*, (March–April), 99–110.

Tzu, Sun (1988), *The Art of War*, translated by Thomas Cleary. Boston: Shambhala Publications.

About the Authors

Reed K. Holden is President of the Strategic Pricing Group Inc., Marlborough, Mass., where he has conducted numerous industry seminars in the United States and Asia on pricing and competitive strategy, business market research, and loyal buyer behavior. He also works with corporate clients as an educator and strategic analyst. Reed has more than 11 years of experience as a sales and marketing manager in the electrical and electronics industries. During that time, he specialized in the development and implementation of sales training and industrial marketing programs. He also was an Assistant Professor at Boston University's Graduate School of Management for nine years. He coauthored the second edition of *The Strategy and Tactics of Pricing* and "Profitable Pricing: Guidelines for Management" which was published in the third edition of the *AMA Management Handbook*.

Thomas T. Nagle is Chairman of the Strategic Pricing Group Inc., which helps firms in such diverse industries as telecommunications, pharmaceuticals, computer software, semiconductors, wholesale nursery, consumer retailing, and financial services develop pricing strategies. His seminars are offered in public programs and at major corporations in North and South America and in Europe. The second edition of Tom's book, *The Strategy and Tactics of Pricing: A Guide to Profitable Decision Making*, is used extensively as a text on the subject. He is the author of "Managing Price Competition," published in *MARKETING MANAGEMENT* (Spring 1993), and "Financial Analysis For Profit-Driven Pricing," published in *The Sloan Management Review* (1994). His articles also have appeared in the *AMA Handbook of Business Strategy*. Tom has taught at the University of Chicago and at Boston University and is currently on the executive program faculties of the University of Chicago.

Reprinted with permission from *Marketing Management*, Summer 1998, pp. 30-39. © 1998 by the American Marketing Association, Reed K. Holden, and Thomas T. Nagle.

THE MONEY ISSUE

WHICH PRICE IS RIGHT?

PREPARE FOR THE COMING REVOLUTION IN HOW BUSINESS SETS PRICES

It is an urgent question: How can we increase profits if we can't raise prices? The answer demands revolutionary thinking—new insights about strategy and human behavior, turbocharged with software, mathematics, and rapid-fire experimentation. Is your company ready to master the new era of pricing? Are you prepared to pay the price of failure?

By Charles Fishman

AIRLINE TICKETS cost 40% less than they did 25 years ago. A two-liter bottle of Diet Coke often has the same price tag as it did in 1985. Light-bulbs, laptops, heck, even the "cost" of a mortgage—all are at historic lows. It's been a good 20 years to be a consumer.

But for companies, the pressure is on. Most companies are desperate to raise prices. And virtually every company has the same lament: We can't. Customers won't stand for it. Competitors will undercut us. And technology will disrupt us—again. Jack Welch saw it back in 1996, when he famously complained, "There is no pricing power at all." The environment is even tougher today.

Anyone who sells anything knows that price is the pivot of business, the ultimate leverage. If you can raise prices—even a bit—you can increase profits dramatically. If you can't raise prices, you feel like your business is struggling, regardless of what is happening with cost, quality, or service.

Meanwhile, anyone who buys anything knows that almost nothing has a single price anymore. Want to know the price of something? Well, you get back a series of questions: Who are you? How long have you been a customer? How much are you buying? How good are you at unblinking negotiation? Did you bring your frequent-shopper card?

So I set out on a mission: to enter the hidden world of prices and pricers. I wanted to talk candidly with the smartest experts, the savviest executives, and the most nimble tacticians about the most urgent subject in business today: pricing. I sensed trouble when the first person I called to interview said after a few minutes, "Wait. I hear typing. I always get nervous when I hear typing." Next came a woman from American Airlines. She kept repeating the official position: "Absolutely not. We just don't discuss prices." Finally, she pleaded, "If I talk about prices, I could go to jail." The spokeswoman for a telecom company said, "We're not going to talk about prices, and the fact that we're not going to talk about it is off the record. You can't use the fact that we won't talk about prices in a story."

But it was not until I traveled to Chicago, to a Professional Pricing Society conference, that I got a full picture of how sensitive the subject is. On my first day, I was asked to leave the trade-show exhibits—the place where vendors beg for attention. A guard was posted at the door, in case I tried to slip in. On the second day, Eric Mitchell, president of the PPS, spotted me standing in the lobby outside the meeting rooms and scowled. I would approach someone and introduce myself, and Mitchell would tag along and stand with his arms crossed as I asked questions. Eventually, his dignity overcame his paranoia, and he assigned an aide to follow me. It didn't matter. Shortly, I was approached by a man who was large enough to play nose tackle for the Chicago Bears. Leval worked security for Marriott. He was extremely polite, and he told me that I would be leaving the hotel. *Immediately.*

So there I was, standing in a biting breeze on Michigan Avenue, wondering what it is about prices that makes otherwise reasonable businesspeople so paranoid. One factor is strategic secrecy: Prices are so important to business that most executives don't want to disclose what they know. But the bigger factor, I came to appreciate, is fear of embarrassment: Most executives are surprisingly in the dark when it comes to setting prices. They guess; they say a prayer; they cross their fingers. They are afraid to disclose what they *don't* know.

Kent Monroe, a professor at the University of Illinois at Urbana-Champaign, is one of the deans of pricing. He's been teaching the subject for nearly 37 years, and he knows that sloppy thinking about pricing is widespread across the U.S. economy. Both consumers and businesspeople assume that price has everything to do with cost. *Wrong.* "You have to know the cost so that you can understand the profitability implications of price," says Monroe, "but not for the purpose of setting price." Businesspeople assume that if they are in a competitive situation, and prices drop, they have to match. *Wrong.* "The natural tendency to match is foolish," he says. Executives who are devoted to using "data" in all kinds of other arenas think it's perfectly acceptable to set prices based on "history" or "experience" or "instinct." *Wrong again.*

Monroe tells a pricing story that shows how even the simplest situation can confound accepted wisdom about prices. "A company is making two versions of the same product," says Monroe. "One has a little more gold and foil on it, but they're essentially the same. One is $14.95; the other is $18.95." Not surprisingly, the $14.95 item is selling better. It's also the lower-profit product.

"Then a competitor comes in with a third product. Again, it's essentially the same thing, but a fancier version. And it's much higher priced: $34.95."

For our original company, asks Monroe, "what becomes the best-seller? Why, the $18.95 version, of course."

It's a small story, but it's true. In fact, you can *feel* how right Monroe is. "The point," he says, "is that economic theory says that can't happen. But it does."

The neat curves and crisp laws of supply and demand, elasticity, and rational behavior that everyone learns in microeconomics class don't work in the real world.

Business is at the start of a new era of pricing. This era is being shaped by a new set of insights into business strategy and human behavior, and these insights are turbocharged with software, mathematics, and rapid experimentation. The result is what might be called "scientific pricing." There is even a blossoming industry of a dozen companies that offer scientific-pricing services.

Changes in pricing will alter every part of the economy. The way that business gets done will change, and companies will flourish or be crushed based in part on their ability to grasp and master the new science of pricing. Among those already using the new techniques are Best Buy, DHL, Ford Motor Co., the Home Depot, JC Penney, Safeway, Saks, Staples, UPS, and Winn-Dixie. General Electric, perhaps taking Jack Welch's warnings to heart, is not only working with at least two different pricing companies—it has also invested in one.

PRICE CHECK (I): BEFORE THE BAR CODE

The oldest records of prices ever found are clay tablets with pictographic symbols found in a town known as Uruk, in what was ancient Sumer and what is now southern Iraq. These price records are from 3300 BC—they've survived 5,300 years. The documents—records of payment for barley and wheat, for sheep, and for beer—are really receipts. "Uruk was a large city, at a minimum 40,000 people," says UCLA professor Robert Englund, one of the few experts on the Uruk documents. "So some of the quantities are very high—hundreds of thousands of pounds of barley, for instance."

But here's the really remarkable thing. The earliest Uruk tablets aren't just the oldest pricing records ever found. They are the oldest examples of human *writing* yet discovered. In other words, when humans first took stylus to wet clay, the first thing that they were compelled to record was… prices.

INSIDE A PERMANENT PRICE WAR: "YOU'RE ONLY AS SMART AS YOUR DUMBEST COMPETITOR"

If there are pioneers in the world of scientific pricing, they are the airlines. In the 25 years since deregulation, the airlines have honed an obsession with prices—their own and each other's—that is legendary. We all live with the seemingly bizarre inconsistencies that result, such as two people on the same plane, sitting across the aisle from each other, one of whom paid $290 to fly from New York to Miami, one of whom paid $1,290. We also benefit from the pricing obsession: With just a little bit of planning, you can fly for the same price today that you did in 1980.

The airlines know full well that we are puzzled by the frantic pricing and repricing that they do—puzzled, that is, when we aren't infuriated. Jim Compton, senior vice president of pricing and revenue management at Continental Airlines, not only wasn't scared of going to jail if he talked about prices, he was happy to pull back the curtain, to show fliers what he and his 150-person staff are up against. "I do not set the prices," says Compton, a patient, thoughtful man. "The market sets prices." That's point one. Point two: "I have a really perishable product. It's gone when the door of the plane closes. An empty seat is lost revenue."

But here's the first of many oddities of airline pricing. Most other perishable products—milk, bananas, trendy sweaters—get cheaper the closer they are to being "expired." Airline seats get more valuable the closer they get to being "expired." The most valuable airline seat is the one that somebody *must have* an hour before takeoff and is willing to pay almost any price for. Unlike a banana, an airline seat gets more profitable with time—right up to the moment it goes from being worth $1,000 one-way to being worth $0.

Here's how Compton and his colleagues think about this: You always want that seat available to sell at full price—just in case someone wants it. You want to sell every seat on the plane, except that you also want to have a handful left at the very end, for your most profitable (not to mention most grateful) customers.

The airlines could easily sell out every seat, every flight, every day. They'd price 'em pretty low, book 'em up, and wait for takeoff. But that would mean there'd never be any seats available two or three weeks before a flight took off. How exasperated are we to call and find no seats three days out? What if there were no seats three *weeks* out?

When you understand that dilemma, all of a sudden, airline prices don't seem so exploitive. Although all of the seats on that New York–Miami flight are going to the same place, they aren't the same product. You pay less when you commit to a ticket four weeks in advance; Continental assumes a risk for holding a seat until the end—and wants to be paid a lot to balance the times when saving that last seat for you means that the seat flies empty. A ticket sold a month out and a ticket sold a day out are very different things.

The complexity required to pursue this balance is mind-boggling. Continental launches about 2,000 flights every day. Each flight has between 10 and 20 prices. Continental starts booking flights 330 days in advance, and every flying day is different from every other flying day. Monday is a different kind of day than Tuesday; the Wednesday before Thanksgiving is different from the Wednesday before that. At any given moment, Jim Compton and Continental may have nearly 7 million prices in the market.

And that's just the beginning. All of those prices need to be managed, all the time. All of the major airlines (except Southwest) participate in a joint fare-publishing enterprise called ATPCO. ATPCO collects fares and rules (such as advance-purchase requirements, refundability, and so on) from each airline. ATPCO then publishes those fares back out to the airlines and to the reservation services. In the 1980s, fare changes were filed once a day. If someone changed fares, you found out on Monday and filed your competitive response on Tuesday. ATPCO was closed on weekends. Now ATPCO accepts fare changes three times every weekday—at 9 AM, 11:30 AM, and 7 PM Central Time—and once each on Saturday and Sunday. From 5 fare changes a week to 17.

As much as it can look like a kind of silly game—why not just take a pass on a couple of those changes?—it's not. "If a sale comes in at 7 PM from a competitor," says Continental's senior director of pricing, Bob Lancaster, "and you miss the 9 AM filing the next morning—you don't get your changes in until 11:30—you're in trouble." So when Continental has 7 million prices in the market, those prices can change not just every day, but several *times* a day. Typically, says Lancaster, the airlines collectively change 75,000 prices a day. On the morning after someone files a 7 PM sale, there might be 400,000 price changes across the markets.

This frantic tail chasing—which is done with the help of sophisticated computers and software that predicts ticket demand the way "models" predict the weather—is not lost on the smart people who do it. The wry, informal motto of the Continental pricing department is: "You're only as smart as your dumbest competitor." If some airline is taking prices on the Atlanta-Houston route into the ditch, then by gosh, Continental is going right down into the ditch with 'em. Usually.

It's easy to be cynical about the airlines; they could do many things better. But they also live in a business environment that would wilt the rest of us—and might soon. In the airline industry, every competitor knows the price of every product that every other competitor offers and knows instantly of any changes. How would you fare if your competitors knew your prices, and your price changes, automatically?

In the airline business, every customer instantly knows every fare available, and a ticket from any airline is equally easy to buy. How would your business fare if your customers instantly knew the prices of your competitors—and could buy their products just as easily as yours?

"Are we addicted to the complexity of our pricing?" asks Continental's chief economist, Paul Thomas. "Yes, we are. But we aren't naive about it. We talk about it all the time."

And this complexity that goes with what the airlines do—this is what's going to sweep through the rest of the economy. Because in just the past few years, the kind of software that the airlines use has become available to any company.

PRICE CHECK (II): SHOPPING FOR AMERICA

Cindy Whittington is standing in a sea of women's coats in a department store in suburban Washington, DC. It is the thick of the Christmas-shopping season, and there are 29 racks of winter coats—perhaps 700 in all. Whittington has a pencil in her teeth, a three-ring binder on her left arm, and a look of calm determination in her eye. She's shopping, and the fate of the nation is balanced on her arm along with her binder.

Whittington is gathering prices used to calculate the U.S. Consumer Price Index. The mood of the stock market, the wages of millions of union workers, and the Social Security checks of nearly 50 million retirees all depend on the CPI. Given the complexity of the consumer economy, the way that the CPI is assembled remains oddly handcrafted. Some 80,000 prices are gathered each month, mostly in person, by 400 people like Cindy Whittington. For the moment, the prices are recorded on paper and keypunched into computers, although pricers will get touch-screen laptops later this year.

It is, in fact, the very complexity of the economy that sends people out into the stores every month. The goal of the CPI is to measure an unchanging (or at least slowly evolving) basket of goods—so that when Whittington plunges into the women's coats this season, she's got a detailed description of the four coats she's seeking. "My friends are very envious, because I get to go 'shopping' for a living," she says. "But it's not shopping, it's pricing." Still, Whittington says she spends so much time in stores, her friends call her "the queen of the deals."

As for the CPI itself, what's the price of that statistic? In an annual economy of $10.2 trillion, measuring the CPI costs $50 million—18 cents a year for each U.S. consumer.

THE SMART WAY TO LOWER PRICES: DISCOUNT LESS, BUT DISCOUNT SOONER

According to a recent study, 63% of noncouture clothing sold in the United States in 2002 was on sale. One way or another, if you're in apparel, managing markdowns matters. Over the years, clothing retailers have gone from being local shops to national chains, and buyers often haven't visited the stores that they are buying for. And even though the buyers have computers on their desks, the buying and pricing process has remained remarkably unchanged in half a century.

"Most retail companies still do a lot of things manually," says Steven Schwartz, senior vice president of planning and allocation at the Casual Male Retail Group, a chain of 475 clothing stores. "Our buyers and planners got reports on sales and inventory weekly," says Schwartz. "And they evaluated those reports, looking for what was selling, what to discount, and deciding the markdown. But they were going through paper 12 inches thick. We took a markdown. If it worked, great. If it didn't work, we took another markdown."

A couple of years ago, Schwartz began to look for a better way, and he found a half-dozen companies offering software to automate the markdown process. It works somewhat like airline-pricing software: The computers absorb several years' worth of data, look at what's in stores and how it's selling, and spit out recommendations for prices on specific clothing items. Casual Male picked ProfitLogic, a company based in Cambridge, Massachusetts that is also working with the Home Depot, JC Penney, and Old Navy. During the first year, Casual Male did a test across six departments in all of its stores. Schwartz's buyers would tell the ProfitLogic software what inventory they wanted to move, what the price was, and, most importantly, when Casual Male wanted to be sold-out (or when the chain wanted to have a certain amount left to be sold at its outlet chain).

ProfitLogic's system not only gave guidance on what to discount, and by how much, it also allowed Casual Male's buyers to ask their own questions, like, "What happens if we mark down 10% instead of 20%?"

The software inspired one basic change in the Casual Male markdown world: Discount less, but discount a lot sooner. "Merchants tend to get emotionally committed to what they buy," says David Boyce, ProfitLogic's vice president of marketing. "Buyers pick styles, colors. In general, they get it right, but once in a while, they don't. They always say, 'Just one more week! It will sell!'"

At Casual Male, the results were immediate. "Sell throughs"—selling all of something—"were much faster, much sooner," says Schwartz. The clothing was still on sale—but not as deeply discounted as it would have been a month later in the season. Schwartz is protective about the exact improvement in profitability. But in June 2002, the software was rolled out for all items at all stores—after Casual Male upgraded its national point-of-sale system.

Saks, with $6.5 billion in sales, is using similar software designed by a ProfitLogic competitor, Spotlight Solutions. After a test done during Christmas 2001, Saks rolled out the software widely this past Christmas. Like at Casual Male, the system is recommending smaller markdowns, but sooner. "What has surprised me," says Bill Franks, CIO of Saks, "is the accuracy of the software's algorithm predicting sales if we move the price. It is uncanny how accurate the software is."

Franks thinks that as the software becomes commonplace, it could have an unintended effect: that of lowering list prices. "What we've had to do up to now is overprice things at the beginning, to compensate for underpricing at the end of the season," he explains. "Ultimately, everything may be a little cheaper, because we won't have to absorb the cost of those deep markdowns at the end."

PRICE CHECK (III): HOW MUCH FOR A COKE?

One of the great moments in the history of price foolishness involved Coca-Cola. On October 28, 1999, the *New York Times* reported that Coke was testing a vending machine that could sense the outside temperature and "automatically raise prices for its drinks in hot weather."

The story came from Coke's then-chairman, Douglas Ivester. He was describing the technology to a Brazilian magazine, bragging that it could increase price during a sports championship in summer heat "when it is fair that it should be more expensive." Coke confirmed the testing; Pepsi said that it would never "exploit" customers in hot weather.

The story ran around the world and was met with outrage. On the day that the story broke, Coke backpedaled furiously, a spokesman saying of temperature-controlled pricing, "We don't see [that] happening anytime soon, if ever."

Of course, Ivester was right according to economic theory and market experience. His customers *already* paid a wild variety of prices for Coke, depending on the setting. What Ivester got wrong was the human part, the perception of price. Consider what the reaction might have been to this headline: "Coke testing machine that automatically discounts prices in cool weather." The tale of the temperature-controlled Coke machine is now taught in business schools across the country.

THE NEW SCIENCE OF PRICING: TEST AND TEST AGAIN

Larry Warnock has only been a new-wave scientific pricer for a few months, but he talks with the zeal of a convert—a zeal that comes from having discovered after 20 years in business something that's been sitting there all along. "How do companies set their prices?" asks Warnock. "Three ways. There's cost-plus. There's 'because my competitor did it.' And then there's what we call OTA pricing. Politely, that's 'out of the air.' Companies say, 'We price what the market will bear.' But they do nothing to *measure* what the market will bear."

Warnock is an executive vice president at Zilliant, an Austin, Texas-based company at the forefront of measuring what the market will bear. Zilliant's offices hardly seem to sit at the epicenter of a strategic revolution. The workspace is pedestrian. The software, however, is not. Zilliant pulls together a growing body of math that can analyze huge amounts of data and then use even more math to predict human behavior in the face of price changes. This isn't the kind of problem solving that even most math-team alumni have any experience with. Zilliant's chief scientist, Ahmet Kuyumcu, sent along a couple of algorithms of the sort that Zilliant uses. Here's one: $P_{win}(R)=\Sigma_N f_N \chi P(R)^N$.

The leap isn't just the computing power, though, or the math. The real leap of Zilliant, and its competitors, is a shrug of modesty. Zilliant says, We're not actually going to get the price *right*. What we're going to do is *look for* the right price.

Zilliant's software runs experiments. You pick a goal—maximizing total profits, for instance—and then you start selling stuff, the *same* stuff, in fact, just at slightly different prices. You don't just take a flier and raise your prices 5% and see if anyone flees to a competitor; you don't just drop your prices 15% and hope that the price brings in 20% more business. You test, you sell, you gather data—you see what works. Then you change your prices—maybe 4% up, maybe 6% down—when you know what's going to happen.

Small changes can make all the difference: Jim Compton and his colleagues at Continental Airlines boarded 44 million passengers in 2001, at an average ticket price of $193. Charging two bucks more per ticket would have swung the firm to profit. That's a price change of 1.04%.

Scientific pricing is really pricing using the scientific method. Let's not guess what's going to happen; let's change prices in a controlled way, watch what happens, then change prices for real after that. And by the way, we'll begin the next set of experiments the next day.

These experiments can reshape how and what companies charge for their services. One of Zilliant's first customers was DHL, the $6 billion-a-year shipping firm. DHL hadn't changed its list prices in five years, and its walk-up (or call-up) business was shrinking in the face of competition from FedEx and UPS.

The typical way that DHL might adjust prices would be to do a market-research study—to *ask* consumers whether they'd ship a five-pound package from Houston to Lyons, France for, say, $81. How about $71? The problem is instantly clear. A "study" like that is marginally better than a guess. As Aman Adinew, director of pricing and yield management for DHL North America, was considering his options, he stumbled onto Zilliant.

"I saw a huge difference between this software and the [survey]," says Adinew. "It is actually testing my customers. They call; we quote a price; they are actually shipping." In DHL's case, the Zilliant software measures something just as important: customers who called, got a quote, and *didn't* ship—a failed price.

The stakes were huge. In the international markets where they competed, FedEx and UPS were underpricing DHL by 20% to 30%. But DHL has a strong international reputation. Did it need to match those discounts to hold its customers? Would less of a discount do the job?

The scale of the problem, in ordinary terms, was vast. DHL was looking at prices in 43 different markets (United States to Mexico, for instance, or United States to Japan), in a range of weights. Just the basic price grid had hundreds of boxes—and DHL needed to test prices in every market for every product.

And the deadline was brutal. DHL and Zilliant talked in September 2001. Prices had to be set by December 17, to make the price-change date of February 1. After Adinew hired Zilliant, the company got its software installed at DHL's Tempe, Arizona call center in 14 days.

The Zilliant software would sit behind DHL's own systems, randomly offering customers the "experimental" prices, then recording the results. "We're taking real orders," says Adinew. "If something happens, and they shut it down, well," he laughs, "I wouldn't be talking to you right now."

Adinew and his staff had guesses about where raising and lowering rates would change volume and profitability. But Zilliant tested a range of prices for every product and every market, just to see. In the end, the system gathered tens of thousands of data points. DHL wound up changing hundreds of prices. And there were plenty of surprises. "Most of our prices went down," says Adinew. "But did we have to match the competition? Not at all." In fact, by lowering prices just a bit, DHL's "ad hoc" business not only stabilized, it grew. People were willing to pay more for DHL.

One key measure of the success of DHL's walk-up rates is the "quote-to-book" ratio. Of people who call to get a quote, how many actually ship? Before the Zilliant test, the number was about 17%. The new prices have increased the ratio to nearly 25% who call and ship. Revenue is up and profitability is up—in the shipping business, in a recession. "That's the beauty of it," says Adinew. The Zilliant experiment paid for itself, he says, "ten thousand times over. I can't tell you the number, but it's huge."

Prices make the world's economy go round. OPEC looks like it's about power; it's really about price. CNBC looks like it's about business; it's really a TV network devoted to prices. Even money, for all its ostensible power, is just a solvent for price. And yet, for all their significance, prices have most often been taken for granted. Scientific pricing ends that.

Adinew, with his airline background, knows the power of what he did. "This was no guessing game," he says. "We will never do this the old way again. This is science." DHL is now starting to use the Zilliant software across all kinds of other segments of its business. And Adinew has seen the future: "In 10 years, no major company will be able to survive without this kind of software. You just won't be able to compete."

Charles Fishman (cnfish@mindspring.com), a FAST COMPANY senior editor, considers himself "extremely price sensitive." His colleagues just think he's cheap.

---

most VALUABLE *PLAYERS*

SLASHING PRICES TO KEEP UP WITH THE BIG CHAINS CAN SPELL DISASTER FOR THE AVERAGE ENTREPRENEUR. IT'S BETTER TO STICK WITH WHAT YOUR BUSINESS DOES BEST: OFFERING CUSTOMERS VALUE-ADDED SERVICES.

By Joshua Kurlantzick

John Reid should be worried. The owner of SPC Office Products, a chain of office supply stores, Reid has watched as self-service giants like Staples and Office Depot have come to dominate his industry. The closest self-service behemoth is only 45 miles from one of his SPC locations in western Oklahoma—a distance that, Reid says, "in our area is like nothing, since people drive that far for dinner." But Reid, 47, is not concerned. Over the past decade, SPC has expanded from one to six stores, kept sales up—revenues were $7.2 million last year—and expanded its roster of large clients. How has Reid competed against the two office behemoths, which have more than 2,000 stores combined and enormous catalog and Web-based supply systems? Reid has convinced residents of western Oklahoma that, even if Staples or Office Depot offer products for slightly less, SPC can provide crucial value-added services—services that, in Reid's view, "are just enough to convince people they should come to us rather than drive 45 miles away."

SEARCHING FOR NEW VALUE

Reid's situation is hardly unique. Over the past 10 years, consumers have been presented with many new avenues for buying products and services. Industries from office supplies to health food to books have become dominated by huge chains—chains that can offer lower prices on high-value products in predictable retailing environments, and that can blanket areas with mass-market advertising. Target is a prime example: Once known as a low-end chain, Target now sells designer clothing on the cheap and has poached thousands of customers from small fashion shops. Meanwhile, the Internet has made it easier for consumers to seek high-value products online and comparison shop among many stores.

Entrepreneurs have scrambled to survive. The number of independent bookstores has fallen by nearly half over

GOOD ADVICE

Entrepreneurs at a loss for how to add value to their businesses can draw on a range of resources for ideas and assistance.

Many marketing and branding consultants have Web sites full of free information and advice about competing on value. Some of the best sites include Helios Consulting (www.heliosconsulting.com) and business and marketing strategist Arnold Sanow's site, www.arnoldsanow.com. And don't forget Entrepreneur.com.

Consultants are also happy to provide more extensive (paid) advice. Try smaller consulting firms for more reasonable prices. Other potential sources of assistance include Small Business Development Centers and university marketing departments.

Though a range of experts have written books on adding value to your business, very few are readable and useful. Paco Underhill's *Why We Buy: The Science of Shopping* (Touchstone Books), which gives some suggestions about offering value to consumers, is an exception. Well-reported and lively, it mixes readable prose and useful tips. Other useful books include Al and Laura Reis' *The 22 Immutable Laws of Branding* (HarperCollins) and Jack Trout's *Differentiate or Die* (John Wiley & Sons).

the past 10 years, says the American Booksellers Association, a trend repeated in many other industries. In western Oklahoma, Reid says, nearly every other local chain of office supply stores has gone out of business.

SINGING A NEW TUNE: To keep their Web-based music business humming, John and Marianne Turton provide customers with something the bigger guys don't—commentaries on hard-to-find vintage LPs.

According to business and marketing strategist, Arnold Sanow, many entrepreneurs have tried to compete with the larger chains on price—almost surely a losing move. "Small businesses cannot win price wars since they do not have the bulk purchasing and margins," Sanow says. "They have to use a different tack."

THE REAL THING

Increasingly, this tack means not competing on price, but convincing customers that small businesses offer more value. To do so, successful entrepreneurs adopt several strategies. Like Reid, many emphasize value-added services. These services can cement customers' trust and foster the belief that entrepreneurial businesses provide more homespun authenticity. According to branding experts like Paco Underhill, author of the bestselling book *Why We Buy: The Science of Shopping* (Touchstone Books), authenticity is a value highly sought after these days—hence the popularity of Saranac, Sierra Nevada and other micro-brewed beers that project an image of locally made authenticity.

Services that make consumers think they're receiving more value can take on several forms. For many companies, service means regularly traveling around the country to meet with large customers and gauge their needs. Judy George, founder of Norwood, Massachusetts-based Domain Home Fashions, a small chain of home furnishing shops in the Northeast, says she spends as much time as possible on the road chatting with her clients. Candy Nichols, owner of a chain of children's clothing stores in New York City's suburbs, uses a similar tack: She sends personal shoppers to some customers' homes with racks of clothes so clients don't have to leave their houses to shop.

DAVID vs. GOLIATH: John Reid battles the office supply giants by emphasizing value-added customer service at his SPC Ofice Products store.

In other cases, value-added service simply means always having a knowledgeable employee available to handle customers' needs, something very few large corporations can do. (Large companies like Dell Computer and Southwest Airlines that do offer a high level of service and a human touch have prospered enormously.) For Reid, this level of service requires spending the money to have more employees on the floor than his giant competitors.

John Moretti, owner of Fountain of Youth, a health-food store in Westport, Connecticut, provides this level of service by personally greeting every customer who comes through his door and asking each one what he or she is looking for. "We actually have benefited from having [health-food chain] Wild Oats open near us," says Moretti, 54. "People see some things at Wild Oats, don't understand what they are and come into my store. I greet them, they get advice about these products they saw, and they wind up buying many things." (Moretti answered *Entrepreneur*'s questions via cellphone, and he occasionally broke off the interview to welcome each customer who came in.)

SHOW 'EM WHAT YOU'RE WORTH

When Angela Llamas-Butler, president of Delta System Designs Inc., a Pittsburgh-area information consulting firm with seven employees, decided. three years ago to seek out more public-sector clients, she worried that her company would struggle to demonstrate its value. "Dealing with the public sector is a totally different game than pleasing private-sector clients, and we had not sought out government contracts before," Llamas-Butler says. "The ways we showed we were valuable to our older clients did not necessarily translate to government clients like police forces."

Still, Llamas-Butler's company showed that entrepreneurs can learn to provide value to a range of customers. Delta System took extra time to work with its new public-sector clients, find out about their most pressing problems and learn to deal with the bureaucracy. Issues had to be managed while satisfying all the relevant authorities who needed to sign off on a given deal. "We would make sure any consulting services we provided jibed with that local government or department's traditional approach to handling problems [to] build our credibility," Llamas-Butler says. "We tried to understand their culture rather than just saying 'We have the answers.'"

For Audiophile International cofounders John and Marianne Turton, 49 and 47, respectively, this level of service necessitates educating themselves so thoroughly about old records that they can provide more information about each LP than nearly any music store owner in the country. Operating their Web-based vintage records business from their home in Fair Oaks, California, the Turtons outsource tasks they know less about, like Web design, and spend nearly all their waking hours listening to records, writing commentaries about each LP, and personally communicating with customers by e-mail.

To provide this level of service, you must empower your employees. "Allow your employees to educate themselves about the business and make important decisions so they have a stake in the company," says Sanow.

Though large companies often can pay slightly higher salaries, entrepreneurial companies are better able to offer employees a variety of roles and greater involvement in the business, allowing them to more easily empower employees, notes business consultant Jerome Klein, president of JHK Marketing in San Rafael, California.

Many successful entrepreneurs also back up their commitment to value-added service with a guarantee. The Turtons vow that customers can return anything for any reason, and despite that risky strategy, Audophile has prospered, garnering almost 3,000 regular customers. Other entrepreneurs take even larger risks—risks necessary to show customers the value of their services. Angela Llamas-Butler, 38-year-old founder of Pittsburgh software company Delta System Designs Inc., got a contract from the local police department in 1999. When one of the other firms working on the contract went out of business, Llamas-Butler decided her firm would take on the defunct company's workload—for free. By doing so, she sacrificed hundreds of thousands of dollars in potential fees. The gamble worked: Her dedication to providing service impressed the police department, which ultimately gave her a new, larger contract.

SELLING VALUE

Marketing experts believe entrepreneurs should move away from accepted methods of advertising to promote their value-added services. For one, they say, entrepreneurs should not shy away from comparing their services to those of large chains. "There used to be a bit of accepted wisdom that small businesses should not even mention big retailers," says Sanow. "But in today's incredibly tough retail environment, break that wisdom— emphasize your service by comparing it to big companies' lack of service." To draw these comparisons, many successful entrepreneurs spend much of their time studying large competitors to find their weaknesses. On the road, Judy George often interviews random people as they exit other furniture stores. The Turtons frequently surf eBay to compare the auction site to their operation. John Reid spends hours each week examining Staples' and Office Depot's Web sites, quarterly reports and other public information.

Marketing consultants also suggest that entrepreneurs generally avoid radio and TV advertisements. "If you want to emphasize that you provide a high degree of personal service and, therefore, differentiate yourself on value, you really can't get that message across in a TV ad," says Klein. "To push your personal service, you need a personal style of advertising, like newsletters or face-to-face contact" Armed with information comparing SPC Office Products to Office Depot and Staples, Reid's employees travel through Oklahoma visiting potential customers in person. Sanow suggests entrepreneurs periodically send frequent customers an invoice that says "no charge" on it, thereby offering them a free product or service in an innovative way.

Personalizing service means using technology judiciously. Zipcar, a Boston-based car rental company battling giants like Avis, uses the Web to handle most reservations, but, unlike its competitors, it bans automatically generated confirmations for Web reservations. Instead, a Zipcar customer service representative sends a personal reply to each customer, explaining the car rental and its policies.

MOVIN' ON UP

In other cases, entrepreneurs convince consumers they are providing value by actually charging more for their products. "Small businesses need to find niches to survive, and often one of the best ways to survive is to move into higher-end versions of what you have been doing," says Klein. "In the higher-end market, it is easier to compete with large companies, and since people have a 'you get what you pay for' mentality, becoming more expensive and specialized creates an idea of value to your consumers."

In the mid-1990S, when it was struggling to break even, Seghesio Family Vineyards, a wine grower in Healdsburg, California, decided it could convince customers of its wines' value and boost revenues by reducing production and raising prices. Seghesio slashed output by nearly 75 percent, abandoned some of its lower-end wines, and boosted its average price to $20 per bottle. Sales have rebounded, and Seghesio has once again become one of the most popular California producers. Similarly, Sanow notes, one of his clients, a travel agency, gave up its general business and focused on making bookings for a few specific Hollywood production companies. In so doing, it became established as a higher-end company that offered more attention and value to its clients. Of course, while taking their business upscale, entrepreneurs must remember to avoid big chains' core products or services.

JOSHUA KURLANTZICK *is a writer in Washington, DC.*

The Old Pillars of New Retailing

*Looking for the silver bullet that will solve your retailing woes? It doesn't exist.
The best retailers lay a foundation for success by creating
customer value in a handful of fundamental ways.*

by Leonard L. Berry

EVERYONE WHO GLANCES AT A newspaper knows that the retailing world is brutally competitive. The demise of Montgomery Ward in the realm of bricks and mortar as well as the struggles of eToys on-line—to choose only two recent examples—make it clear that no retailer can afford to be complacent because of previous successes or rosy predictions about the future of commerce.

Despite the harsh realities of retailing, the illusion persists that magical tools, like Harry Potter's wand, can help companies overcome the problems of fickle consumers, price-slashing competitors, and mood swings in the economy. The wishful thinking holds that retailers will thrive if only they communicate better with customers through e-mail, employ hidden cameras to learn how customers make purchase decisions, and analyze scanner data to tailor special offers and manage inventory.

But the truth of the matter is, there are no quick fixes. Yes, technology can help any business operate more effectively, but many new advances are still poorly understood—and in any case, retailing can't be reduced to tools and techniques. Over the past eight years, I've analyzed dozens of retail companies to understand the underlying differences between outstanding and mediocre performers. My research includes interviews with senior and middle managers and frontline employees, observations of store operations, and extensive reviews of published and internal company materials. I've found that the best retailers create value for their customers in five interlocking ways. Doing a good job in just three or four of the ways won't cut it; competitors will rush to exploit weakness in any of the five areas. If one of the pillars of a successful retailing operation is missing, the whole edifice is weakened.

The key is focusing on the total customer experience. Whether you're running physical stores, a catalog business, an e-commerce site, or a combination of the three, you have to offer customers superior solutions to their needs, treat them with real respect, and connect with them on an emotional level. You also have to set prices fairly and make it easy for people to find what they need, pay for it, and move on. These pillars sound simple on paper, but they are difficult to implement in the real world. Taking each one in turn, we'll see how some retailers have built successful operations by attending to these commonsense ways of dealing with customers, and how others have failed to pay them the attention they require.

Pillar 1: Solve Your Customers' Problems

It has become commonplace for companies to talk about selling solutions rather than products or services. But what does this really mean for retailers? Put simply, it means that customers usually shop for a reason: they have a problem—a need—and the retailer hopes to provide the solution. It's not enough, for example, just to sell high-quality apparel—many retailers do that. Focusing on solutions means employing salespeople who know how to help customers find clothing that fits and flatters, having tailors on staff and at the ready, offering home delivery, and happily placing special orders. Every retailer hopes to meet its customers' pressing needs; some do it much better than others.

The Container Store provides its customers with superior solutions. The 22-store chain, based in Dallas, averages double-digit annual sales growth by selling something that absolutely everyone needs: storage and organization products. From boxes and trunks to hangers, trays, and shelving systems, each store carries up to 12,000 different products.

The Container Store's core strategy is the same today as it was in 1978, when the company was founded: to improve customers' lives by giving them more time and space. The company accomplishes this mission well. It starts with the selection of merchandise, which must meet criteria for visibility, accessibility, and versatility. The company's philosophy is that its products should allow people to see what they've stored and get at it easily. The merchandise must also be versatile enough to accommodate customers' particular requirements.

Store organization is another key ingredient of superior solutions at the Container Store. The merchandise is organized in sections such as kitchen, closet, laundry, office, and so on. Many products are displayed in several sections because they can solve a variety of problems. A sweater box, for example, can also store office supplies. Plastic trash cans can also be used for dog food and recyclables. Individual products are often combined and sold as a system—thus, parents in the store who want to equip their children for summer camp may find a trunk filled with a laundry bag, a toothbrush case, a first-aid pouch, leakproof bottles, a "critter catcher," and other items.

Great service is another component of the Container Store's ability to solve its customers' storage problems. The company is very careful about hiring; it patiently waits until it finds just the right person for a position. Container Store employees are well trained to demonstrate how products work and to propose solutions to complex home organizational problems. They are also treated very well, both in terms of pay and in less tangible ways. In fact, the Container Store was ranked the best place to work in the country in 1999 and 2000 by *Fortune* magazine.

A relentless focus on solutions may sound simple, but it's not. The Container Store has many imitators, but none have matched it. Many businesses have only the fuzziest concept of selling solutions. Department store chains, for example, have stumbled in recent years. They lost their one-stop shopping advantage by eliminating many merchandise categories outside of apparel and housewares. And even as they focused on apparel, they lost ground both to specialty retailers that have larger category selections and to discounters that have lower prices. Finally, they lost their customer service advantage by employing salespeople who often are little more than poorly trained order takers. As a result, these stores do a relatively poor job of solving customers' problems. That's probably why only 72% of consumers shopped in department stores in 2000 compared with 85% in 1996.

Clearly, the lesson here is that you must understand what people need and how you're going to fill that need better than your competitors. The Container Store has figured this out; many department stores and other struggling retailers must go back to the beginning and answer these basic questions.

Pillar 2: Treat Customers with R-e-s-p-e-c-t

The best retailers show their customers what Aretha Franklin sang about: respect. Again, this is absolutely basic, and most retail executives would say that of course they treat customers with respect. But it just isn't so.

Everyone has stories to tell about disrespectful retailing. You're in an electronics store, looking for assistance to buy a DVD player or a laptop computer. You spot a couple of employees by their uniforms and badges, but they're deep in conversation. They glance in your direction but continue to ignore you. After awhile, you walk out, never to return.

Or you're in a discount store, looking for planters that have been advertised at a low price. You go to the store's garden center but cannot find the planters. This time, you succeed in flagging down an employee. You ask about the planters, but she just mumbles "I dunno" and walks away. Frustrated, you go to the customer service desk and ask the clerk where you might find the advertised planters. He suggests that you try the garden center. Once again, you head for the exit.

It's easy to go on. Stories about women trying to buy cars, as everyone knows, are enough to make your hair curl. The fact is, disrespectful retailing is pervasive. In the 2000 Yankelovich Monitor study of 2,500 consumers, 68% of those surveyed agreed with the statement that "Most of the time, the service people that I deal with for the products and services that I buy don't care much about me or my needs."

Disrespectful retailing isn't just about bored, rude, and unmotivated service workers. Cluttered, poorly organized stores, lack of signage, and confusing prices all show lack of respect for customers.

The best retailers translate the basic concept of respect into a set of practices built around people, policies, and place:

- They select, prepare, and manage their people to exhibit competence, courtesy, and energy when dealing with customers.
- They institute policies that emphasize fair treatment of customers—regardless of their age, gender, race, appearance, or size

of purchase or account. Likewise, their prices, returns policy, and advertising are transparent.

- They create a physical space, both inside and outside the store, that is carefully designed to value customers' time.

In 1971, a 30-year-old entrepreneur named Len Riggio bought a floundering Manhattan bookshop called Barnes & Noble. Today, Barnes & Noble is the nation's largest bookseller, with fiscal 1999 sales of $3.3 billion. Respect for the customer has been at the heart of the company's rise.

Riggio's biggest idea was that books appeal to most everyone, not just to intellectuals, writers, and students in cosmopolitan cities. Riggio listened to prospective customers who wanted bigger selections of books, more convenient locations, and less intimidating environments. He put superstores in all types of communities, from big cities like Atlanta and Chicago, to smaller cities like Midland, Texas, and Reno, Nevada. His respect for the customer led him to create stores with spacious and comfortable interiors, easy chairs for relaxing with a book, and Starbucks coffee bars. To this day, he considers his best decision the installation of easy-to-find public restrooms in the stores. As he said in a recent speech, "You work so hard and invest so much to get people to visit your store, why would you want them to have to leave?"

Besides the large selection of books, the stores also have an active calendar of author signings, poetry readings, children's events, and book discussion groups. Many Barnes & Noble superstores have become a social arena in which busy consumers—who normally rush in and out of other stores—linger.

Riggio sees the Internet as much more than a way to deliver books to customers; it's another opportunity to listen to them and thus show respect for them. He views the store network and Barnesandnoble.com as portals to each other. Customers can ask salespeople at Internet service counters to search Barnesandnoble.com for out-of-stock books, for customer reviews of titles that interest them, and for information about authors, such as other books they've published. Customers in a superstore can order the books they want on-line and have them shipped either to that store or to any other address. If a return is necessary, customers can bring their on-line purchase back to the store.

The value of respect often gets little more than lip service from retailers. Some companies wait until it's too late to put words into action.

Pillar 3: Connect with Your Customers' Emotions

Most retailers understand in principle that they need to connect emotionally with consumers; a good many don't know how to (or don't try to) put the principle into practice. Instead, they neglect the opportunity to make emotional connections and put too much emphasis on prices. The promise of low prices may appeal to customers' sense of reason, but it does not speak to their passions.

Many U.S. furniture retailers are guilty of ignoring consumers' emotions. Although the average size of new homes in the country has grown by 25% since 1980, furniture accounts for a lower percentage of total U.S. consumer spending today (1%) than it did in 1980 (1.2%). Making consumers wait up to two months to receive their furniture contributes to these poor results. How can consumers get emotionally involved in products they know they won't see for weeks?

Poor marketing also hurts the industry. Most furniture stores focus strictly on price appeals, emphasizing cost savings rather than the emotional lift that can come from a new look in the home. "We don't talk about how easy it can be to make your home more attractive," says Jerry Epperson, an investment banker who specializes in the furniture industry. "All we talk about is 'sale, sale, sale' and credit terms."

Great retailers reach beyond the model of the rational consumer and strive to establish feelings of closeness, affection, and trust. The opportunity to establish such feelings is open to any retailer, regardless of the type of business or the merchandise being sold. Everyone is emotionally connected to some retailers—from local businesses such as the wine merchant who always remembers what you like; to national companies like Harley-Davidson, which connects people through its Harley Owners Group; to catalog retailer Coldwater Creek, which ships a substitute item to customers who need to make returns before the original item is sent back.

One retailer that has connected especially well with its target market in recent years is Journeys, a Nashville, Tennessee-based chain of shoe stores located primarily in shopping malls. The chain focuses on selling footwear to young men and women between the ages of 15 and 25. Started in 1987, Journeys didn't take off until 1995 when new management took over. The chain has achieved double-digit comparable-store sales increases in five of the six years since then and is now expanding by as many as 100 new stores per year.

Journeys has penetrated the skepticism and fickleness that are characteristic of many teens. By keeping a finger on the pulse of its target market, the company consistently has the right brands available for this especially brand-conscious group of consumers. Equally important, it creates the right store atmosphere—the stores pulsate with music, video, color, and brand merchandising.

A Journeys store is both welcoming and authentic to young people; it is simultaneously energetic and laid-back. Journeys' employees are typically young—the average age of a store manager is about 25—and they dress as they please. Customers frequently visit a store in groups just to hang out; salespeople exert no pressure to buy. And everyone, whether they've made a purchase or not, usually leaves with a giveaway—for instance, a key chain, a compact-disc case, a promotional T-shirt, or one of the 10 million or so stickers the stores give out over the course of a year. The stickers, which usually feature one of the brands Journeys sells, often end up on backpacks, skateboards, school lockers, or bathroom mirrors. Journeys also publishes a bimonthly magazine, *Dig*, that is available in the stores, and it runs a Web site that seeks to replicate the atmosphere of its stores. The number of site visits explodes whenever the company's commercials appear on MTV.

Journeys works in large part because it has created an atmosphere that connects emotionally with the young people it serves. Other retailers should bear in mind that it takes more than a room full of products with price tags on them to draw people in.

Pillar 4: Set the Fairest (Not the Lowest) Prices

Prices are about more than the actual dollars involved. If customers suspect that the retailer isn't playing fair, prices can also carry a psychological cost. Potential buyers will not feel comfortable making purchases if they fear that prices might be 30% lower next week, or if certain charges have only been estimated, or if they are unsure whether an advertised sale price represents a genuine markdown.

Consider some of the pricing tactics commonly used by certain home improvement retailers. One well-known company advertises products as "special buys" even though it has not lowered the regular prices. Another purposely misrepresents a competitor's prices on price-comparison signs within its stores. Still another company promotes lower-grade merchandise implying that it is top quality. One retailer puts a disclaimer in its ads that reads: "Prices in this ad may be different from the actual price at time of purchase. We adjust our prices daily to the lumber commodity market." The disclaimer paves the way for the retailer to raise its prices regardless of the advertised price.

Excellent retailers seek to minimize or eliminate the psychological costs associated with manipulative pricing. Most of these retailers follow the principles of "everyday fair pricing" instead of "everyday low pricing." A fact of retail life is that no retailer, not even Wal-Mart, can truthfully promise customers that it will always have the lowest prices. An uncomfortable truth for many retailers is that their "lowest price anywhere" positioning is a crutch for the lack of value-adding innovation. Price is the only reason they give customers to care.

Retailers can implement a fair-pricing strategy by clearing two hurdles. First, they must make the cultural and strategic transition from thinking value equals price to realizing that value is the total customer experience. Second, they must understand the principles of fair pricing and muster the courage needed to put them into practice. Retailers who price fairly sell most goods at regular but competitive prices and hold legitimate sales promotions. They make it easy to compare their prices with those of competitors, and they avoid hidden charges. They don't raise prices to take advantage of temporary blips in demand, and they stand behind the products they sell.

Zane's Cycles in Branford, Connecticut, is one of the most successful independent bicycle retailers in the United States. Zane's has grown its one-store business at least 20% every year since it was founded in 1981, selling 4,250 bicycles in 2000 along with a full array of accessories. The company's success illustrates the appeal of fair pricing.

Zane's sells better bike brands with prices starting at $250. It stands behind what it sells with a 30-day test-drive offer (customers can return a bike within 30 days and exchange it for another) and a 90-day price protection guarantee (if a buyer finds the same bike in Connecticut at a lower price within 90 days, Zane's will refund the difference plus 10%). Zane's also offers free lifetime service on all new bicycles it sells; it was likely the first bicycle retailer in the United States to take this step. The promise of lifetime service includes annual tune-ups, brake and gear adjustments, wheel straightening and more.

Zane's holds only one promotional sale a year, a three-day spring weekend event featuring discounts on all products. Vendors and former employees come to work at the huge event—some even fly in to participate. Customers who purchase a bicycle at Zane's within 90 days before the sale are encouraged to return during the event for a refund based on the discounted price of their bike. The company refunded about $3,000 during the 2000 sale, but most of that money remained in the store because customers bought more gear. Zane's sold 560 bicycles during the 2000 sale—that's more than the typical one-store U.S. bicycle retailer sells in an entire year. And yet the limited duration of the sale means that Zane's sells about 85% of its bicycles at the regular price.

When Connecticut passed a bike-helmet law in 1992, Zane's sold helmets to kids at cost rather than take advantage of legislated demand. Owner Chris Zane convinced area school administrators to distribute flyers to students under 12 announcing that policy. "We sold a ton of helmets and made a lot of new friends for the store," Zane says. "Our customers trust us. They come in and say, 'I am here to get a bike. What do I need?' They have confidence in our ability to find them just the right bike at a fair price and to stand behind what we sell."

Constant sales, markdowns on over-inflated prices, and other forms of pressure pricing may boost sales in the short term. Winning customers' trust through fair pricing will pay off in the long term.

Are Your Retailing Pillars Solid—or Crumbling?

	Inferior Retailers...	Superior Retailers...
Solutions	gather products, stack them on shelves, put price tags on them, and wonder where their customers are.	consider what people really need and how they can meet that particular need better than competitors can.
Respect	are staffed by people who don't know what customers want and aren't about to interrupt their conversations to find out.	actually train and manage the salespeople they hire so that they are courteous, energetic, and helpful to customers.
Emotions	act as if their customers are Spock-like Vulcans who make purchases solely according to cold logic.	recognize that everything about a retail experience sends a message to customers that goes to the heart, not just the brain.
Pricing	focus exclusively on their supposed low prices, often because they have nothing else of value to offer customers.	focus on having fair prices instead of playing mind games with "special offers," fine print, and bogus sales.
Convenience	are open for business when it's convenient for them, close checkout lanes when it's convenient for them, deliver products when it's convenient for them, and so on.	understand that people's most precious commodity in the modern world is time and do everything they can to save as much of it as possible for their customers.

Pillar 5: Save Your Customers' Time

Many consumers are poor in at least one respect: they lack time. Retailers often contribute to the problem by wasting consumers' time and energy in myriad ways, from confusing store layouts to inefficient checkout operations to inconvenient hours of business. When shopping is inconvenient, the value of a retailer's offerings plummets.

Slow checkout is particularly annoying to busy people. Managers usually know how much money they are saving by closing a checkout lane; but they may not realize how many customers they've lost in the process. For a food shopper waiting behind six other customers in the "10 Items or Fewer" lane to buy a carton of milk, the time invested in the purchase may outweigh the value of the milk. The shopper may follow through this time but find another store next time. Studies by America's Research Group, a consumer research company based in Charleston, South Carolina, indicate that 83% of women and 91% of men have ceased shopping at a particular store because of long checkout lines.

To compete most effectively, retailers must offer convenience in four ways. They must offer convenient retail locations and operating hours and be easily available by telephone and the Internet (access convenience). They must make it easy for consumers to identify and select desired products (search convenience). They need to make it possible for people to get the products they want by maintaining a high rate of in-stock items and by delivering store, Internet, or catalog orders swiftly (possession convenience). And they need to let consumers complete or amend transactions quickly and easily (transaction convenience).

ShopKo, a discount chain based in Green Bay, Wisconsin, illustrates how shopping speed and ease can create value. ShopKo's more than 160 large discount stores operate in 19 midwestern, mountain, and northwestern states; 80% of the customer base is working women. With fiscal 1999 sales of $3.9 billion (including its small-market subsidiary, Pamida), ShopKo is much smaller than Wal-Mart, Kmart, or Target, yet it competes successfully against all three. Since 1995, following the arrival of new management a year ear-

lier, ShopKo has more than doubled sales and achieved record earnings growth.

ShopKo takes possession convenience seriously and is in-stock 98% of the time on advertised and basic merchandise. Search convenience is another strength. ShopKo stores are remarkably clean and neat. Major traffic aisles are free of passage-blocking displays. Customers near the front of the store have clear sight lines to the back. Navigational signs handing from the ceiling and on the ends of the aisles help point shoppers in the right direction. Clothing on a hanger has a size tag on the hanger neck; folded apparel has an adhesive strip indicating the size on the front of the garment. Children's garments have "simple sizing"—extra small, small, medium, and large—with posted signs educating shoppers on how to select the proper size.

ShopKo has a "one-plus-one" checkout policy of opening another checkout lane whenever two customers are waiting in any lane. Ready-to-assemble furniture is sold on a pull-tag system. The customer presents a coded tag at checkout and within three minutes the boxed merchandise is ready to be delivered to the customer's car. These ways of operating give ShopKo an edge in transaction convenience.

ShopKo is succeeding in the fiercely competitive discount sector by focusing on the total shopping experience rather than on having the lowest prices. Shopping speed and ease combined with a pleasant store atmosphere, a well-trained staff, and a carefully selected range of merchandise creates a strong mix of customer value.

While ShopKo creates real convenience for its customers, the term is often used carelessly in retailing. Consider that Internet shopping is commonly referred to as convenient. The Internet does indeed offer superior convenience for some stages of the shopping experience; it is inferior for other stages. On-line shoppers who save a trip to a physical

store must wait for delivery. Christmas shoppers who receive gifts ordered on-line *after* the holiday learn a lesson about possession inconvenience. This is one reason that the most promising path for most retailers is a strategy that combines physical and virtual stores. Increasingly, the best-managed retailers will enable customers to take advantage of the most effective features of physical and virtual shopping, even for the same transaction.

Retail competition has never been more intense or more diverse than it is today. Yet the companies featured in this article, and hundreds of other excellent retailers, are thriving. They understand that neither technology nor promises of "the lowest prices anywhere" can substitute for a passionate focus on the total customer experience. These retailers enable customers to solve important prob-

lems, capitalize on the power of respectfulness, connect with customers' emotions, emphasize fair pricing, and save customers time and energy. In an age that demands instant solutions, it's not possible to combine those ingredients with Redi-Mix, crank out a concrete-block building, and hope the structure will stand. But retailers who thoughtfully and painstakingly erect these pillars will have a solid operation that is capable of earning customers' business, trust, and loyalty.

Leonard L. Berry is Distinguished Professor of Marketing and holds the M.B. Zale Chair in Retailing and Marketing Leadership at Texas A&M University in College Station, Texas. He founded Texas A&M's Center for Retailing Studies and directed it from 1982 to 2000. He is the author of Discovering the Soul of Service *(Free Press, 1999).*

When Worlds Collide

*E-tailers are groping for a way to integrate their online
and offline stores. It isn't easy.*

By Tim Hanrahan

Here's an e-commerce riddle: What do most companies' online stores and physical stores have in common?

The answer: Too often, very little. And retailers are trying to change that.

During the Internet boom, many merchants with online and offline outlets ended up confusing customers. Prices weren't consistent between the different sales channels, and neither was the product mix—if you spotted an item in a store, sometimes you couldn't find it on the Web site, and vice versa.

So, over the past couple of years, retailers have been trying to integrate their channels. The idea: to present customers with a seamless shopping experience. If you order something online, the logic goes, you should be able to return it to an actual store. Conversely, if you go into a store and can't find what you want, it should be easy to locate and order the item on the retailer's Web site. And prices should be consistent from channel to channel.

The results have been all over the map. Many retailers with an online arm have attempted *some* form of integration—but, in most cases, it doesn't go beyond in-store pickups and returns. A handful have gone much further, finding creative ways to let their channels complement each other, such as putting Web kiosks in stores, so customers can order out-of-stock items. Meanwhile, at the other end of the spectrum, some retailers have decided the best approach is not to integrate at all.

Most retailers have consistent pricing across channels. But some companies use their online channel to clear out excess inventory, offering Web-only sales, for instance. And some retailers offer better prices or special discounts in a store or online to lure shoppers across channels.

Overall, a recent Forrester Research survey of 100 large U.S. retailers found that 63 currently sell online, and 52 of those accept in-store returns of items bought online. Thirteen allow store pickup of online orders, often a preference for buyers of bulky consumer electronics.

In Europe, integration is in a similar muddle. A study by Forrester Research last year found that 70% of European retailers weren't fully integrated—defined as having integrated marketing, computer systems and customer experience among channels, among other items.

Supermarket chain **Ahold NV,** for instance, offers a loyalty card for online and store purchases in the Netherlands, and allows online customers to check what's in stock at their local store. But they can't return online goods to stores, nor pick up goods ordered online. Wal-Mart Europe allows returns to its stores—but no pickups.

With retailers trying to figure out a model for integration, there are many potential paths to take. Here's a look at three companies and the different approaches they took.

STAPLES

For an idea of **Staples** Inc.'s integration goals, consider its motto. For years, the office-products retailer emphasized its selection with "Yeah, we got that." But it recently changed its slogan to "Staples. That was easy," highlighting the fact that customers can buy from Staples' catalog, stores or Web site—and that each of those channels is designed to serve as a sales pitch and a backup for the others.

In terms of channels, there's "absolutely no effort to sway customers one way or the other," says Demos Parneros, president of Staples' U.S. superstores.

"Whatever makes their life easier," adds Paul Gaffney, the company's chief information officer.

Walk into a Staples store, and amid the aisles you'll see Internet kiosks that let you connect to Staples.com and order products that aren't in stock. Signs on the shelves, and sales associates, point customers toward the kiosks if they can't find what they're looking for in the store.

The kiosks make life easier in another way: Customers who are skittish about online ordering can print out a bar-code receipt containing their order and pay at the cash register.

The integration continues with Staples' catalog and Web site. The stores stock copies of the catalog for customers who want to keep browsing at home, and each copy features the Staples.com Web address on the cover, along with the retailer's fax and phone numbers. The Web site, in turn, offers a link for ordering a catalog or finding a local store.

Pricing is also integrated. Most Staples products cost the same online and offline, thanks to a nightly price download to the company's stores, catalog call center and Web site. (There are some small variations from store to store based on location and competition.) In addition, Staples offers free next-day shipping on orders over $50, and products ordered online can be returned to a store.

Integration has been a key part of Staples' recent strategy of focusing on higher-margin small-business customers. As its stores have been slimmed down to focus on items aimed at such customers, Staples' Web outpost has become all the more important for finding items that aren't in stock.

The program has seen strong results. Revenue rose 30% to $11.6 billion in fiscal 2002, ended Feb. 1, from $8.9 billion in fiscal 1999, ended Jan. 29, 2000. Online sales for fiscal 2002 totaled $1.6 billion, up from $94 million in fiscal 1999. Sales from Staples' kiosks, meanwhile, rose to $250 million in fiscal 2002 from $200 million in fiscal 2001.

To be sure, there have been problems. For one thing, when the integration program began, prices weren't coordinated across the company's various channels. The company won't specify the price differences, but says they were minor. Nonetheless, the discrepancy caused confusion: Customers would sometimes call and ask why the prices were different.

Staples already had in place an "everyday low price" strategy. But to reassure customers that its prices remained competitive, Staples unveiled a 110% price-match guarantee, which promises to make up the difference, plus 10%, if a customer finds a cheaper item within 14 days of a Staples purchase. (Staples' stores only match other stores, while the Web site matches stores and other Web sites.)

Another hurdle: Even though the company allowed customers who bought online or by catalog to return products to stores starting in 2000, the sorting was done largely by hand, slowing things down behind the scenes. The company has been steadily syncing up these back-end systems to make returns go more smoothly.

GAP

Gap Inc.'s integration efforts don't go as far as Staples', but the San Francisco clothing retailer uses its Web sites to complement its stores in numerous ways.

Gap carries odd sizes on the sites and offers free shipping to customers if they can't find a particular item in its Gap, Banana Republic and Old Navy brick-and-mortar stores. While the sites carry mostly the same items as the stores, Gap also uses the Web to test-market new products, including petites at Banana Republic and maternity clothes at Gap and Old Navy. Based on customer response to the maternity lines—started at Gap.com in 2000 and OldNavy.com in 2001—the company rolled out maternity apparel into a dozen Gap stores and 54 Old Navy stores earlier this year. A Gap spokeswoman says that its online operation has helped get "early gauges" on customer reaction to new product lines.

Last year, Gap says, it significantly increased its customer e-mail database and combined its online and in-store customer research. So, for example, online surveys help shape the product selection available in real-world stores, and surveys of customers in stores help Gap create targeted e-mail campaigns. The company, which doesn't disclose financial results for its online stores, says this research has helped improve sales, increase repeat customers and improve conversion rates.

Merchandise prices are consistent across channels, and shoppers can return or exchange online purchases in any store. Gift cards purchased across channels are valid online, in-store or by phone, and online customers can download coupons to use in-store or by phone.

This summer, Gap is rolling out a new point-of-sale system in its stores that will allow customers to buy clothes from the store and the Web operation at the same time, on one receipt. So, a customer who went into a store and found an item was out of stock could purchase it in the store and have it delivered, using the new point-of-sale system to link up to Gap's Web sites.

BORDERS

While Staples and Gap are pushing to integrate their channels, other companies have gone the opposite way.

Borders Group Inc. was late to the online-bookselling game. The Ann Arbor, Mich., retailer was wary of the free-wheeling Internet environment because it didn't focus on traditional guideposts for success, such as profit margins and operating costs. But Borders came to feel pressure from investors, employees and the media. "Our stock price was punished for our decision not to rush in," says Anne Roman, a company spokeswoman.

The company didn't begin selling on the Web until 1998, ceding a three-year head start to upstart **Amazon.com** Inc. That year, Borders.com rang up less than $5 million in sales—a fraction of Amazon's $610 million. Running the online site was "a huge drain," says Tami Heim, president of Borders Books & Music Stores and Borders Online.

But the bookseller wanted to stay online. The company says that its research showed that its target customers tended be affluent and early to embrace new technologies. Also, the company cited Forrester research that showed Borders customers have a high tendency to search for information online and then purchase in-store, as well as to search in-store, then return home and buy online. "It was a critical strategic decision to be able to meet their needs through both channels," says Ms. Heim.

So, instead of duking it out, Borders embraced its online enemy: In 2001, it struck a deal with Amazon to handle its online book sales. Go to Borders.com today, and you end up at an Amazon page with a Borders logo up top. When a visitor orders a book, Amazon bills the customer, ships the book and records the sale as revenue, while Borders gets a referral fee. The books come out of the same inventory that Amazon uses for its own customers. (The companies won't disclose the terms of the deal.) The arrangement also lets Amazon users reserve books online, then pick them up from Borders and pay Borders prices.

By partnering, Borders "took a lower-risk, lower-reward approach," says Matt Fassler, an analyst at Goldman Sachs.

Borders stuck with in-store technology it developed, however. Its TitleSleuth kiosks, rolled out in 2000, tell store shoppers whether a book is in stock and its rough aisle location. The BordersStores.com Web site, meanwhile, lets surfers see what's in stock at their local store, and how much it costs. From the site, users can reserve titles to pick up later, or can buy them immediately at the Borders.com store on the Amazon site.

All of this makes books easier to track down, but it also means price disparities are laid bare. A paperback copy of "The Nanny Diaries," for instance, costs $13.95 at a Borders store in Denver, but $11.16 at Amazon's Border.com site. Buy from Borders stores and pay Borders prices; buy from Borders.com and pay Amazon prices.

Ms. Heim says Borders gets few complaints from customers about pricing: Most of them, she says, understand prices may differ depending on the channel. "There was never a fear of customers shifting between channels," she says. "We wanted to keep them loyal to the brand."

Critics say that retailers may run into problems down the road if they don't control all the channels. "You need to have an integrated view of what your customers are doing," such as how much they spend online and what books they order, says Peter Fader, a professor of marketing at the University of Pennsylvania's Wharton School. "Borders doesn't have that because Amazon owns the data."

And, he says, Borders "handed the keys to a direct competitor, [which] sends an implicit message to customers that they don't know how to manage this channel."

Ms. Heim says Borders is "very pleased" with the Amazon partnership. As to aiding a rival, she says that the Borders brand "enhances Amazon and brings greater value to ours."

True, she says, Amazon owns the sales data from Borders transactions online. "They do, however, share information with us that allows us to directionally serve our customers better," she says. "We know what is selling and all the key performance metrics associated with the site. We are satisfied with the intelligence and quality of information we receive."

Most important, says Ms. Heim, is that the deal lets Borders focus on its core mission: selling books in its stores. "Every time you try to take on something you don't have the talent and full infrastructure to support, it becomes a distraction."

Mr. Hanrahan is a news editor of The Wall Street Journal Online in New York. He can be reached at tim.hanrahan@wsj.com

10 top stores put to the test

What makes a successful online retailer? Revolution tries out some of the online giants to figure out why they're attracting customers, and then parting them from their money

Just because Wall Street held a barbecue of internet retailers the other week doesn't mean the internet is dead as a retail medium. People are still shopping online, and will continue to do so in growing numbers. But it is becoming clear that in many sectors not all the current retailers are going to survive. They are insufficiently differentiated, and in many cases the brick and mortar world is biting back with its own online offerings.

So what makes a winning internet retailer? What is it that makes people buy things from one store and not another? It's a question that has been exercising retailers ever since retailing was just dusty market squares in mud-walled villages. And you only have to look at the number of stores that go out of business in main streets and local malls every year to know that we don't have all the answers yet, by any means. And online, things are more complicated, because the elements that make people prefer one store to another in the physical world do not necessarily have the same importance online.

Shopping is as much about the experience of buying things as it is about the products you're buying. In the brick-and-mortar world, it's everything from the layout of the store, the signposting and lighting, to the smiles on the faces of the shop assistants. Online, the essential ingredients of the shopping experience are to do with web site navigation, ease of finding what you're looking for, the clarity of reassurance that your personal and credit card details are secure, how well the business handles queries or unusual requests, and other related issues.

Internet retailers have to figure out new rules, and they're all still learning. But some are definitely doing better than others. The question is why. We decided to take 10 of the top internet retailers and try them out firsthand.

We talked to them to find out a little bit about their marketing strategy, how they're attracting customers and turning them into cash. And where possible, we bought something. But as you'll see, that was an occasion easier said than done. In the process we tried to figure out whether they're living up to the promise of their marketing, and how. And where they have a physical world presence, how comfortably does their online business sit with that? What is it that they're doing well? What can other retailers learn from them?

You may well disagree with some of our choices. This is not a league table, and choosing who to write about for reports like this is always somewhat subjective. These aren't flawless online stores (in this game nobody's perfect), but each is a giant in its space, with a powerhouse brand and serious numbers of customers. All of them are doing things that we think are interesting, so no matter what your line of business, we think they're worth your spending a bit of time with.

EBAY

Proposition

Founded by the supportive husband of a Pez dispenser collector, eBay's mission is simple: "We help people trade practically anything on Earth." And with some four million items on sale on any given day, practically everything is just what consumers will find. The company has grown profitable with its online version of the classic auction model: a commission on every single item sold on the site.

The company acquired San Francisco-based traditional auctioneer Butterfield & Butterfield in the fall of last year. The resulting auctions of high-end items have been joined by other niche plays, such as eBay Motors, a collaboration with Autotrader.com. Local auctions mean more yard-sale level merchandise is now available and further serve to erode classified advertising revenues for local newspapers. People are selling all types of household items through the site.

As perhaps the original online business-to-business trading service, the company has also sought to cash in on the investor cachet of an explicit B-to-B play. "EBay Business Exchange is a natural evolution of the eBay business model, enabling businesses to obtain new, used and refurbished business merchandise and providing businesses of varying sizes a targeted way to reach buyers of business items," says eBay chief operating officer Brian Swette.

Marketing

eBay built its user base during The Great Beanie Baby Craze. Indeed, tens of thousands of its daily auctions are still accounted for by Beanie Baby traders. The site consistently tops Media Metrix's ranking of e-commerce destinations. An online-centric approach to building its brand has concentrated on affiliate stores, where other online retailers (including Buy.com) are able to offer a co-branded version of the auction site, putting auctions of their own products to the fore.

User Experience

Buying and selling on eBay is not for the fainthearted. The site's huge number of concurrent auctions make navigation a nightmare. EBay does a good job of enabling searches and making popular categories easy to access. But registration is close to indispensable, and over 10 million have already signed up. A My eBay page is a necessity for tracking multiple auctions. And for the truly active (and addicted), eBay a-go-go is a service for wireless devices that lets traders keep track of when they are outbid, when a bid has been successful and when an item sells.
While online fraud remains at a level comparable with traditional sales channels, every user who has lied about his or her age, hair color or profession in an online chatroom will feel justified in worrying about buying on eBay. But those worries are dissipated by eBay's user-feedback feature: sellers are ranked according to the comments of previous customers, indicating whether they were satisfied or not.

Mark Dolley

AMAZON

Proposition

Amazon is still based on "our founding commitment to customer satisfaction and the delivery of an educational and inspiring shopping experience." It has, however, thrown in a dozen new categories since it started as a books-only site in 1996. With the boast of Earth's Biggest Selection to uphold, this marriage of selection and service is watched from Wall Street to Main Street.

Amazon puts its money where its mouth is. All of its 13 product areas offer a well-presented and wide array of brands, price points and personalities. For example, the look and feel of the art and collectibles site is more upscale than the book area. But the same accessible layout and graphic scheme pervades.

"We want to be less about push and more about inviting the consumer in," says marketing director Bill Curry. "We have a rich amount of information that helps consumers find what they want, rather than having someone tell them what they should buy."

What Amazon.com will tell consumers about next is anyone's guess. The company has actively added new categories and services. About the only hot e-commerce area they've stayed out of is financial services. Stay tuned.

Marketing

Amazon has built arguably the most extensive and active affiliate network of any online retailer. It is the official book retailer of Excite@Home and the official link for Yahoo!Search, as well as myriad other revenue producing alliances. Because it has expanded into so many areas, it has a huge audience target to hit. Marketing is accomplished more through specific areas than through the overall site. For example, full-page ads in regional Sunday newspaper book review sections only advertise the site's book business. The kitchen store may find its best audience in women 35 to 54 years of age, but the music audience may skew much younger. According to Curry, the site experience has to be a key marketing element to make sure the wide audience comes back to Amazon. "The nature of the business is that we want to get to anyone who is online and has a credit card," he says. "The individual areas need to appeal to each demographic group through their offerings and the way the site is navigated.

User Experience

We decided to take Amazon up on its claims by searching for a recent record release from a critically acclaimed but under-distributed artist, Neko Case. The site definitely invites more than pushes, as Curry says. After registering information (privacy policy plainly displayed), we entered "Neko Case" in the search box and got a quick page featuring the artist's most recent release, *Furnace Room Lullaby*. The page showed many different ways to learn about the artist and the release. Front and center were reviews from Amazon staff. More intelligent, complete and absent of hype were the user reviews.

When we clicked the selection into the shopping cart and hit continue to place the order, it was clear the order was "secure" and stored on Amazon's servers. Everything about the process was clearly explained, including what to expect in terms of shipping times and costs. On the final order confirmation page, big thank you messages were prominently posted at the top and the bottom. And you could even sign up for more information via email on artists like Neko Case.

John Gaffney

PRICELINE

Proposition

Priceline's value to online consumers is based on a business model protected by US Patent No. 5,794,207. Granted in 1998, it reads: "The present invention allows prospective buyers of goods and services to communicate a binding purchase offer globally to potential sellers, for sellers conveniently to search for relevant buyer purchase offers, and for sellers potentially to bind a buyer to a contract based on the buyer's purchase offer." In plain terms, it's a name-your-price model, where you can trade off naming a lower price against the correspondingly lower chance of getting what you want.

The company's initial focus was airline tickets. By signing up 34 airlines, Priceline was able to provide compelling deals on domestic and international fares and claims to have picked up some three percent of the US leisure fare market.

But even on the airline front, Priceline has found itself challenged by Microsoft's Expedia.com. Showing scant regard for Priceline's patent, Expedia.com offers an identical service, its Flight Price Matcher ("Flights At A Price You Like: Yours!").

Expansion has brought new categories of goods and services to Priceline's home page, including hotel stays, cars, mortgages and even groceries and telephone calls. "Further down the line, we'll add cruises, vacation packages and more. You can also expect priceline.com to begin its international expansion, beginning with Asia, later this year," says CEO Dan Schulman.

Despite charging a commission on every successful bid, the venture remains unprofitable.

Marketing

Priceline's advertising will forever be remembered for two things: making William Shatner very rich, and resurrecting radio as a means to promote dot-coms. The company combined Shatner's well-known voice with the bombardment of an uncluttered medium to earn almost overnight recognition.

Shatner cleverly chose to emulate savvy Silicon Valley landlords and take payment in equity, netting him an eight figure sum. With national radio now overrun by dot-com commercials, Priceline's more recent campaigns (still featuring Shatner) have concentrated on national TV. Local cable buys have been added in markets where the company offers specific services, such as its WebHouse Club grocery shopping scheme.

User Experience

Bidding on Priceline is no guarantee of satisfaction. In measuring its own success, the company looks at "reasonable" bids falling within 30 percent of the regular price for a product or service. In the first quarter of 2000, it was only able to satisfy 43.5 percent of those bids.

Even where users win on price, they lose on convenience. Online status checking, real-time online customer support and other helpful features abound. But to achieve maximum scalability with minimum investment, Priceline.com makes consumers sweat for their savings. For instance, first-time grocery buyers must compile their list, make their bids, pay up via credit card and then wait for a WebHouse Club Card to arrive in the mail before trekking to a participating store.

Mark Dolley

BUY.COM

Proposition

Buy.com was started as one of the truly visionary business models of the web. Its premise was one of buying computer hardware and software from Ingram Micro (a wholesaler that supplies many other dot-coms) and then selling those products at a loss. The company hoped to make up that loss with revenues from advertising shown to its customers as they shopped. Now though, post reality check, the company is regularly mentioned in reports of impending dot-com demise.

In fairness, the company widely diversified its offering. Books, CDs and DVDs form part of an online superstore that now numbers some 850,000-plus SKUs. But it still relies heavily on Ingram Micro as a supplier (for all its books, for example), and competition has driven margins to razor-thin levels. With a low price guarantee, Buy.com locked itself into the business of stacking product high and selling it cheap, though this is no bad thing for the consumer.

International expansion has seen Buy.com affiliates open in the UK, Australia and Canada. The company has also gone beyond the web, with a compact version of the store accessible on various wireless devices, including the Palm VII and Sprint PCS phones with the Wireless Web option. "Buy.com is increasing its presence within the wireless sector, says CEO Greg Hawkins. "We're catering to the growing number of consumers, professionals and corporations that recognize the importance of extending data access into the mobile, wireless internet environment."

Marketing

Buy.com tried it all: from billboards to banners and even Super Bowl ads. And not without success. The company has served more than two million unique customers. Unfortunately, those customers proved costly to acquire and as fickle as one might image for a store whose main claim has been cheapness.

User Experience

Buy.com's eSearch facility, combined with separate store departments for the main categories (book, computers, music etc.), make navigation relatively easy. But with such a breadth of items, Buy.com doesn't offer the depth of product descriptions users of other sites take for granted. Try buying a book, and you'll only find detailed information for the top 25 sellers. Lower down the list, you'll be lucky to find a one-line synopsis.

Shipping times, a key piece of information determining online purchases, are present throughout Buy.com. And for those who want to make extra sure, an ordertracker is available. The company boasts about its Anytime Customer Service, and a telephone call in the middle of the night was answered within two minutes.

Mark Dolley

EGGHEAD

Proposition

The name "Egghead" enjoys almost 70 percent brand recognition among online users, largely the by-product of Egghead's brick and mortar days gone by. The firm wants to parlay that advantage into a top place in the hierarchy of web retailers.

"We want to become the leading internet destination for technology products and services," says Bari Abdul, senior VP of marketing for the site. While online retailers have been aggressive in their fight for supremacy over the book and toy categories, which together represent a $25-billion-a-year industry, there still is no clear online leader in the $150-billion-a-year computer supplies market, Abdul says. Egghead may soon be able to claim that crown for itself. In 1999 it was the third-largest e-commerce site by sales volume after Amazon and Buy.com, with some $515 million in sales.

Marketing

The site's advertising promotes the idea of a "computer store inside a computer." Its print campaign has targeted the *Wall Street Journal, USA Today* and business publications such as *Inc.* and *Entrepreneur* magazine. Online ads have appeared on small-business sites and at portals such as CNET and ZDNet.

Egghead also sends out 20 million emails a month to its 3.7 million users who registered for email. These messages feature promotions such as private auctions that are listed only through email and five-percent-off deals on superstore sales.

The big sell here is variety. The site includes a retail "superstore," an auction area and a "Smart Deals" section offering surplus and overstock items at deep discounts.

"Most important is the selection," says Abdul. "At egghead.com we have up to 50,000 of the latest products on the site every day, and at the auction site we have about 10,000 more daily."

User Experience

This variety of offerings comes as the result of a deal last fall in which the auction site OnSale.com bought out Egghead and the OnSale.com leadership effectively took over management of the site.

On a recent test drive, we found variety—Egghead's chief selling point—to also be the site's main weakness. With no specific product in mind, we found it difficult to get a clear sense of what was available on the site. The superstore listed three categories of goods—computer products, software and electronics—each with a dozen or so subcategories to navigate. The auction half of the house has four categories, including (and we found this mystifying) travel and sports and fitness.

These seemingly mismatched offerings are perhaps part of a larger plan. Egghead wants to be the site of choice for small- and home-based business operators, and these categories may be aimed at that market. More logical is the site's plan to leap into the office products market this spring. "They need a place that they can go to get information and also get huge selection and good customer service. That is what the market is looking for," Abdul says.

Functionality on this sprawling site is sufficient. A search feature allows shoppers to track down products simultaneously in the retail store, in auctions and in the discount shop. If you know what you are looking for, that is helpful. In the travel section we found a large Samsonite suitcase that was going for $60, reduced from $150. It shipped the day after we ordered and arrived six business days later—a genuine bargain.

Adam Katz-Stone

TRAVELOCITY

Proposition

In March of this year Travelocity was the 30th most active site on the web, with over seven million unique visitors, according to the research group Media Metrix. The site's proud parents say they offer "a new way to plan and buy travel."

That phrase comes from Mike Stacy, senior VP of marketing, who explained that Travelocity is all about empowering consumers to research and plan their personal travel itineraries and vacation plans.

"All the airlines, all the hotels and vacation packages are surrounded by destination content information, and that presents a much different customer experience than you find in the traditional world," he says. "The consumer now is in control."

Marketing

Travelocity's TV ad campaign hawks the "control" message with emotional visuals. A grandfather arrives to see a new baby for the first time. A woman in the tropics awaits her lover.

In the online realm, Travelocity's innovative banner ads allow users to enter an origination city through an ad and immediately receive a list of the day's lowest fares to 10 or 15 destinations. The banner appears on all the major portals, at college sites and at financial sites.

With a target audience of 35- to 45-year-old homeowners whose income tops $75,000 per household, Travelocity seems to have a working formula. In 1998 the site did $285 million in gross sales. In 1999 the gross topped $1.1 billion, and in the first quarter of this year sales had already topped $500 million.

User Experience

We went to www.Travelocity.com to book a weekend room in Virginia Beach. This should have been easy, but it was not. Since we already knew where we wanted to go, we took control by going straight to "Find/Reserve a Hotel" and entered the city and state: Virginia Beach, VA.

Travelocity could not find that city, so we went to another site to track down the ZIP code for the resort town and then tried again, still without success. Eventually we queried Travelocity to search for a hotel "near a point of interest" and—lo and behold—the search engine recognized Virginia Beach as a point of interest.

Asked about the problem, a customer service representative said on the phone that the hotel booking tool gets a little funky sometimes. This is disappointing, but perhaps not surprising, since Travelocity has set its sights chiefly on the competitive arena of air travel bookings.

Stacy touted as a unique feature a "best fare finder," in which a traveler may enter a desired destination and get a report back detailing the lowest available airfares. Likewise, the "alternate airports" feature will search out less expensive fares that can be obtained by flying into nearby airports and then calculate the mileage from those airports to the traveler's destination.

Still, you'd think they could find Virginia Beach.

Adam Katz-Stone

TOYSRUS

Proposition

Despite some well-publicized stumbles last holiday season, Toysrus.com still finds itself the best-positioned toy e-commerce site going forward. As a division of the global Toys 'R' Us retail chain, Toysrus.com is able to leverage its parent company's incredible name recognition as well as its skills in managing inventories, giving it a huge advantage over pure online retailers such as eToys.

"They just have great brand awareness," notes Jupiter Communications Ken Cassar, in predicting Toysrus.com will likely lead online toy retailers this year.

Toysrus.com's weaknesses are the same ones faced by toy retailers in general—it is a seasonal and hits-driven business. The site will do as much as 70 percent of its annual revenues during the fourth quarter. That puts a lot of pressure on all aspects of Toysrus.com, from site management to fulfillment. Last year, Toysrus.com ended up alienating some consumers by failing to fulfill orders by Christmas. The site has since built two additional fulfillment centers to better meet surges in seasonal demand.

Marketing

The best thing Toysrus.com has going for its brand values. Plain and simple, Toys 'R' Us is the best known name in the lucrative US toy retail sector. "Our Q scores, measuring popularity and awareness, rank Toys 'R' Us equal with the likes of Disney and McDonalds," boasts John Barbour, CEO of Toysrus.com.

Toys 'R' Us leverages that stellar brand equity by including the site's URL in newspaper circulars and other advertisements, generating 50 million impressions during the last post-Thanksgiving shopping period. The URL is also displayed on in-store signage and shopping bags.

"All of these bricks and mortar assets allow us to spend far less on the important aspects of marketing and customer acquisition costs—which gives us a much faster track to profitability than pure online toy retailers," Barbour says.

User experience

The Toysrus.com interface is very clean looking with lots of white space to facilitate fast load times. Consumers can search for items by age group, brand, category (i.e. dolls, games) and character and theme. This search function appears on every page within the site, as does a selection of channels that include video games, Pokemon Central and collectibles. Products are displayed with age range and a small thumbnail picture, with more information available at a single click. Toysrus.com also offers "The Toy Guy," who provides brief reviews of products.

Toysrus.com offers a reasonably helpful FAQ page, as well as the ability to check on the status of an order. Customer service can be accessed through both email and 1–800 number. Both were required during initial attempts to shop, since the screen froze several times during the shipping and billing process. The site's technical support blamed the problem on later versions of the Netscape Navigator browser, adding that it was being addressed. A later attempt using Internet Explorer was completely free of problems.

David Ward

BARNES & NOBLE

Proposition

Barnes and Noble may be the internet's best example to date of using an offline brand to build an online business. Barnesandnoble.com is constructed on the brand's offline strengths, plain and simple. Barnes & Noble was the first book superstore and the first retail brand name in the book business. Since launching its online business in May 1997, it fought through the challenge of Amazon.com to become the sixth largest e-commerce site, according to Media Metrix.

Marketing

By the company's own admission, it does not do a lot in the way of unique branding for the site, or even the promise of a unique internet experience. Like its competitors in this space B&N relies heavily on affiliate marketing. In 1998 it launched a mybnlink.com program with BeFree, which essentially made every user an affiliate. For example, if you recommend a book via email to 20 of your friends and they all buy it from BarnesandNoble.com, you get 10 percent of the total revenue generated. The site relies heavily on brick and mortar power to drive online business. One recent promotion gave consumers a 10 percent discount on any online purchase in return for filling out a demographic information card in the store. B&N maintains strategic alliances with major Web portals and content sites, such as AOL, Lycos and MSN.

User Experience

More than its competitors, Barnes & Noble's approach seems to be aimed at the 35- to 54-year-old demographic. The day we shopped, users could pre-order *The Beatles Anthology* book, not due until late summer at best, but certainly an attention-getter for this age group. The featured music entry was Carly Simon's new record, when the site could easily have opted for the new Britney Spears or Pearl Jam records, released on that very day. It is definitely book-centric. Other product lines seem to get minimal attention. Links from the home page directed readers to subsets of book interests such as the Discover New Writers program and the wildly successful Oprah's Book Club. (Both are also in-store features.)

The site was unique in its grouping of books by winners of various literary awards. We clicked on the IMPAC Dublin Literary Prize and found a great description of the winner, a novel called *Wide Open* by Nicola Barker.

Upon ordering, the site seems to become more of an AOL affiliate than Barnes & Noble. Orders are handled by a co-branded AOL Quick Checkout system. New York City customers were urged to take advantage of a new home or office delivery service.

John Gaffney

CDNOW

Proposition

CDNow is trying to stress the "now" in its company's name. After making a living off its first-mover status for the past three years, the company has repositioned its brand. The site is now more in step with the broadband era of music e-commerce, content and community. In fact, its new tagline is: "Never miss a beat."

"We want to be a music destination. Buying a CD is only part of that," says senior brand marketing director Sam Liss. "We're looking to offer the user specificity. We're not looking to be the Wal-Mart of the internet. We're looking to offer an immersive experience that will make it easier for the user to find the product they're looking for and learn a lot about other product available on the way."

Marketing

CDNOW is in a state of transition financially, and that will affect its marketing plans. It has put a lot of PR muscle behind its new interview section and other broadband applications. It has also been chastised by some analysts for overpaying for some extensive portal deals. Time Warner and Sony will explore a broader strategic relationship with the company and have committed $51 million to it. CDNOW has also hired an investment banker, Allen & Company, to investigate other strategic opportunities and partnerships.

User Experience

CDNOW gets a number one with a bullet for being a fun site to surf. The company's vision of a "destination site" for music is executed with an obsessive attention to detail, presenting literally dozens of informational and commerce choices on the home page alone.

The day we shopped, the page had a broad array of artists featured (from Matchbox 20 to Jeff Buckley to Primal Scream) in the new release section. Album reviews were broken out by editor's picks, staff picks and featured reviews. Our favorite was the artist's pick, where an artist picks their top 10 records.

Looking for jazz selections, we opted for pianist Kenny Barron's picks. On the jump page his picks and an audio sample were listed together. We listened to a mid-1960s McCoy Tyner record titled *Inception*, which had a great smoky club feel.

Meanwhile, we found something else that will help CDNOW appeal to music fans: the company sells vinyl records, where available. But they're more expensive than compact discs.

The order process seemed suspiciously similar to Amazon.com's, both in the graphic interface and the actual process. One segment of the process that could stand more direct explanation is one of supreme importance: the availability of the product is not listed until you place your order. So if an item is backordered, the customer has no information, unless he or she calls the help line, as to when it will be delivered.

John Gaffney

DELL

Proposition

Founded in 1984 as a direct supplier of built-to-order computers Dell had long realized the importance of efficient fulfillment, billing and customer service even before the advent of e-commerce and the formation of Dell.com.

Thanks in part to a growing e-commerce business, Dell current ranks number two in the PC market, with a market capitalization of $130 billion and more than 35,000 employees. Dell.com now generates nearly $40 million dollars each day, a growing percentage of which is in high-end business-to-business services and infrastructure offerings.

Over the past year Dell.com intensified its efforts in the consumer space with Dell Gigabuys, which carries both PC and consumer electronics products such as digital cameras. It also launched the Dell4Me.com initiative to raise consumer awareness about the site's ability to provide everything from PCs to an ISP service. "It gives people a reason to visit the site more than once a year," comments Jupiter analyst Cassar.

Marketing

Dell.com leverages its direct mail channel to drive traffic for the web site. Catalogs sent to businesses and homes carry the URL on the cover and on inside pages. Dell.com also maintains its brand identity through print advertising in business, trade and technical publications.

Dell offers one of the most recognizable names in computing, one that many home consumers have already come in contact with at the office. "Dell projects the image of being a leader in providing customers customized solutions for their computing and internet needs," says company spokesman Bryant Hilton, adding that TV advertising is primarily the vehicle for corporate branding campaigns. Dell has also aggressively paired with companies such as America Online in promotions.

User Experience

Shopping at Dell.com is a utilitarian experience. Pages often have a cluttered look, but information is easily retrievable. The home page has multiple channels that segment users: consumers are directed to once section while government customers are sent to another. Though Dell.com primarily highlights its own products, especially in the build-to-order segment, the Gigabuys section has over 30,000 offerings, many from brands other than Dell. The site features a selection of exclusives, as well as a top-10 list chosen by customers. The most popular items were products such as laser printers, reflecting the site's business audience.

Dell.com customers can search through categories such as printers/scanners and software and accessories, or use a keyword to locate what they want. There were no attempts at cross- or up-selling, but the site does allow you to group four products together for comparison shopping. With its foundation in direct mail, Dell.com excels in fulfillment. A CD writer ordered on Sunday evening arrived on our doorstep Thursday morning via standard delivery. Repeat customers have the option of one-click checkout, and all customers have the ability to monitor the status of their order. Customer service consists of FAQs as well as an e-mail section.

David Ward

Tips for distinguishing your ads from bad ads

By Bob Lamons

So you think you know a good ad?

It's one of the crosses we have to bear in advertising. Everybody is a creative expert; you may not know one thing about how to go about creating an ad, but by golly, you certainly know a good one when you see it. And conversely, you know a bad ad when you see it, too.

Or do you?

Most people, including many of us on the creative side, have a hard time remembering that our likes and dislikes aren't necessarily the same as those with whom we're trying to communicate. We reason that if the ad doesn't appeal to us, it won't be effective with our target audience, which may or may not be accurate.

But let's assume for the sake of argument that our personal tastes are much the same as the audiences we're attempting to reach. Here are a few suggestions for distinguishing a good ad from others that aren't so:

◆ Does it have a powerful visual?

The purpose of the primary visual in an ad is to stop the reader and begin the process of interesting him or her in the selling proposition. The purpose is not to show all the product's many features or its inner workings, unless by doing so, you can demonstrate something that differentiates your product from others the prospect may be considering. Too many technical managers simply want to show the product because they think clients will be as intrigued by it as they are, which usually isn't the case. They also think a beauty shot of the product will be a stopper. It's not.

Go ahead and take some liberties with your product shots. Baldor makes its electric motors shiny gold; Miller welding equipment is always blue (hence, "The Power of Blue" tagline), and its photography is always dramatically lighted. For Cooper Cameron, we use a photo-illustration technique that shows the product transitioning to a blueprint-like effect at the outer edges, because it fits with our message of technology leadership.

Producing powerful ads is more costly, but it's definitely worth any extra effort.

Some advertisers invest in sexy, diaphanous computer art showing the product's inner layers in an interesting but surreal way. There's no limit to the creative ways you can portray your products in magazine ads. Just don't use the photo you took for the technical bulletin; its boring.

◆ Does it have an intriguing headline?

I definitely subscribe to what I call the Law of Offering a Benefit in ad heads. Not only does this help the visual stop readers, but it sorts the prospects from the nonprospects.

Even writers of powerful headlines have to work a little harder to craft a benefit statement that is uniquely yours. For example, I like the way SAS Institute projects headlines on the foreheads of people in its series of thoughtful black-and-white (only the logo is four-color) ads for its data mining and e-intelligence software products. One recent headline was, "Opportunity no longer knocks. These days, it darts past the door before you can even react." And how about this one from Gartner/G2 Growth Research: "Growth opportunities reside in every nook and cranny of this economy. Be the tweezers."? I dare you not to read at least some of that ad to find out what they mean by "Be the tweezers."

There are many ways to offer a benefit. I favor writing magazine ad headlines that reach out and grab both eyeballs, because that's how you break through clutter.

◆ Is your selling proposition clear?

Too many trade ads these days are so clever, you can hardly figure out what they promote. They somehow confuse shock value with selling—or maybe it's not shocking at all, but many of them are so vague, you find yourself turning the page without even considering the message. I guess that's good, because nobody has time these days to read every ad, and these abstract concepts are actually performing a public service by making the goods ad stand out even more.

Still, I hate to see advertisers waste money; it perpetuates the myth that business-to-business advertising is superfluous and can be cancelled without repercussions. (Of course, bad advertising *is* superfluous and *should* be cancelled, but that's another story altogether.)

Here's one reason I like Harvey Studies: They provide verbatim comments about your ads—the good, the bad and the ugly. I usually go through the comments, marking the good ones in yellow and the bad ones in pink. If the yellow doesn't outnumber the pink by a wide margin, we have a problem.

◆ Is there a good call to action?

Most advertisers don't give much thought to the call to action, but I think it's just as important as the headline and primary visual. What do you want people to do as a result of reading your ad? If you said, "Call our 800 number for full details," or "Log on to our Web site at www.(fill in the blank).com," you need to go back to the drawing board.

A good call to action can actually start the selling process. Promise a test report; offer a product demonstration; direct them to a special section of the Web site where they have to log in before they see something of value. If nothing else, compare how your product stacks up to others in the field. Everyone is superbusy these days, and if you can offer something that helps them expedite or narrow their research, you're giving them something money can't buy: free time.

Power ads seek out the ideal prospects and cause them to pay attention in ways that serve the prospect's self interests ("What's in it for me?"). It will cost you more to produce a powerful ad, because you and the agency team will have to put more effort into it. But the results will be well worth the extra investment.

The real value in b-to-b advertising can only be achieved by making sure your ad pulls its share of the load. Marketers must stamp out lazy advertising, and you can help by knowing what to look for.

Bob Lamons is president of Robert Lamons & Associates in Houston. He can be reached at lamons@ama.org.

MARKETING

LIVING UP AND DOWN THE DIAL

As more companies pump up the volume of their radio advertising, here
are 10 tips for making the most of your airtime.

RADIO HAS BEEN very good to the Vermont Teddy Bear Company. By advertising its stuffed animals on stations nationwide, the business has grown from $5 million to $39 million in sales. "We do some stuff in other media, but 95% of our advertising has been with radio," says Gerry Howatt, the company's media-buying manager. "We started doing a lot of it in 1991, and the company took off." Today, Howatt oversees a staff of five and a budget of $9.1 million a year—a rich 23% of total revenue. "We're in 140 major markets, and I know all their radio stations and which ones work for us," Howatt says.

Sure, the Shelburne, Vt., company's focus on radio is extreme, but it is not alone. Spending on radio ads is expected to grow 6% to 8% in 2003. And while a lot of that growth is likely to come from campaigns for beer and new movies, smaller businesses are flocking to the airwaves, too. "By my experience, we've seen dramatically more local businesses this past year," says Jeff Delvaux, who manages six stations in Duluth, Minn., for Midwest Communications.

In an era of permission e-mail and even cell-phone marketing campaigns, why are companies taking to the airwaves? Because radio is just so dependable—it can be bought overnight, it can be relatively cheap to get into, and it's a medium where the basics run deep. Here are 10 tips to work it:

Be smart when setting a budget. The cost of buying radio time varies regionally and is based on factors such as the time of day and the size of the market. Delvaux advises service companies to set aside 6% to 8% of gross sales for radio ads. And he counsels retailers to take 12% of projected gross sales, subtract the cost of rent, and voila: the result should be their ad budget. This formula, which Delvaux credits to ad guru Roy Williams, generally works for retail companies that sell at a 100% markup. Delvaux likes the plan because it takes into account the value of foot traffic. If you're paying a premium for rent, you shouldn't have to spend as much on advertising; but if you're off the beaten track, you'll have to advertise more to get noticed. (For more on budgets, see box, Fine-Tuning Your Ad Budget.)

Hold production costs to zero. Radio stations will happily produce most ads for free and even pass them over to competing stations as a favor to their clients. "With MP3s it's easy to e-mail them, and it costs the radio station next to nothing," Delvaux says.

Keep the script simple. "Radio is good for generating excitement, although it's lousy for giving details," say Peter Kern, who, with his wife, Pamela, runs Kern Media, a media-buying company in New Gloucester, Maine. Radio spots can be effective even if they're not especially clever—the slightly insulting ads you've heard a thousand times (think guy screaming about car sales) really do work. Use radio to tout discounted merchandise or the launch of a new service. Save details for newspapers or direct mail.

Avoid the rush hour and long commercial breaks. Kern advises his clients to buy time in the morning and at midday, when the rates are cheaper and stations have more listeners, rather than at 5 p.m., the time that many advertisers request. He also suggests picking radio stations that limit the number of ad spots they run to 14 an hour. Ideal is a station that runs from three to four spot breaks an hour, with four to five commercials per break. Stay away from those stations that carry 8 to 10 spots per break because your ad will just get lost on them.

Saturate the airways. "The biggest mistake businesses make is not buying a lot [of radio ads] in a continuous period of time," says Kern. "You should be buying more frequently over two weeks instead of spread out over a month, and buying 30 spots on two stations instead of 18 spots on three." A rough rule of thumb, he says, is that listeners need to hear your ad a minimum of three times a week "before you start to break through the clutter." This is particularly true if your company is relatively unknown. "Burger King doesn't have to tell you who they are," says Kern. "But most businesses need to convey where they're located, what they do, and what the special is."

Follow the numbers. Dan Paisner, president of the 10-location car-wash chain ScrubaDub Auto Wash Centers Inc., looks carefully at station demographics, ratings, and ad costs. He then calculates his cost-per-ratings point, which helps him figure out where he needs to advertise to most efficiently reach men and women ages 25 to 54 without duplication. "It's like any dollar invested in your business," says Paisner, whose company is based in Natick, Mass."You want the greatest return from it."

Buy up during soft markets. ScrubaDub buys time almost entirely in the first quarter of the year, when radio ad rates are their cheapest—and cars happen to be their dirtiest. Similarly, Vermont Teddy Bear moves quickly when stations offer discounts. When rates dipped last fall, for example, the company locked in spots that will run from January through June of this year.

Talk to your customers. Proflowers, an Internet florist business based in San Diego, provides passwords in its ads. The

FINE-TUNING YOUR AD BUDGET

Each of the six Minnesota radio stations Jeff Delvaux manages for Midwest Communications works with 100 to 200 customers a month, and "the No. 1 problem we see with small business is that they don't allocate their resources," he says. Here's how he walks customers with retail businesses through a budgeting plan. (Service companies can generally follow the same rules, although they may not have sales in the same way that retailers do.)

1. DETERMINE AN OVERALL ADVERTISING BUDGET. Using the sales minus rent equation (see main story), for a company with $1 million in gross sales, 12% would be $120,000. If your rent is $70,000 a year, then your ad budget should be $50,000.

2. ASSIGN 50% OF YOUR BUDGET OVER 12 MONTHS. Break down spending month by month according to the national sales averages for your industry or your own operating history. In other words, if your industry does 10% of its business in April, budget 10% of your money for April. Using our example, 50% of the total budget is $25,000, so the April budget would be $2,500.

3. ASSIGN 25% OF YOUR BUDGET TO REGULAR SALES. In this example, that would be $12,500 annually, or $3,125 for a sale every quarter, which is typical for retail companies.

4. ASSIGN 15% OF YOUR BUDGET TO SPECIAL OPPORTUNITIES. This is another trouble spot for businesses—they get a great idea but don't have the cash to execute it. "This is also the money you can spend if you get to the middle of the month and sales are slow and you need a little push," says Delvaux. At $7,500 for the year, or $625

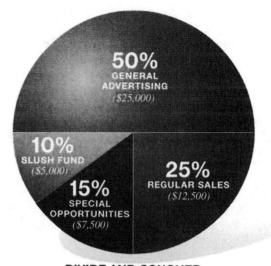

DIVIDE AND CONQUER
*Breaking down a sample
annual advertising budget*

a month, this money can be spent, accrued to the next month, or put to the bottom line.

5. ASSIGN 10% OF YOUR BUDGET TO A SLUSH FUND. "Hold this money for October, November, December," says Delvaux of the final $5,000 in this sample budget. "If you're on track to meet your goals, then keep it in your pocket. If not, spend it."

---

company—which has $70 million in annual sales, according to Steve Bellach, chief marketing officer—prompts customers to enter their passwords when they visit Proflowers.com. "The passwords allow us to track down to the detail the performance of each channel," says Bellach. Vermont Teddy Bear also asks telephone customers which radio ad they remember, and then calculates $X sales for $Y investment. Based on the data, the company buys additional time on stations that draw the best response. "Say we got $500 in sales from a $100 ad," says media buyer Howatt. "The next time we'd run two ads and see if we got $1,000." If the company ran a third ad and made only $1,200, its interest in the station would level off. "It's trial and error," Howatt says.

Shop for baritones online. If you want professional audio talent, Kern recommends ProComm Studio Services (procommss. com), based in Fletcher, N.C., which works with audio talent nationwide. "They're great on the customer end," he says. "Very affordable." You call an 800 number for an estimate for

the job, and then direct your recording session over the phone. Clients whose work is posted on the site include the cheese company Cabot Creamery, car dealerships, banks, and restaurants.

Expect the unexpected when dealing with radio personalities. Vermont Teddy Bear buys lots of "live reads"—premium-priced ads that are delivered and embellished upon on-air by radio personalities. A few years ago, Howatt was ushered in to meet Don Imus as a thank-you for buying live reads on his show. But Imus, who apparently had just had an argument over the phone, was in no mood: He threw the teddy bear media buyer out of his office a minute into the meeting. Then something amazing happened. The next day Imus apologized on the air for the outburst—and apologized, and apologized. "We ended up with a 35-minute infomercial on Vermont Teddy Bear," Howatt laughs. Ah, the magic of radio.

Leslie Brokaw

From *Inc.*, March 2003, pp. 46, 48. © 2003 by Leslie Brokaw.

The Demographics of Media Consumption

COUNTING EYES ON BILLBOARDS

Major media organizations are vying to create detailed audience measurements for outdoor advertising. The industry is finally poised to gain new credibility as it prepares to enter the ratings game.

BY SANDRA YIN

The outdoor ad—displayed on bus shelters, subways, phone booths, newsstands and billboards—has long had a reputation as a low-end form of promotion. But its biggest problem may be its perceived lack of accountability.

Unlike print, TV and radio, whose audience demographics are based on readership surveys, ratings and audits, outdoor advertising offers only crude measurements of its audience. Today, it's possible to find out, for example, how many cars pass an ad at a particular location, but not the share of 18- to 34-year-old males in those cars. Because the outdoor ad industry can't determine precise audience delivery, media planners and advertisers have difficulty gauging the value of an ad buy. "What [advertisers] are demanding," admits Kevin Gleason, chairman of the Washington, D.C.-based Outdoor Advertising Association of America (OAAA) and president and CEO of Adams Outdoor Advertising, an Atlanta-based firm that controls 15,000 billboards nationwide, "they're not getting from outdoor."

That may soon change. Two major media measurement organizations—Arbitron, Inc. and VNU Media Measurement & Information, corporate parent of Nielsen—are vying to devise detailed audience measurements of outdoor ads. After completing a test in Atlanta this past June, Arbitron, a New York City-based media and market research firm, announced plans to create an outdoor audience ratings service. The service will likely involve collecting travel patterns through diaries and lay-

ering the locations on top of the travel patterns to define a particular consumer's "opportunity to see" an ad, says Jacqueline Noel, director of sales and marketing for Arbitron Outdoor, an Arbitron subsidiary. The company—which received $300,000 in backing from the OAAA—expects to have the ratings tool completed by early 2003, depending on industry feedback on a prototype.

Meanwhile, Nielsen Outdoor, a newly formed unit of VNU Media Measurement & Information, a New York City-based media information services company, plans to launch its own outdoor ratings service in early 2003. The service Nielsen plans to introduce in the U.S. will be based significantly on what the company learned in South Africa, according to Lorraine Hadfield, Nielsen's managing director. Last October, when the company tested global positioning devices there, members of a randomly chosen, demographically balanced sample carried small meters that tracked their movements at 20-second intervals. This information was then matched to a map of outdoor sites to determine the participants' opportunity to see an ad.

Why the race to build an outdoor audience measurement tool? The stakes are rising for the $5 billion outdoor industry.

Why the race to create an outdoor audience measurement tool now? In some ways, it's long overdue, as the stakes are rising for the $5 billion outdoor industry. Although it represents only 2.2 percent of all ad spending, outdoor has been growing at a steady clip. With average annual growth of 6.7 percent over the past five years, spending in the outdoor ad industry has outpaced that in newspapers, consumer magazines and TV, which grew an average of 3.5 percent, 5.7 percent and 5.8 percent, respectively, over the same period, according to Veronis Suhler Stevenson, a New York City-based media merchant bank. Over the past 10 years, spending on outdoor ads has risen a cumulative 97 percent. And the outlook for the next 10 years is bright. Merrill Lynch predicts that in 2012, $8.6 billion will be spent on outdoor advertising media, up two-thirds from a projected $5.2 billion for 2002.

BOARDS RULE

Billboards dominate the outdoor advertising landscape, bringing in nearly two-thirds of the industry's revenues.

ANNUAL REVENUE BY TYPE OF AD, 2001 (BILLIONS):

- Alternative outdoor $.3 billion (6%)
- Transit $.9 billion (17%)
- Street furniture* $.9 billion (17%)
- Billboards $3.1 billion (60%)
- Total revenue $5.2 billion

*Includes bus shelters, newsstands and phone booths.
Source: Outdoor Advertising Association of America

Once a credible audience measurement tool is available, continued growth is virtually guaranteed, say industry observers and insiders. And as more upscale brands advertise outdoors, the industry's clout will be bolstered and diversified. While Anheuser-Busch and Miller are still among top spenders outdoors, other brands in the top 20 in 2001 included Apple, Cingular and the Gap. Among the newer categories to show up in outdoor ads are insurance, retail and finance. Other new players on the outdoor operator side include global media conglomerates Viacom (which owns CBS, Nickelodeon and MTV) and Clear Channel (which owns 1,225 radio stations).

How well have outdoor ads performed? So far, measurements have been based on basic traffic studies involving "claimed recall," in which consumers specify whether or not they saw an outdoor ad. More reliable numbers available through the Traffic Audit Bureau, a nonprofit organization based in New York City, amount to gross traffic numbers or circulation counts. "Traffic counts are hardly enough," says Susan Nathan, senior vice president and director of Media Knowledge, which runs Universal McCann's media research group.

When it comes to outdoor ads, many media planners actually dismiss the numbers offered by the industry. For example, an ad's cost per thousand (CPM) is based on traffic counts, which media planners are skeptical about, often believing just 25 percent of the reported traffic count, says Erwin Ephron, a partner at New York City-based media and marketing consultancy Ephron, Papazion & Ephron. So a planner may assume that for a location with a reported traffic count of 80,000, only 20,000 people pass by the site a day. "Those [numbers] are based upon smoke," says Ephron.

That's not to say accurate data on the outdoor audience is nonexistent. Scarborough Research, a New York City-based market research company, for one, gauges the percentage of adults in a market traveling certain roads, their commuting habits and even the auto dealerships where they are most likely to shop. For instance, almost 1 in 5 (18 percent) adults in the Atlanta area has a commute that lasts 30 to 59 minutes. Half of all adults in the area travel on Interstate 285—for any purpose. This information tells media planners which roads in the market are heavily trafficked. But though half of Atlanta adults who travel on Interstate 285 may pass by an ad, the data doesn't reveal how many people actually see it or who those people are. Of Arbitron's ratings system under development, Martin Aliaga, the OAAA's research director, says, "It will elevate the credibility of our numbers and look at outdoor as consumed by a consumer—from the consumer's point of view."

IN MY BACKYARD

Local ad sectors spend the most on outdoor advertising.

TOP 10 OUTDOOR ADVERTISING CATEGORIES BY PERCENT OF TOTAL 2001 REVENUES:

Local services and amusements	12.8%
Public transportation, hotels and resorts	11.4%
Retail	10.0%
Media and advertising	8.8%
Restaurants	7.8%
Automotive dealers and services	6.6%
Insurance and real estate	5.4%
Financial	5.3%
Automotive accessories and equipment	4.9%
Telecommunications	4.7%

Source: Outdoor Advertising Association of America

Industry leaders are hoping that a better audience measuring tool will help encourage wider acceptance of outdoor advertising. A nagging obstacle has been its perception as primarily a local medium. Local businesses have always known the power of their markets, so they weren't that interested in audience data. Only after mergers in the late 1990s left the majority of the industry in the hands of three operators (Viacom, Clear Channel

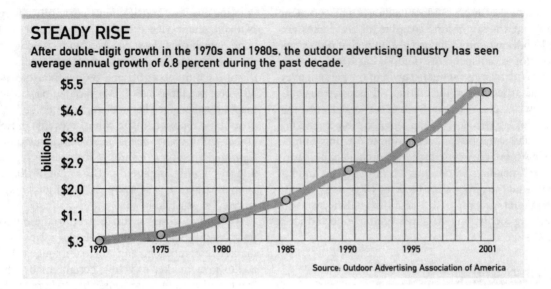

STEADY RISE

After double-digit growth in the 1970s and 1980s, the outdoor advertising industry has seen average annual growth of 6.8 percent during the past decade.

Source: Outdoor Advertising Association of America

and Lamar Advertising) did it shift to a more national outlook, according to Cynthia Evans, chair of the New York City-based Advertising Research Foundation's Outdoor Council and senior partner of the New York City-based Medialab division of Media Edge: CIA, a media investment organization owned by WPP.

The industry also faces an image problem: Ads aren't always kept clean. Lack of maintenance and the risk that graffiti will deface an ad have caused some advertisers to shun this form of marketing. "There's no way you're going to put Chanel perfume on a newsstand like [those sheds in New York]," says Jean-Luc Decaux, co-CEO of JCDecaux North America, a branch of French company JCDecaux, the world leader in outdoor advertising. In fact, many advertisers do not want their brand associated with something as plebeian as a bus shelter, says Evans.

However, JCDecaux has taken steps to create outdoor ad vehicles that high-end brands consider viable. Seven years ago, the newsstands in San Francisco were graffiti-covered wooden barricades chained to trees at night. JCDecaux offered to buy, replace and maintain all the newsstands to create a vehicle for premium outdoor ads. The new kiosks are columns that carry ads on two sides; the third side has a door that opens for the newsstand vendor. When the stands first launched, most advertisers wanted only a few panels downtown for two weeks, says Decaux, and they complained that they were too expensive.

But Calvin Klein, Inc. apparently saw the potential of the medium in December 1995. The company bought up the ad space on all 115 newsstands in San Francisco for the month before Christmas. As soon as the perfume ads went up, the phone started to ring. Marketers wanted to know what Calvin Klein had bought and said they wanted to buy the same thing. "The concept has been extremely successful over the last five years," says Decaux. "Why? It's simple. It delivers the audience. The format is standard. It's backlit. It's well-maintained. It's got great locations. And if you combine all that—that makes a great medium."

More such offerings throughout the U.S., says Decaux, would spur spending on out-of-home advertising and ultimately grow the base of the outdoor ad business. To that end, his company is developing the street furniture business in the U.S. Come 2003, it will introduce 2,000 bus shelters in Chicago, bringing 4,000 new ad panels to the Windy City. (Before, there had been no bus shelters in that market.) As better offerings become available or are created in top markets, it should become easier to sell nationally, says Decaux. But the lack of audience measurements is still a source of client resistance. "There is no tool available that you can take to a client and say, 'You have to buy 50 boards in New York to get proper coverage,' " he says. "Right now, you can't go to your client and say, 'I've got this measurement system that will tell you how you'll do.' Once that's available, I think outdoor will be a lot better received by marketers."

Outdoor advertising can also be a way to reach people who are not big consumers of traditional mass media, such as TV and newspapers. When the American Cancer Society wanted to reach underserved and low-income women in Michigan who were eligible for free cancer screenings and treatment, Meridian Advertising, a Troy, Mich.-based advertising agency, ran ads on bus shelters and public phone booths in urban neighborhoods, where the majority of the women who were eligible lived. So far, the year-long campaign, which launched in October 2002, has surpassed expectations. "We're thrilled," says Gary McMullen, vice president of corporate communications for the American Cancer Society's Great Lakes division. "We're getting over 100 calls a day, where before we fielded under 10 a day."

To promote brand awareness and differentiate itself from other energy companies, London-based BP, the largest oil and gas producer in the U.S., chose to go outdoors as part of its multimedia campaign. Research had shown that the oil industry is not highly regarded, says Dave Welch, BP's director of advertising. So the company mounted its "Beyond Petroleum" outdoor campaign, created by New York City ad agency Ogilvy &

Mather. At least 36 billboards were deployed in New York, Washington, D.C. and Chicago last August (and were to stay in place through December). High-impact marquee or foot traffic locations, such as Times Square and a point of entry to D.C. from a major artery in Virginia, were chosen to reach an audience of opinion-makers and create buzz. Some of the billboards and bus shelter ads exude more attitude than is typical of the industry, with slightly tongue-in-cheek messages. One reads: "Solar, natural gas, wind, hydrogen. And oh yes, oil." Research has shown that familiarity with the company, favorable views of it and a general awareness have all increased, relative to the industry as a whole. "We're very pleased with the results of the campaign to date," says Welch.

Still, while Welch's initial reaction is positive, he does contend that measurements of outdoor ads leave something to be desired. "I would be happier with outdoor if it had more detailed audience results," he says, noting that most of the data is based on impressions, which makes it hard to compare the medium with TV or radio's detailed audience ratings. "We as advertisers, always hunger for information that gives us more precision about the value of certain ad vehicles."

The expectation of an audience measurement tool has brought new optimism to the outdoor ad industry. Says Tom Teepell, chief marketing officer of Baton Rouge, La.-based Lamar Advertising, "We're looking forward to the day we'll be considered on a level playing field with other media."

UNIT 4
Global Marketing

Unit Selections

Key Points to Consider

- What economic, cultural, and political obstacles must an organization consider that seeks to become global in its markets?

- Do you believe that an adherence to the "marketing concept" is the right way to approach international markets? Why, or why not?

- What trends are taking place today that would suggest whether particular global markets will grow or decline? Which countries do you believe will see the most growth in the next decade? Why?

- In what ways can the Internet be used to extend a market outside the United States?

 **Links: www.dushkin.com/online/**
These sites are annotated in the World Wide Web pages.

CIBERWeb
  http://ciber.centers.purdue.edu
Emerging Markets Resources
  http://www.usatrade.gov/website/ccg.nsf
International Business Resources on the WWW
  http://globaledge.msu.edu/ibrd/ibrd.asp
International Trade Administration
  http://www.ita.doc.gov
World Chambers Network
  http://www.worldchambers.net
World Trade Center Association On Line
  http://iserve.wtca.org

It is certain that marketing with a global perspective will continue to be a strategic element of U.S. business well into the next decade. The United States is both the world's largest exporter and largest importer. In 1987, U.S. exports totaled just over $250 billion—about 10 percent of total world exports. During the same period, U.S. imports were nearly $450 billion—just under 10 percent of total world imports. By 1995, exports had risen to $513 billion and imports to $664 billion—roughly the same percentage of total world trade.

Whether or not they wish to be, all marketers are now part of the international marketing system. For some, the end of the era of domestic markets may have come too soon, but that era is over. Today it is necessary to recognize the strengths and weaknesses of our own marketing practices as compared to those abroad. The multinational corporations have long recognized this need, but now all marketers must acknowledge it.

International marketing differs from domestic marketing in that the parties to its transactions live in different political units. It is the "international" element of international marketing that distinguishes it from domestic marketing—not differences in managerial techniques. The growth of global business among multinational corporations has raised new questions about the role of their headquarters. It has even caused some to speculate whether marketing operations should be performed abroad rather than in the United States.

The key to applying the marketing concept is understanding the consumer. Increasing levels of consumer sophistication are evident in all of the world's most profitable markets. Managers are required to adopt new points of view in order to accommodate increasingly complex consumer wants and needs. The markets in the new millennium will show further integration on a worldwide scale. In these emerging markets, conventional textbook approaches can cause numerous problems. The new marketing perspective called for by the circumstances of the years ahead will require a long-range view that looks from the basics of exchange and their applications in new settings.

The selections presented here were chosen to provide an overview of world economic factors, competitive positioning, and increasing globalization of markets—issues to which each and every marketer must become sensitive. "Segmenting Global Markets: Look Before You Leap" reflects the importance of understanding local and global issues before implementing a global market segmentation strategy. The second article stresses that international marketing research is a very serious and critical undertaking. The third article reveals that to sell to rural India, global giants are thinking small—offering Indians an array of new products in sample sizes. "Time for Marketers to Grow Up?" describes that as the world's birthrates slow and its population ages, multinational companies are forced to reconsider strategies for selling diapers, arthritis medicine, and everything in between. "Cracking China's Market" describes the dawning reality that China is turning into a profitable global market for foreigners in a relatively short time. "The Lure of Global Branding" provides some guidelines for proper global brand leadership.

Segmenting Global Markets:
Look Before You Leap

Before implementing a global market segmentation strategy,
it's critical to understand both local and global issues.

By V. Kumar and Anish Nagpal

*"I am a citizen, not of Athens or Greece,
but of the world."*

Today we live in a global marketplace that makes Socrates' famous words more valid than ever before. As you read this article, you may be sitting on a chair from Paris, wearing a shirt made in Britain, and using a computer, without which you are handicapped, that probably was made in Taiwan. Have you ever wondered why and how this happens?

Global marketing refers to marketing activities of companies that emphasize four activities: (1) cost efficiencies resulting from reduced duplication of efforts; (2) opportunities to transfer products, brands, and ideas across subsidiaries in different countries; (3) emergence of global customers, such as global teenagers or the global elite; and (4) better links between national marketing infrastructures, which paves the way for a global marketing infrastructure that results in better management and reduced costs.

As the business world becomes more globalized, global market segmentation (GMS) has emerged as an important issue in developing, positioning, and selling products across national boundaries. Consider the global segment based on demographics, global teenagers. The sharing of universal needs and desires for branded, entertaining, trendy, and image-oriented products makes it possible to reach the global teen segment with a unified marketing program. For example, Reebok used a global advertisement campaign to launch its Instapump line of sneakers in the United States, Germany, Japan, and 137 other countries worldwide.

WHAT IS GMS?

Global market segmentation can be defined as the process of identifying specific segments—country groups or individual consumer groups across countries—of potential customers with homogeneous attributes who are likely to exhibit similar buying behavior.

The study of GMS is interesting and important for three reasons. First of all, considering the world as a market, different products are in different stages of the product life cycle at any given time. Researchers can segment the market based on this information, but the membership of the countries in each segment is fleeting. This makes it difficult to re-evaluate and update the membership of each segment.

Second, with the advent of the Internet, product information is disseminated very rapidly and in unequal proportions across different countries. The dynamic nature of this environment warrants a continuous examination of the stability of the segment membership. Third, the goal of GMS is to break down the world market for a product or a service into different groups of countries/consumers that differ in their response to the firm's marketing mix program. That way, the firm can tailor its marketing mix to each individual segment.

Targeted segments in GMS should possess some of the following properties:

Measurability. The segments should be easy to define and measure. Objective country traits such as socioeconomic variables (e.g., per capita income) can easily be gauged, but the size of the segments based on culture or lifestyles is much harder to measure. Thus, a larger scale survey may be required for segmenting global markets depending upon the basis of GMS.

EXECUTIVE SUMMARY

The primary purpose of this article is to shed more light on the more complex challenges of global market segmentation (GMS). To provide a complete understanding, we discuss some of the well-known issues in segmenting foreign markets and move on to state the various properties of global target markets. We conclude that companies can implement GMS most effectively by first gaining a full understanding of both local and global concerns.

Size. Segments should be large enough to be worth going after. Britain and Hong Kong can be grouped together in the same segment, because of previous British supremacy in Hong Kong, but their population sizes differ.

Accessibility. The segments should be easy to reach via the media. Because of its sheer size, China seems to be an attractive market. However, because of its largely rural population, it has less access to technology.

Actionability. Effective marketing programs (the four Ps) should be easy to develop. If segments do not respond differently to the firm's marketing mix, there is no need to segment the markets. Certain legal issues need to be considered before implementing an advertisement campaign. For example, many countries, such as India, do not allow direct slandering of the competitor's products.

Competitive Intensity. The segments should not be preempted by the firm's competition. In fact, in global marketing, small companies often prefer entry of less competitive markets and use this as one of the segmentation criteria when assessing international markets.

Growth Potential. A high return on investment should be attainable. Typically, marketers face a trade-off between competitive intensity and growth potential. Currently, Latin American markets have good growth potential, but the instability of local currencies causes major problems.

Companies typically employ the following six-step process for implementing GMS:
- Identify purpose (by introducing a new or existing product and choosing appropriate marketing mix programs in groups of countries)
- Select segmentation criteria (traditional vs. emerging)
- Collect relevant information
- Segment the countries/consumers according to criteria
- Reevaluate the fit of the segment after implementation of the intended program
- Update/reassign segment membership

An interesting aspect of the GMS process is the need to constantly reevaluate segment membership. The process of assigning membership to countries into a segment could be done using traditional procedures, or by evaluating the countries by using emerging techniques.

TRADITIONAL SEGMENTATION BASES

The choice of the segmentation basis is the most crucial factor in an international segmentation study. That a segmentation approach is essential in international markets is no longer questioned. Rather, the basis for segmentation becomes the focus. For example, for its Lexus brand, Toyota would segment the market based upon household income. On the other hand, if Marlboro were planning to introduce a new brand of cigarettes, it would segment the market based on population.

Individual- and country-based segmentation includes the following categories:

Demographics. This includes measurable characteristics of population such as age, gender, income, education, and occupation. A number of global demographic trends, such as changing roles of women, and higher incomes and living standards, are driving the emergence of global segments. Sony, Reebok, Nike, Swatch, and Benetton are some firms that cater to the needs of global teenagers.

Culture. This covers a broad range of factors such as religion, education, and language, which are easy to measure, and aesthetic preferences of the society that are much harder to comprehend. Hofstede's classification scheme proposes five cultural dimensions for classifying countries: Individualism vs. Collectivism, Power Distance (PD), Uncertainty Avoidance (UA), Masculinity vs. Femininity, and Strategic Orientation (long-term vs. short-term). For example, Austria, Germany, Switzerland, Italy, Great Britain, and Ireland form one cluster that is medium-high on Individualism and high on Masculinity. These cultural characteristics signify the preference for "high performance" products and a "successful achiever" theme in advertising.

Geography. This is based upon the world region, economic stage of development, nation, city, city size and population density, climate, altitude, and sometimes, even the ZIP code. It is easy to form country segments using regional blocks such as NAFTA, European Union, MERCOSUR, or Asia-Pacific. However, the value of such segments may vary depending on the need. These groupings are viable for developing trade policies, but not for marketing products/services given tremendous variation in other factors.

Environment. GMS is further complicated by different political, legal, and business environments in each country. Economic indicators such as Gross Domestic Product (GDP) may be used. However, it may not be relevant to refer to country segments based on this criterion because a country can move from one level of GDP to another, making this criterion obsolete.

Behavior-based segmentation includes three categories, which are shown in Exhibit 1.

EXHIBIT 1   Traditional segmentation basis (behavior-based)

Segmentation Basis	Brief Description	Example
Psychographics	This segment groups people in terms of their attitudes, values, and lifestyles and helps predict consumer preferences in products, services, and media.	Porsche AG divided its buyers into five distinct categories: Top Guns, Elitists, Proud Patrons, Bon Vivants, and Fantasists—each group having a particular characteristic.
Benefit	This approach focuses on the problem a product solves, regardless of location. It attempts to measure consumer value systems and perceptions of various brands in a product class.	Toothpaste consumers can be segmented into Sensory, Sociable, Worrier, and Independent segments. Sociable consumers seek bright teeth; Worriers seek healthy teeth. Aqua packaging could indicate fluoride for the Worrier segment, and white (for a white smile) for the Sociable segment.
Behavior	This examines whether or not people buy and use a product, as well as how often and how much. Consumers can be categorized in terms of usage rates (heavy, medium, and light).	ABB classifies customers according to their switchability criterion—oyal customers, those loyal to competitors, and those who can be lost to or won from the competition.

EMERGING SEGMENTATION BASES

Countries also can be segmented by means of product *diffusion patterns* and *response elasticities*. Some countries are fast adopters of the product, whereas some countries require a lag period to adopt the product. With this in mind, a firm could introduce its products in countries that are innovators (fast adopters) and later in those countries that are imitators (lag countries).

Rather than using macro-level variables to classify countries, a firm might consider segmenting markets on the basis of new-product diffusion patterns. As Exhibit 2 indicates, country segments formed on the basis of diffusion patterns may differ by product.

This type of segmentation allows the global marketer to segment countries on the basis of actual purchase patterns. Having knowledge of purchase patterns can help marketers make mode-of-entry decisions and help determine the sequence of countries in which the product should be introduced.

Consumers in lag countries can learn about the benefits of the product from the experience of adopters in the lead country, and this learning can result in a faster diffusion rate in the lag markets. Thus, countries can be grouped according to the degree of learning they exhibit for a given lead country. Lag countries that exhibit strong learning ties are potential candidates for sequential entry (using a waterfall strategy). Entry into countries that exhibit weak learning effect can be accelerated since there is not much to gain by waiting. Here, a sprinkler strategy (simultaneous entry into the relevant markets) would work well.

If a firm wants to introduce its innovation into a new country, it must be aware that the diffusion rate depends upon the kind of innovation. The diffusion pattern of a continuous innovation (one that has a majority of features in common with earlier products plus some new features that improve performance or add value) is very different from a discontinuous innovation (which is new or drastically different from earlier forms in several relevant features or attributes).

In the case of continuous innovations, such as home computers, the introduction of a successive generation will influence not only its diffusion but also the diffusion of the earlier generations. In such cases, diffusion will occur more quickly since consumers have some related knowledge. Hence, when a new generation of the product is introduced in the lead market while the lag markets are still adopting the existing (older) generation, information on the added benefits of the new generation travels faster from the lead market to potential adopters in the lag markets. The users in the lag markets will be familiar with the innovation and can easily absorb the benefits of the next generation.

Another interesting way to group countries is according to their response elasticities. Consumers across countries respond in different ways when the price of the product changes. Grocerystore scanner systems store a wealth of information that can then be used to find customer buying patterns. If the data shows the customers are price sensitive toward a particular product, couponing strategies can help target that segment, where legal.

IMPLEMENTING GMS

It is important to consider some of the conceptual and methodological issues so GMS can fulfill its high potential. Exhibit 3 gives a brief description of the four critical types of equivalencies that should be taken into account when implementing GMS.

Construct equivalence refers to whether the segmentation basis has the same meaning and is expressed similarly in different countries and cultures. Different countries under study must have the same perception or use for the product being researched. Otherwise, comparison of data becomes meaningless. If, for example, a firm is studying the bicycle market, it must realize that, in the United States, bicycles are classified under the recreational-sports industry, whereas in India and China they are considered a basic means of transportation.

EXHIBIT 2   Segments based upon diffusion patterns

Product Categories

Segment	VCRs	Cellular phones	Home computers	Microwave ovens	CD players
1	Germany, UK, France, Sweden	Denmark, Norway	Belgium, UK, Netherlands	Germany, Italy, Denmark, Austria	Belgium, Netherlands, Sweden, Austria, Finland
2	Belgium, Denmark, Spain, Austria, Finland	Finland, France	France, Italy, Sweden, Norway, Austria, Germany	Belgium, UK, Netherlands, France, Spain	Spain, Denmark, Germany
3	Italy, Portugal	Germany, UK, Italy, Switzerland	Spain, Portugal	Norway	Switzerland, Italy

Source: Kumar, V., Jaishankar Ganesh, and Raj Echambadi, "Cross-National Diffusion Research: What Do We Know and How Certain Are We?" *Journal of Product Innovation Management*, 15, 1998.

Similar activities also may have different functions in different countries. For example, for many U.S. families, grocery shopping is a chore to be accomplished as efficiently as possible. However, in India and many other countries interaction with vendors and local shopkeepers plays a very important social function.

Construct equivalence is easier to establish for the general bases, such as geographic variables. However, for bases such as values and lifestyles, construct equivalence is much harder to achieve. VALS-2 identifies eight segments based on two main dimensions: self-orientation and resources. Another VALS system was developed for Japan, presumably because the U.S.-based VALS-2 system was not appropriate for that country. Instead it identifies 10 segments based on two key dimensions: life orientation and attitudes toward social change.

Scalar equivalence means that scores from different countries should have the same meaning and interpretation. The first aspect used to determine scalar equivalence concerns the specific scale or scoring procedure used to establish the measure. The standard format of scales used in survey research differs across countries. For example, in the United States a 5- or 7-point scale is most common. However, 20-point scales are used in France.

EXHIBIT 3   Types of equivalence

Equivalence

Construct	Scalar	Measurement	Sampling
Are we studying the same phenomena in Brazil, India, and Britain?	Do the scores on consumers in the U.S., Argentina, and Japan have the same meaning?	Are the phenomena in France, Singapore and South Africa measured in the same way?	Are the samples used in Hong Kong, China, and Romania equivalent?

The second aspect concerns the response to a score obtained in a measure. Here the question arises as to whether a score obtained in one research context has the same

meaning and interpretation in another context. For example, on an intention-to-purchase scale, does the proportion of likely buyers indicate a similar likelihood of purchase from one country to another, or does a position on the Likert scale have the same meaning in all cultures?

Differences in response styles often result in a lack of scalar equivalence. Some of these response styles include "extreme" responding and "social desirability" responding. Research shows Chinese respondents show a "marked degree of agreeability," while Americans show a "marked willingness to dissent." These differences can cause problems in the data-collection process, which can lead to erroneous grouping of countries.

Measurement equivalence refers to whether the measures used to operationalize the segmentation basis are comparable across countries. For example, consider the level of education. The United States uses one educational scale while in Europe the educational system is quite different, and the term "college" is not appropriate. Also, household income is difficult to compare across countries owing to differences in the tax structure and purchasing power.

Some items of a segmentation basis have measurement equivalence, but the others do not. For example, research shows that in the U.S. consumer innovativeness is expressed both in terms of purchase of new products and in social communication about new products. In France, however, the latter does not apply. Hence, only items pertaining to the person's tendency to purchase new products have measurement equivalence across the two countries. The researcher thus faces the dilemma of either using the same set of items in each country (etic scale) or adapting the set of items to each country (emic-scale). A compromise would be a combined emic-etic scale with some core items common to all countries and some country-specific items.

Sampling equivalence deals with problems in identifying and operationalizing comparable populations and selecting samples that are simultaneously representative of other populations and comparable across countries. One aspect of sampling equivalence deals with the decision-making process, which varies across countries. For example, in the United States, office supplies are often purchased by the office secretary, whereas this decision is made by a middle-level manager or CEO in some countries.

It is also important to consider whether the sample is representative of the population. In most developed countries, information on potential markets and sampling frames is easily available. However, in Japan, the most popular residential list for sample studies was made inaccessible to researchers. Developing countries do not have extensive databases and so obtaining the sampling frame to suit the needs of the research could be difficult.

Equivalence presents a dilemma in the minds of managers. On one end, it would be wise to develop scales specifically for each culture; on the other, responses collected in this manner may not mean the same thing. This issue can be resolved to some extent by using a combination of items in the scale.

THINK GLOBALLY, ACT LOCALLY

Used effectively, segmentation allows global marketers to take advantage of the benefits of standardization (such as economies of scale and consistency in positioning) while addressing the needs and expectations of a specific target group. This approach means looking at markets on a global or regional basis, thereby ignoring the political boundaries that define markets in many cases.

The greatest challenge for the global marketer is the choice of an appropriate base for segmentation. Pitfalls that handicap global marketing programs and contribute to their suboptimal performance include market-related reasons, such as insufficient research and overstandardization, as well as internal reasons, such as inflexibility in planning and implementation. If a product is launched on a broad scale without formally researching regional or local differences, it may fail.

The successful global marketers will be those who can achieve a balance between the local and the regional/global concerns. Procter and Gamble's Pampers brand suffered a major setback in the 1980s in Japan when customers favored the purchase of diapers of rival brands.

The diapers were made and sold according to a formula imposed by Cincinnati headquarters, and Japanese consumers found the company's hard-sell techniques alienating. Globalization by design requires a balance between sensitivity to local needs and global deployment of technologies and concepts.

GMS offers a solution to the standardization vs. adaptation issue because it creates the conceptual framework for offering standardized products and marketing programs in multiple countries by targeting the same consumer segments in different countries. The formulation of a global strategy by a firm may result in the choice of one particular segment across markets or multiple segments. However, in implementing the marketing mix for maximum effect, the principle "Think globally, act locally" becomes a critical rule for guiding marketing efforts.

ADDITIONAL READING

Ganesh, Jaishankar, V. Kumar, and Velavan Subramaniam (1997), "Learning Effect in Multinational Diffusion of Consumer Durables: An Exploratory Investigation," *Journal of the Academy of Marketing Science*, 25 (3), 214–228.

Hofstede, Geert (1984), *Culture's Consequences: International Differences in Work-Related Values*. California: Sage Publications.

Kotabe, Masaaki, and Kristiaan Helsen (1998), *Global Marketing Management*. New York: John Wiley & Sons Inc.

Kumar, V. (2000), *International Marketing Research*. New Jersey: Prentice Hall.

V. Kumar (VK) is Marvin Hurley Professor of Business Administration, Melcher Faculty Scholar, Director of Marketing Research Studies and Director of International Business Programs at the University of Houston, Bauer College of Business, Department of Marketing. He may be reached at vkumar@uh.edu.

Anish Nagpal is a doctoral student at the University of Houston, Bauer College of Business, Department of Marketing.

International marketing research: A management briefing

Many firms expand globally with little marketing research. But noteworthy business failures have occurred that could have been prevented with a minimal amount of study. Products and marketing campaigns usually need to be adapted overseas. The same is true for marketing research methods. Accepted approaches to conducting research are based on methods that were developed to study the U.S. market. Different conditions overseas, however, especially in emerging markets, make these methods difficult to apply. A look at typical problems in conducting research overseas can help in developing some guidelines for adapting methods in foreign countries.

Tim R. V. Davis
Professor of Management and International Business,
Cleveland State University, Cleveland, Ohio

Robert B. Young
Market Research Director, Stores Division,
ICI Paints/Glidden, Cleveland, Ohio

International marketing research is much more crucial than many managers think. With a burgeoning number of companies pursuing global strategies, managers are in great need of dependable information on foreign markets. Attempting to expand overseas without doing adequate research too often means having to face the crippling costs of business failure. Moreover, American market research techniques often don't work well abroad; managers must confront different challenges when conducting research overseas, especially in developing countries.

Corporate blunders in foreign markets frequently occur because of a lack of understanding of the Four Ps in the marketing mix—Product, Price, Place, and Promotion. Failure to investigate and, where necessary, reinterpret the Four P's abroad has proved costly.

Product and packaging problems

The failure of many products that lack acceptability overseas could have been predicted with minimal market research. Chase & Sanborn's attempt to introduce instant coffee in France failed because brewing real coffee is a cherished culinary delight for most French people. Instant coffee was considered a somewhat vulgar substitute.

In other cases, the problem may not be the product but the packaging. Snapple encountered difficulty marketing its bottled drinks through vending machines in Japan, where cans load more easily and are less fragile than glass. In China, Procter & Gamble marketed diapers in pink packaging that conveyed a preference for female babies. But many Chinese consumers shunned the product; under the country's one-child-per-family rule, the preference in many families is for a son. This type of product image problem could have been uncovered with prior research.

Pricing problems

Many companies do too little research on product or service pricing in overseas markets. In some cases, the price a company charges is simply the foreign currency equivalent of the domestic price, which may bear little relationship to what the customer is willing to pay. Ford recently tried to sell its economy model Escort car in India for more than $21,000. But in an emerging market like India, only a small percentage of the total population have incomes of $20,000 or more. So most Indians saw the Escort as a luxury automobile that very few could afford.

Even when managers are aware of acceptable pricing levels, they may still price products or services too high or too low. Exporters often set high prices to recover special labeling and packaging charges, overseas transportation, and import tariffs—costs that local competitors do not have to incur. These expenditures may prevent a company from pricing the product competitively. On the other hand, management may price products lower than the competition and be willing to take a loss early with a view to achieving profits later when more volume is achieved. Frequently, sufficient volume is never achieved and the foreign venture fails to break even. The lack of adequate cost analysis and pricing research is another major cause of business failure.

Place (distribution) problems

How products are placed or distributed in overseas markets can be the most important international business decision a company makes. Firms can try to break into established wholesale, retail, or direct sales networks, piggyback on other firms' distribution systems, or build their own channels, which can be costly and time-consuming. Neilson, Canada's largest manufacturer and marketer of confectioneries, has distributed its products successfully in such far-flung markets as Japan, China, and the Middle East. But success has eluded it in the market it would most like to succeed in: the United States. The reason for this is Neilson's choice of distributor. In the early 1990s, the company chose Pro Set, a collectible trading card producer, as its distributor. However, Pro Set's sales force lacked experience in selling confectionery and never achieved significant penetration in the US market. The firm was poorly managed and eventually filed Chapter 11 bankruptcy, leaving Neilson with a huge outstanding receivables balance and a severely damaged reputation with customers.

Promotional problems

Promotional methods and advertising media vary around the world. The lack of understanding of branding, selling, advertising, and promotion practices in different countries may also land companies in difficulty. Lincoln Electric, a US-based manufacturer of electric motors and welding equipment, acquired an arc welding firm in Germany and immediately slapped its own brand on the products that were made by the firm. Many customers

had a strong "Buy German" attitude and were contemptuous of American engineering, so they immediately switched to other German products. Although Lincoln's problems in Germany ran considerably deeper, the company never recovered from its poor start and eventually had to close its operation there. Royal Applicant, an American manufacturer of small, hand-held vacuum cleaners like the "Dirt Devil," suffered a similar disaster. The company assumed that its successful domestic promotional strategy would work equally well in Europe. In the United States, expenditures on television advertising were closely correlated with predictable increases in sales volume. But in the different European countries, the growth in TV ad spending did not produce the predicted increases. Even though sales had risen to over $20 million by 1993, they never produced a return on investment. The company eventually withdrew entirely from the European market.

It is critical for managers to investigate the Four Ps in every country in which they do business and make modifications when and where they are needed. As these and other examples illustrate (see the box on the next page), mistakes are often made by well-known corporations, not just small firms. The tendency to take market knowledge for granted is the most insidious problem in international business, and often a fatal one.

Difficulties in conducting global marketing research

Even if managers are convinced of the need for foreign market research, they may have little understanding of the differences involved in carrying it out. They must become acquainted with the challenges it will bring—challenges they may not encounter at home.

More diverse research projects

The main types of marketing research projects are basically the same whether they are conducted at home or abroad. Studies typically deal with market entry, customer satisfaction, buyer behavior, and aspects of the Four Ps, and focus mainly on differences across countries. This may involve straight comparisons between a single foreign country and the domestic market or comparisons among multiple countries. But international research studies must contend with wide-ranging cultural diversity, which may include marked differences in language, religion, race, and ethnic origin that affect the sale of products and services. Domestic studies often examine regional differences, but they generally do not approach the level of diversity that is encountered in country comparisons.

More unknowns

Most managers know considerably more about their own domestic market than they do about conditions overseas. International research must shed light on more unknowns, providing insight on issues that may be clearly understood in the domestic market. Considering the lack of published information on many foreign markets, researchers have a heavy burden to bear. There are limits to the type and amount of data they can collect. The scope of what is to be studied will be constrained by the amount of time and resources available. So choices must be made about the focus of market research and what issues can be investigated.

Longer completion time

Generally, each phase of international marketing research—planning, design, execution, and interpretation of findings—requires more time to complete than in domestic research. The studies take longer to plan because they tend to be more complex and more difficult to arrange. Research designs must take into account viable data collection methods. Execution of the study will take longer if multiple countries are involved because of the separation in time and distance. In vast countries like China and India, the distance between markets makes large-scale studies extremely difficult to conduct. Interpreting the findings also takes time because of the logistics of coordinating comparison studies across countries.

Higher costs

Because of such factors as the different data collection techniques, the need for translation, and long-distance travel, conducting international marketing research is usually much more expensive than at home. Consumer telephone surveys that are a bargain in the United States cost much more abroad. In Japan, studies are mainly conducted door-to-door. In many developing countries, telephone ownership is low and interviewers must often travel vast distances to contact a representative sample of respondents. The time and cost required to collect primary data may make the research prohibitively expensive.

Suspect samples

Census data are unreliable or unavailable in many developing countries. Street maps and phone directories may not exist. Unreliable population statistics often make surveys of the general population difficult to conduct. In planning studies, market researchers need to question the accuracy of available demographic information and the study subjects: Are there any inherent biases in the sample? What proportion of the universe is covered? How are the data verified to ensure proper market coverage? Does

Gaffes, twists, and trials abroad

Many managers view foreign markets as being no different from domestic ones. They assume that successful marketing strategies and tactics used at home will work equally well overseas. But when Gerber first marketed baby foods in Africa, consumers thought the pictures of babies on the bottles meant that the jars contained ground-up babies! Research can also uncover unexpected uses to which products are put, such as the use of Jolly Green Giant sweet corn as fishing bait in Italy.

Obtaining adequate distribution for products is a real challenge when entering emerging markets, particularly transporting them over vast distances. The well-developed air, rail, and highway systems of the US and Europe that offer a variety of transportation options are virtually nonexistent in many developing countries, so research needs to be conducted on how products can reach far-flung markets. Wrigley, which has long been attempting to introduce chewing gum in China, had to face this problem. It discovered from its own market research that only about 17% of the Chinese population could be reached by conventional transportation. Bicycles, tricycles, carts, and motorbikes are used to reach small towns and villages, where products are sold through street kiosks and plywood stands. Wrigley found that many consumer products took eight months to reach the marketplace. After lengthy negotiations with state agencies, the company decided to use a combination of its own representatives and state-owned distributors to get its product to market. The typical route covered by a shipment of chewing gum consists of traveling 1,000 miles by truck, an additional leg by freighter, and finally by bicycle to small street stands. The process requires two weeks to complete, but the product is still freshly soft and sugar dusted at the time it is sold. This distribution method helped Wrigley sell more than 400 million sticks of chewing gum in China during 1999.

Some famous examples of translation errors have occurred in print, poster, TV, and radio advertising. In the late 1980s, Hispanics in the US were encouraged to fly on Braniff Airlines. A radio commercial mentioned flying Braniff *en cuero*, which means "in leather." But a very similar Spanish expression, *en cueros*, means "naked," and the two phrases sound identical when spoken quickly. Clairol, a popular marketer of hair care products, introduced a curling iron in Germany called the "Mist Stick," then discovered that the word "mist" is German slang for "manure." All these problems could have been averted with prior market research.

the sample cover all regions or cities? Is the sample source updated regularly?

Representative sampling may be less of a problem in countries with more homogeneous populations like Japan and South Korea, but it may be a serious concern in places where the population is more diverse, such as Hong Kong and Indonesia. More culturally diverse populations will require larger research samples or more subsamples. Researchers may also have to deal with population movement and migration. For instance, approximately two-fifths of the population of the gulf states of the Middle East consist of expatriate males working in the region for only four to five years. An unstable population is an additional headache when trying to establish a representative sample.

In one study, when asked to choose which of several brands of vodka she would buy, a Russian woman replied, "I would buy all of them because they won't be in the stores tomorrow."

Data collection difficulties

Few countries provide such open access and freely available information as the United States. In many countries, business, government, and the population at large may be less willing to discuss issues, share information, and open up to questioning. People may be unwilling to talk to strangers without formal introductions, referrals, or invitations. An interviewer arriving at a home unannounced may be seen as a threat and treated hostilely. Moreover, the usual data collection methods used at home may be inappropriate in other countries. High levels of illiteracy may rule out written surveys. Mail surveys may be hindered by unreliable postal delivery. Other methods of collecting data may be unavailable. The mall or shopping center interviews common in the US are rarely used in Asia because there are so few shopping malls. In India, electronic point-of-sale cash registers and scanners are virtually nonexistent, so retail checkout data must be collected manually. In most Middle Eastern countries, few women would consent to be interviewed by a man, so female interviewers must be recruited.

Gathering data on certain types of products can also be difficult. For instance, the idea of discussing grooming and personal care products with a stranger would be considered too personal and perhaps offensive in many countries. These data collection difficulties may result in the number of completed interviews and usable questionnaires being quite low.

Translation errors and unintended meanings

A common problem in international marketing research is the errors that occur in translation. The literal translation of brand names and terms from one language to another sometimes creates misunderstandings. Managers of Schweppes tonic water decided to shorten the name in Italy when they learned that the phonetic equivalent of the brand name translated to "bathroom water" in Italian. Questionnaires developed in one country may be difficult to translate because of differences in idioms, the vernacular, and phrasing. This can occur in the US as well, where a large section of the population are bilingual. But it is a much bigger problem in, say, India, where 13 major languages are spoken and salient cultural differences exist across regions. Questions may also take on an entirely different meaning in another country. In one study, when asked to choose which of several brands of vodka she would buy, a Russian woman replied, "I would buy all of them because they won't be in the stores tomorrow."

Measurement problems

Attitude measurement is not universal around the world. As the example of the Russian woman illustrates, participants' responses may be partly culturally determined. Skewed results on attitude scales are common. Products and services routinely achieve well above 60 or 70 percent approval ratings on five-point scales in Latin American countries. Indeed, a product has to be very poor to receive anything less. Latin Americans do not like to hurt others' feelings, including marketers. In contrast, a response of "not bad" in France would be almost the equivalent of "extraordinary." And a response of "somewhat interested" would represent a much stronger commitment than in England, where the term "somewhat" has a less enthusiastic connotation.

Respondent incentives and biased results

The use of incentives as a means to increase participation is another issue. A common criticism of paying respondents for their opinions is that it invites biased answers. But in many countries, incentives are necessary for getting respondents to participate at all. In some countries, such as Brazil, a drink and a willingness to socialize may be enough for an interview to be granted. In other countries, incentives may be considered somewhat insulting.

Reliance on outside research firms

MNCs must work closely with market research firms that collect data for them in different countries. Decisions must be made over how much autonomy will be given to these outside researchers and how closely their work will be supervised or monitored. MNCs with marketing research departments in foreign subsidiaries will be able to work more closely with local firms in different countries. But even large corporations do not have in-house marketing research staff in every country in which they do business. MNCs can send out their own staff to brief people in each country, but inevitably they must place considerable reliance on local researchers. Differences in data collection techniques and concerns about the comparability of findings across countries are significant issues when using various research firms in different countries.

Restrictive laws and disclosure of results

A more sinister threat may be the imposition of legal regulations that make it more difficult to keep research results confidential. For example, new laws enacted in the summer of 1999 control the conduct of market research in China, where government officials monitor questionnaire construction and insist on seeing survey results. Not only is this is in direct conflict with the required nondisclosure of proprietary research studies, in which the results are made known only to the clients commissioning the work, but the new disclosure requirements may unwittingly leak new product plans and marketing proposals to competitors. Managers need to be fully aware of such laws and regulations in various countries.

Inadequate use of findings

The real value of market research depends on how the findings are used. International research will add little value to management decision-making if the findings are not interpreted and acted upon appropriately. Reports from domestic market studies may languish on the shelf because management sees little relevance in the research, or disagrees with the findings. This tendency is greater in international research, where studies may be commissioned at the headquarters level but the findings may need to be implemented in foreign subsidiaries. When managers in the local subsidiaries conduct their own research, they will tend to have more ownership and belief in the findings. But corporate management at headquarters may want to control the questions that are investigated and compare the findings across countries or regions. In this case, local management may resent corporate interference and question the usefulness of the research.

Proposals for improving global marketing research

Given all these difficulties, what can marketers do to make their international research both efficient and effec-

tive? Most companies will need to adapt their approach to conducting research. Here are some guidelines for doing that.

Look for ways to cut costs

It is essential to stretch marketing research dollars so that the maximum benefit can be obtained from budgeted resources. Two excellent ways of doing this are by making the fullest use of published sources and tapping available government assistance.

Make extensive use of secondary sources

The United States and most of Western Europe have a wealth of secondary market data that can be accessed online at little or no cost. All market entry studies should begin by consulting published sources. Many international business texts urge managers to organize relevant macro region or country data (political stability, economic stability, currency strength, quality of infrastructure) and micro industry data (current sales by product, distribution access, raw material availability, labor costs, competitive activity) into a matrix where they can be weighed, ranked, and scored. Although the value of this assessment will depend on the availability of published sources, the objectivity of the data, and the accuracy of the rankings, it is generally a useful first pass for comparing countries, considering alternative selection criteria, and narrowing market entry choices. No attempt should be made to collect primary data before secondary sources have been thoroughly investigated and analyzed.

Seek help from government agencies

Most developed countries and many developing ones have state agencies that aid businesses. Virtually all governments try to promote the development of exports. The Export Market Information Center offers assistance to exporters in the UK. In the US, the International Trade Administration, a division of the Department of Commerce, provides a wide variety of market intelligence on different countries. It conducts low-cost market surveys and searches for sales agents and distributors for companies. Many export-driven emerging countries also provide assistance to help local businesses contribute to a balance-of-trade surplus.

Appoint a single market research coordinator for major studies

The use of a coordinating market research vendor with a network of affiliated offices around the world can improve the consistency and accuracy of results across countries and languages. One major vendor can organize and coordinate the work. With a single point of contact, special instructions and changes can be communicated and implemented simultaneously across multiple countries. Leading MNCs tend to appoint coordinating agencies that have offices in multiple countries. VeriFone uses a single vendor that has extensive experience in global market research and a network of branch offices throughout the world. The vendor's branch office personnel conduct most of the fieldwork. Project briefings, interviewer training, and pilot tests can be conducted and monitored much more easily. Other well-known MNCs like IBM, Compaq, Carrier, and Federal Express also use a single global vendor to manage large-scale research projects around the world.

Walker Information is a leading international research firm with more than 60 years of experience. Based in Indianapolis, it has a network of affiliate offices in more than 50 countries helping global clients conduct research studies that take into account cultural and language differences. Walker provides a diverse range of services, including studies of customer loyalty, employee commitment, corporate reputation, supplier relationships, and corporate philanthropy. Its clients include consumer packaged goods companies, heavy manufacturing firms, consumer and business services, trade associations, not-for-profits, and government agencies.

Pay close attention to the translation of questionnaires

The validity of market research can be improved by having strict, formalized guidelines governing questionnaire preparation and translation. Using a small number of translators can help reduce errors by lowering the potential for different interpretations of terms. Back translation—the process of translating questionnaires from one language to another, then back again with the aid of a second, independent translator—can reveal unintended losses of meaning. The back translator is usually a person whose native tongue is the language that will be used for the final questionnaire. Pilot tests can also help ensure better quality in the final study.

For many years, IBM has been conducting a strategic tracking study across its major markets in Europe, North and South America, and Asia. Conducted in 14 languages across 27 countries, this survey assesses IBM's products against competitors' offerings on such strategic issues as product demand, marketing channels, and preferred information sources. The study reveals broad information on trends rather than in-depth information on customer wants and needs. IBM uses only two translation firms to reduce inconsistency in terms, one for the various European languages and another for Asian languages. It also makes sure these firms use back translators to improve questionnaire accuracy. Local IBM employees in engineering, manufacturing, or sales may also be called upon

to double-check technical terms. All surveys are piloted in the field prior to conducting full-scale studies.

Develop a core set of questions to enhance comparability across countries

To compare countries and regions, many MNCs develop a core set of questions that will be used worldwide. At Carrier Corporation, a core set of 25 questions was used in a global study. Allowance was made for differences in each region by giving subsidiaries the opportunity to ask an additional five questions that were tailored to their area. Compaq uses a Customer Satisfaction Council to develop and maintain a consistent set of customer satisfaction measures across business units and geographic areas. Headed by the vice president of customer satisfaction and quality, this global, cross-divisional, interdisciplinary team meets regularly and invites representation from manufacturing and functions worldwide. Its goal is to establish internal metrics that are linked to customer satisfaction. Consistent validity and reliability among each customer segment across each country is a key strategic objective. Study results are used globally as well as locally. Some measures are customized and modified by market. The Council is responsible for integrating customer satisfaction information into product planning initiatives and process improvements.

In some countries, class, caste, or racial differences determine who speaks and who does not.

Use alternative data collection methods

The difficulties in collecting data overseas often mean that researchers need to adapt their approach to each country or region. Greater use may have to be made of qualitative methods in developing countries. The lack of accurate census and demographic information may sometimes rule out probability sampling. As a result, researchers may have to rely more on nonprobability sampling techniques such as convenience and quota sampling. Convenience sampling is often used for populations that are difficult to approach. The sample size gradually grows through introductions and referrals. Drawing quotas from different segments of society may help reduce sample bias (respondents with the same class, caste, or kinship ties, for example).

Methods will depend partly on the stage of the research, the market knowledge required, and the need for statistical precision. The lack of representative samples may be less of a handicap if the research is in the discovery stage and the objective is to obtain broad qualitative data. Indepth interviews and focus groups will often be the best method for exploring a broad range of issues.

Cultural differences may determine whether to use individual interviews or focus groups. American-style focus groups usually consist of eight to ten selected respondents who freely express their perceptions, attitudes, opinions, and feelings on pertinent research issues under the guidance of a moderator. Such discussion often provides rich qualitative data reflecting a diversity of opinions. Similar diverse results are often achieved in male focus groups carried out in the Middle East. The main problem there may be getting participants to show up on time and controlling the discussion when everybody starts talking at once. However, in collectivist cultures such as Japan and Southeast Asia, individuals may be reluctant to speak out, especially if their opinions are contrary to other group members. In some countries, class, caste, or racial differences may also determine who speaks and who does not. In these circumstance, individual interviews may encourage more openness and candor than focus groups.

Approaches to running focus groups may also partly reflect research traditions in different countries. American focus groups typically emphasize direct questioning, specific issues, and more direct interpretations. In Europe, discussions are more open-ended, with greater use of projective techniques and broader interpretations of the findings.

Recruit native language interviewers and moderators

Many consumers are reluctant to be interviewed for marketing research studies. Often, individual interviewers and group discussion moderators may have to build rapport with them. Companies can raise the comfort level of respondents by using native language interviewers and moderators who can converse in the local dialect. This is also a matter of courtesy. Native language interviewers and moderators can enhance the quality of interviews or focus groups when subtle nuances are important. Both telephone and personal interviews are influenced by country cultural norms. Local interviewers and moderators need to be able to interpret facial gestures and body language and to clarify respondent questions.

Select lead countries as a starting point

Lead countries should be chosen as a data collection point prior to conducting research elsewhere. These may be the wealthiest economies in the region or those with the best prospects. They can sometimes be used as proxies for other countries in the area. For instance, some broad cultural similarities have been found among Southeast Asian countries. Handled with care and prudence, this is another way firms can cut the costs of international mar-

keting research. Selected lead countries can also be used to iron out problems before rolling the research out on a broader scale. Surveys may be vetted for consistency and accuracy. A thorough debriefing following the initial research allows new learning to be taken into neighboring countries.

Test market in smaller countries to maintain secrecy

Secrecy or confidentiality can be a problem in conducting marketing research. Regulations need to be investigated in each country. Given the recently announced disclosure requirements in China, that may not be the best place to test new products. Smaller countries may sometimes be used to keep new product plans more private. Carewell Industries test-marketed its Dentax toothbrush in Singapore before introducing it in the United States because of the country's remoteness from the American market. It is also a relatively self-contained, low-cost environment for testing new products.

Use start-up offices and stores as research labs

An alternative method of collecting intelligence overseas is to establish a branch office, small-scale assembly operation, or service store as a research lab. This may be especially helpful for introducing new products and services into different countries. Marketing research studies rely heavily on people's perceptions and opinions—views that may be suspect when respondents have little direct experience with a new product or service. By establishing an office, factory, or store, management may learn a great deal more from having a direct presence in a country than simply relying on others' opinions about a product's or service's acceptability. Setting up a small-scale test site on a joint venture basis with a local partner can also lower risk and expense.

Citibank maintained a branch office in Tokyo while researching the market before setting up a successful retailing operation throughout Japan. Outpost factories have been used widely in manufacturing. Small, experimental assembly plants are often set up in developing countries to test the feasibility of manufacturing there and establishing local supplier relationships. Outpost factories may also be set up close to major competitors to gather intelligence. McDonald's and Pizza Hut opened experimental stores in Moscow to test the feasibility of selling fast food in Russia. KFC did the same thing in China. These outpost stores were used to adapt the menu, adjust store policies and procedures to local requirements, and explore alternative supplier relationships. Having established a successful, experimental prototype, management could then roll out more stores with a considerable degree of confidence.

Encourage broad participation by those who must use the findings

When corporate managers coordinate marketing research studies around the world, they need to build ownership at the local level. A wide range of stakeholders should be involved if the findings are to be interpreted and used properly. This is especially important when international studies are first conceived and when the implications of the findings are explored. It may necessitate involving general management at the central, regional, and local levels as well as sales, R&D, manufacturing, and other affected functions. Outside entities such as advertising agencies and local distributors may also need to be closely involved. More participation at critical stages in the research can help eliminate resistance and lead to fuller use of the study findings.

Capture and share findings in corporate marketing information system

By capturing research findings in the corporate marketing information system and sharing them across countries, management can build an understanding of the differences and similarities among markets. Marketing research information is not widely shared across the subsidiaries of most MNC's. Country managers know very little about the findings from studies that have been carried out in other foreign subsidiaries, or of product, pricing, distribution and promotional differences, brand names, slogans, and value propositions in other countries. Sharing such information can promote better understanding and collaboration between foreign subsidiaries.

Keep a close watch on the Net

The recent emergence of Internet-based research is making international marketing research easier to conduct. As more people go online, the Net is helping to define global user communities for different products. Direct contact with subjects in different countries over the Web may shrink the time and cost of conducting the research. The main methods of gathering research data over the Net are (1) e-mail based surveys, (2) Web site surveys, (3) online discussion groups, and (4) computer-assisted interviewing. With only a small portion of the world's population online, these methods are largely untried and untested. But online market studies could eventually help replace onsite interviewing and mail surveys for certain types of studies. Innovations in Net-based research need to be closely monitored. They have the potential to create major advances in international marketing research.

Many US firms are latecomers to doing business globally. With the munificence of the US market, most have not had to venture into foreign markets. Thus, few American managers have extensive international business experience. Many are unaware of the differences overseas. They may be surprised by how little is known about many foreign markets and how little has been written about international marketing research. Managers need to be educated about these differences as well as the research methods that can be used to uncover them. Ultimately, global business success depends on a foundation of valid foreign market information.

References and selected bibliography

Axtell, R. E. 1993. *Do's and taboos around the world.* 3rd ed. New York: Wiley.

Bartlett, C. A., and S. Ghoshal. 1989. *Managing across borders: The transnational solution.* Boston: Harvard Business School Press.

Byfield, S., and L. Caller. 1997. Horses for courses: Stewarding brands across borders in times of rapid change. *Journal of the Market Research Society* 39/4: 589–601.

Ceteora, P. R., and J. L. Graham. 1999. *International Marketing.* 10th ed. New York: Irwin/McGraw-Hill.

Childs, R. 1996. Buying international research. *Journal of the Market Research Society* 38/1: 63–66.

Craig, C. S., and S. P. Douglas. 2000. *International Marketing Research.* 2nd ed. New York: Wiley.

Crampton, M. F. 1996. Where does your ad work? *Journal of the Market Research Society* 38/1: 35–53.

Frevert, B. 2000. Is global research different? *Marketing Research* 12/1: 49–51.

Goodwin, T. 1999. Measuring the effectiveness of online marketing. *Journal of the Market Research Society* 41/4: 403–406.

Iyer, R. 1997. A look at the Indian market research industry. *Quirk's Marketing Research Review* (November): 22–26.

Jeffries-Fox, B. C. 1995. Dance with me: US firms need good international partners to keep in step. *Marketing Research* 7/2: 15–18.

Keillor, B., D. Owens, and C. Pettijohn. 2001. A cross-cultural/ cross-national study of influencing factors and socially desirable response biases. *International Journal of Market Research* 43/1: 63–84.

Kent, R., and M. Lee. 1999. Using the Internet for market research: A study of private trading on the Internet. *Journal of the Market Research Society* 41/4: 377–385.

Lee, B., and A. Wong. 1996. An introduction to marketing research in China. *Quirk's Marketing Research Review* (November): 18–19, 37–38.

Leonidou, L. C., and N. Rossides. 1995. Marketing research in the Gulf States: A practical appraisal. *Journal of the Marketing Research Society* 37/4: 455–467.

Lewis, S., and M. Hathaway. 1998. International focus groups: Embrace the unpredictable. *Quirk's Marketing Research Review* (November): 36–41.

McIntosh, A. R., and R. J. Davies. 1996. The sampling of nondomestic populations. *Journal of the Market Research Society* 38/4: 431–446.

McKie, A. 1996. International research in a relative world. *Journal of the Market Research Society* 38/1: 7–12.

Meier, G. M. 1998. *The international environment of business.* New York: Oxford University Press.

Moseley, D. 1996. Information needs for market entry. *Journal of the Market Research Society* 38/1: 13–18.

Mytton, G. 1996. Research in new fields. *Journal of the Market Research Society* 38/1: 19–33.

Pawle, J. 1999. Mining the international consumer. *Journal of the Market Research Society* 41/1: 19–32.

Prahalad, C. K., and K. Lieberthal. 1998. The end of corporate imperialism. *Harvard Business Review* 76/4 (July–August): 69–79.

Ricks, D. A. 1983. *Big business blunders: Mistakes in multinational marketing.* Homewood, IL: Dow Jones Irwin.

Robinson, C. 1996. Asian culture: The marketing consequences. *Journal of the Market Research Society* 38/1: 55–62.

Root, F. R. 1994. *Entry strategies for international markets.* Rev. ed. New York: Lexington.

Rydholm, J. 1996. Leaping the barriers of time and distance. *Quirk's Marketing Research Review* (November): 10–11, 42–45.

Soruco, G. R., and T. P. Meyer. 1993. The mobile Hispanic market: New challenges in the 90s. *Marketing Research* 5/1: 6–11.

Valentine, C. F. 1988. *The Arthur Young international business guide.* New York: Wiley.

Wilsden, M. 1996. Getting it done properly: The role of the coordinator in multicountry research. *Journal of the Market Research Society* 38/1: 67–71.

Zikmund, W. 2000. *Exploring marketing research.* 6th ed. Orlando, FL: Dryden Press.

MARKETING

Small Packets, Big Business

To sell to rural India, global giants are thinking small—offering Indians an array of new products in sample sizes

By Rasul Bailay/HAPUR, INDIA

ON A COLD WINTER afternoon in this dusty village, Rashmi Chaudhury walks up to a small roadside shop for her weekly indulgence: a tiny plastic packet of Head & Shoulders shampoo. The 32-year-old housewife gives the shopkeeper a two-rupee (eight U.S. cents) coin and says she has no desire for anything bigger. "We shampoo our hair once a week," she explains.

People like Chaudhury form the bulk of the clientele at Arora Provisional Store in Hapur, about 60 kilometres east of New Delhi, where small, sample-size packets of produce—from tobacco, shampoo and ketchup to detergent powder and jam—dangle from the store's roof.

Marketers have long known that India is a big country where it pays to think small—very small. Now, global giants like Amway, Gillette and Coca-Cola are using the formula to change consumer behavior and jump-start sales of products that many Indians have never tried before. In tiny pillow-like plastic packets that contain about 20 millilitres of product, they're selling shaving gel, dishwashing liquid and toothpaste, to name just a few items.

The secret of sachets is simple: They answer the needs of low-income consumers who can't afford—and aren't used to—buying larger sizes. In India, where annual per-capita income is just $450, a bottle of shampoo is beyond the reach of many customers. People receive their wages "daily or weekly and they calibrate their purchases based on their incomes," says Vijay Bhat, regional strategy director for advertising firm Ogilvy & Mather in Hong Kong. That means buying a single cigarette instead of a pack, one egg instead of a dozen, or a sachet of shampoo instead of a bottle.

Nano-marketing hit the big time in India in the late 1980s when Hindustan Lever, the Indian arm of Anglo-Dutch conglomerate Unilever, followed the example of local firms by launching its own brand of shampoo in sachets. In the past two years, a clutch of consumer-goods companies have followed in its footsteps with a new selection of goods in small packets. Amway introduced shampoo, body lotion, car wash and dishwashing liquid.

Gillette tried to woo Indian men away from soap and water with shaving gel. And Coca-Cola and Kraft Foods offered villagers powdered drinks in an effort to woo them from the traditional refreshment, a local lemon-water drink known as *nimbu pani*.

Some companies are going a step further in their efforts to use sachets to switch consumer behaviour. Products like perfume, for example, are widely perceived as a luxury item and therefore are used by less than 1% of the population. Earlier this year, however, CavinKare, a consumer-goods firm in Madras, set out to alter that with the launch of its Spinz brand of perfume in 0.4-millilitre sachets selling for just two rupees.

"We looked at how we can get more people to use perfume at a price they wouldn't mind trying out," says S. Jagdish of CavinKare. "We knew that to break into this category we needed to change the rules of the game." The company says the response has been good, but declined to give sales figures.

When Hindustan Lever launched its sachets of shampoo in the late 1980s, the volume of shampoo sold this way soon outsold that in bottles. This prompted the company to market toothpaste in the same fashion, winning over millions of villagers who traditionally use branches of the Indian *neem* tree to clean their teeth. Today, Hindustan Lever says its shampoo sachets are sold in around 400,000 of India's 600,000 villages. Now there is hardly any shampoo brand in India that is not available in sachets. According to a study last year by market-research company ACNielsen, in 2001 rural Indians bought 90% of their shampoo in sachet form.

LITTLE TRICKS TO REACH THE MASSES

"The success of the sachet concept in shampoo egged marketers on to try it out in other categories," says Neerja Wable, senior vice-president at the Indian Market Research Bureau in New Delhi. "You name a product and it is available in sachets."

Today, the trickle of sachets has turned into a flood. Small packets of detergent powder, tomato paste, jam, shaving lotion, mosquito repellent and medicines, among other products, dangle from ramshackle shops in rural India and beyond. In Hapur, the Arora Provisional Store stocks only about 100 bottles of shampoo, but its stockpile of shampoo in sachets runs into thousands. "Most of my customers are 'earn today, spend today' kind of people," explains Pankaj Arora, the store's 24-year-old owner.

Companies have realized that the best way to reach those customers—part of the huge, albeit not-so-affluent rural market—is to furnish products in small quantities at rock-bottom prices. "The real market in India is in the rural areas," says Nantoo Banerjee, a spokeswoman for Coca-Cola India. "If you can crack it, there is tremendous potential."

With that in mind, Coca-Cola launched its Sunfill powdered drink in 2001 in 25-gram sachets to target rural consumers.

Kraft Foods, a unit of Philip Morris Co., had already introduced its Tang powdered drink in sachets the same year.

"Sachets are aimed at breaking the price barrier for rural people as Indians are very price sensitive," says Hemendra Mathur, a manager at New Delhi-based market-research firm KSA Technopak. "With sachets, they are converting nonusers into users."

Packaging costs are higher for sachets but companies are able to keep the price down, thanks partly to lower government duties on small packs. "It's actually cheaper for a consumer in some cases to buy many sachets instead of a bottle," says Rahul Malhotra, country marketing manager for Procter & Gamble India. Indeed: a 100-millilitre of Pantene shampoo sells for 61 rupees while an equal amount in sachets costs around 40 rupees. Small really is beautiful.

Time for Marketers to Grow Up?

By CRIS PRYSTAY and SARAH ELLISON

IF DEMOGRAPHY is destiny, then consumer products companies are facing an aging future. As the world's birthrates slow and its population ages, multinational companies are being forced to reconsider strategies for selling diapers, arthritis medicine and everything in between.

But some remain reluctant to let go of their fixation on youth. Lois Coleman, who organizes focus-groups for consumer companies, says she is almost never asked to study people over age 50. Even for the bran flakes she helped launch in Mexico, she was asked to talk to consumers under 35. "It was a bran cereal," she says, pausing. "Now who do you think really needed that product—the kids in their 20s?"

For now, many companies find themselves straddling a widening gap between the relatively young populations of developing countries and the aging populations of the developed world—and trying to find growth opportunities in both.

"For decades, our industry took for granted that population growth in the developed countries would deliver a substantial part of the sales growth," said A.G. Lafley, chief executive of **Procter & Gamble** Co., at a recent conference on laundry detergent. "Few imagined the day would come when we would see zero population growth—let alone decline—in major markets. Yet that is what we are facing today."

Growth has to come from developing markets, Mr. Lafley says—so, the company built a low-cost diaper factory in Vietnam, where it sells diapers for 15-cents a piece, less expensive than in the West. Population growth in other "young" countries such as Mexico and Brazil are a critical source of sales growth, providing the extra bodies to buy more toothpaste and laundry detergent and other staples. But pricing is an issue, too: On average, prices of laundry products in developing countries can be half or even less than half the price in developed markets, P&G says.

Meanwhile, P&G has focused on one of the clear advantages of selling in developed markets: affluent, albeit aging, con-

sumers. In the fall, P&G launched a toothpaste for aging women, called "Rejuvenating Effects" in the U.S. One of P&G's latest blockbuster beauty products is its Olay anti-aging cream, which it rolled out first in Western Europe and the U.S. The best opportunities for its $500 million osteoporosis drug, Actonel, are (in descending order) Japan, Italy, France, the rest of Western Europe and then the U.S.

Some big multinationals are still clinging to dated ideas about the demographic makeup of new markets. "There is a big gap between the realities of demographics and the way advertisers approach it," says Mike Townsin, regional director of MediaCom Asia Pacific, the media planning and research arm of ad agency Grey Worldwide.

In Asia, for example, the young adults that attracted multinational marketers in the 1980s now have grown up and become so-called empty-nesters—that is, people from the age of 40 to 59 whose youngest child is nearing financial independence, according to research company Asian Demographics Ltd., of Auckland, New Zealand. At the peak of their careers and newly dependent-free, empty-nesters are a fast-growing group in powerful economies such as Hong Kong, Singapore, Korea and Taiwan. Their numbers are forecast to grow by 30% to 10.9 million in the next decade. Meanwhile, the youth market will shrink by 10% to 11.4 million in the same decade, according to the research company.

Yet multinationals are, for the most part, still obsessed with romancing Asia's youth. Coca-Cola Japan, for example, isn't yet targeting Baby Boomers, says a spokesman. The company has been making canned teas and coffees for years but hasn't yet created ads pitching them to seniors.

Motorola Inc. makes phones with features that aging consumers like, such as a zoom function to bump up the font size on the tiny screen and even internal speakers that can connect with hearing aids. But still the company hasn't developed ad campaigns highlighting these features or targeting seniors. "Our strategic direction is to focus on the youth," says Mabel Tay, Motorola's director of brand and consumer communications for Asia Pacific.

Half of Japan's population will be over 50 by 2025, yet multinationals keep romancing Asia's youth.

In Japan, several domestic companies have already begun to get with the program, reorienting their marketing to the senior set. They have little choice: Half of Japan's population will be over 50 by 2025, according to the U.S. Census Bureau's International Database on Aging. In the U.S., in comparison, 36% of the population will be over 50 by that time.

Toymaker Takara Co. Ltd. is trying to gain a foothold in the growing adult market with creations including a two-seater mini electric car, home karaoke systems and robots that open beer cans. Two years ago, Meiji Dairies Corp., which had long pitched its yogurts to children and health-conscious young adults, started making a yogurt for people over 40, called LG21. The product contains a bacteria that kills off another type of bacteria that many older Japanese carry and that is believed to cause stomach ulcers and even cancer. The company forecasts LG21 sales will make up 25% of its total expected yogurt sales for the year ending March 31, 2003. Says Seichi Sato, manager of Meiji's yogurt-marketing department: "The advantage of the [older] market is there is virtually no competitors."

Yamaha Corp. recognized Japan's ranks of teenagers had thinned over the past decade. Two years ago, the company created an easy-to-play electronic guitar for Baby Boomers who grew up on the Beatles and Japanese folk rock and always wanted to play.

"The population of younger people is decreasing in Japan, and at the same time there's many entertainment products, like Playstation and Nintendo, competing for their interest," says Yasuhiko Asahi, of Yamaha's EZ EG Guitar product. "We're now looking at people 50 years old and up. They'll retire in the near future, and generally have more money and more time."

Of course, there are many good reasons why global marketers have learned to shy away from older consumers, in Asia and other places. Young adults do spend more freely than older adults: They are quicker to pick up on new technologies, and quicker to open their wallets. And children exert a strong influence over their parents' spending.

Young people "don't hesitate to buy new products compared to elderly people, who take time to consider and closely examine any new purchase," says Setsuo Sakamoto, executive director of Japanese ad agency Hakuhodo Inc.'s "elder business development unit."

Pitching products to Asia's elders means learning more about the cultural and historical nuances shaping their values, says Richard Pinder, regional managing director at ad agency Leo Burnett. Asia's middle class youth, on the other hand, all speak MTV. "They are easier to understand," says Mr. Pinder. "They're more willing to spend. They're more Western."

Still, he notes, sooner or later the demographic reality will force a change. "It's going to become a major issue" he says.

Cracking China's Market

Adapting to Chinese Customs, Cultural Changes, Companies From U.S., Europe Find Profit

By LESLIE CHANG And PETER WONACOTT

Beijing

LONG-HELD perception: China is a perpetual market of tomorrow, sucking money from foreign companies tantalized by visions of a billion new consumers, even as hope of profit recedes year by year.

Dawning reality; China has turned into a profitable market for foreigners in relatively short order.

Capitalizing on dramatic changes that include the emergence of urban consumers, more open local governments, the spread of modern retail outlets and the entrepreneurialism of the Chinese, a critical mass of foreign companies are now making money in China. According to an August report by the American Chamber of Commerce, 64% of about 200 companies surveyed in China say they are profitable.

As multinational

consumer-products companies such as Coca-Cola, Eastman Kodak and Motorola make further inroads—and more money—in a rapidly changing China, their logos are becoming an integral part of the nation's landscape

China is now **Eastman Kodak** Co.'s second-biggest film market after the U.S., and sales here are growing faster than in any other major market, the film firm says. Food conglomerate **Groupe Danone** SA of France has in the past six years built a $1.2 billion business in China that is profitable in all its divisions. Germany's **Siemens** AG, selling everything from washing machines to high-speed railways, saw double-digit profit growth last year in China, now its No. 3 market after the U.S. and Germany. **Procter & Gamble** Co. has invested $1 billion in China and says its operation here is profitable. The KFC restaurant chain, owned by **Yum Brands** Inc., opens a new store every other day in China, all funded by its Chinese prof-

its, "China is an absolute gold mine for us," Yum's chief executive David Novak told analysts recently.

China continues to be one of the most challenging markets around owing to brutal price wars, backstabbing business partners, widespread counterfeiting and a slow-moving judicial system. But here is how some of the most successful players in China are turning a profit:

Kodak: Just $12,000 to Run an Outlet

Under a tropical evening sky in Xiamen, executives from Eastman Kodak pile out of a minibus to be greeted by hundreds of cheering workers. They climb to a stage festooned to red-and-gold Kodak colors, and a worker reads a poem commemorating production of the 20-millionth Kodak disposable camera in this seaside city. "Kodak, I love you," he gushes.

Kodak is loving China back. "There were a lot of people that were burned and hurt and called China a shattered dream," says one of the executives, Ying Yeh, a vice president for Kodak. "But I never had any doubt."

Kodak, which is based in Rochester, N.Y., has nearly 8,000 photo stores across China, one of the country's largest retail networks in any sector. The company taps the desire of many Chinese to run their own businesses while helping them negotiate the ins and outs of setting up shop on their own. Because of China's vast size, foreign companies seeking national reach must rely to an unusual extent on such a far-flung network of people, then find ways to tie their interests to the company's own.

One Kodak campaign, "99,000 Will Make You a Boss," offered all the necessary photo-development equipment, training, and a store license for the equivalent of a one-time fee of 99,000 yuan, less than $12,000. Kodak negotiated a deal with the Bank of China and other big banks to arrange financing for individual operators lacking capital. As its numbers of distributors and outlets boomed, Kodak factories have fed these "mini-bosses" with competitively priced cameras and film. That's thanks to a big

Opening Doors for Big Business

Multinational companies are expanding their operations in China and turning profits. Some examples:

COMPANY	SCALE OF OPERATIONS	EMPLOYEES	TOTAL INVESTMENT	PROFIT DETAILS
Coca-Cola	31 bottling plants with three joint-venture partners and two concentrate plants	20,000	$1.1 billion	Profitable for eight years
Danone	More than 50 manufacturing plants for biscuits, beverages and dairy products	25,000	NA	Operating profit margins higher than the company's global average, amounting to at least $140 million in 2001
Kodak	Five manufacturing plants for cameras, chemicals and film and more than 8,000 outlets	5,000	$1.2 billion	Company says it's profitable
Motorola	Two manufacturing plants for mobile-phone handsets, cellular networks and semiconductors	12,000	$3.4 billion at end of 2001	Company says it's profitable
Procter & Gamble	Five plants for food, personal care and household consumer goods	4,000	$1 billion	Company says it's profitable
Siemens	40 companies with businesses including telecommunications, machine automation, power, transport and home appliances	21,000	More than $610 million	Profit grew at double-digit rates in 2002
Yum Brands	Close to 800 KFC restaurants and 100 Pizza Hut restaurants	40,000 to 50,000	More than $400 million	China is expected to account for 29% of international profits for 2002

Source: The companies

bet Kodak made on manufacturing in China in 1998, when it picked up three debt-laden state firms and many of their workers for over $1 billion. In return, Beijing barred new foreign-invested film factories for four years.

The gamble helped Kodak, a distant fourth when it arrived in China in 1994, leapfrog rivals including Japan's **Fuji Photo Film** Co., which relies on imports to stock its stores. Today, Fuji's market share has shrunk to 25% compared with Kodak's 63%.

Kodak is now expanding in China's poorer west. In a country where fashion and new lifestyles spread at warp speed, many are buying cameras for a first time to record the change. Says Paul Walrath, a plant manager in Xiamen and a 26-year Kodak veteran, "We're counting on great performance in China to drive the company where we want to go."

Danone: Master of Piggybacking

Like Kodak, France's Danone was a relative latecomer when it started building its China business around 1996. It decided to piggyback off the successes of domestic brands rather than to build all its businesses from scratch, in 1996 buying a controlling stake in Hangzhou Wahaha Group Co., an enterprising maker of vitamin-enriched milk drinks targeted at children.

Danone embarked on a massive expansion for Wahaha—building multiple plants across the country, backed by a huge advertising campaign—that pushed annual sales from 800 million bottles when it bought the company to four billion bottles within two years. It then

quickly leveraged that scale, distribution network and brand-name recognition into a new business: bottled water, for China's increasingly health-conscious population. Through the same obsessive focus on scale and speed, Danone has built Wahaha into China's biggest water company—and made China into Danone's biggest water market, with $908 million in revenue in 2001.

In launching a new drink, Danone expects that prices will collapse by 50% within three years, thanks to local competition. Only through investing heavily up-front is it possible to achieve economies of scale and, hence, profitability. "You need to recover your investment before the price wars start," says Simon Israel, Danone's Asia-Pacific chairman. "I've never seen anything move so fast as it does in China."

Rare for multinationals, Danone acquires Chinese companies but continues to sell their products under their own brands. The strategy has smoothed the way for a steady diet of acquisitions and curried favor with Chinese executives and officials, who are loath to see national brands go under.

Today, 80% of Danone's sales here are under Chinese brands. The company has so played down its multinational origins that it was asked by the government to help Wahaha manufacture a "domestic" cola to take on Coke and Pepsi. Thus did Danone, which does not sell soft drinks anywhere else in the world, become the parent of Future Cola, which holds the No. 3 spot in China and is known as "the Chinese people's own cola."

The moves have handed Danone dominance despite its late start. The company had $1.2 billion in sales here in

2001 and is one of China's largest food and beverage concerns. Danone has more than 50 plants and 25,000 employees around the country, all built up in the past six years.

Coca-Cola Co. which has seen eight straight years of profit in China, says sales are growing faster here than anywhere in the world. The Atlanta-based company already reaches 600 million consumers in China's large and medium-size cities, but its latest drive focuses on reaching the other half.

A survey the company conducted in Yunnan, a largely rural province in the southwest, revealed that most consumer offerings, from ice cream to drinks, cost between six cents and 36 cents, which means a 30-cent can of Coke was too expensive for many. Coke's solution: ramp up its business in returnable bottles, in which a customer drinks a Coke on the premises of a shop or restaurant. The business, which drives down costs because bottles and crates can be reused many times, brings the price of a Coke servicing down to a single yuan—about 12 cents.

"We're looking for this to be a solution for our rural markets," says Nick Moore, region manager for the North and Southwest China Region.

Such minute price distinctions are crucial in China. At an Internet cafe in Tangshan, where customers can surf the Web for an hour for a mere 24 cents, 2,000 cases of Coke sold last year, compared with 300 cases in 2001, before Coke launched its cheaper drinks in returnable bottles. "Customers always want the cheapest thing to drink," says the cafe's owner. "Now, the Coke is the same price as the water."

Yum Brands: Localize, Localize

When KFC set up its first China store in 1987, the venture was seen as so politically sensitive that the site required the approval of the Beijing mayor, and foreign novelty was a big part of its appeal. Recently, it took Yum Brands only a day to get most of the approvals it needed to set up a new Pizza Hut restaurant in the central city of Zhengzhou.

Globalization is taking hold in China faster than anyone expected, and fast food has become part of the Chinese landscape. Catering to national tastes, KFC offers soup, rice and Chinese breakfast porridge. It does its own tests and product launches with minimal input from the home office in Louisville, Ky. "We're free to create our own products. Our company is not a company that micromanages from a distance," says Sam Su, president of Greater China for Yum Restaurants China.

KFC now has about 800 restaurants here and plans to open 200 a year for some time to come, and China is the company's biggest source of profit after the U.S.

Article 43

The Lure of Global Branding

Brand builders everywhere think they want global brands.
But global brand leadership, not global brands, should be the priority.
Successful companies follow four principles to meet that goal.

by David A. Aaker and Erich Joachimsthaler

AS MORE AND MORE companies come to view the entire world as their market, brand builders look with envy upon those that appear to have created global brands—brands whose positioning, advertising strategy, personality, look, and feel are in most respects the same from one country to another. It's easy to understand why. Even though most global brands are not absolutely identical from one country to another—Visa changes its logo in some countries; Heineken means something different in the Netherlands than it does abroad—companies whose brands have become more global reap some clear benefits.

Consolidating all advertising into one agency and developing a global theme can cause problems that outweigh any advantages.

Consider for a moment the economies of scale enjoyed by IBM. It costs IBM much less to create a single global advertising campaign than it would to create separate campaigns for dozens of markets. And because IBM uses only one agency for all its global advertising, it carries a lot of clout with the agency and can get the most talented people working on its behalf. A global brand also benefits from being driven by a single strategy. Visa's unvarying "worldwide acceptance" position, for example, is much easier for the company to manage than dozens of country-specific strategies.

Attracted by such high-profile examples of success, many companies are tempted to try to globalize their own brands. The problem is, that goal is often unrealistic. Consolidating all advertising into one agency and developing a

global advertising theme—often the cornerstone of the effort—can cause problems that outweigh any advantages. And edicts from on high—"Henceforth, use only brand-building programs that can be applied across countries"—can prove ineffective or even destructive. Managers who stampede blindly toward creating a global brand without considering whether such a move fits well with their company or their markets risk falling over a cliff. There are several reasons for that.

First, economies of scale may prove elusive. It is sometimes cheaper and more effective for companies to create ads locally than to import ads and then adapt them for each market. Moreover, cultural differences may make it hard to pull off a global campaign: even the best agency may have trouble executing it well in all countries. Finally, the potential cost savings from "media spillover"—in which, for example, people in France view German television ads—have been exaggerated. Language barriers and cultural differences have made realizing such benefits difficult for most companies.

Second, forming a successful global brand team can prove difficult. Developing a superior brand strategy for one country is challenging enough; creating one that can be applied worldwide can be daunting (assuming one even exists). Teams face several stumbling blocks: they need to gather and understand a great deal of information; they must be extremely creative; and they need to anticipate a host of challenges in execution. Relatively few teams will be able to meet all those challenges.

Third, global brands can't just be imposed on all markets. For examples, a brand's image may not be the same throughout the world. Honda means quality and reliability in the United States, but in Japan, where quality is a given for most cars, Honda represents speed, youth, and energy. And consider market position. In Britain, where Ford is number one, the company positioned its Galaxy minivan as the luxurious "nonvan" in order to appeal not only to soccer moms but also to executives. But in Germany, where Volkswagen rules, Ford had to position the Galaxy as "the clever alternative." Similarly, Cadbury in the United Kingdom and Milka in Germany have preempted the associations that connect milk with chocolate; thus neither company could implement a global positioning strategy.

For all those reasons, taking a more nuanced approach is the better course of action. Developing global brands should not be the priority. Instead, companies should work on creating strong brands in all markets through global brand leadership.

Global brand leadership means using organizational structures, processes, and cultures to allocate brand-building resources globally, to create global synergies, and to develop a global brand strategy that coordinates and leverages country brand strategies. That is, of course, easier said than done. For example, companies tend to give the bulk of their brand-building attention to countries with large sales—at the expense of emerging markets that may represent big opportunities. But some companies have successfully engaged in global brand management. To find out how, we interviewed executives from 35 companies in the United States, Europe, and Japan that have successfully developed strong brands across countries. (About half the executives were from companies that made frequently purchased consumer products; the rest represented durables, high-tech products, and service brands.)

Four common ideas about effective brand leadership emerged from those interviews. Companies must:

- stimulate the sharing of insights and best practices across countries;
- support a common global brand-planning process;
- assign managerial responsibility for brands in order to create cross-country synergies and to fight local bias; and
- execute brilliant brand-building strategies.

Sharing Insights and Best Practices

A companywide communication system is the most basic element of global brand leadership. Managers from country to country need to be able to find out about programs that have worked or failed elsewhere; they also need a way to easily give and receive knowledge about customers—knowledge that will vary from one market to another.

Creating such a system is harder than it sounds. Busy people usually have little motivation to take the time to explain why efforts have been successful or ineffective; furthermore, they'd rather not give out information that may leave them exposed to criticism. Another problem is one that everyone in business faces today: information overload. And a feeling of "it won't work here" often pervades companies that attempt to encourage the sharing of market knowledge.

To overcome those problems, companies must nurture and support a culture in which best practices are freely communicated. In addition, people and procedures must come together to create a rich base of knowledge that is relevant and easy to access. Offering incentives is one way to get people to share what they know. American Management Systems, for example, keeps track of the employees who post insights and best practices and rewards them during annual performance reviews.

Regular meetings can be an effective way of communicating insights and best practices. Frito-Lay, for example, sponsors a "market university" roughly three times a year in which 35 or so marketing directors and general managers from around the world meet in Dallas for a week. The university gets people to think about brand leadership concepts, helps people overcome the mind-set of "I am different—global programs won't work in my market," and creates a group of people around the world who believe in and understand brands and brand strategy. During the week, country managers present case studies on packaging, advertising, and promotions that were tested in one country and then successfully applied in another. The case studies demonstrate that practices can be transferred even when a local marketing team is skeptical.

Formal meetings are useful, but true learning takes place during informal conversations and gatherings. And the personal relationships that people establish during those events are often more important than the information they share. Personal ties lead to meaningful exchanges down the road that can foster brand-building programs.

In addition to staging meetings, companies are increasingly using intranets to communicate insights and best practices. (Sharing such information by e-mail isn't as effective—there is simply too much e-mail clutter. E-mail is useful, however, for conveying breaking news about competitors or new technology.) The key is to have a team create a knowledge bank on an intranet that is valuable and accessible to those who need it. Mobil, for example, uses a set of best-practice networks to do just that. The networks connect people in the company (and sometimes from partner organizations) who are experts on, for example, new product introduction, brand architecture, and retail-site presentation. Each network has a senior management sponsor and a leader who actively solicits postings from the experts. The leader ensures that the information is formatted, organized, and posted on an easy-to-use intranet site.

Field visits are another useful way to learn about best practices. Honda sends teams to "live with best practices" and to learn how they work. In some companies, the CEO travels to different markets in order to energize the country teams and to see best practices in action.

Procter & Gamble uses worldwide strategic-planning groups of three to 20 people for each category to encourage and support global strategies. The teams have several tasks. They mine local knowledge about markets and disseminate that information globally. They gather data about effective country-specific marketing efforts and encourage testing elsewhere. They create global manufacturing sourcing strategies. And they develop policies that dictate which aspects of the brand strategy must be followed everywhere and which ones are up to country management.

Who's Responsible for the Brand?

Business Management Team

Brand Champion

Global Brand Team

Global Brand Manager

Deciding who has ultimate responsibility for global brands is the first step toward going global and ensuring buy-in among country teams. To fight local bias and exploit cross-country synergies, a company must assign managerial responsibility for its brands. Depending on the company's makeup, responsibility for global brand leadership can follow one of four possible configurations: business management team, brand champion, global brand manager, and global brand team. The first two are led by senior executives; the latter two by middle managers.

Another way that companies can communicate information about their brands is by sharing research. Ford operates very differently from country to country in Europe, but its businesses share research methods and findings. Ford UK, for example, which is very skilled at doing direct mail and research on segmentation, makes its technology and research methods available to other countries. That's especially important for businesses in small markets that are short on budget and staff.

Supporting Global Brand Planning

Two years ago, the newly appointed global brand manager of a prominent packaged-goods marketer organized a brand strategy review. He found that all the country brand managers used their own vocabularies and strategy templates and had their own strategies. The resulting mess had undoubtedly contributed to inferior marketing and weakened brands. Another packaged-goods company tried to avoid that problem by developing a global planning system. Brand managers weren't given incentives or trained

properly to use the system, however, and the result was inconsistent, half-hearted efforts at planning.

Companies that practice global brand management use a planning process that is consistent across markets and products—a brand presentation looks and sounds the same whether it's delivered in Singapore, Spain, or Sweden, and whether it's for PCs or printers. It shares the same well-defined vocabulary, strategic analysis inputs (such as competitor positions and strategies), brand strategy model, and outputs (such as brand-building programs).

There is no one accepted process model, but all models have two starting points: it must be clear which person or group is responsible for the brand and the brand strategy, and a process template must exist. The completed template should specify such aspects of a strategy as the target segment, the brand identity or vision, brand equity goals and measures, and brand-building programs that will be used within and outside the company. Although various process models can work, observations of effective programs suggest five guidelines.

First, the process should include an analysis of customers, competitors, and the brand. Analysis of customers must go beyond quantitative market research data; managers need to understand the brand associations that resonate with people. Analysis of competitors is necessary to differentiate the brand and to ensure that its communication program—which may include sponsorship, promotion, and advertising—doesn't simply copy what other companies are doing. And an audit of the brand itself involves an examination of its heritage, image, strengths, and problems, as well as the company's vision for it. The brand needs to reflect that vision to avoid making empty promises.

Second, the process should avoid a fixation on product attributes. A narrow focus on attributes leads to short-lived, easily copied advantages and to shallow customer relationships. Most strong brands go beyond functional benefits; despite what customers might say, a brand can also deliver emotional benefits and help people express themselves. A litmus test of whether a company really understands its brands is whether it incorporates the following elements into the brand strategy: brand personality (how the brand would be described if it were a person), user imagery (how the brand's typical user is perceived), intangibles that are associated with the company (its perceived innovativeness or reputation for quality, for example), and symbols associated with the brand, such as Virgin's Branson, the Coke bottle, or the Harley eagle. A simple three-word phrase or a brief list of product attributes cannot adequately represent a strong brand.

Third, the process must include programs to communicate the brand's identity (what the brand should stand for) to employees and company partners. Without clarity and enthusiasm internally about the associations the brand aspires to develop, brand building has no chance. A brand manual often plays a key role. Unilever has a detailed manual on its most global brand, Lipton Tea, that puts the answer to any question about its brand identity (What does the brand stand for? What are the timeless elements of the brand? What brand-building programs are off target?) at the fingertips of all employees. Other companies use workshops (Nestlé), newsletters (Hewlett-Packard), books (Volvo), and videos (the Limited) to communicate brand identity. To engage people in this process, Mobil asked employees to nominate recent programs or actions that best reflected the core elements of the Mobil brand—leadership, partnership, and trust. The employees with the best nominations were honored guests at a car race sponsored by the company.

Fourth, the process must include brand equity measurement and goals. Without measurement, brand building is often just talk; yet surprisingly few companies have systems that track brand equity. Pepsi is an exception. In the mid-1990s, Pepsi introduced a system based on what it calls a "marketplace P&L." The P&L measures brand equity by tracking the results of blind taste tests, the extent of a product's distribution, and the results of customer opinion surveys about the brand. In the beginning, country managers were strongly encouraged—but not required—to use the system. But the value of the marketplace P&L soon become clear, as country managers compared results at meetings and used the shared information to improve their brand-building efforts. In 1998, CEO Roger Enrico made the system mandatory—a dramatic indication of its value given Pepsi's decentralized culture and the home office's general reluctance to impose companywide rules.

Finally, the process must include a mechanism that ties global brand strategies to country brand strategies. Sony and Mobil, among others, use a top-down approach. They begin with a global brand strategy; country strategies follow from it. A country brand strategy might augment the global strategy by adding elements to modify the brand's identity. For example, if the manager of a Mobil fuel brand in Brazil wants to emphasize that the brand gives an honest gallon (because other brands of fuel in Brazil are not considered reliable in their measurements), he would add "honest measures" to the country brand identity. For example, although the term "leadership" may mean "technology leadership" in most countries, the strategist may change it to mean "market leadership" in his or her market. In the top-down approach, the country brand team has the burden of justifying any departures from the global brand strategy.

In the bottom-up approach, the global brand strategy is built from the country brand strategies. Country strategies are grouped by similarities. A grouping might, for example, be made on the basis of market maturity (underdeveloped, emerging, or developed) or competitive context (whether the brand is a leader or a challenger). While the brand strategy for these groupings will differ, a global brand strategy should also be able to identify common elements. Over time, the number of distinct strategies will usually fall as experiences and best practices are shared. As the number shrinks, the company can capture synergies. Mercedes, for example, uses one advertising agency to create a menu of five campaigns. Brand managers in different countries can then pick the most suitable campaign for their market.

Assigning Responsibility

Local managers often believe that their situation is unique—and therefore, that insights and best practices from other countries can't be applied to their markets. Their belief is based in part on justifiable confidence in their knowledge of the country, the competitive milieu, and the consumers. Any suggestion that such confidence is misplaced can feel threatening. Moreover, people are comfortable with strategies that have already proven effective. The local brand managers may fear that they will be coerced or enticed into following a strategy that doesn't measure up to their current efforts.

Most companies today have a decentralized culture and structure. They find it difficult, therefore, to persuade country teams to quickly and voluntarily accept and implement a global best practice. To ensure that local teams overcome such reluctance, an individual or group must be in charge of the global brand. Our research suggests that responsibility for global brand leadership can follow four possible configurations: business management team, brand champion, global brand manager, and global brand team. The first two are led by senior executives; the latter two by middle managers.

Business Management Team. This approach is most suitable when the company's top managers are marketing or branding people who regard brands as the key asset to their business. P&G fits that description. Each of its 11 product categories is run by a global category team. The teams consist of the four managers who have line responsibility for R&D, manufacturing, and marketing for the category within their region. Each team is chaired by an executive vice president who also has a second line job. For example, the head of health and beauty aids in Europe also chairs the hair care global category team. The teams meet five or six times a year.

Because the teams are made up of top-level line executives, there are no organizational barriers to carrying out decisions. At the country level, P&G's brand and advertising managers implement the strategy. Thus local bias cannot get in the way of the company's global brand leadership.

The 11 teams strive to create global brands without weakening brand strength locally. They define the identity and position of brands in their categories throughout the world. They encourage local markets to test and adopt brand-building programs that have been successful elsewhere. And they decide which brands will get new product advances. For example, Elastesse, the chemical compound that helps people eliminate "helmet head," was first added to the company's Pantene product line rather than one of its three sister brands.

Brand Champion. This is a senior executive, possibly the CEO, who serves as the brand's primary advocate and nurturer. The approach is particularly well suited to companies whose top executives have a passion and talent for brand strategy. Companies like Sony, Gap, Beiersdorf (Nivea), and Nestlé meet that description. Nestlé has a brand champion for each of its 12 corporate strategic brands. As is true for the leaders of P&G's business management teams, each brand champion at Nestlé has a second assignment. Thus the vice president for nutrition is the brand champion for Carnation, and the vice president for instant coffee is the brand champion for Taster's Choice (known as Nescafé outside the United States). At Nestlé, brand leadership is not just talk. The additional work that the brand champion takes on has resulted in a change in the company's performance-evaluation and compensation policies.

Most global brand managers have little authority and must create a strategy without the ability to mandate.

A brand champion approves all brand-stretching decisions (to put the Carnation label on a white milk chocolate bar, for example) and monitors the presentation of the brand worldwide. He or she must be familiar with local contexts and managers, identify insights and best practices, and propagate them through sometimes forceful suggestions. In some companies, such as Sony, the brand champion owns the country brand identities and positions and takes responsibility for ensuring that the country teams implement the brand strategy. A brand champion has credibility and respect not only because of organizational power but also because of a depth of experience, knowledge, and insight. A suggestion from a brand champion gets careful consideration.

P&G plans to evolve over the next decade toward a brand champion approach. It believes that it can achieve greater cooperation and create more global brands by concentrating authority and responsibility in the hands of high-level brand champions. At the moment, P&G regards only a handful of its 83 major brands as global.

Global Brand Manager. In many companies, particularly in the high-tech and service industries, top management lacks a branding or even marketing background. The branding expertise rests just below the top line managers. Such companies are often decentralized and have a powerful regional and country line-management system. Effective global brand managers are necessary in these cases to combat local bias and spur unified efforts across countries.

Some local brand managers have sign-off authority for certain marketing programs, but most have little authority. They must attempt to create a global brand strategy without the ability to mandate. There are five keys to success in these situations:

- Companies must have believers at the top; otherwise global brand managers will be preoccupied with convincing the executive suite that brands are worth supporting. If there are no believers, a brand manager can try to create them. The global brand manager for MasterCard did just that by convincing the organization to form a "miniboard" of six board members and nominating one to be its chair. That person became the brand's voice during board meetings.

- A global brand manager needs to either create a planning process or manage an existing one. To make the process effective, all country managers should use the same vocabulary, template, and planning cycle. This is the first step toward fighting local bias.

- A global brand manager should become a key part of the development, management, and operation of an internal brand communication system. By traveling to learn about customers, country managers, problems, and best practices, he or she will be able to maximize the opportunities for cooperation.

- In order to deal with savvy country brand specialists, global brand managers must have global experience, product background, energy, credibility, and people skills. Companies need a system to select, train, mentor, and reward prospects who can fill the role. At Haagen-Dazs, the global brand manager is also the brand manager for the United States, the lead market for its ice cream. The latter position gives the manager credibility because of the resources and knowledge base that come with it.

- Companies can signal the importance of the role through the title they give the manager. At IBM, global brand managers are called brand stewards, a title that reflects the goal of building and protecting brand equity. At Smirnoff, the global brand manager is given the title of president of the Pierre Smirnoff Company, suggesting how much the company values his position.

Global Brand Team. A global brand manager, acting alone, can be perceived as an outsider—just another corporate staff person contributing to overhead, creating forms, and calling meetings. Sometimes adding people to the mix—in the form of a global brand team—can solve this problem. With a team working on the issue, it becomes easier to convince country brand managers of the value of global brand management.

Global brand teams typically consist of brand representatives from different parts of the world, from different stages of brand development, and from different competitive contexts. Functional areas such as advertising, market research, sponsorship, and promotions may also be represented. The keys to success with these teams are similar to those for the global brand manager.

One problem with a global brand team (unless it is lead by a global brand manager) is that no one person ultimately owns the brand globally. Thus no one is responsible for implementing global branding decisions. In addition, team members may be diverted from their task by the pressures of their primary jobs. And the team may lack the authority and focus needed to make sure that their recommendations are actually implemented at the country level. Mobil solves that problem in part by creating "action teams" made up of people from several countries to oversee the implementation.

Some aspects of the brand's management will be firm, but others will be adaptable or discretionary.

Some companies partition the global brand manager or team across business units or segments. For example, Mobil has separate global brand teams for the passenger car lubricant business, the commercial lubricants business, and the fuel business because the brand is fundamentally different in each. A global brand council then coordinates those segments by reconciling the different identities and looking for ways to create brand synergy.

And consider how DuPont handles its Lycra brand. The 35-year-old synthetic is known worldwide for the flexibility and comfort it lends to clothing; its identity is embodied in the global tagline "Nothing moves like Lycra." The problem for Lycra is that is has a variety of applications—it can be used, for example, in swimsuits, in running shorts, and in women's fashions. Each application requires its own brand positioning. DuPont solves the problem by delegating responsibility for each application to managers in a country where that application is strongest. Thus the Brazilian brand manager for Lycra is also the global lead for swimsuit fabric because Brazil is a hotbed for swimsuit design. Similarly, the French brand manager takes the lead for Lycra used in fashion. The idea is to use the expertise that is dispersed throughout the world. The global brand manager for Lycra ensures that those in charge of different applications are together on overall strategy; he or she also pulls together their ideas in order to exploit synergies.

When local management is relatively autonomous, it may be necessary to give the global brand manager or team a significant degree of authority. Doing so can also reduce the chances that the manager or team will get smothered by organizational or competitive pressures; in addition, it can signal the company's commitment to brand building.

The team or manager may have authority over its visual representation and brand graphics, for example. In that case, the group or the individual would have to approve any departures from the specified color, typeface, and layout logo. Or a global brand team may have authority over the look and feel of a product. The IBM ThinkPad is black and rectangular; it has a red tracking ball and a multicolored IBM logo set at 35 degrees in the lower right corner. The global brand team must approve any deviations from that look. In another example, the global brand manager at Smirnoff has sign-off authority on the selection of advertising agencies and themes.

While companies are spelling out the authority of the global brand manager or team, they must also make clear what authority resides with the country team. Some aspects of the brand's management will be firm—the definition of what the brand stands for, say—but others will be adaptable or discretionary, such as the advertising presentation or the use of product promotions. The job of the person or group responsible for the brand is to make sure that everyone knows and follows the guidelines.

Delivering Brilliance

Global brand leadership, especially in these days of media clutter, requires real brilliance in brand-building efforts—simply doing a good job isn't enough. The dilemma is how to balance the need to leverage global strengths with the need to recognize local differences. Our research indicates that those who aspire to brilliant execution should do the following:

First, consider what brand-building paths to follow—advertising, sponsorship, increasing retail presence, promotions. The path you choose may turn out to be more important than the way you follow through with it. Experience shows that if the path starts with advertising, as it usually does, other sometimes more innovative and more effective brand-building approaches get the short end of the stick. Second, put pressure on the agency to have the best and most motivated people working on the brand, even if that means creating some agency-client tension. Third, develop options: the more chances at brilliance, the higher the probability that it will be reached. Fourth, measure the results.

P&G finds exceptional ideas by encouraging the country teams to develop breakthrough brand-building programs. Particularly if a brand is struggling, country brand teams are empowered to find a winning formula on their own. Once a winner is found, the organization tests it in other countries and implements it as fast as possible.

For example, when P&G obtained Pantene Pro-V in 1985, it was a brand with a small but loyal following. The company's efforts to expand the product's following in the United States and France did not increase the product's popularity. In 1990, however, brand strategists struck gold in Taiwan. They found that the image of models with shiny healthy hair resonated with Taiwan's consumers. The tagline for the ads was "Hair so healthy it shines." People recognized that they couldn't look just like the models but inside they said, "I've got to have that hair." Within six months, the brand was the leader in Taiwan. The concept and supporting advertising tested well in other markets and was subsequently rolled out in 70 countries.

Another way to stimulate brilliant brand building is to use more than one advertising agency. It's true that a single agency can coordinate a powerful, unified campaign; using only one agency, however, means putting all your creative eggs in one basket. On the other hand, using multiple agencies can lead to inconsistency and strategic anarchy.

In Europe, Audi gets the best of both approaches by following a middle course. It has five agencies from different countries compete to be the lead agency that will create the brand's campaign. The four agencies that lose out are nonetheless retained to implement the winning campaign in their countries. Because the agencies are still involved with Audi, they are available for another round of creative competition in the future. A variant on this approach would be to use several offices from the same agency. That may not lead to as much variation in creative ideas, but it still provides more options than having just one group within one agency.

Adapting global programs to the local level can often improve the effectiveness of a campaign. Take Smirnoff's "pure thrill" vodka campaign. All of its global advertising shows distorted images becoming clear when viewed through the Smirnoff bottle, but the specific scenes change from one country to another in order to appeal to consumers with different assumptions about what is thrilling. In Rio de Janeiro, the ad shows the city's statue of Christ with a soccer ball, and in Hollywood, the "w" in the hillside sign is created with the legs of two people. The IBM global slogan "Solutions for a Small Planet" became "small world" in Argentina where "planet" lacked the desired conceptual thrust.

And yet managers won't be able to tell how well they're building brands unless they develop a global brand measurement system. The system must go beyond financial measures—useful as they are—and measure brand equity in terms of customer awareness, customer loyalty, the brand's personality, and the brand associations that resonate with the public. When these measures of the brand are available, a company has the basis to create programs that will build a strong brand in all markets and to avoid programs that could destroy the brand.

All multinational companies should actively engage in global brand management. Any company that tries to get by with unconnected and directionless local brand strategies will inevitably find mediocrity as its reward. In such cases, an exceptionally talented manager will, on occasion, create a pocket of success. But that success will be isolated and random—hardly a recipe that will produce strong brands around the world.

David A. Aaker *is the E. T. Grether Professor of Marketing Strategy at the University of California at Berkeley's Haas School of Business and is a partner in Prophet Brand Strategy, a consulting firm based in San Francisco and New York.* ***Erich Joachimsthaler*** *is a visiting professor at the University of Virginia's Darden Graduate School of Business in Charlottesville and is the chairman of Prophet Brand Strategy.*

Industry/Company Guide

This guide was prepared to provide an easy index to the many industries and companies discussed in detail in the selections included in *Annual Editions: Marketing 04/05*. It should prove useful when researching specific interests.

INDUSTRIES

Industry/Company Guide

COMPANIES AND DIVISIONS

Glossary

This glossary of marketing terms is included to provide you with a convenient and ready reference as you encounter general terms in your study of marketing that are unfamiliar or require a review. It is not intended to be comprehensive, but taken together with the many definitions included in the articles themselves, it should prove to be quite useful.

acceptable price range
The range of prices that buyers are willing to pay for a product; prices that are above the range may be judged unfair, while prices below the range may generate concerns about quality.

adaptive selling
A salesperson's adjustment of his or her behavior between and during sales calls, to respond appropriately to issues that are important to the customer.

advertising
Marketing communication elements designed to stimulate sales through the use of mass media displays, direct individual appeals, public displays, give-aways, and the like.

advertorial
A special advertising section in magazines that includes some editorial (nonadvertising) content.

Americans with Disabilities Act (ADA)
Passed in 1990, this U.S. law prohibits discrimination against consumers with disabilities.

automatic number identification
A telephone system that identifies incoming phone numbers at the beginning of the call, without the caller's knowledge.

bait and switch
Advertising a product at an attractively low price to get customers into the store, but making the product unavailable so that the customers must trade up to a more expensive version.

bar coding
A computer-coded bar pattern that identifies a product. *See also* universal product code.

barter
The practice of exchanging goods and services without the use of money.

benefit segmentation
Organizing the market according to the attributes or benefits consumers need or desire, such as quality, service, or unique features.

brand
A name, term, sign, design, symbol, or combination used to differentiate the products of one company from those of its competition.

brand image
The quality and reliability of a product as perceived by consumers on the basis of its brand reputation or familiarity.

brand name
The element of a brand that can be vocalized.

break-even analysis
The calculation of the number of units that must be sold at a certain price to cover costs (break even); revenues earned past the break-even point contribute to profits.

bundling
Marketing two or more products in a single package at one price.

business analysis
The stage of new product development where initial marketing plans are prepared (including tentative marketing strategy and estimates of sales, costs, and profitability).

business strategic plan
A plan for how each business unit in a corporation intends to compete in the marketplace, based upon the vision, objectives, and growth strategies of the corporate strategic plan.

capital products
Expensive items that are used in business operations but do not become part of any finished product (such as office buildings, copy machines).

cash-and-carry wholesaler
A limited-function wholesaler that does not extend credit for or deliver the products it sells.

caveat emptor
A Latin term that means "let the buyer beware." A principle of law meaning that the purchase of a product is at the buyer's risk with regard to its quality, usefulness, and the like. The laws do, however, provide certain minimum protection against fraud and other schemes.

channel of distribution
See marketing channel.

Child Protection Act
U.S. law passed in 1990 to regulate advertising on children's TV programs.

Child Safety Act
Passed in 1966, this U.S. law prohibits the marketing of dangerous products to children.

Clayton Act
Anticompetitive activities are prohibited by this 1914 U.S. law.

co-branding
When two brand names appear on the same product (such as a credit card with a school's name).

comparative advertising
Advertising that compares one brand against a competitive brand on a least one product attribute.

competitive pricing strategies
Pricing strategies that are based on a organization's position in relation to its competition.

consignment
An arrangement in which a seller of goods does not take title to the goods until they are sold. The seller thus has the option of returning them to the supplier or principal if unable to execute the sale.

consolidated metropolitan statistical area (CMSA)
Based on census data, the largest designation of geographic areas. *See also* primary metropolitan statistical area.

consumer behavior
The way in which buyers, individually or collectively, react to marketplace stimuli.

Consumer Credit Protection Act
A 1968 U.S. law that requires full disclosure of the financial charges of loans.

consumer decision process
This four-step process includes recognizing a need or problem, searching for information, evaluating alternative products or brands, and purchasing a product.

Consumer Product Safety Commission (CPSC)
A U.S. government agency that protects consumers from unsafe products.

consumerism
A social movement in which consumers demand better information about the service, prices, dependability, and quality of the products they buy.

convenience products
Consumer goods that are purchased at frequent intervals with little regard for price. Such goods are relatively standard in nature and consumers tend to select the most convenient source when shopping for them.

cooperative advertising
Advertising of a product by a retailer, dealer, distributor, or the like, with part of the advertising cost paid by the product's manufacturer.

corporate strategic plan
A plan that addresses what a company is and wants to become, and then guides strategic planning at all organizational levels.

countersegmentation
A concept that combines market segments to appeal to a broad range of consumers, assuming that there will be an increasing consumer willingness to accept fewer product and service choices for lower prices.

customer loyalty concept
To focus beyond customer satisfaction toward customer retention as a way to generate sales and profit growth.

demand curve
A relationship that shows how many units a market will purchase at a given price in a given period of time.

demographic environment
The study of human population densities, distributions, and movements that relate to buying behavior.

derived demand
The demand for business-to-business products that is dependent upon a demand for other products in the market.

differentiated strategy
Using innovation and points of difference in product offerings, advanced technology, superior service, or higher quality in wide areas of market segments.

direct mail promotion
Marketing goods to consumers by mailing unsolicited promotional material to them.

direct marketing
The sale of products to carefully targeted consumers who interact with various advertising media without salesperson contact.

discount
A reduction from list price that is given to a buyer as a reward for a favorable activity to the seller.

discretionary income
The money that remains after taxes and necessities have been paid for.

disposable income
That portion of income that remains after payment of taxes to use for food, clothing, and shelter.

dual distribution
The selling of products to two or more competing distribution networks, or the selling of two brands of nearly identical products through competing distribution networks.

dumping
The act of selling a product in a foreign country at a price lower than its domestic price.

durable goods
Products that continue in service for an appreciable length of time.

economy
The income, expenditures, and resources that affect business and household costs.

electronic data interchange (EDI)
A computerized system that links two different firms to allow transmittal of documents; a quick-response inventory control system.

entry strategy
An approach used to begin marketing products internationally.

environmental scanning
Obtaining information on relevant factors and trends outside a company and interpreting their potential impact on the company's markets and marketing activities.

European Union (EU)
The world's largest consumer market, consisting of 16 European nations: Austria, Belgium, Britain, Denmark, Finland, France, Germany, Greece, Italy, Ireland, Luxembourg, the Netherlands, Norway, Portugal, Spain, and Sweden.

exclusive distribution
Marketing a product or service in only one retail outlet in a specific geographic marketplace.

exporting
Selling goods to international markets.

Fair Packaging and Labeling Act of 1966
This law requires manufacturers to state ingredients, volume, and manufacturer's name on a package.

family life cycle
The progress of a family through a number of distinct phases, each of which is associated with identifiable purchasing behaviors.

Federal Trade Commission (FTC)
The U.S. government agency that regulates business practices; established in 1914.

five C's of pricing
Five influences on pricing decisions: customers, costs, channels of distribution, competition, and compatibility.

FOB (free on board)
The point at which the seller stops paying transportation costs.

four I's of service
Four elements to services: intangibility, inconsistency, inseparability, and inventory.

four P's
See marketing mix.

franchise
The right to distribute a company's products or render services under its name, and to retain the resulting profit in exchange for a fee or percentage of sales.

freight absorption
Payment of transportation costs by the manufacturer or seller, often resulting in a uniform pricing structure.

functional groupings
Groupings in an organization in which a unit is subdivided according to different business activities, such as manufacturing, finance, and marketing.

General Agreement on Tariffs and Trade (GATT)
An international agreement that is intended to limit trade barriers and to promote world trade through reduced tariffs; represents over 80 percent of global trade.

geodemographics
A combination of geographic data and demographic characteristics; used to segment and target specific markets.

green marketing
The implementation of an ecological perspective in marketing; the promotion of a product as environmentally safe.

gross domestic product (GDP)
The total monetary value of all goods and services produced within a country during one year.

growth stage
The second stage of a product life cycle that is characterized by a rapid increase in sales and profits.

hierarchy of effects
The stages a prospective buyer goes through when purchasing a product, including awareness, interest, evaluation, trial, and adoption.

idea generation
An initial stage of the new product development process; requires creativity and innovation to generate ideas for potential new products.

implied warranties
Warranties that assign responsibility for a product's deficiencies to a manufacturer, even though the product was sold by a retailer.

imports
Purchased goods or services that are manufactured or produced in some other country.

integrated marketing communications
A strategic integration of marketing communications programs that coordinate all promotional activities—advertising, personal selling, sales promotion, and public relations.

internal reference prices
The comparison price standards that consumers remember and use to judge the fairness of prices.

introduction stage
The first product life cycle stage; when a new product is launched into the marketplace.

ISO 9000
International Standards Organization's standards for registration and certification of manufacturer's quality management and quality assurance systems.

joint venture
An arrangement in which two or more organizations market products internationally.

just-in-time (JIT) inventory control system
An inventory supply system that operates with very low inventories and fast, on-time delivery.

Lanham Trademark Act
A 1946 U.S. law that was passed to protect trademarks and brand names.

late majority
The fourth group to adopt a new product; representing about 34 percent of a market.

Glossary

lifestyle research
Research on a person's pattern of living, as displayed in activities, interests, and opinions.

limit pricing
This competitive pricing strategy involves setting prices low to discourage new competition.

limited-coverage warranty
The manufacturer's statement regarding the limits of coverage and noncoverage for any product deficiencies.

logistics management
The planning, implementing, and moving of raw materials and products from the point of origin to the point of consumption.

loss-leader pricing
The pricing of a product below its customary price in order to attract attention to it.

Magnuson-Moss Act
Passed in 1975, this U.S. law regulates warranties.

management by exception
Used by a marketing manager to identify results that deviate from plans, diagnose their cause, make appropriate new plans, and implement new actions.

manufacturers' agent
A merchant wholesaler that sells related but noncompeting product lines for a number of manufacturers; also called manufacturers' representatives.

market
The potential buyers for a company's product or service; or to sell a product or service to actual buyers. The place where goods and services are exchanged.

market penetration strategy
The goal of achieving corporate growth objectives with existing products within existing markets by persuading current customers to purchase more of the product or by capturing new customers.

marketing channel
Organizations and people that are involved in the process of making a product or service available for use by consumers or industrial users.

marketing communications planning
A seven-step process that includes marketing plan review; situation analysis; communications process analysis; budget development; program development integration and implementation of a plan; and monitoring, evaluating, and controlling the marketing communications program.

marketing concept
The idea that a company should seek to satisfy the needs of consumers while also trying to achieve the organization's goals.

marketing mix
The elements of marketing: product, brand, package, price, channels of distribution, advertising and promotion, personal selling, and the like.

marketing research
The process of identifying a marketing problem and opportunity, collecting and analyzing information systematically, and recommending actions to improve an organization's marketing activities.

marketing research process
A six-step sequence that includes problem definition, determination of research design, determination of data collection methods, development of data collection forms, sample design, and analysis and interpretation.

mission statement
A part of the strategic planning process that expresses the company's basic values and specifies the operation boundaries within marketing, business units, and other areas.

motivation research
A group of techniques developed by behavioral scientists that are used by marketing researchers to discover factors influencing marketing behavior.

nonprice competition
Competition between brands based on factors other than price, such as quality, service, or product features.

nondurable goods
Products that do not last or continue in service for any appreciable length of time.

North American Free Trade Agreement (NAFTA)
A trade agreement among the United States, Canada, and Mexico that essentially removes the vast majority of trade barriers between the countries.

North American Industry Classification System (NAICS)
A system used to classify organizations on the basis of major activity or the major good or service provided by the three NAFTA countries—Canada, Mexico, and the United States; replaced the Standard Industrial Classification (SIC) system in 1997.

observational data
Market research data obtained by watching, either mechanically or in person, how people actually behave.

odd-even pricing
Setting prices at just below an even number, such as $1.99 instead of $2.

opinion leaders
Individuals who influence consumer behavior based on their interest in or expertise with particular products.

organizational goals
The specific objectives used by a business or nonprofit unit to achieve and measure its performance.

outbound telemarketing
Using the telephone rather than personal visits to contact customers.

outsourcing
A company's decision to purchase products and services from other firms rather than using in-house employees.

parallel development
In new product development, an approach that involves the development of the product and production process simultaneously.

penetration pricing
Pricing a product low to discourage competition.

personal selling process
The six stages of sales activities that occur before and after the sale itself: prospecting, preapproach, approach, presentation, close, and follow-up.

point-of-purchase display
A sales promotion display located in high-traffic areas in retail stores.

posttesting
Tests that are conducted to determine if an advertisement has accomplished its intended purpose.

predatory pricing
The practice of selling products at low prices to drive competition from the market and then raising prices once a monopoly has been established.

prestige pricing
Maintaining high prices to create an image of product quality and appeal to buyers who associate premium prices with high quality.

pretesting
Evaluating consumer reactions to proposed advertisements through the use of focus groups and direct questions.

price elasticity of demand
An economic concept that attempts to measure the sensitivity of demand for any product to changes in its price.

price fixing
The illegal attempt by one or several companies to maintain the prices of their products above those that would result from open competition.

price promotion mix
The basic product price plus additional components such as sales prices, temporary discounts, coupons, favorable payment and credit terms.

price skimming
Setting prices high initially to appeal to consumers who are not price-sensitive and then lowering prices to appeal to the next market segments.

primary metropolitan statistical area (PMSA)
Major urban area, often located within a CMSA, that has at least one million inhabitants.

PRIZM
A potential rating index by ZIP code markets that divides every U.S. neighborhood into one of 40 distinct cluster types that reveal consumer data.

product
An idea, good, service, or any combination that is an element of exchange to satisfy a consumer.

product differentiation
The ability or tendency of manufacturers, marketers, or consumers to distinguish between seemingly similar products.

product expansion strategy
A plan to market new products to the same customer base.

product life cycle (PLC)
A product's advancement through the introduction, growth, maturity, and decline stages.

product line pricing
Setting the prices for all product line items.

product marketing plans
Business units' plans to focus on specific target markets and marketing mixes for each product, which include both strategic and execution decisions.

product mix
The composite of products offered for sale by a firm or a business unit.

promotional mix
Combining one or more of the promotional elements that a firm uses to communicate with consumers.

proprietary secondary data
The data that is provided by commercial marketing research firms to other firms.

psychographic research
Measurable characteristics of given market segments in respect to lifestyles, interests, opinions, needs, values, attitudes, personality traits, and the like.

publicity
Nonpersonal presentation of a product, service, or business unit.

pull strategy
A marketing strategy whose main thrust is to strongly influence the final consumer, so that the demand for a product "pulls" it through the various channels of distribution.

push strategy
A marketing strategy whose main thrust is to provide sufficient economic incentives to members of the channels of distribution, so as to "push" the product through to the consumer.

qualitative data
The responses obtained from in-depth interviews, focus groups, and observation studies.

quality function deployment (QFD)
The data collected from structured response formats that can be easily analyzed and projected to larger populations.

quotas
In international marketing, they are restrictions placed on the amount of a product that is allowed to leave or enter a country; the total outcomes used to assess sales representatives' performance and effectiveness.

regional marketing
A form of geographical division that develops marketing plans that reflect differences in taste preferences, perceived needs, or interests in other areas.

relationship marketing
The development, maintenance, and enhancement of long-term, profitable customer relationships.

repositioning
The development of new marketing programs that will shift consumer beliefs and opinions about an existing brand.

resale price maintenance
Control by a supplier of the selling prices of his branded goods at subsequent stages of distribution, by means of contractual agreement under fair trade laws or other devices.

reservation price
The highest price a consumer will pay for a product; a form of internal reference price.

restraint of trade
In general, activities that interfere with competitive marketing. Restraint of trade usually refers to illegal activities.

retail strategy mix
Controllable variables that include location, products and services, pricing, and marketing communications.

return on investment (ROI)
A ratio of income before taxes to total operating assets associated with a product, such as inventory, plant, and equipment.

sales effectiveness evaluations
A test of advertising efficiency to determine if it resulted in increased sales.

sales forecast
An estimate of sales under controllable and uncontrollable conditions.

sales management
The planning, direction, and control of the personal selling activities of a business unit.

sales promotion
An element of the marketing communications mix that provides incentives or extra value to stimulate product interest.

samples
A small size of a product given to prospective purchasers to demonstrate a product's value or use and to encourage future purchase; some elements that are taken from the population or universe.

scanner data
Proprietary data that is derived from UPC bar codes.

scrambled merchandising
Offering several unrelated product lines within a single retail store.

selected controlled markets
Sites where market tests for a new product are conducted by an outside agency and retailers are paid to display that product; also referred to as forced distribution markets.

selective distribution
This involves selling a product in only some of the available outlets; commonly used when after-the-sale service is necessary, such as in the case of home appliances.

seller's market
A condition within any market in which the demand for an item is greater than its supply.

selling philosophy
An emphasis on an organization's selling function to the exclusion of other marketing activities.

selling strategy
A salesperson's overall plan of action, which is developed at three levels: sales territory, customer, and individual sales calls.

services
Nonphysical products that a company provides to consumers in exchange for money or something else of value.

share points
Percentage points of market share; often used as the common comparison basis to allocate marketing resources effectively.

Sherman Anti-Trust Act
Passed in 1890, this U.S. law prohibits contracts, combinations, or conspiracies in restraint of trade and actual monopolies or attempts to monopolize any part of trade or commerce.

shopping products
Consumer goods that are purchased only after comparisons are made concerning price, quality, style, suitability, and the like.

single-channel strategy
Marketing strategy using only one means to reach customers; providing one sales source for a product.

single-zone pricing
A pricing policy in which all buyers pay the same delivered product price, regardless of location; also known as uniform delivered pricing or postage stamp pricing.

slotting fees
High fees manufacturers pay to place a new product on a retailer's or wholesaler's shelf.

social responsibility
Reducing social costs, such as environmental damage, and increasing the positive impact of a marketing decision on society.

societal marketing concept
The use of marketing strategies to increase the acceptability of an idea (smoking causes cancer); cause (environmental protection); or practice (birth control) within a target market.

specialty products
Consumer goods, usually appealing only to a limited market, for which consumers will make a special purchasing effort. Such items include, for example, stereo components, fancy foods, and prestige brand clothes.

Standard Industrial Classification (SIC) system
Replaced by NAICS, this federal government numerical scheme categorized businesses.

standardized marketing
Enforcing similar product, price, distribution, and communications programs in all international markets.

stimulus-response presentation
A selling format that assumes that a customer will buy if given the appropriate stimulus by a salesperson.

strategic business unit (SBU)
A decentralized profit center of a company that operates as a separate, independent business.

Glossary

strategic marketing process
Marketing activities in which a firm allocates its marketing mix resources to reach a target market.

strategy mix
A way for retailers to differentiate themselves from others through location, product, services, pricing, and marketing mixes.

subliminal perception
When a person hears or sees messages without being aware of them.

SWOT analysis
An acronym that describes a firm's appraisal of its internal strengths and weaknesses and its external opportunities and threats.

synergy
An increased customer value that is achieved through more efficient organizational function performances.

systems-designer strategy
A selling strategy that allows knowledgeable sales reps to determine solutions to a customer's problems or to anticipate opportunities to enhance a customer's business through new or modified business systems.

target market
A defined group of consumers or organizations toward which a firm directs its marketing program.

team selling
A sales strategy that assigns accounts to specialized sales teams according to a customers' purchase-information needs.

telemarketing
An interactive direct marketing approach that uses the telephone to develop relationships with customers.

test marketing
The process of testing a prototype of a new product to gain consumer reaction and to examine its commercial viability and marketing strategy.

TIGER (Topologically Integrated Geographic Encoding and Reference)
A minutely detailed U.S. Census Bureau computerized map of the U.S. that can be combined with a company's own database to analyze customer sales.

total quality management (TQM)
Programs that emphasize long-term relationships with selected suppliers instead of short-term transactions with many suppliers.

total revenue
The total of sales, or unit price, multiplied by the quantity of the product sold.

trade allowance
An amount a manufacturer contributes to a local dealer's or retailer's advertising expenses.

trade (functional) discounts
Price reductions that are granted to wholesalers or retailers that are based on future marketing functions that they will perform for a manufacturer.

trademark
The legal identification of a company's exclusive rights to use a brand name or trade name.

truck jobber
A small merchant wholesaler who delivers limited assortments of fast-moving or perishable items within a small geographic area.

two-way stretch strategy
Adding products at both the low and high end of a product line.

undifferentiated strategy
Using a single promotional mix to market a single product for the entire market; frequently used early in the life of a product.

uniform delivered price
The same average freight amount that is charged to all customers, no matter where they are located.

universal product code (UPC)
An assigned number to identify a product, which is represented by a series of bars of varying widths for optical scanning.

usage rate
The quantity consumed or patronage during a specific period, which can vary significantly among different customer groups.

utilitarian influence
To comply with the expectations of others to achieve rewards or avoid punishments.

value added
In retail strategy decisions, a dimension of the retail positioning matrix that refers to the service level and method of operation of the retailer.

vertical marketing systems
Centrally coordinated and professionally managed marketing channels that are designed to achieve channel economies and maximum marketing impact.

vertical price fixing
Requiring that sellers not sell products below a minimum retail price; sometimes called resale price maintenance.

weighted-point system
The method of establishing screening criteria, assigning them weights, and using them to evaluate new product lines.

wholesaler
One who makes quantity purchases from manufacturers (or other wholesalers) and sells in smaller quantities to retailers (or other wholesalers).

zone pricing
A form of geographical pricing whereby a seller divides its market into broad geographic zones and then sets a uniform delivered price for each zone.

Sources for the Glossary
Marketing: Principles and Perspectives by William O. Bearden, Thomas N. Ingram, and Raymond W. LaForge (Irwin/McGraw-Hill, 1998);
Marketing by Eric N. Berkowitz (Irwin/McGraw-Hill, 1997); and the *Annual Editions* **staff.**

Index

Index

Test Your Knowledge Form

We encourage you to photocopy and use this page as a tool to assess how the articles in *Annual Editions* expand on the information in your textbook. By reflecting on the articles you will gain enhanced text information. You can also access this useful form on a product's book support Web site at *http://www.dushkin.com/online/*.

NAME: DATE:

_____

TITLE AND NUMBER OF ARTICLE:

_____

BRIEFLY STATE THE MAIN IDEA OF THIS ARTICLE:

_____

LIST THREE IMPORTANT FACTS THAT THE AUTHOR USES TO SUPPORT THE MAIN IDEA:

_____

WHAT INFORMATION OR IDEAS DISCUSSED IN THIS ARTICLE ARE ALSO DISCUSSED IN YOUR TEXTBOOK OR OTHER READINGS THAT YOU HAVE DONE? LIST THE TEXTBOOK CHAPTERS AND PAGE NUMBERS:

_____

LIST ANY EXAMPLES OF BIAS OR FAULTY REASONING THAT YOU FOUND IN THE ARTICLE:

_____

LIST ANY NEW TERMS/CONCEPTS THAT WERE DISCUSSED IN THE ARTICLE, AND WRITE A SHORT DEFINITION:

We Want Your Advice

ANNUAL EDITIONS revisions depend on two major opinion sources: one is our Advisory Board, listed in the front of this volume, which works with us in scanning the thousands of articles published in the public press each year; the other is you—the person actually using the book. Please help us and the users of the next edition by completing the prepaid article rating form on this page and returning it to us. Thank you for your help!

ANNUAL EDITIONS: Marketing 04/05

ARTICLE RATING FORM

Here is an opportunity for you to have direct input into the next revision of this volume.
We would like you to rate each of the articles listed below, using the following scale:

1. **Excellent: should definitely be retained**
2. **Above average: should probably be retained**
3. **Below average: should probably be deleted**
4. **Poor: should definitely be deleted**

Your ratings will play a vital part in the next revision.
Please mail this prepaid form to us as soon as possible.
Thanks for your help!

RATING	ARTICLE	RATING	ARTICLE
_____	1. The Next 25 Years	_____	33. When Worlds Collide
_____	2. High Performance Marketing	_____	34. 10 Top Stores Put to the Test
_____	3. Marketing High Technology: Preparation, Targeting, Positioning, Execution	_____	35. Tips for Distinguishing Your Ads From Bad Ads
_____	4. The Customer Profitability Conundrum: When to Love 'Em or Leave 'Em	_____	36. Living Up and Down the Dial
_____	5. Entrepreneurs' Biggest Problems—And How They Solve Them	_____	37. Counting Eyes on Billboards
_____	6. Marketing Myopia (With Retrospective Commentary)	_____	38. Segmenting Global Markets: Look Before You Leap
_____	7. Why Customer Satisfaction Starts With HR	_____	39. International Marketing Research: A Management Briefing
_____	8. Start With the Customer	_____	40. Small Packets, Big Business
_____	9. What Drives Customer Equity	_____	41. Time for Marketers to Grow Up?
_____	10. Services Communications: From Mindless Tangibilization to Meaningful Messages	_____	42. Cracking China's Market
_____	11. Why Service Stinks	_____	43. The Lure of Global Branding
_____	12. Trust in the Marketplace		
_____	13. A Matter of Trust		
_____	14. A Different Approach for Developing New Products or Services		
_____	15. Product by Design		
_____	16. Surviving Innovation		
_____	17. A Beginner's Guide to Demographics		
_____	18. Defining Luxury: Oh, the Good Life		
_____	19. Emailing Aging Boomers vs. "Seniors"		
_____	20. Race, Ethnicity and the Way We Shop		
_____	21. Asian-American Consumers as a Unique Market Segment: Fact or Fallacy?		
_____	22. Defining Moments: Segmenting by Cohorts		
_____	23. What Are Your Customers Saying?		
_____	24. Tough Love		
_____	25. The Very Model of a Modern Marketing Plan		
_____	26. In Praise of the Purple Cow		
_____	27. Have It Your Way		
_____	28. The Hole Story: How Krispy Kreme Became the Hottest Brand in America		
_____	29. Kamikaze Pricing		
_____	30. Which Price is Right?		
_____	31. Most Valuable Players		
_____	32. The Old Pillars of New Retailing		

(Continued on next page)

ANNUAL EDITIONS: MARKETING 04/05

BUSINESS REPLY MAIL
FIRST-CLASS MAIL PERMIT NO. 84 GUILFORD CT
POSTAGE WILL BE PAID BY ADDRESSEE

McGraw-Hill/Dushkin
530 Old Whitfield Street
Guilford, Ct 06437-9989

llnnllnnlnlnlnlllnnllnlnlnlnlnlnlnllnnlnl

ABOUT YOU

Name _____   Date _____

Are you a teacher? ☐   A student? ☐
Your school's name _____

Department _____

Address _____   City _____   State _____   Zip _____

School telephone # _____

YOUR COMMENTS ARE IMPORTANT TO US!

Please fill in the following information:
For which course did you use this book?
_____

Did you use a text with this ANNUAL EDITION?   ☐ yes ☐ no
What was the title of the text?
_____

What are your general reactions to the *Annual Editions* concept?
_____

Have you read any pertinent articles recently that you think should be included in the next edition? Explain.
_____

Are there any articles that you feel should be replaced in the next edition? Why?
_____

Are there any World Wide Web sites that you feel should be included in the next edition? Please annotate.
_____

May we contact you for editorial input?   ☐ yes ☐ no
May we quote your comments?   ☐ yes ☐ no